123

£8

Boeing
B-17 Flying Fortress

Boeing B-17
FLYING FORTRESS

Martin W. Bowman

The Crowood Press

First published in 1998 by
The Crowood Press Ltd
Ramsbury, Marlborough
Wiltshire SN8 2HR

© Martin W. Bowman 1998

British Library Cataloguing-in-Publication Data
A catalogue record for this book is available from
the British Library.

ISBN 1 86126 170 5

Photograph previous page: B-17E 41-2633 *Sally*, its
bomb-bay doors open, and three other Es of the 19th
Bomb Group, prepare to bomb the Japanese airfield
at Lae, New Guinea. The B-17E below *Sally's* tail is
41-2461, piloted by Lt Bernice 'Bernie' Barr, who
had taken over the crew from Major Conrad F.
Necrason when the latter had been ordered to India
for further duty. 41-2633 is fitted with the Sperry
ball turret whose gunner controlled the movement of
the two machine guns by hand and foot pedals while
sighting with his eye. The gunner could enter the
turret from inside the aircraft by having the ball turret rotated until the door opening faced the interior
of the plane, but since this required the turret to be
positioned so that the guns were pointed downwards,
this meant that he could not enter it from inside
while the B-17 was on the ground. USAF

Typefaces used: Goudy (*text*),
Cheltenham (*headings*)

Typeset and designed by
D & N Publishing
Membury Business Park, Lambourn Woodlands
Hungerford, Berkshire.

Printed and bound by Butler & Tanner, Frome.

Acknowledgements

I would particularly like to thank the fol-
lowing people for all their help and exper-
tise in helping make this book possible:
Steve Adams; R.V. 'Bob' Bailey, 483rd
Bomb Group (H) Assoc.; Mike Bailey; B-17
combat crewmen and wingmen; Richard E.
Bagg; Bernice 'Bernie' S. Barr, 99th Bomb
Group (H) Assoc.; Gp Capt Antony J. Bar-
wood OBE, RAF retd; Joseph F. Baugher;
A.D. Beaty; D.R. Black; Gp Capt Roy Boast
CBE, DFC, RAF retd; Boeing Aircraft Ltd;
Theo Boiten; Les Bostock; Patrick Bunce;
City of Norwich Aviation/100 Group
Museum; William M. Cleveland; Alfred B.
Cohen; Collings Foundation; Mrs Diane L.
Cook; Howard K. Corns; Sqn Ldr Bob
Davies AFC, RAF retd; Colin Deverell;
Graham Dinsdale; Bill Donald; Jack P.
Dorfman; Douglas Aircraft Ltd; Sandy Ellis;
Erwin H. Eckert, 301st Bomb Group
Assoc.; Kenneth W. Fields; John Wallace
Fields; Reuben 'Ruby' Fier; Thomas J. Fit-
ton; Norman L.R. Franks; C.E. 'Ben'
Franklin; Jim French; Harry Friedman MD;
Robert M. Foose; Capt Al D. Garcia,
USAF; J.J-V. Glazebrook; Lt Col Harry D.
Gobrecht; Larry Goldstein; Andrew
Height; Gerhard Heilig; J.A. Hey; Jules
Horowitz, USAF retd; Col E.C. 'Ned'
Humphreys; Col Raymond F. Hunter; Air
Cdr Tom Imrie; Philip Jarrett; Mick Jen-
nings; Mike Johns; Fred A. Johnsen;
Richard R. 'Dick' Johnson; Antonio Claret
Jordao, Museu Aerospacial; Michael W.
Kellner; Joe C. Kenney; Jack Krause;

Arthur Lange; William T. Larkins; Geoff
Liles; Jerry Linderman; Lockheed-Califor-
nia; Ron Mackay; Ped G. Magness; Ed Mal-
oney; Armand Miale; Arvin 'Mac'
McCauley; Brian S. McGuire; Ian McLach-
lan; Gus Mencow; Richard C. Muchler;
Musée de l'Air; Charles M. Nekvasil; Mike
O'Leary; Roy W. Owen USAF retd; Murray
Peden QC, RCAF retd; Milo Peltzer; Tony
Plowright; Lt Col John A. Plummer USAF
retd; Sue Reilly; Connie and Gordon
Richards; Elly Sallingboe, B-17 Preserva-
tion Ltd; Jerry C. Scutts; Bill Somers; Derek
Smith; Hans Heiri Stapfer; George Steb-
bings; Phil Sweeney; Frank Thomas; R.
Thomas; Thorpe Abbotts Memorial Muse-
um; Paul Tibbets; Walter A. Truax; Geoff
Ward; Brig Gen Robert W. Waltz; Gordon
W. Weir; Angela Westphal; Truett L.
Woodall Jr.; Richard Wynn; Larry D. Yan-
notti; Sam Young.

Numerous reference books on B-17s have
been published, and space does not permit
listing them all, but I would like to pay
homage in particular to the leading reference works on B-17s by the 'B-17 Grandad-
dy' of them all, Peter M. Bowers. Last, but by
no means least, I would like to thank the
dedicated staff of the US 2nd Air Division
Memorial Library in Norwich: Derek S.
Hills, Trust Librarian; Linda J. Berube,
American Fulbright librarian; Lesley Fleet-
wood, and Christine Snowden; all of whom
were most helpful and who provided much
willing assistance with research.

Contents

1 BRAVE NEW WORLD
Design and Development of the Model 299   7

2 SWIFTLY THEY STRIKE
The Pioneers of 90 Squadron RAF   23

3 ON WINGS WE CONQUER
War in the South-West Pacific, 1942–1943   35

4 THE CACTUS AIR FORCE
War in the South Pacific, 1942–1943   53

5 THE BIG LEAGUE
European Theatre of Operations 1942–October 1943   65

6 MEDITERRANEAN MISSIONS
15th Air Force Operations, Italy, October 1943–May 1945   87

7 'HIGHER, STRONGER, FASTER'
Round-the-Clock Bombing, ETO, October 1943–Summer 1944   107

8 AN 'ABUNDANCE OF STRENGTH'
8th Air Force Operations, August 1944–May 1945   127

9 TO OBSERVE UNSEEN
RAF Coastal Command and 100 Group (Bomber Support)   147

10 POST-WAR POSTSCRIPT   155

Appendix I   Equipment Diagrams   179

Appendix II   USAAF B-17 Medal of Honor Recipients 1942–44   183

Appendix III   Surviving B-17 Flying Fortresses Around the World   184

Appendix IV   B-17 Serials   186

Glossary   188

Index   190

Magnificent study of a 96th BG, 8th AF, B-17G.

CHAPTER ONE

Brave New World

Design and Development of the Model 299

During the isolationist period between the two world wars America had relied on a small, peacetime organization that would be capable of rapid expansion in war. For several years the striking force based in the USA therefore consisted of just three groups: the 1st Pursuit, the 2nd Bombardment and the 3rd Attack. There was also one observation group, and there was one observation squadron for each of the Army corps, with three composite groups overseas – the 4th in the Philippines, the 5th in Hawaii and the 6th in Panama.

The Air Corps had been created by the Air Corps Act of 2 July 1926, and the composition, organization and command of the combat elements of the Air Corps throughout the 1920s and early 1930s were mainly restricted to observation duties. Bombardment aviation had but a minor role, with the mission of destroying military objectives in the combat theatre and in the enemy's zone of interior. In addition, it placed aviation under the command of ground officers at division, corps, army and GHQ levels. Within the air arm there was conflict between air and ground officers over the composition, organization and command of military aviation.

General Billy Mitchell and other Air Service officers wanted aviation units organized as an air force under the command of airmen. However, it was not until 1 March 1935 when the War Department established General Headquarters Air Force (GHQAF) to serve as an air defence and striking force, that an air officer was at last appointed to command: Brig Gen Frank M. Andrews was given this post, while Brig Gen Oscar Westover became chief of the Air Corps on 24 December that same year. They also knew that observation aviation was no longer as important as more pursuit units. Above all, they wanted to increase the number of bombardment groups: bombardment they felt was now the major instrument of warfare, and deserved priority above all else.

In 1921 the Army, led by Mitchell, set out to prove the Navy admirals wrong when they said that a bomber could not sink a battleship. Mitchell had wanted to bomb one of Germany's largest World War I battleships, the *Ostfriesland*, at anchor off the Capes of Virginia after the surrender. It had widely been proclaimed as unsinkable, but on 21 July 1921 Mitchell's eight Martin MB-2 Bombers dropped seven bombs and capsized and sank her, and two other warships. It was a milestone in US Army aviation history. The feat was repeated in 1923 when two obsolete US battleships suffered the same fate.

Following the loss of the Navy dirigible *Shenandoah* in 1925, Mitchell publicly accused the high command of the Army and the Navy of being guilty of 'incompetency, criminal negligence and almost treasonable administration of the national defense.' In December 1925 Mitchell was court-martialled, found guilty, and suspended from the Air Service for five years. He resigned his commission in 1926. (Ten years after his death from a heart attack in 1936, Mitchell was posthumously awarded the Medal of Honor.)

During 1927–1932 only eight new aviation groups – five of them pursuit, one observation, and two bombardment (the 7th and the 19th) – were activated, bringing the number of bombardment squadrons to twelve. Even so, by the end of 1932 thirteen of the forty-five squadrons in service were observation. The standard bombers from 1928 to 1932 were the Keystone series and the Curtiss B-2 Condor; however, the Keystone could only manage speeds of just over 100mph (160km/h), and the Condor's performance was less.

On 1 March 1935 the War Department established General Headquarters Air Force (GHQAF) to serve as an air defence and striking force, and significantly, all of the attack and pursuit, and five bombardment units in the US became part of the

new combat force, organized into three wings. In 1935 the change in designation of the 9th Group from observation to bombardment, and the inactivation of the 12th Observation Group in 1937, finally signalled the decline in observation and the growth of bombardment aviation.

In the 1930s it was accepted that a formation of unescorted bombers could get through to their target if they were properly arranged and adequately armed. During air manoeuvres in 1933, pursuits repeatedly failed to intercept the bombers and there was even talk of eliminating pursuits altogether. From 1931 onwards a largely strategic bombing doctrine was adopted at the Army Air Corps Tactical School at Maxwell Field, Alabama, mainly through the instigation of its chief, Captain (later Major) Harold L. George, and a small, influential group of officers, including Major Donald Wilson, 1st Lt Kenneth L. Walker, and 2nd Lt Haywood S. 'Possum' Hansell Jr. They believed that air power – that is, long-range bombers, properly equipped, with defensive fire-power, and organized into massed formations – could directly affect the outcome of future wars by penetrating an enemy's defences and destroying his industrial infrastructure, and therefore his will to exist. These beliefs, which were taught to students, became the unofficial doctrine of air power, and as the 1940s beckoned, they would be put into practice in World War II.

The Emergence of Boeing

Where would the new bombers come from? Funds for new aircraft were very limited and mostly it was manufacturers who funded new developments which in turn might attract orders from the Army. The early fame of the Boeing Airplane Company of Seattle, Washington, was earned as a result of its position as the leading American supplier of single-seat fighter aircraft from 1924 to 1936. In 1929 ninety examples of the Boeing P-12B were ordered, the largest single Army order for fighters since 1921. Altogether, 586 aircraft in the P-12/F-4B series were delivered to the Army and the Navy (and a few overseas), the last on 28 February 1933. Boeing's Model 248, which appeared in March 1932, was the first all-metal monoplane fighter. Boeing built three prototypes at its own expense, and after testing as the XP-936, the Army purchased these and went on to order 136 P-26 production models.

In the early 1930s, Boeing switched production to the more potentially lucrative transport business. One of the most revolutionary designs in commercial aviation history was the Model 200 Boeing Monomail, which first flew in May 1930. Designed initially as a mail and cargo aircraft, it achieved major performance increases mainly through structural and aerodynamic refinement. The traditional biplane design with drag-producing struts and wires was replaced by a single, smooth, all-metal low wing of clean cantilever construction. The wheels retracted into the wings in flight, and the drag of the single air-cooled 600hp Pratt & Whitney Hornet engine was greatly reduced by enclosing it in a newly developed 'anti-drag' cowling.

Boeing Air Transport was formed to operate the San Francisco–Chicago airmail route which had been bought in 1927. The success of this venture encouraged the company to design larger, passenger-carrying aircraft, and the airline was expanded into the Boeing Air Transport System. In 1929 the Boeing airline and aeroplane operations merged with other manufacturers in the American aviation industry, including Pratt & Whitney, a leading manufacturer of aircraft engines, and the Standard Steel Propeller Co, to form United Aircraft and Transport Corporation. The airlines operated under their own names within a holding company called United Air Lines.

The Model 247 was the first airliner produced in quantity by Boeing, and the first all-metal streamlined monoplane transport. A decision was made to completely re-equip the Boeing Air Transport System (soon to become United Air Lines) with the innovative new twelve-seater transport. It was powered by two supercharged Pratt & Whitney 550hp S1D1 Wasps (the first time superchargers had been used on a transport type), and featured a retractable landing gear, an enclosed cabin, autopilot, trim tabs and de-icing equipment. An order for sixty Model 247s was placed while the design was still in the mock-up stage.

The Model 247 first flew in February 1933, and all sixty were delivered within a year. Fifteen more Model 247s were built, including two for Deutsche Lufthansa, the German national airline. In 1934 a 247 was modified for Roscoe Turner and Clyde Pangborn as the 247D, to fly as an American entry in the Melbourne Centenary Air Race from Mildenhall, England, to Australia. The 247D was placed third in the overall race and second in the transport category. That same year, Congress passed legislation which forced aircraft and engine manufacturers to sever their links with airline operations. The Boeing Aircraft Company resumed independent operation and moved into the bomber business.

Boeing Enters the Bomber Business

Boeing and Martin funded their first all-metal monoplane bomber designs, the five-seat B-9, and the B-10 respectively. Boeing's Model 214 and 215, which became the US Army Y1B-9 and YB-9, were logical military developments of the all-metal Model 221 Monomail, and in turn these greatly influenced the Model 247 design. The Model 215 (YB-9) was 51ft 6in (15m 69cm) long and 76ft 10in (23m 42cm) wide with open cockpits, and could carry a 2,200lb (998kg) bomb load externally. Power was provided by two 600hp Pratt & Whitney Hornet engines. The YB-9 was completed first, and the aircraft made its first flight on 13 April 1931. Following US Army tests, the Model 214 (Y1B-9), originally powered with two 600hp liquid-cooled Curtiss Conqueror engines, was changed to Hornet powerplants. Boeing had to content themselves with a service test order placed in August 1931 for five Y1B-9As, and the Army did buy the two prototypes, but the B-9 raised the speed of bombers to 186mph (299km/h), a point 5mph (8km/h) above that of contemporary fighters, and marked the beginning of a modern US bombardment force.

On 14 April 1934 the US Army's general staff at Wright Field, which in 1933 had conducted a design study to determine the feasibility of an extremely heavy bomber, finally issued a request for design proposals for 'Project A', an aircraft capable of carrying a one-ton bomb 5,000 miles (8,045km), to hit targets in Hawaii or Alaska. Boeing proposed the Model 294, or the XBLR-1 (experimental bomber, long range), as it was known. On 28 June 1934 Boeing were awarded a contract for design data, wind-tunnel tests and a mock-up. The only other contender, the Martin XB-16, became too expensive to build.

The XBLR-1 was a massive four-engined bomber. It took three years to build, weighed over 35 tons, and was almost 88 ft (26.8m) long. It had a 149ft (45.4m) span and passageways were built inside the wing to enable the crew to make minor repairs to the four Pratt & Whitney R-1830-11 radial engines while the aircraft was in flight. The original designation was changed to XB-15 by Edmund 'Eddie' T. Allen, test pilot and director of Aerodynamics and Flight Research, before its first flight on 15 October 1937. (Allen was killed testing the XB-29 on 21 September 1942.) The XB-15 (35-277) was now the largest aircraft in the world. The new bomber, which was armed with six machine guns, also contained complete living and sleeping quarters with sound-proofed, heated, ventilated cabins. The XB-15 joined the 2nd Bomb Group in August 1938 and established a number of records, carrying a 31,167lb (14,137kg) payload to 8,200ft (2,500m) on 30 July 1939. On 2 August it remained airborne for 18 hours, 40 minutes and 47 secs, carrying a 4,409lb (2,000kg) payload for 3,107 miles (5,000km). In 1940 it made a 2,839-mile (4,568km) flight to the Galapagos Islands. In 1942 the aircraft was converted to the XC-105 transport with cargo doors and hoist, and continued to serve in this role until 1945, when it was dismantled.

The Model 299

Meanwhile on 18 July 1934, the Air Corps at Wright Field issued a specification for a multi-engined four- to six-place bomber to replace the Martin B-10. The new bomber had to be capable of carrying a 2,000lb (907kg) bomb load at a speed of 200–250mph (322–402km/h) over a distance of 1,020–2,000 miles (1,640–3,218km). On 18 July 1934 Boeing learned that competing manufacturers were to build prototypes at their own expense. The Army Corps also stipulated that a flying prototype had to be available for trials in August

A YIB-9A, the Army's first all-metal cantilever monoplane bomber, in flight with the Boeing XP-936, the prototype for the P-26A Peashooter. The YIB-9 made its first flight on 13 April 1931 and it raised the speed of bombers to 186mph (300km/h), a point 5mph (8km/h) above that of contemporary fighters; but all Boeing got was a service test order for five YIB-9AS and two prototypes. The company therefore applied the B-9 design concept to a similar civil transport plane, which became the successful Model 247; however, by 1934 247 production was winding down, and the only business Boeing had was unfinished contracts for P-26A and C fighters. In August 1,100 of its 1,700 workforce were laid off. Cash on hand was barely $500,000, and on 16 September 1934, $275,000 of this was boldly invested in the Model 199. Boeing

X13372, the Model 299, shown here at its roll-out at Boeing Field, Seattle, 17 July 1935, when, because its wingspan was greater than the width of the hangar door, it had to be rolled out sideways on wheeled dollies. The Model 299 was flown for the first time on 28 July by the company test pilot, Leslie Tower. The clean lines of the Model 299 owed much to the sleek Model 247 airliner which was scaled up into the much bigger Model 299 by using many of the engineering innovations that had been developed on the earlier Model 294 (XB-15) project. Boeing

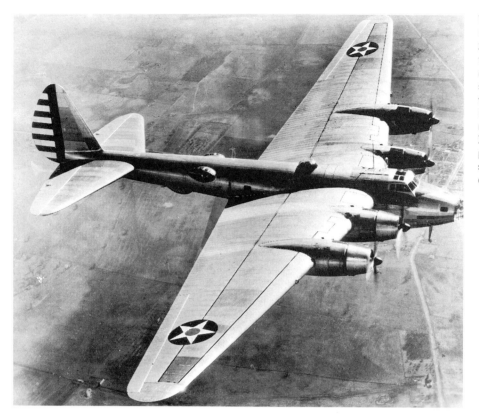

When the XB-15 35-277 made its first flight on 15 October 1937 (twenty-eight months after the Model 299), it was at that time the largest aircraft in the world. The new bomber, which was armed with six machine guns, also contained complete living and sleeping quarters with sound-proofed, heated, ventilated cabins. The XB-15 joined the 2nd Bomb Group in August 1938 and established a number of records. In 1942 the aircraft was converted to the XC-105 transport with cargo doors and hoist, and popularly known as 'Grandpappy', it continued to serve in this role until 1945, when it was dismantled. Boeing

1935; the winner could expect to receive an order for some 220 bombers. The term 'multi-engine' had generally been used to indicate two engines. However, Boeing were already working on a new concept for a four-engined bomber (the Model 299, or X-13372, to use its company designation, was already in the design stage), so on 26 September 1934 Boeing President, Clairmont L. Egtvedt, and his board made certain that 'multi-engined' also permitted four, as well as two engines before they voted to risk $275,000 of company capital on the new venture. Eventually the project to build a prototype would cost $432,034.

The Model 299's lineage could be traced back to the Monomail, the Model 215 (B-9 bomber) of 1931, and the Boeing 247 transport of 1933, and further data was available as a result of the work on the XB-15. E. Gifford Emery had been appointed project engineer, with Lambert 'Ed' C. Wells as his assistant (in December 1935 the 24-year-old former Stanford University graduate was promoted to the post of project engineer). The design team looked to the 247 and the XB-15 and decided to base construction on the Model 247, while the engine arrangement, fuselage cross-section and military equipment fit came from the XB-15.

Construction and On-Going Development

The design team utilized tubular strutting to produce a structure of great strength. The fuselage was a conventional semi-mono-coque all-metal structure of basically circular configuration consisting of four main sub-assemblies bolted together. Major assemblies were made up of nine sub-assemblies riveted together into stressed elements. A series of circumferential frames and vertical bulkheads with longitudinal stringers and covered with stressed skin provided a very strong structural unit.

Eighteen sub-assemblies made up an extremely efficient wing with a low weight/strength ratio. Truss-type main spars were capped with sheet metal and gusseted girders. Sections between spars were covered with corrugated aluminium sheet, and stressed skin was riveted to corrugated areas and to the tube and channel truss-type ribs. The entire structure produced a wing with an exceptional ability to absorb punishment without loss of structural integrity. A symmetrical NACA airfoil was used, and the ailerons were of all-metal structure with fabric (and later aluminium skin) covering. The tail surfaces were made up of cantilevered vertical and horizontal stabilizers.

Sheet metal covered the stabilizers, while fabric was used on the rudder and elevators.

The Model 299 was the first US aircraft to have air brakes in the landing-gear wells. The unique landing gear was an electrically operated, twin yoke arrangement with a retracting screw. Each main gear had to be operated separately. The tail wheel too was retractable, and all three wheels, when retracted, were half exposed. The Model 299 was also the first to be equipped with flaps on the rear edges of its wings to serve as air brakes on landing. The split flaps were of all-metal construction. The landing lights, which were in protruding cylinders, were later faired into the wings on subsequent models.

Unlike its other antecedent, the B-9, the Model 299 (X13372) would carry all bombs internally. In fact it could carry 4,800lb (2,177kg) in eight vertical stacks of 600lb (272kg) bombs each, and could transport 2,500lb (1134kg) of bombs 2,040 miles (3,282km). Five defensive single-mount .30 or .50 calibre machine-gun positions were provided. A streamlined machine-gun cupola was located on each side of the sleek fuselage, which tapered to a shark-fin vertical tail, with two more in blisters on top and bottom of the fuselage, behind the crew compartment and wing, while a rather inelegant blister, which could be turned 360 degrees, contained a single machine-gun in the nose. The bombardier's sighting panel was installed in a nook under the fuselage and directly behind the nose. All told, the Model 299 had a crew of eight consisting of a pilot, co-pilot, bombardier, navigator/ radio operator, and four gunners. The prototype was powered by four tried and tested 750hp single-row Pratt & Whitney S1E-G (R-1690) Hornet radials.

Rushed to completion in only a year, the highly polished aluminium Model 299 was rolled out at Boeing Field on 17 July 1935. Following thorough engine runs, systems tests and ground-handling runs, the aircraft was flown for the first time on 28 July at Boeing Field, Seattle, by the company test pilot, 32-year old Leslie Tower. Richard L. Williams, a *Seattle Times* reporter, wrote 'Declared to be the largest land plane ever built in America, this 15-ton flying fortress, built by Boeing Aircraft Company under

Army specifications, today was ready to test its wings ...' While the role of later versions was to be offensive, the Model 299 was conceived for a purely defensive mission: the protection of the American coastline from foreign surface fleets. It was this designation, and not the later, formidable defensive machine-gun armament, which suggested the famous name 'Flying Fortress'.

Only a month after the roll-out, on 20 August, Tower, his assistant and co-pilot Louis Wait, with C.W. Benton Jr as mechanic, and Henry N. Igo of Pratt & Whitney on board to maintain the engines, flew the Model 299 from Seattle to Wright Field at Dayton, Ohio, to begin service trials in competition with the twin-engined Martin 146 and the Douglas DB-1. The Model 299 completed the 2,100-mile (3,380km) trip, much of the way on auto-pilot, in a record-breaking nine hours non-stop with an unbelievable average speed of 233mph (375km/h). A delighted

Egtvedt and Wells were on hand to tell the crew that the Air Corps did not expect them to arrive for another two hours.

Air Corps pilot Lt Donald Putt was assigned to the Model 299 as project test pilot. Competitive testing soon proved that the Boeing aircraft was in a class of its own, and it went on to exceed all the Army specifications for speed, climb and range. Major Ployer P. 'Pete' Hill (chief of Wright Field's flight testing section) took over the final tests from Putt. Testing was almost complete, and the Air Corps about to confer the title XB-17 to the aircraft, when on 30 October 1935 Hill took the controls for yet another flight. Putt sat beside him in the right-hand seat and Les Tower stood behind them on the flightdeck. The Model 299 raced down the runway and began its climb, and then appeared to stall: it then crashed and burst into flames. Putt, Benton and Igo scrambled clear of the

Specification – XB-17 (Model 299)	
Crew:	8
Powerplant:	Pratt & Whitney S1EG Hornets 750hp @ ♦,000ft (2,134m)
Performance:	Maximum speed 236mph (380km/h)
	Cruise speed 140mph (225km/h) @ 70% power
	Rate of climb 8 mins to 10,000ft (3,048m)
	Ceiling 24,620ft (7,504m)
	Range 3,101 miles (4,990km)
Weights:	Empty weight 21,657lb (9,824kg); gross weight 38,053lb (17,261kg)
Dimensions:	Length 68ft 9in (20m 96cm); height 14ft 11in (4m 55cm); wingspan 103ft 9in (31m 62cm); wing area 1,420sq ft (132sq m)
Armament:	5 × .30 cal. machine guns; maximum bomb load 8 × 600lb (272kg)

Testing was almost complete and the Air Corps about to confer the title XB-17 to the Model 299 when, on 30 October 1935, the aircraft crashed with Major Ployer P. 'Pete' Hill (chief of Wright Field's Flight Testing Section) at the controls. Hill died later in the day and Leslie Tower, Boeing test pilot, died a few days later. The subsequent investigation concluded that the crash was a result of the mechanical ground locks not having been unlocked prior to take-off. Boeing

wreckage, but Hill and Tower who were trapped inside were bravely pulled clear by 1st Lts Robert K. Giovannoli, of the Wright Field powerplant branch, and Leonard F. Harman, project engineer. John Cutting, test observer, and Mark Koegler, Wright Field mechanic, were injured in the crash. Pete Hill never regained consciousness and died later in the day. Tower died a few days later. The subsequent investigation concluded that the crash was a result of the mechanical ground locks (which were operated from the cockpit) not having been unlocked prior to take-off; this prevented movement of the main surfaces and the pilots could only control movement in the servo tabs.

Enter the Y1B-17

Before the crash of the Model 299, the Army Air Corps had been considering an order for sixty-five B-17 bombers. On 17 January 1936, however, production contracts were awarded to Douglas for 133 twin-engined B-18 Bolos, while Boeing received only a service test order for thirteen improved B-299Bs and a static test model (at a total cost of $4 million), under the designation YB-17. (This was changed to Y1B-17 on 20 November 1936.) The major significant change from the Model 299 was the substitution of Wright SGR-1820-39 Cyclone engines of 1,000 take-off horsepower, for the earlier Hornets, and the crew was decreased from eight to six.

The landing gear was also changed to a single strut oleo arrangement instead of the earlier double legs, to permit easier changing of the wheel and tyre assembly, and minor changes were made to the armament systems.

36-149, the first Y1B-17, was rolled out on 30 September 1936, and it flew for the first time on 2 December. The flight was made by a five-man Air Corps crew, with Major John D. Corkille, Air Corps plant representative at the Boeing plant, at the controls. His co-pilot was Captain Stanley Umstead, chief of the Wright Field Flight Test Section. The fifty-minute flight went well, as did the second, two days later, when the press photographed the new aircraft from a Boeing 247 transport.

On 7 December 1936, on the third flight from Boeing Field, the Y1B-17 (36-149) crashed on landing with Captain Stanley Umstead at the controls. The brakes had failed and the bomber came to a sickening halt and nosed over. No one was hurt, but in January 1937 Boeing had to endure a nerve-racking congressional investigation. Boeing

Captain Stanley Umstead AAC. Boeing

Specification – Y1B-17 (Model 299B)	
Crew:	6
Powerplant:	Wright Cyclone R-1820-39 of 775hp @ 14,000ft (4,267m)
Performance:	Maximum speed 256mph (412km/h) @ 14,000ft (4,267m)
	Cruise speed 217mph (349km/h)
	Rate of climb 6½ mins to 10,000ft (3,048m)
	Ceiling 30,600ft (9,327m)
	Range 1,377miles (2,215km)
Weights:	Empty weight 24,465lb (11,097kg); gross weight 30,000lb (17,690kg)
Dimensions:	Length 68ft 4in (20m 83cm); height 18ft 4in (5m59cm); wingspan 103ft 9in (31m 62cm); wing area 1,420sq ft (132sq m)
Armament:	5 × .30 cal. machine guns; maximum bomb load 8 × 600lb (272kg)

On 7 December, 36-149 was flown by Capt Stanley Umstead on the third flight from Boeing Field, and it almost ended in complete disaster for the company. While taxiing, Umstead applied the brakes so hard that the bi-metal discs overheated. He took off, and instead of leaving the gears down to let the brakes cool, retracted the wheels immediately; by now the brake plates had welded themselves into a solid mass. During the short flight one of the engines overheated and had to be shut down, and on the way back a second engine failed. Umstead touched down and discovered to his cost that the wheels would not rotate: the bomber came to a sickening halt and nosed over. No one was hurt, but in January 1937 Boeing had to endure a nerve-wracking congressional investigation, while the aircraft's detractors (those who favoured less complex, twin-engined bombers especially) gained ground. No official action was taken, however, but any further accidents in the tale of bad luck which seemed to dog the new bomber would have resulted in the cancellation of the entire project. The Model 299 was repaired, and was flying again by 2 January. Rubber de-icer boots were fitted to the leading edge of the wing, and aluminium covering was substituted for fabric on the flaps.

The First of the 'Shark Fins'

The thirteen test Y1B-17s went into service with the 20th, 49th and 96th Bomb Squadrons of the 2nd Bombardment

Nos. 61, 50 (36-152) and 80 (36-151), of the 96th, 20th and 49th Bomb Squadrons respectively, were among the first thirteen Y1B-17s received by the 2nd Bomb Group in March–September 1937. No. 80 took part in the goodwill trip to South America in 1938. USAF

Group, commanded by Lt Col Robert C. Olds, at Langley Field, Virginia. The first arrived on 1 March 1937, and the last on 5 August. The 2nd Bomb Group flew over 1,800,000 miles (2,896,200km) and logged 9,293 flying hours over land and sea without ever losing a plane. The Y1B-17 therefore gained a well-earned reputation for rugged construction and safe operation. Pre-flight checklists were introduced by Olds to prevent a repetition of the Model

equally successful trip to Rio de Janeiro, Brazil. Apart from confirming the 2nd Bomb Group's navigational skill and airmanship, it also reminded any would-be aggressor that the AAC now had the ability to fly bombers over long distances.

Despite these wonderful achievements (for which the 2nd was awarded the MacKay Trophy in 1939) the War Department chose to ignore the earlier words of GHQ Air Force commander Gen Frank

experimentation and development would be confined to aircraft 'designed for the close-in support of ground troops'. It also stated that aircraft production would be restricted to 'medium and light aircraft, pursuit and other light aircraft'.

In an attempt to ram the point home fully regarding the need for a strategic bombing capability, and at the same time fire a warning shot over the US admirals' bows, on 12 May 1938 three Y1B-17s in

The six Y1B-17s of the 2nd Bomb Group which made the Goodwill flight from Langley Field to Buenos Aires, Argentina, in February 1938, pictured over New York City. They covered a total of 12,000 miles (19,308km) without serious incident. Boeing

299 crash. Men such as Harold L. George, Curtis E. LeMay, Robert B. Williams, Neil Harding and Caleb Haynes, who were to become synonymous with USAAF achievements in World War II, served in the 2nd Bomb Group. On 15 February 1938 six Y1B-17s, led by Colonel Olds, took off from Langley and made a very successful 'goodwill' trip to South America, visiting Peru and Buenos Aires, Argentina, and returning on 27 February. Seven other Y1B-17s, led by Major Vincent Meloy and Maj Gen Delos C. Emmons, later made an

Andrews, who in June 1937 had urged the War Department that all future bombers purchased should be four-engined. Twin-engined bombers meant that the Air Corps would be tied to a support role for the ground troops in any future battle. Andrews, like General Billy Mitchell before him, was convinced of the need for a genuine strategic bomber which could destroy America's enemies before they reached the battlefields. Instead, in May 1938 the War Department declared that for the fiscal years 1939 and 1940

the 49th Bombardment Squadron, 2nd Bomb Group, were given a 'navigational exercise' to intercept the Italian liner Rex at sea. At 12:23 hours Col Olds and his lead navigator, Lt Curtis E. LeMay, located the luxury liner some 725 miles (1,167km) east of New York City, and dropped a message onto the deck. (In 1940 LeMay navigated the XB-15 on a 2,839-mile (4,568km) flight to the Galapagos Islands.) This brilliant feat of navigation proved that an invasion force at sea *could* be intercepted before it could harm coastal

(Left) The first Y1B-17 (Model 299B), one of thirteen service test machines, comes in for its first landing, on 2 December 1936, at Boeing Field, Seattle. The 50-minute flight was made by an AAC crew. At first the aircraft were designated YB-17, but this changed to the Y1B-17 on 20 November 1936 when the regular AAC appropriated funds to category F-1 funds. The models were virtually identical with the XB-17, but differed in having the new Wright R-1820-39 Cyclone engines of 1,000hp in place of the 750hp Hornets, and single-leg landing gear instead of the double-strut type. Also, much framework of the gun blisters was replaced with clear plastic domes. Boeing via Phil Jarrett

Workers put the finishing touches to a Y1B-17 at Seattle before delivery to the AAC. In September 1939, when war broke out in Europe, the Air Corps had only twenty-three Flying Fortresses in active inventory. Boeing

defences – but instead of championing the B-17's cause, Gen Malin Craig, AAC chief of staff, under pressure from the US Navy, issued an order limiting the Air Corps' area of operation to not more than 100 miles (160km) from the American shore!

Meanwhile, on 12 May 1937, a static test aircraft (37-369, the fourteenth Y1B-17) was ordered for completion to be used in a controlled experiment to discover just how much stress the aircraft could take before it disintegrated. However, the experiment was deemed unnecessary after a 2nd Bomb Group Y1B-17 (36-157) flown by Lt William Bentley, emerged intact after being thrown onto its back in a violent thunderstorm during a flight to Langley Field in the summer of 1938. Later, the static test aircraft, now redesignated Y1B-17A and fitted with supercharged R-1820-51 engines, was used to test Moss/General Electric turbosuperchargers, which would be needed for high altitude flight. 37-369 flew for the first time on 29 April 1938 with the supercharger turbines mounted on top of the R-1820-51 engine nacelles (because the current Air Corps' specification stipulated that the exhaust be at the top of the nacelle). The experiment was a failure, but confidence was restored when the Y1B-17A flew again on 20 November with the turbos operating successfully mounted under the nacelles. The Y1B-17A was delivered to the Matériel Division at Wright Field on 31 January 1939 for experimental testing. With the turbosuperchargers engaged, the R-1820-

Boeing Y1B-17A 37-369, the fourteenth Y1B-17, which flew for the first time on 29 April 1938, photographed in the vicinity of Boeing Field, Seattle, Washington, on 24 November 1938. Boeing via Phil Jarrett

Boeing Y1B-17A 37-369, photographed on 30 January 1939, was originally intended for completion as a static test aircraft but was subsequently redesignated Y1B-17A, and used to test supercharged R-1820-51 engines. Boeing

Y1B-17 36-156, No. 51, in the 20th Bombardment
Squadron, and other Y1B-17s of the 2nd
Bombardment Group at Langley Field, Virginia,
during filming of Louis D. Lighton's 1938 MGM
classic movie Test Pilot. Early in 1938 Colonel
Robert C. Olds, 2nd Bombardment Group
commanding officer, flew a Y1B-17 to set a new
east-to-west transcontinental record of 12 hours 50
minutes. He immediately turned around and broke
the west-to-east record, averaging 245mph
(394km/h) in 10 hours, 46 minutes. USAF

A Boeing engineer illustrates the use of the
Y1B-17A's belly gun position with the .30 calibre
Browning machine gun. Boeing

Y1B-17s of the 20th Bomb Squadron, 2nd Bombardment Group, pictured at Langley Field, Virginia, in the late 1930s. The display of bombs represents the group's insignia which is of four aerial bombs 'dropping bend sinisterwise azure' on a shield. *Boeing via Phil Jarrett*

Specification – Y1B-17A (Model 299F)	
Crew:	6
Powerplant:	Wright Cyclone R-1820-51 of 800hp @ 25,000ft (7,620m)
Performance:	Maximum speed 295mph (475km/h) @ 25,000ft (7,620m) Cruise speed 183mph (294km/h) Rate of climb 7 mins 48 secs to 10,000ft (3,048m) Ceiling 38,000ft (11,582m) Range 1,377 miles (2,215km)
Weights:	Empty weight 31,160lb (14,134kg); gross weight 45,650lb (20,707kg)
Dimensions:	Length 68ft 4in (20m 83cm); height 18ft 4in (5m 59cm); wingspan 103ft 9in (31m 62cm); wing area 1,420sq ft (132sq m)
Armament:	5 × .30 cal. or .50 cal. machine guns; maximum bomb load 8 × 600lb (272kg)

51 Cyclones could each produce 800hp at 25,000ft (7,620m) in comparison to the Y1B-17's -39s which could only generate 775hp at 14,000ft (4,267m). With this sort of power, the Y1B-17A was able to reach a top speed of 295mph (475km/h) at 25,000ft. Turbos now became standard on the B-17B and all future USAAF B-17 models. (Since the power produced by a piston engine is directly related to the amount of air passing through it in a given time, the greater the mass of air that can be 'rammed' into the cylinders, the greater the high-altitude performance will be. For this

purpose, a supercharger or 'blower' was developed by Dr Sanford Moss of General Electric, and it was first used in flight tests in 1920. The supercharger is driven by the crankshaft of the engine, while the turbo-supercharger is driven by the exhaust gases of the engine.)

B-17B: First of the Stratosphere Bombers

In January 1939 Franklin D. Roosevelt asked Congress to strengthen America's

air power, declaring that it was 'utterly inadequate'. The AAC clamoured for more four-engined bombers but by June that year the AAC had barely thirteen operational B-17s, and more orders were painfully slow in coming. A production requirement for just ten B-17Bs (Model 299E, later Model 299M) had been received by Boeing on 3 August 1937, and by 30 June 1938, orders had risen to a paltry thirty-nine. The Air Corps was anxious to proceed with the B-17B and prove the strategic bomber concept, but financial wranglings soured relations. Boeing was a small, independent company, with just 600 employees, with no cash reserves. It had tooled up in anticipation of large B-17B production orders, and had spent $100,000 on the supercharger development. Although the Air Corps had previously agreed to pay $205,000 per aircraft, they now offered only $198,000 – so not only was Boeing faced with a bill for the superchargers, they were also losing $12,000 on each aircraft! Eventually a compromise was worked out where the Army would pay $202,500 per aircraft.

Problems with the superchargers, which tended to fail at a very frequent rate, meant that the first B-17B (38-211) did not fly until 27 June 1939. The units were very sensitive to heat and cold, and would crack if not operated properly. On occasion the turbosuperchargers would even burst into flames, with the resultant fire burning its way through the aluminium wing if not extinguished quickly. The B-17B had the same Wright R-1820-51 Cyclones as the previous model, giving 900hp up to 25,000ft (7,620m). The kinked forward fuselage and small rotating turret on the nose were deleted to produce a new, more streamlined nose, 7in (18cm) shorter than that of the Y1B-17. The Plexiglass had a flat bomb-aiming panel with a simple socket for a .30-calibre Browning machine-gun. The navigator became a separate crew member and was moved

Specification – B-17B Model 299M	
Crew:	8
Powerplant:	Wright Cyclone R-1820-51 of 1,200hp @ 25,000ft (7,620m)
Performance:	Cruise speed 225mph (362km/h) Rate of climb 7 mins to 10,000ft (3,048m) Ceiling 30,000ft (9,144m) Range 2,400–3,600 miles (3,864–5,796km) with 4,000lb (1,814kg) bombs
Weights:	Empty weight 27,652lb (12,543kg);gross weight 37,997lb (17,235kg)
Dimensions:	Length 67ft 9in (20m 65cm); height 18ft 4in (5m 59cm); wingspan 103ft 9in (31m 62cm); wing area 1,420sq ft (132sq m)
Armament:	1 × .30 cal. and 6 × .50 cal. machine guns; maximum bomb load 4 × 1,100lb (500kg) or 20 × 100lb (45kg)

Boeing B-17B, which flew for the first time on 27 June 1939. Except for minor changes in the fairing of the machine-gun blister into the fuselage, the remainder of the B-17B armament was the same as used on the Y1B-17. Internally, some crew members were relocated, and improved R-1820-51 engines delivered 1200hp for take-off. Boeing

from behind the pilots to a more practical position in the new nose section on the left-hand side behind the bombardier.

Other changes were made. The flaps, which were returned to metal covering, were enlarged by moving the ends of the inner wing panels outboard five main rib spaces, and by shortening the ailerons. The rudder was of increased area, and a Plexiglas dome was added to the cabin roof for the aircraft commander, who sat behind the pilot. External bomb racks could be added to carry a further 4,000lb

(1,814kg) of bombs if required. In-fuselage flotation bags were deleted, and provision made to carry two auxiliary fuel tanks in the bomb-bay. The brakes were changed from the pneumatic type of the Model 299 and Y1B-17, to hydraulic type.

B-17B models were delivered to the 2nd Bomb Group at Langley Field, and to the 7th Bomb Group at Hamilton Field near San Francisco, during the period October 1939–30 March 1940. (In October, the 2nd Bomb Group's original B-17s were transferred to the 19th Bomb Group at March

Field, California.) Meanwhile 38-211, the first B-17B, was retained at Wright Field pending new armament installations planned for the subsequent B-17C version. The B-17B's ability to reach uncharted altitudes posed new problems, not least among the crews who had to operate in very cold temperatures, while oil and other lubricants tended to take on the consistency of tar. A B-17B belonging to the 41st Reconnaissance Squadron, 2nd Bomb Group, in Newfoundland, was the first US Air Force Bomber to drop its bombs in anger when it

The thirty-nine B-17Bs were procured in small batches of thirteen, thirteen, two, one and ten, and were delivered to the 2nd and 7th Bomb Groups between 29 July 1939 and 30 March 1940. A B-17B serving with the 41st Reconnaissance Squadron, 2nd Bomb Group, based in Newfoundland, attacked a German U-boat on 27 October 1941. Although the submarine was undamaged in the attack, this incident (which went unheralded because America was not yet at war with Germany) was the first in which bombs were dropped in anger by the AAC.
Boeing via Phil Jarrett

(Below) Headed by Senator Elmer Thomas of Oklahoma, a Congressional delegation inspect a line-up of B-17Bs of the 19th Bomb Group at March Field, California, on 29 November 1939, led by Colonel Harvey S. Burwell, the CO. The committee visited the field during inspection of Army stations in the US and Panama. The first B-17B in line carries the 19th Bomb Group insignia. Note the 'BS' codes applied to the tail fins. The first B in the 1939–40 unit identification indicated 'bomber', the second letter identified the group (2nd letter of the alphabet; the seventh was BG, and the nineteenth, BS, S being the nineteenth letter of the alphabet. In May 1940 the identification changed to 2B, 7B and 19B, respectively). Senator Thomas declared ominously, after his March Field inspection: 'The Air Force is the best off of any of the elements of the Army, but even that must be strengthened.' By 1940, Douglas B-18A Bolos, like these in the back line, equipped most of the US bomber squadrons, and the type was still in service when Japan attacked the US. Those that survived were replaced, in 1942, by B-17s.
via Phil Jarrett

B-17B 38-211 MD105 (assigned to the Air Corps' Material Division at Wright Field on 2 August 1939 – hence 'MD' unit designator) in flight. The offset aircraft commander's blister behind the cockpit was moved to the centreline on the B-17D. Boeing via Philip Jarrett

attacked a U-boat on 27 October 1941. The US was not yet at war with Germany and the incident was kept secret.

In 1940–41, many B-17Bs were revamped and fitted with new devices such as flush-type waist windows for .50-calibre guns. In 1940 the 2nd and 7th Groups, equipped with B-17B high altitude bombers, practised precision bombing using the top secret gyro-stabilized Norden bombsight, which was originally developed by Carl L. Norden and Capt Frederick I. Entwistle. Experienced bombardiers placed their practice bombs within yards of the target from as high as 20,000ft (6,096m); a feat which led to claims that bombs could be place in a pickle barrel from such heights. Precision bombing called for attacks in daylight, but the ideal conditions prevailing on the ranges at Muroc Dry Lake in the Californian Mojave Desert were not to be found in Europe where first the *Luft-waffe* and then RAF Bomber Command discovered that day bombing was too costly. During the first few months of the war unescorted RAF bombers on daylight raids fell easy victim to *Luftwaffe* single- and twin-engined fighters and forced them to operate only at night.

B-17C, the First Combat-Worthy Fortress

The B-17C (Model 299H), which flew for the first time on 21 July 1940, was a more combat-worthy model following recommendations made by Britain and France as a result of their experience with bombers in air combat. Armour plate (albeit only in the tail behind the waist positions) and self-sealing fuel tanks were fitted, and all machine-guns, except the nose-gun, were standardized at .50 calibre. (By using a .30 calibre gun in the nose, the socket could be mounted in the Plexiglas instead of the framework; therefore three separate sockets were placed in the nose-cone, one in the forward top window on the right-hand side, and another in the second window on the left, making six positions in all.) The two limited-vision gun cupolas on the sides of the fuselage were replaced with streamlined, Plexiglas, teardrop-shaped flush windows, and the guns moved inside onto swivel posts.

Combat experience in Europe had also revealed a need for all-round defence, and this could only be addressed by installing power-operated gun turrets with belt-fed guns (aboard the B-17C all six guns were pannier-fed). However, the top gun blister was replaced only by a removable sliding Plexiglass hatch, while a large 'bath-tub', which the gunner had to kneel in to fire his gun, replaced the under gunner's blister. Both only provided for rearward defence. Nevertheless, the B-17C was considered well armed, and it possessed an impressive top speed of 325mph (523km/h) at around 29,000ft (8,932m) and could cruise at 230mph (370km/h) at 30,000ft (9,144m). The bomb load remained the same (4,996lb (2,266kg)) as on the B-17B. Other changes included adding boost and transfer pumps to allow each fuel tank to feed a separate engine, and the oxygen system was changed to a manifold type. Dual in place of single brakes were fitted on each main wheel.

Thirty-eight B-17Cs were ordered on 10 August 1939 (the first B-17C was retained by Boeing for test purposes) as part of an overall US requirement for 461 new B-17, B-24, B-25 and B-26 bombers. Only the B-17 had flown in prototype form and, as we will see, twenty of these new aircraft (Model 299U) were acquired by Britain. In 1940 the requirement for these four types of bomber had risen to 3,214; in the interim, companies like Boeing were in a dire financial situation. In April 1940 the Army finally exercised its option for forty-two additional B-17Cs, but only after Boeing had been forced to lay off part of its workforce. On 18 May Boeing received a very timely contract from the French government for 240 DB-7 attack bombers (subsequently taken over by Great Britain) to be built under licence from Douglas. Hirings replaced firings and Boeing borrowed big to wipe out outstanding debts and to expand their plant. On 12 July 1940 Boeing was advised by the War Department that orders for 512 more B-17s in two lots (277 and 235) would be made. The military defeat in the West had done somebody some good.

Planning for The US Bombing Offensive

On 21 July 1941 the Army Air Forces came into being, with Maj Gen Henry H. Arnold as its chief. That same month, President Franklin D. Roosevelt asked the Secretaries of War and of the Navy to produce estimates for bringing their forces to an effective war footing. Arnold used the opportunity to gain permission for the AAC's Air War Plans Division to prepare their own report, forcing the War Plans Division to concentrate solely on the needs of its land forces. Arnold's staff officers at AWPD, headed by

Col Harold L. George, and including Lt Col Kenneth Walker, Maj Haywood 'Possum' Hansell and Maj Larry S. Kuter, formulated a policy (AWPD/1) of a relentless air offensive against Nazi Germany and a strategic defence in the Pacific. If Japan entered the war, it too would be subjected to aerial bombardment after Germany had surrendered. The planning team listed 154 targets for its strategic bombing concept, the principal ones being the German airframe assembly plants and associated metal production, fifty electrical generating or switching stations, forty-seven key points in the German transportation network, and all of the twenty-seven petroleum plants in Germany. Six months' strategic bombing of these targets, together with the neutralization of the *Luftwaffe*, submarine and naval facilities, might, it was thought, render a land campaign unnecessary.

AWPD/1 calculated that German industry could be destroyed by daylight precision bombing because it was expected that 90 per cent of the bombs dropped on a clear day would explode within 1,250ft (380m) of the MPI. Events would prove otherwise, however, and to achieve this objective, 1,060 medium bombers, 1,700 B-17 and B-24 heavy bombers (in twenty groups), 2,040 B-29 and B-32 very heavy bombers

and 3,412 fighters needed to be deployed against Nazi Germany from bases in Great Britain and Egypt, together with 3,740 intercontinental B-36 bombers, based in the US. AWPD maintained that 6,800 medium, heavy and very heavy bombers based in Europe and North Africa could bring about the downfall of Germany. This was fine in theory, but America's ability to build bombers in sufficient numbers to achieve this aim was impossible. In the summer of 1941 for instance, only 700 bombers of all types were available. The B-32 never entered full-scale production, and the sheer enormity of the B-36 project prevented the bomber reaching wartime production. Although sixteen pursuit groups were deemed necessary to protect the bombers' bases, no provision was made for long-range escort fighters to accompany the bombers.

One thing was for certain: when the US entered the war it would direct its greater strength against Germany and it would be the B-17s, based in the United Kingdom, which would form the main offensive weapon. In the interim, it was RAF Bomber Command which first used the B-17 in combat operations, and the experience was used to improve successive versions of the Flying Fortress.

B-17 Production Totals			
Model	Boeing Co	Douglas Aircraft	Lockheed Vega
Model 299	1		
Y1B-17	13		
Y1B-17A	1		
B-17B	39		
B-17C	38		
B-17D	42		
B-17E	512		
B-17F-BO	2,300		
B-17F-DL		605	
B-17F-VE			500
(Total F production 3,405)			
B-17G-BO	4,035		
B-17G-DL		2,395	
B-17G-VE			2,250
(Total G production 8,680)			
Grand Total	6,981	3,000	2,750

Swiftly They Strike

The Pioneers of 90 Squadron RAF

The British Purchasing Commission had first taken an interest in the B-17C and had ordered twenty aircraft (designated 299U) from the 1939 contract. In the spring of 1941 these were duly supplied to Britain, together with the necessary personnel to instruct and assist in bringing them into RAF service. These aircraft, serial numbered AN518/AN537, were intended as trainers pending deliveries of the B-17E, and were not to be used operationally. However, the aircraft situation in Britain at this time was acute, and so it was decided to modify these B-17Cs to an operational standard. In June 1941 the first five Fortress Is, as they were known in RAF service, were delivered to No. 90 Squadron for high-altitude bombing operations.

The first aircraft to arrive flew the Atlantic Ferry Route on 14 April 1941 with Maj Mike Walsh, USAAC, who was to head the American advisory personnel, at the controls. AN521 crossed the Atlantic in the then record time of 8 hours and 26 minutes, but for security reasons the news was not released. It was intended that the new type equip 21 Squadron, but as this would mean taking a first-line squadron off operations, on 7 May 1941 90 Squadron (Motto: 'celer' meaning 'swift') was officially reformed at Watton in Norfolk under the command of Wg Cdr J. McDougall in No. 2 Group. This group was unique in RAF Bomber Command in that it specialized in daylight bombing.

The twenty (Model 299U) Fortress Is (B-17Cs) for the RAF photographed at McChord Field, Washington, in February 1941. At first, 'AM' serial letters were applied in error but they were changed later to 'AN'. AN518 (40-2043) B-Bertie joined 90 Squadron on 9 August 1941, went on to serve as MB-B in 220 Squadron Detachment in the Middle East, then went to India in July 1942, where it was handed over to the USAAF on 1 December 1942; AN522 (40-2053) J-Johnny joined 90 Squadron on 4 June 1941 and broke up in the air over Catterick on 22 June; AN527 (40-2061) and AN530 (40-2066) joined 90 Squadron and later served with 220 Squadron, Coastal Command, being SOC in 1943; AN529 (40-2065) C-Charlie joined 90 Squadron on 11 May 1941 and force-landed in Libya, behind enemy lines, on 8 November 1941. Boeing via Philip Jarrett

Fortress I (40-2064), which became **AN528** B-Baker **in 90 Squadron RAF, pictured during an early test flight in Washington state.** B-Baker **joined 90 Squadron on 4 June 1941 but her career was short-lived: she caught fire running up her engines at dispersal at Polebrook on 3 July and was burnt out.** Boeing

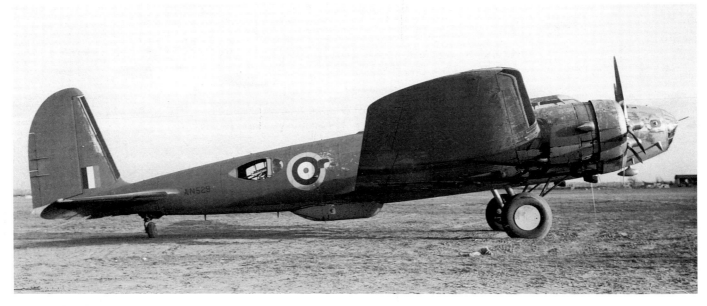

Fortress I AN529 (40-2065), **C-Charlie pictured at Squires Gate, Blackpool, in April 1941, shortly after arrival in the UK. AN529, together with AN534 (40-2073) WP-E, were the first two B-17Cs taken on charge by 90 Squadron at RAF Watton, on 11 May 1941. AN529 was finally lost on 8 November following a daylight raid on Benghazi from 20,000ft (6,000m) when it ran out of fuel and had to be put down in a desert wadi about 200 miles (320km) south-east of Tobruk.** British official via Philip Jarrett

Four days later the squadron took delivery of two B-17Cs, AN534 and AN529.

On 5 May a group of young airmen, most of them veterans of RAF night bombing or low-level daylight operations, arrived at Watton to train on an aircraft they had never seen before and one which they were to fly in broad daylight and at high altitude. All were recent graduates of a rigorous decompression test at Farnborough; this had involved 'climbing' at 3,000ft (914m) a minute to 35,000ft (10,668m) and remaining there for five hours. The B-17C's range was poor, and only American bombs up to 1,100lb (500kg) could be carried. The top-secret Norden precision bombsight, developed by the US Navy and able to place a bomb in 'a pickle barrel', had been deleted and replaced by the Sperry sight. Depending on one's point of view, it was either very bad ('one needed a bloody big barrel'), or an excellent device but limited because it was only calibrated for automatic operation to 25,000ft (7,620m) and bomb aimers had to 'guestimate' by feeding in pre-set calculations supplied by Sperrys at higher altitudes.

On 7 May the aircraft AN521, now called *K-King*, was flown to Burtonwood, near Liverpool, for modifications; Maj Walsh was at the controls, with Roy Boast (later Gp Capt CBE, DFC) as navigator. Boast had previously flown on Whitleys, and more recently the Halifax, and had 'foolishly' volunteered to go to Farnborough for a day's high-altitude test 'to get a night in London' – only to find himself posted to 90 Squadron forthwith. Like many other old hands in 90 Squadron, he yearned for a return to night 'ops'. Also on the 7th, AN534 arrived at Watton to become the squadron's first Fortress I. On 11 May, Maj Mike Walsh, accompanied by Tom Imrie and others, flew AN529 to Watton from Burtonwood. The only potentially dangerous incident which occurred was when the 2nd pilot forgot to lock the throttles and the Fortress began heading for the barrage balloons over Liverpool.

Next day, flying training was started from Watton's satellite airfield at Bodney. It proved a very short sojourn, in fact lasting only two days, because the undulating grass runways proved most unsuitable for Fortress training. On 13 May Sgt Tim (Mick) Wood, an Australian who had completed seven Wellington operations with 115 Squadron, made his first Fortress flight on conversion to type in AN534 with Capt James T. Connally, USAAC, a veteran of the 19th Bomb Group

90 Squadron Fortress I crew get suited up for high-altitude flight. All crew-members had been sent to Farnborough where they had been exposed to a routine 'bends' test in the decompression chamber, as the Fortress I was expected to fly at heights well in excess of 30,000ft (9,000m). At first, electrically heated one-piece suits made by Seibe-Gorman with electrically heated gloves and boots were worn, but they restricted movement, which was so essential for the gunners, were bulky, and not very reliable. In August 1941 one-piece 'Taylor' suits, but much more easily donned, with an electrically heated lining, glove lining and socks, became available. The suit also provided built-in flotation, was reliable, and much easier to move in. These were used with fleecy-lined flying boots and soft leather gauntlets. IWM

operations in the Pacific. This was followed the next day by an intercom test in AN529, again with Capt Connally (as CO, 504th Bomb Group, Connally was killed leading a B-29 raid on Japan in February 1945). Wood and the other pilots also received instruction from Maj Walsh and Lt Bradley, son of US General Omar Bradley. Altogether the USAAC provided five experienced airmen, while other American advisors included Franklyn Joseph, an expert on the Sperry 01 bombsight, and a number of Boeing representatives including Bob Crawford and Tex O'Camb, an expert on Wright Cyclones and superchargers and a USAAC reservist who joined the RAF as a Flight Lieutenant on condition that he could transfer to the USAAC if America entered the war.

On 15 May Fortress training flights continued, this time from Great Massingham, a satellite of RAF West Raynham, while Fortresses went for overhaul at West Raynham. Despite the constant upheaval,

training was beginning to pay dividends; Wg Cdr McDougall chose Mick Wood as his second pilot, and nineteen-year-old Sgt (later Air Cdr) Tom Imrie DFM became one of his gunners. Imrie was a veteran of thirty-four operations as a WOP-AG (wireless operator-air gunner) on Whitley bombers with No. 51 Squadron at Dishforth, Yorkshire. A young medical officer, Fg Off Antony J. Barwood (later Gp Capt Barwood OBE), was posted to 90 Squadron in May to deal with the problems of high-altitude flying. He had been sent to Farnborough where he had been exposed to a routine 'bends' test in the decompression chamber. The Fortress was expected to fly at heights well in excess of 30,000ft (9,144m), an altitude not achieved by operational RAF bombers (except for the pressurized experimental Wellington Mk V/VI). Barwood recalls:

I was still very young, but much older than most of the aircrew. Later, my job became the selection of aircrew at Polebrook where we operated a mobile decompression chamber; this could take six men to a simulated 35,000ft [10,668m], driven by a Coventry Victor single-cylinder engine. Crews were young and keen, and were declared fit to fly B-17Cs after they had passed the decompression test. I always flew with them on their first training sortie. Wg Cdr Noel Singer, senior air staff officer to the AOC, and also AM Sir Richard Peirse, came to Polebrook to fly in a B-17; I said he had to be 'bends'-tested first, and he didn't pass, and was not allowed to fly.

Sqn Ldr Edgar Bright (another aviation medicine specialist who retired as Air Cdr Bright AFC) came in as station SMO at Polebrook and did some of the training. Before each sortie we always checked every crew's oxygen supply to make sure that the cylinders were correctly filled and that the regulators at each crew position were fully functional. We also briefed the crews on oxygen systems and clothing, and attended operation debriefings to see if there had been any problems.

There were many problems with the oxygen and intercom systems which needed sorting out before the aircraft could be operated at altitude. We started with the American oxygen system, eight individually controlled regulators and BLB re-breather bag masks with hand-held carbon-granule microphones. However, the regulators seized up, the masks froze and the microphones became progressively more useless above 15,000ft [4,570m] as they depended on air density to excite the carbon granules within the diaphragm of the microphone. We then changed to British Mk VIII oxygen regulators and Type E masks with an incorporated electromagnetic microphone, which also required amplifier changes in the aircraft. The masks still froze, and were modified with an additional valve. I covered the diaphragm on the microphone with a French letter to prevent them freezing!

An oxygen economizer invented by Professor – later Sir – Brian Matthews KBE was introduced. It stored the oxygen flowing through the regulator while the user was not breathing in, which is only about one third of the breathing cycle. The original economizers were hand made by 'metal bashers' within the Royal Aircraft Establishment and at the Physiology Laboratory, as the IAM then was. They effectively reduced the weight of the oxygen cylinders which the aircraft had to carry by 50 per cent and produced a more effective oxygen system. The final change was to a Mk 10 regulator, controlled centrally by the captain who could deliver oxygen to each crew position.

The bitter cold at altitude was made far worse by the aircraft having to fly with all four of the rear fuselage blisters off; high air blast therefore affected all the rear crew so that effective flying clothing was of vital importance. Tom Imrie DFM recalls that there were technical problems to contend with, too:

We had constant engine oil problems caused by the pressure differences. The oxygen system and the intercom were bad, and the armament was prehistoric, with free-mounted .5s in the waist and one .300 in the nose. Ammunition was contained in heavy 50lb [23kg] containers, and it was a hell of a struggle trying to lift them onto the mountings at 30,000-plus feet. The guns jumped around all over the place and hosepiped on the free mountings, and often they didn't fire. Also they iced up at altitude and we had to wash them in petrol. The windscreens iced up, too, and eventually had to be double-glazed.

By 26 May four crews had converted successfully to the Fortress and now there were five on squadron strength. Training took on a new importance with regular cross-country, bombing and altitude flights being made throughout East Anglia, and on occasions further afield. Tom Imrie recalls: 'We moved about so much we hardly ever had time to unpack – but morale always remained high. At West Raynham we shared the station with two Blenheim squadrons which at that time had high losses on the Channel ports.' Imrie, for one, was finding the transition from night operations to very high-altitude daylight operations 'terrifying! It was nerve-racking flying in broad daylight, and on one test flight over Cornwall on 4 June we even got the B-17 up to 41,000ft [12,500m]. We could see the earth's curvature, and the sky had turned a dark purple colour instead of blue.'

However, there were welcome features which were absent on RAF aircraft. Imrie continues: 'On one occasion, at Abingdon, we were visited by HM King George VI and Queen Elizabeth and the two princesses. The young Princess Elizabeth enquired about the incongruous dark grey carpets throughout and thermos flasks on the bulkhead. These were a leftover from the Fortress's early role on long, over-water operations when crew comfort was important. Tony Barwood adds:

My first training sortie was to be a routine training flight from West Raynham on the afternoon of 22 June. I was fully briefed and kitted by Sqn Ldr D.A.H. Robson, the station medical officer at West Raynham, and himself a pilot. However, the flight was delayed as Flt Lt William K. Stewart (later AVM, CBE, DFC, commander of the RAF Institute of Aviation Medicine) and a test pilot, Flt Lt Henderson, were on their way from Farnborough to gain experience of a Fortress sortie, and I was turned off. The Fort, AN522 J-Johnny was flown by Fg Off Mike Hawley, with Lt Jim Bradley as instructor pilot. But at high altitude the aircraft hit some cumulo nimbus at around 30,000ft [9,000m] over Catterick, Yorkshire, and broke up. Flt Lt Stewart was trapped in the tail section which broke away from the fuselage; it fell 12,000ft [3,660m] but he managed to bale out at about 3,000ft [900m]. He was the only survivor.

During 27–29 June, McDougall and his available crews flew to Polebrook, their new, permanent home near Peterborough. Much of the base was still under construction, and crews, used to pre-war brick-built barracks at other bases, were taken aback to find themselves billeted in highly uncomfortable wooden huts little better than the leaky Nissens with their iron stoves used on other bases. The airfield tended to flood, but at least the concrete runway was a vast improvement over grass.

The squadron's new tenancy was marred by the loss of AN528 on 3 July when B-Baker burst into flames during an engine test on the airfield. Gradually, twelve aircraft were gathered at Polebrook, although maintenance problems often reduced the available number of Forts to just three. Meanwhile, bombing practice continued apace, and by 6 July bomb aimers were deemed to have reached acceptable proficiency. However, as Roy Boast recalls, practice bombing only took place at low altitude, well below that required for operational bombing: 'We did not do any practice bombing above 25,000ft [7,620m] during training. I logged the dropping of thirty-three practice bombs from altitudes between 8,000 and 20,000ft [2,450 and 6,100m].'

Meanwhile, calls were mounting for an operation over Germany, and at 1500 hours on 8 July, three Fortress Is, each carrying four 1,100lb (500kg) ground-burst bombs (armour-piercing bombs were not yet available) taxied out at Polebrook for the first RAF Fortress operation, to the docks at Wilhelmshaven. The outcome was awaited with great interest by RAF and USAAC personnel alike. McDougall piloted AN526 G-George while Flt Sgt Mick Wood flew as second pilot. The rest of the crew consisted of Fg Off Eddie Skelton, the squadron navigation officer, Fg Off Barnes, the squadron gunnery leader, and Sgts Tom Danby, Danny 'Mophead' Clifford, both gunners, and Tom Imrie, who flew as signaller. Skelton and Barnes had been in McDougall's crew in Blenheims.

Behind them came AN529 C-Charlie piloted by Plt Off Alex Mathieson and AN519 H-Harry flown by Sqn Ldr Andy MacLaren and Plt Off Mike Wayman, both ex-Blenheim pilots, with Roy Boast as Navigator/bomb aimer. Despite the small size of the operation, crews never questioned whether this and subsequent raids did any good. Roy Boast recalls: 'I had been in single aircraft operations in Whitleys, so the attitude was, "Let's do the job and get out!"'

The loose vic formation cleared the coast and half-way over the North Sea began climbing to 27,000ft (8,230m). With light armament and little armour plate, the Fortress 1s relied almost entirely on height for protection against Bf 109s and FW 190s. Roy Boast recalls: 'We started losing oil from the breathers in two engines at 25,000ft [7,620m], it streamed back and started freezing on the tailplane, and the aircraft began vibrating very badly. MacLaren was forced to abandon the attack, and I aimed our bomb-load on an airfield on Nordeney.'

Meanwhile McDougall dropped all four demolition bombs on Wilhelmshaven, but two of Mathieson's bombs 'hung up' and were released over the Frisians on the return journey. Both aircraft climbed to 32,000ft (9,750m) as two Bf 109Es rose to intercept, but the German fighters lost control at such high altitude and failed to close the attack. It was just as well, because the RAF gunners reported that all guns and mountings had frozen. Bombing results at Wilhelmshaven could not be determined because the cameras also failed to function. Tom Imrie was 'pretty relieved' to get back: 'Condensation trails were a dead giveaway at our height of 28,000-plus, but fortunately we didn't encounter any fighters. We were on oxygen for almost the entire flight.'

On 23 July, Prime Minister Winston Churchill planned to make a speech in the House of Commons to coincide with a raid on Berlin by Fortresses of 90 Squadron. Because the Fortresses would be operating at their extreme range, additional fuel tanks were installed in the bomb-bay at the expense of two of the bombs, which reduced the high-explosive load to just 2,200lb (1,000kg). Even so, engine and throttle set-

tings would be crucial. Meanwhile a blackout was imposed, and crews were confined to camp at Polebrook, much to the chagrin of Tom Imrie and the other airmen, who felt 'boot-faced' (fed up) about it.

Despite the grandiose scheme, again only three Fortresses were available for the raid, which began at 09:00 hours. Wg Cdr McDougall was at the controls of AN530 F-Freddie, with MacLaren in AN523 D-Dog and Mathieson in AN529 C-Charlie. MacLaren's navigator/bomb aimer, Roy Boast, recalls:

> It was a beautiful summer's day, 'gin-clear' without a cloud in the sky. We had been told to stick to the throttle and engine settings as briefed, but we tended to exceed them. Even so, we could not keep up with the other two aircraft, and by the time we crossed the Dutch coast we were only at 23,000ft [7,000m]. Mike Wayman and 'Mac' didn't want our aircraft to arrive over Berlin on our own and at such a low altitude, so after 'Mac' had checked the fuel and found we had used more than we should have, and we were making vapour trails anyway, he decided to abort. MacLaren dived for the deck and we flew home at 100ft [30m] – being ex-Blenheim pilots, 'Mac' and Mike were used to this. We were alive, but we thought the other two would get their posthumous VCs.

However, increasingly thick cloud had forced McDougall and Mathieson to abort too. McDougall instructed Imrie to radio to base, and Churchill was presumably warned in time to change his speech in the Commons. All three aircraft returned safely, although Sgt Denny had passed out through lack of oxygen and experienced frostbite to the side of his face. The New Zealander was saved by Tom Danby who gave him a walk-around oxygen bottle; generous tots of rum helped to revive him completely and he suffered no lasting effect apart from a huge hangover!

The following day the same three crews were required as part of Operation Sunrise, an all-out attack by Nos 5 and 2 Group squadrons on the battle cruisers Gneisenau and Prinz Eugen, which were berthed in harbour at Brest. McDougall and MacLaren began the attack, dropping their 1,100-pounders (500kg) from 27,000ft (8,380m). Although bursts were seen on the torpedo station and the outer corner of the dry dock, targets of this nature really required armour-piercing bombs if they were to cause any lasting damage.

Five Bf 109s rose to intercept the Fortresses, but they soon gave up and veered away to attack the incoming stream of ninety lower-flying Hampdens and Wellingtons. In fact the Fortress crews had not been briefed that a large RAF formation would be inbound after they came off the target; one of MacLaren's gunners saw the formation at 10,000ft (3,000m), mistook the twin-tailed Hampdens for Bf 110s and shouted that a hundred Messerschmitts were below them! MacLaren bolted for home. Nine bombers were lost, and no hits were made on the ships.

The Brest raid was the last that McDougall flew with 90 Squadron: after, he handed over his crew to Mick Wood, and Wg Cdr Peter F. Webster DSO, DFC, took over as squadron commander. On 26 July, Sgt Mick Wood flew as first pilot of F-Freddie, and with C-Charlie, flown by newly promoted Sqn Ldr Mathieson, headed for Hamburg. Thunderstorms prevented an attack on the primary target, so Wood dropped his bomb-load on Emden. Mathieson returned to base with his bomb-load intact, but Wood's aircraft developed engine trouble and he was forced to land at Horsham St Faith near Norwich.

Two days later the squadron's second flying accident occurred, claiming AN534 which crashed at Wilbarston, Northants after encountering turbulence during a test flight. F/Sgt Brook and Lt Hendricks, USAAC, and the crew were all killed. Once again, Tony Barwood escaped certain death. He had been briefed to make the flight, but was delayed after an airman in a routine chamber test developed the 'bends' during a session in the mobile decompression chamber and he had to cope with his descent and possible after-effects.

On 2 August, AN529 C-Charlie, flown by Sqn Ldr Mathieson, and AN530 F-Freddie, flown by Plt Off Frank Sturmey, took off to attack Kiel. After twenty minutes into the flight Sturmey was forced to abort with engine problems and brought his bombs back to Polebrook, only to burst his tail-wheel tyre on landing. Mathieson carried on to the target alone and successfully dropped all four 1,100lb (500kg) bombs on the target.

At 17:15 hours, his tail-wheel tyre repaired, Sturmey took off again and this time headed for Bremen. However, thick cloud made bombing impossible and he headed for the seaplane base at Borkum in the Frisian Islands; Roy Boast dropped his bombs from 32,000ft (9,750m). On the way

Fortress I AN530 F-Freddie joined 90 Squadron on 10 July 1941 and operated with them until 12 February 1942, when it joined 220 Squadron, Coastal Command. F-Freddie was scrapped on 11 September 1943. Charles E. Brown via Philip Jarrett

home two Bf 109s intercepted the Fortress at about 20,000ft (6,000m) over the North Sea, one attacking the nose while the other concentrated on the beam. Roy Boast, who hastily manned the nose gun, recalls: 'I fired one round and the machine gun jammed. The fighter came round for another head-on attack and I crouched behind the bombsight. Fortunately he didn't fire (probably out of ammo), but he kept on attacking head-on while the other carried out beam attacks. We had about twenty holes in the fuselage – I think he was trying to put the beam gunners out of action.' Sturmey lost them after some violent evasive action and made it back to Polebrook without sustaining any casualties.

Apprehension was growing as to whether the B-17Cs would remain immune from attack at high altitude; but the operations continued. On 6 August, Sturmey in AN523 *D-Dog* and Mathieson in AN529 *C-Charlie* set off for another

crack at Brest, where the battle cruisers *Gneisenau* and *Scharnhorst* were in harbour. Aboard *C-Charlie* the pilots could only wait, hands off the controls, while Roy Boast took over the lateral control of the Fortress through the Sperry auto-pilot system linked to the bombsight, to place the cross-hairs on the target and keep them there while the bombsight calculated the wind velocity. Suddenly the intercom crackled in his ear: 'Sturmey said, "Where are you going?" and I replied, "Nicely on the run!" only to be interrupted by a shout, "Look out to starboard!" In fact the bombs were going down into the sea, proving that the bombsight was way off.' Mathieson bombed the target from 32,000ft (9,750m) and claimed hits.

On 12 August, four Fortress Is were ordered to take part in diversionary operations to draw the *Luftwaffe* fighters away from Blenheims of No 2 Group which would be making an attack on the Knapsack

power station near Cologne. Because of increasing doubts regarding the proficiency of bomb aimers and/or the bombsight, both Roy Boast and Plt Off Tony Mulligan (who did the setting) flew as bomb aimers with Plt Off Sturmey in *D-Dog*. Sturmey was briefed to bomb De Kooy airfield in Holland, but the target was covered by eight-tenths cloud, and an airfield at Texel was bombed instead. Mulligan released his bombs from 32,000ft (9,750m) after Boast had checked his settings. Boast adds, 'The Sperry was a very good bombsight, in advance of its time. Our problems arose because we tried to use it outside its design capabilities. Sperry's pre-set calculations had not been fully tested, and though they worked well in certain wind conditions, they did not in others.'

Meanwhile Plt Off Wayman in AN532 *J-Johnny* bombed Cologne through cloud from 34,000ft (10,360m) and Plt Off Taylor in AN536 *M-Mother* also bombed through cloud over Emden from 33,000ft

(10,000m). Mick Wood in *C-Charlie* suffered an engine failure over Oxford – to reach altitude before crossing the coast, the aircraft had to fly west, turning over the Midlands, as a loaded B-17's rate of climb was so slow – and was forced to return to Polebrook after only twenty-seven minutes.

Flushed with the success of actually getting four B-17Cs into the air, 90 Squadron was assigned two targets on 16 August. Mick Wood and Plt Off Taylor were allocated Düsseldorf, while two others attacked the *Scharnhorst* and *Gneisenau* at Brest again. Bad weather forced Wood and Taylor to abandon their operation, and they returned to Polebrook with their bomb-loads intact.

Frank Sturmey and Plt Off Tom Franks in *D-Dog*, together with Plt Off Wayman in *J-Johnny*, made a successful attack on Brest – but on the return, Sturmey's Fortress was intercepted by seven enemy fighters at 32,000ft (9,750m). For twenty-five minutes Sturmey and Franks carried out a series of violent evasive manoeuvres all the way down to 8,000ft (3,450m). Tony Mulligan, the bomb aimer, recalled later on the BBC:

Three minutes after our bombs had gone, Flt Sgt Fred Goldsmith, the fire controller, called out that there were enemy fighters coming up to us from the starboard quarter, 1,000ft [300m] below. They closed in, and there was almost no part of the Fortress which wasn't hit – a petrol tank was punctured, bomb doors were thrown open, flaps were put out of action, tail-tab was shot away, tail-wheel stuck half down, brakes not working, only one aileron any good and the rudder almost out of control. The centre of the fuselage had become a tangle of wires and broken cables, and square feet of wing had been shot away

Fred Goldsmith had been badly wounded by shrapnel during the first attack, but he continued to call out the enemy positions to Sturmey so the pilot could take evasive action, and even attempted to cross the open bomb-bay to give first-aid to the gunners. He was prevented from doing so, and an attempt by Mulligan also failed. In fact the gunners were already beyond help: Sgt H. Needle, the WOP-AG, had been hit in the stomach by cannon fire as he tried in vain to fire his frozen dorsal gun; Sgt S. Ambrose, the beam gunner, had also been killed during the fighter attacks; and Sgt M.J. Leahy, the ventral gunner, had been seriously wounded. The *Luftwaffe* pilots

only broke off the attack as the English coast came into view. Sturmey decided Polebrook was out of the question, and put the badly damaged bomber down at Roborough airfield near Plymouth – but he overshot, hit a tank-trap and the aircraft caught fire. A marine sentry sheltering behind the tank-traps was killed in the crash. The survivors evacuated the Fortress, but Leahy died later in hospital.

Düsseldorf was again targeted on 19 August, but bad weather, freezing guns and tell-tale contrails forced Plt Off Wayman and Sgt Wood's crews to abort. Plt Off Wayman also had trouble with a turbo. Throttling back was critical at higher altitude as the engine exhaust drove the turbosuperchargers: if exhaust pressure flow dropped, the turbo would 'stall' and could not be restarted. Wayman's signaller alerted No. 2 Group that they had, in RAF parlance, 'dropped a turbo'; Group radioed back: 'Where did it fall, and could it be recovered, because it is classified!'

Another attempt was made on Düsseldorf two days later when three crews were despatched. Sqn Ldr Mathieson led the operation with Mick Wood in AN518 *B-Baker*, a new aircraft, and Plt Off Wayman in *J-Johnny*. Mathieson was defeated by frozen guns in heavy cloud over Flushing, and Wayman was forced to jettison his bombs in the North Sea after developing engine trouble. Mick Wood's guns also froze, and after producing massive contrails at altitude, he too decided to abandon the operation.

Düsseldorf continued to elude 90 Squadron when on 29 August Mick Wood failed to get airborne in AN533 *N-Nan*, and AN536 *M-Mother*, flown by Fg Off Wayman, took off but returned early after producing heavy contrails at altitude. On 31 August, 90 Squadron opted for individual sorties, and three Fortress Is were despatched to Hamburg, Bremen and Kiel. Mick Wood successfully attacked Bremen in AN518 *B-Baker* with four 1,100lb (500kg) bombs, but Mathieson, who bombed Spikeroge, and Wayman, who bombed Bremen, returned with oil and turbosupercharger problems respectively. Operational problems were now developing at an increasing rate and the shortage of trained ground personnel did not help the cause. The biggest let-down, however, appeared to be the continuing failure of the bombsights. Mr Vose, an American civilian who had been involved in the design of the Sperry bombsight, had taken to heart RAF jibes

about the dubious accuracy of his bombsight. The old World War I Veteran donned RAF uniform and acted as bomb aimer for Mathieson on the operation to Bremen on 2 September. Sturmey and Wood returned with intercom and engine failures respectively, but although Mathieson made it to Bremen, Mr Vose unfortunately placed his bomb wide of the target. At Polebrook he was last seen leaving the Mess, heading for the USA; it was said, to modify his bombsight!

In the back of the crews' minds was the fear that now the *Luftwaffe* could engage them at altitude, something had to give, and they thought it would be sooner rather than later. At the beginning of September, 90 Squadron was alerted to provide four Fortresses for a raid on the German battleship *Admiral von Scheer*, which was sheltering in Oslo Fiord. On 5 September, four Fortresses with Wood, Sturmey, Romans and Mathieson as pilots, were bombed up at Polebrook before flying to Kinloss in northern Scotland. Sqn Ldr MacLaren, the detachment commander, flew a reserve Fortress, AN535, *O-Orange*, with ground personnel and spares on board. Next day four Fortresses set out to bomb the *Admiral von Scheer*. *O-Orange* aborted with supercharger problems, and the other three crews were prevented from bombing by a heavy layer of cloud and smoke which shielded the battleship from view. All three bomb-loads were dropped on targets of opportunity from 30,000ft (9,000m).

Crews were told to stand by for another raid on 8 September while bombs were brought from Polebrook for another attempt. Alex Mathieson tried to convince his friend Roy Boast that he should fly with him, as he recalls: 'His bomb aimer was older, and Alex said, "Come on Roy, my chap will stand down. It's wonderful over the mountains of Norway." I said, "No, I don't think I want to."' At 09:10 Plt Off Sturmey took off and headed for Norway; he was followed five minutes later by Mick Wood. Plt Off David Romans followed, but Sqn Ldr Alex Mathieson in *N-Nan* was delayed. Again he tried to convince Boast that he was 'missing a great experience', but although Boast was 'half tempted', he did not go. Mathieson and his crew were never seen again. Next day Sturmey and Boast carried out a sea search for them but it was in vain.

Sturmey, in *J-Johnny*, carried on to the target but encountered heavy cloud and was forced to return early to Kinloss without dropping his bombs. At 11:27 two Bf 109s intercepted Romans at 27,000ft (8,230m); the Canadian's gunners shot down one fighter before the Fortress erupted in flames and crashed in the Norwegian mountains. Mick Wood in *O-Orange* was about one mile astern when the attack started. He immediately jettisoned his bomb-load and climbed sharply at maximum throttle to 35,000ft (10,670m) in an effort to outclimb the fighters. He gave the order for all crew to be prepared to bale out, but in the rarefied atmosphere the pilot's vocal chords failed to vibrate sufficiently. One of the gunners misunderstood the instruction and switched to his emergency oxygen supply, and then passed out when it was exhausted. A waist gunner who went to help him disconnected from the aircraft oxygen supply but did not connect to his portable oxygen bottle, and he too passed out.

Wood could not contact his gunners on the intercom, and asked his wireless operator to investigate. When he was told of the gunners' plight he immediately dived the aircraft, but at 29,000ft (8,840m) the enemy fighters attacked again and riddled the aircraft with machine-gun fire. Flt Sgt Tates was hit in the arm and Sgt Wilkins was mortally wounded; the wireless operator slipped into unconsciousness when his oxygen lead was severed by a piece of shrapnel; the glycol tank was punctured and began streaming heavy white smoke. Fortunately for the Fortress crew the enemy pilots probably assumed that the smoke meant that the Fortress was finished, and broke off the attack.

The bomb-bay doors had remained open all this time, and now that the fighters had gone, one of the gunners attempted to hand-crank them up. He soon passed out when he lost his oxygen supply, but Dave Hindshaw, the second pilot, went to his aid and quickly connected to him to another supply. Wood nursed the ailing Fortress across the North Sea. One engine was out, and he had no aileron control, but he managed to reach Scotland – only for another engine to fail. The Australian told the crew to take up crash positions, but managed to put down without any further casualties.

90 Squadron were to get involved with *Admiral Scheer* again, as Tony Boast – who, shortly after Oslo, got his wish to rejoin a Halifax squadron – recalls:

On 9/10 April 1945 I was bomb aimer in the deputy master bomber aircraft (405 RCAF Squadron, PFF) on a raid on Kiel. Part of the job

was to mark the target for the main force of nearly 600 aircraft, including Lancasters of 90 Squadron (then in 3 Group). The master and deputy stayed in the target area throughout the raid, directing subsequent waves of aircraft. The *Admiral Scheer* was hit several times and capsized. I like to think that perhaps 90 Squadron had *some* revenge for Oslo.

Only four more individual sorties were flown after the Oslo débâcle, but of these, only Sturmey's attack on Emden on 20 September was successful. His bomb aimer, Tony Mulligan, recalls:

We lost sight of our aerodrome at 2,000ft [600m] and never saw the ground again until we were off the Dutch islands. Foamy white cloud, like the froth on a huge tankard of beer, stretched all over England and for about thirty miles out to sea. The horizon turned, quite suddenly, from purple to green and from green to yellow. It was hazy, but I could see Emden fifty miles away.

I called out to Sturmey, 'Stand by for bombing, bombsight in detent, George in. OK, I've got her!' As the cross-hairs centred over a shining pinpoint in Emden on which the sun was glinting, the bombs went down. We were still two miles away from Emden when we turned away. Almost a minute later one of the gunners told us through the intercom, 'There you are, bursts in the centre of the target,' and back we came through those extraordinary tints of sky. It proved a typical trip in a Fortress, with the temperature at minus 30°C.

Sturmey flew another sortie to Emden five days later, but the operation was aborted when his aircraft began producing the telltale contrails at 27,000ft (8,230m). To all intents and purposes 90 Squadron's brief

career on the B-17C was at an end, although on 26 October four Fortresses, each with two bomb-bay tanks, flew to the Middle East as a 90 Squadron detachment, leaving five in England to continue operations with 90 Squadron.

The four Fortresses flew to Portreath and then out into the Bay of Biscay, over the Pyrenees and the Mediterranean to Malta. Each aircraft carried one additional man. Sqn Ldr Andy MacLaren flew as CO with 'Junior' Jim Taylor as second pilot, Kendrick Cox as spare pilot and Tom Imrie as fire controller. Flt Lt Tex O'Camb, the engineering officer and his assistant, crew chief Flt Sgt Murray, flew with Plt Off Freddie Stokes; and Flt Off Frank Sturmey and Barwood, travelling as the specialist flying doctor, flew with Flt Off James Stevenson, with Flt Sgt Ken Brailsford as his No. 2 and Flg Off Struthers, RCAF, as navigator.

The next day they flew on to Fayoum, south of Cairo, and later went on to Shallufa after the customary 'flying the flag' over Cairo on 31 October. Operations began on 8 November when Stevenson and Brailsford in AN529 *C-Charlie* carried out a daylight raid on Benghazi from 20,000ft (6,000m). As the bomb-bay doors were open throughput the bombing run, the vented hydraulic fluid from the operation of the autopilot swirled up into the bomb-bay and froze the lower bomb releases. Tony Barwood, who was on board to experience the high-altitude operations under desert conditions, recalls:

It was the passenger's job to be ready with two screwdrivers to operate manually the lower releases if the bombs failed to come off. On this occasion manual release under the direction of the bomb aimer over the intercom was necessary.

90 Squadron Fortress I, one of four which transferred from the UK to Egypt, in November 1941. Antony Barwood

Fortress I AN531 (40-2068) which joined 90 Squadron on 1 November 1941, serving until 12 February 1942, before passing to 220 Squadron Coastal Command and later, 206 Squadron. British official via Philip Jarrett

It did not contribute to the accuracy of the bombing! There was some flak, which was a shock, as we weren't expecting any. Shortly after turning for home the aircraft progressively ran out of fuel, engines 1, 2 and 3 being feathered in turn. The crew prepared to bale out, but a convenient wadi came up and Stevenson effectively crashlanded about 200 miles [320km] south-east of Tobruk, then under siege by Rommel's army, and about 200 miles from the wire at the Libyan-Egyptian border. Apart from some sand in the eyes, nobody was injured.

The crew stayed with the aircraft, and after thirty-six hours were spotted by SAAF Marylands, who alerted an armoured unit of the Long-Range Desert Group who rescued them.

From about December 1941, the three remaining Fortress Is operated with the Royal Navy from Fuka satellite on the North African coast between Mersa and Alexandria against shipping in the Mediterranean. A naval observer was attached to 90 Squadron for ship recognition purposes. One aircraft flown by Freddie Stokes with Flt Lt 'Tiny' Nisbet attacked an Italian cruiser, and the fourth bomb in a stick of four very nearly hit the target – but the vessel turned at the last moment. A Bf 110 attacked and badly damaged one of the B-17's engines. Stokes made it back safely to Shallufa where 'Chiefy' Murray and Tony Barwood, bereft

of spares, repaired the inlet manifold with elastoplast and plaster of Paris!

The second Fortress I to suffer a mishap was AN521 on 8 January 1942. Frank Sturmey took *K-King* aloft for a fuel consumption test, but at 20,000ft (6,000m) about six miles (10km) north-west of Shallufa, oil pressure was lost in the No. 3 engine. Tony Barwood was flying this day with a German oxygen regulator salvaged from a Junkers. He had this Draeger device connected to a single 750-litre (165 gallon) oxygen cylinder, and had slightly modified his mask to be compatible with the regulator function. After some time at 20,000ft (6,000m) he saw that the oil pressure on No. 3 was zero, and immediately informed the captain. No. 3 could not be feathered as there was no oil left in the engine sump due to a broken oil pipe, so it ran away and eventually caught fire. He went aft to warn the rest of the crew, whom he found playing cards, blissfully unaware of their predicament! Barwood had no sooner said, 'We have a problem.', when he saw two parachutes floating behind them. He had assumed they were going to land, but a look up the catwalk to the cockpit revealed that Sturmey, Franks and Mulligan had baled out. By now the Fortress was dangerously low. Barwood recalls:

I picked up a chest parachute and baled out at 400ft [120m] at 300 knots. My boots flew off and

two panels in my 'chute were ripped out, but I landed safely. Lt 'Kipper' Baring, a Royal Navy ship recognition expert flying with us on a familiarization exercise, broke both his ankles on landing. Flt Sgt Mennie baled out of the astrodome hatch and was killed when he struck the tail, and Sgt Tuson died after he baled out too low.

On 12 February 1942, 90 Squadron was disbanded at Polebrook and the Shallufa detachment became part of 220 Squadron serving in that theatre. The two surviving B-17Cs were flown to India, complete with groundcrews, while some of the aircrews, including Tom Imrie, embarked on an Imperial Airways Empire flying boat:

We boarded *Cameronian* on the Nile on 10 May and made several two-hour hops totalling 17 hours 15 minutes' flying time across the Middle East and Karachi before landing at Pandaveshwar, near Asanol in Bengal, on 11 May. We never flew any operations; the two B-17Cs were handed over to the USAF in December 1942 and were used for continuation training.

So ended an unfortunate period in RAF Bomber Command operations using Fortress Is. It should not be forgotten, however, that many lessons were learned about high-altitude flight, and these led to improvements in oxygen supply, flying clothing and lubricants, while the Fortress

(Above) **B-17C 40-2052 (Fortress I) AM521, WP-K-King, which crashed near Shallufa, Egypt, on 8 January 1942 after engine failure during a fuel consumption test. Two gunners were killed.** Boeing

Fortress I AN518 (40-2064), WP-B in flight in the Middle East in early 1942. This aircraft served 90 Squadron from 9 August 1941 to 3 February 1942 and was one of four which formed the 220 Squadron detachment at Shallufa, Egypt. Two of the Fortresses Is were lost and it was intended that AN518, and AN532 'J-Johnny', would join other Fortresses in Northern Ireland on maritime patrol duty; but on 1 July 1942 both were despatched to India. Lack of spares restricted their operation, however, and on 1 December 1942 they were handed over to the USAAF, who were operating a few B-17Es in theatre. J-Johnny crashed on a test flight and B-Baker was converted into a USAAF VIP transport. Tony Barwood

design was subsequently improved with the addition of armour plating, self-sealing tanks and better armament; all of which were incorporated in the B-17D which followed the 'C' off the production lines.

The B-17D Delivers

Forty-two B-17Cs, ordered on 17 April 1940, had required thirty-two modifications (in part due to the experience gained by 90 Squadron), and so on 9 September 1940, they had been re-designated as B-17D versions. At first glance the 'D' differed little from the 'C': engine cowl flaps which permitted improved regulation of the cylinder-head temperature were added, and the armament was doubled in the belly (ventral 'bathtub') and upper (top hatch) positions, and additional socket positions were added for the .30 calibre nose-gun, making seven guns in all. The aircraft commander's astrodome was moved from the starboard side of the fuselage behind the cockpit to the centreline, while the lower windows for oblique

photography were deleted. Internally, more armour plate was added, a new bladder-type self-sealing fuel tank system installed, and changes were also made in other areas. The bomb-release system was redesigned to

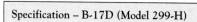

Specification – B-17D (Model 299-H)	
Crew:	10
Powerplant:	Wright Cyclone R-1820-65 1,200hp @ 25,000ft (7,620m)
Performance:	Maximum speed 323mph (520km/h) @ 25,000ft (7,620m) Cruise speed 227mph (365km/h) Rate of climb 7 mins 12 sec to 10,000ft (3,048m) Ceiling 37,000ft (11,278m) Range 2,000–3,400 miles (3,218–5,470km)
Weights:	Empty weight 30,960lb (14,043kg); gross weight 49,650lb (26,612kg)
Dimensions:	Length 67ft 11in (20m 70cm); height 18ft 4in (5m 59cm); wingspan 103ft 9in (31m 62cm); wing area 1,420sq ft (132sq m)
Armament:	1 × .30, 6 × .50 cal. machine guns; maximum bomb-load 8 × 600lb (272kg) or 4 × 1,100lb (500-kg) or 20 × 100lb (45kg)

Dual .50 calibre machine-gun installation in the bathtub of the B-17D. Boeing

B-17D pictured at Seattle on 5 February 1941. The 'D' model incorporated many design changes as a result of the experience gained by the RAF in Europe. Boeing

Specification – B-17E (Model 299-O)	
Crew:	6–10
Powerplant:	Wright Cyclone R-1820-65 1,200hp @ 25,000ft (7,620m)
Performance:	Maximum speed 317mph (510km/h) @ 25,000ft (7,620m) Cruise speed 224mph (360km/h) @ 15,000ft (4,572m) Rate of climb 7 mins 6 secs to 10,000ft (3,048m) Ceiling 36,600ft (11,156m) Range 2,000 miles (3,200km) with 4,000lb bombs
Weights:	Empty weight 33,279lb (15,095kg); gross weight 53,000lb (24,041kg)
Dimensions:	Length 73ft 10in (22m 50cm); height 19ft 2in (6m 5cm); wingspan 103ft 9in (31m 62cm); wing area 1,420sq ft (132sq m)
Armament:	1 × .30, 8 × .50 cal. machine guns; maximum bomb-load 4 × 1,000lb (454kg) or 20 × 100lb (45kg)

B-17E 41-2475 was delivered to Sacrameto on 27 December 1941. It went on to serve at Langley and McDill Fields before crash-landing on 20 April 1943. F. Wilding via Norman Franks

prevent freezing at altitude, a low-pressure oxygen system was used, and the electrical system was changed from 12-volt to 24-volt.

B-17E: the 'Big Ass' Bird

Modifications which resulted from the European combat experience were incorporated into the extensively improved B-17E (Model 299-O), ordered on 30 August 1940. Greatly enlarged tail surfaces, adapted from the Boeing Stratoliner, gave better control and stability for high-altitude bombing. The rear fuselage from the radio compartment on was extensively redesigned to provide more space for the gunners, and the tail was extended 6ft (2m) to include a 'stinger' tail-gun position with two .50 calibre Browning M-2 machine guns; these were fired by the gunner in an uncomfortable half-kneeling, half-sitting position on a bicycle-type seat.

The ventral bathtub was deleted on the first 112 B-17Es, and replaced with a solid Bendix power-operated gun turret with twin .50s fired by a gunner using controls and a periscope sighting arrangement in the fuselage. The turret proved troublesome to operate and was subsequently replaced from the 113th aircraft on, with the Sperry ball turret with the gunner squeezed inside. A Sperry A-1 electrically

(Above) **B-17E 41-2443 in flight. The B-17E first flew on 5 September 1941, was assigned to the 42nd Squadron, 11th Bomb Group at Hickham on 18 October, and was lost on 5 April 1942. Note the power-operated Bendix gun turret, which was installed in the first 112 Es on the production line, and was fired by a gunner lying prone and facing aft, sighting the guns through a periscope arrangement of angled mirrors. A much improved ball turret designed by Sperry finally replaced this cumbersome installation.** Boeing

Kitted out for protection against the elements at high altitude, these B-17E waist gunners at their cramped stations demonstrate how they would use their hand-operated, K-5 post-mounted, .50-calibre machine guns in actual combat. The metal ammunition boxes (note the two spare) each contained 100 rounds, but these were replaced later by belt feeds with two ammunition boxes being fixed to the roof. Later, all .50s were power-operated, armour plate was installed, and beginning with late Model Gs, the waist positions were staggered to ease congestion in the compartment. The sliding hatches which cover the waist windows have been pushed to the rear. Boeing

operated dorsal turret with twin .50s was installed behind the cockpit just in front of the radio room which still carried the normal .50 calibre machine gun. Ammunition feed was from six 125-round boxes mounted below the guns, using disintegrating link belts. The single .30 calibre in the nose was retained, as it was thought no enemy fighter pilots would attempt a head-on attack with such high closing speeds between fighter and bomber.

On The Threshold of War

Boeing received orders for 812 B-17Es, but after 512 aircraft had been built, the remaining 300 aircraft were converted to B-17F production. Material shortages delayed production, and the first B-17E did not make its maiden flight until 5 September 1941, four months behind schedule. Meanwhile deliveries of B-17Ds had begun on 3 February 1941, and twenty-one

were flown from Hamilton Field to Hickam Field, Hawaii, on 21 May 1941. Nine were transferred to the Philippines, staging through Midway and Wake, Port Moresby and Darwin, Australia, during the period 5–12 September. At the end of November, another twenty-six B-17Cs and Ds joined them in Manila. About one hundred B-17Es had been delivered to the AAFs by the time of the Japanese attack on Pearl Harbor, 7 December 1941.

CHAPTER THREE

On Wings We Conquer

War in the South-West Pacific, 1942–1943

At 07:55 hours on Sunday 7 December 1941, Pearl Harbor became a time, not merely a place. Some 190 carrier-borne aircraft of a Japanese strike force reached the island of Oahu in the Hawaiian Islands and split into elements. America had broken the Japanese 'Purple Code' and knew that Japan was preparing for war, but expected that the first bombs would fall on the Philippines or Malaya. Two trainee radar operators on a rudimentary mobile set at Opana, north of Pearl Harbor, reported the large formation, but the Hawaiian base commander assumed the aircraft were some B-17s which were expected and the radar operators were told to stand down. Army personnel watched in awe, then dived for cover as Zero fighters roared over the island at low level, machine-gunning B-17s, P-40s, Catalinas and other aircraft parked in neat rows at Wheeler Field and Kanaohe. Approximately fifteen dive bombers attacked Hickam Field and blew up the Hawaiian air depot and hangar 11.

Among the units on the ground at Hickam were members of the 11th Bomb Group, which had been formed on 1 February 1940 and comprised the 14th, 26th and 42nd Bomb Squadrons and the 50th Reconnaissance Squadron (later redesignated the 431st Bomb Squadron). The first bomb hit about 350ft from the hangar where Ray Storey, the 50th Reconnaissance Squadron armament chief, was working:

It didn't take long for the fellows on the field to figure out what was happening. Actually, the base was on fifty per cent alert because a Japanese midget submarine had been sunk in the harbour on Saturday. The boys who were really taken by surprise were those still in the barracks. Many of them – particularly the younger recruits – thought the Navy was putting on one of its aerial shows. Some started out of their barracks to take a look and were killed right in the doorways. Japanese Zeros were making strafing runs only fifty feet above ground – so low you could see the pilots' faces.

Horst Handrow, an air gunner in the 50th Squadron who had emigrated with his family from Germany as a child in 1932, was in his barracks:

I was just getting out of bed and looking for my Sunday paper which hadn't come yet. Cursing to myself a little I thought I'd take it out on Lester, my buddy, and so I started to beat him on the head with my pillow. The fight was on when an explosion rocked the barracks. Lester fell and I hit the floor. Now what in the hell could have cause that! Lester was dead – I could see a three-inch hole in his neck. Then another explosion. I ran to the window and with the roar of a dive bomber overhead I saw this plane dive, plane and all, right into H.A.D. The H.A.D seemed to leave the ground and then settle again in a blast of burning metal and wood. The red circle on the next plane's wing gave out the story. We were at war … I grabbed a machine gun, and rushed out to my airplane 81, Then I ran back for another. When I got back, some Jap had shot the tail off! Next time the plane went up into the air and settled back a burning mass of metal.

B-17E Yankee on the line. When camouflage was adopted for bombers in February 1941, a star was added to each side of the fuselage, and the rudder stripes were deleted, as was the star on the lower left and upper right wing. On 15 May 1942 the red centre of the star-in-circle insignia was deleted because of its similarity to the Japanese 'hinomaru' or 'rising sun' marking, which Americans called the 'meatball'. USAF

We lost all our planes the same way ... About twelve Zeros strafed the parking ramp with incendiary fire, and set almost all the B-18s and B-17s on fire.

At Pearl Harbor torpedo bombers and dive bombers attacked the eighty-six ships of the American Pacific fleet at anchor, inflicting heavy casualties. Eight battleships were reduced to heaps of twisted, blazing metal. The USS *Arizona* was hit in the forward magazine by a bomb which

two B-17Es of the 88th Reconnaissance Squadron, all of which were en route to the island of Mindanao in the Philippines, flew in from Hamilton Field, arriving over Hawaii during the Japanese attack. Pilots landed wherever they could: Lt Frank Bostrom put down on a golf course, while some, like Maj Richard H. Carmichael and Lt Robert Richards, landed on the small fighter strip at Bellows Field. Lt Brandon and his crew, including the navigator 'Bunky' Snider, jumped from their

mento Air Depot. As soon as we got our planes, we were to report to Hamilton Field and were to have left on the night of 6 December. We were picking up our planes one at a time and there were various things wrong with them, minor things, so we didn't all get them on the same day.

Instead of leaving for Hickam Field on the night of 6 December, Fields flew a 'shakedown' flight with Captain Bill Lewis, the squadron operations' officer and deputy commander. Lewis was an ex-airline pilot

Captain Raymond Swenson's B-17C in the 38th Reconnaissance Squadron was caught on approach to Hickam Field by strafing Japanese fighters, and stands burned out on the tarmac. A flare storage box was struck by cannon fire from the Zeros and the Fortress descended in flames but intact, but it broke in half upon hitting the ground, coming to rest just short of the Hale Makai barracks. All but one of the crew survived. Lt Robert Richards of the 38th Reconnaissance Squadron, 19th Bomb Group, bellied B-17C 40-2049 in at Bellows Field, a fighter strip at Kahuhu, 40 miles from Hickam, while being attacked during the Japanese strike on the Hawaiian Islands on 7 December 1941. The Fortress was landed downwind and it wrecked a P-40 before coming to rest and being strafed by enemy aircraft. Two crew-members were wounded. USAF

pierced several decks, and exploded in a pall of smoke and flame. She sank with over a thousand men still inside. Within about twenty-five minutes, seven other battleships had been either destroyed or reduced to damaged and listing hulks.

Five of the twelve B-17Ds of the 5th Bomb Group, lined up in neat rows at Hickam, were destroyed. Four of the 11th Bomb Group's six B-17Ds were also destroyed. Twelve unarmed B-17Ds of the 7th Bomb Group, and four B-17Cs and

Fortress before the wheels had finished turning. They sheltered in a drainage ditch as their B-17 was destroyed by strafing Japanese fighters.

Fortunately not all of the 7th Bomb Group's B-17s were able to fly to Hawaii on this fateful day, as Lt John W. Fields, a co-pilot/navigator in the 22nd Squadron, recalls:

We were to pick up new B-17Es, the first ones to come off the production line, from the Sacra-

who had been called back into the Air Corps on active duty. The first Fields knew of the attack on Pearl Harbor was when he was awakened on the morning of 7 December at about 11 o'clock by his squadron commander, Major Kenneth D. Hobson. Fields recalls:

He said, 'Pearl Harbor's been attacked. We've got to get our planes off and take them to Muroc Lake' We all immediately began to get our stuff packed and out to the planes.

I flew as co-pilot with Major Hobson, with a crew chief. We didn't have a navigator or any gunners. I was squadron armaments officer, and they immediately told us to take our bomb-bay tanks out and load the ship with bombs because they were fearful that a Japanese fleet was steaming into the west coast, that they were going to move in on the west coast and take it. We dropped our bomb-bay tanks and loaded up with bombs, then they changed their orders again, and we'd take the bombs out and put the bomb-bay tanks back in. This went on for about

vessels in Pearl Harbor and an oil slick all over the water. It was really a mess. On a visit there I was shocked to see the number of capsized and burned boats in the harbour and in the dry docks. I saw the battleships *Utah*, *California*, *Arizona*, *West Virginia* and the *Oklahoma*, as well as several destroyers, either burned or in some other way totally disabled. In some of the ships I learned that many bodies were still unrecovered.

There was a 20mm aircraft gun emplacement just outside the officers' barracks at Hickam where I stayed, and they told me that it was five

They departed for Mindanao but they never got there, although they did make it to Java where they met the 19th Bomb Group (whose motto was *In alis vincimus*: On wings we conquer), which had evacuated from the Philippines.

Attack in The Philippines

At the time of the Japanese attacks America had some thirteen groups equipped with the B-17, but most were well below

At the time of the Japanese attacks, America had some thirteen groups equipped with the B-17; however, most were well below group strength of thirty-two aircraft. During the first week of December, eight B-17Bs (and nineteen B-18s) were delivered to the 6th Bomb Group, which had arrived at Rio Hato, Panama, on 9 December, to defend the Panama Canal. B-17E 41-2504 served in the 6th Air Force in Panama and Guatemala from April 1942 until November 1943 on canal patrol and anti-submarine duties. USAF

seven days, and during all this time we were out chasing imaginary fleets up and down the west coast, flying out of Muroc.

Fields finally left Hamilton Field, California on 16 December, when ten Fortresses set out for Hickam Field.

The runways had been cleared off, but many of the buildings had been bombed, and there were still burned aircraft visible along the side of the runways. There was still smoke from burning

days before they got any ammunition for their gun, so they felt pretty low. They were just not equipped for an attack on Pearl Harbor or Hickam Field.

The Hawaiian Department countermanded our orders, which had been to go to 'Plum', which we knew by then to be the island of Mindanao, impounded our equipment, and put us to work flying patrol missions [for the *Lexington* force] out of Hawaii. Finally, and largely through Major Hobson's insistence, they decided to let three crews go: Major Hobson, J.R. Dubose and Jack Hughes.

the group strength of thirty-two aircraft. Some 150 B-17s, of all models and including twelve YB-17s, were scattered throughout the Pacific seaboard, Alaska and Newfoundland. Twenty-nine remaining B-17Es of the 7th Bomb Group (motto: *Mors ab alto*: Death from above), which left Salt Lake City, Utah, on 5 December for the Philippines, were hurriedly diverted to Muroc to help defend California from possible Japanese attack. Only nineteen B-17Bs could be sent to

Spokane, Washington to join the five B-17Cs of the 19th Bomb Group, while a paltry two B-17Bs were stationed in Alaska. Six B-17Bs (and one B-18) of the 41st Reconnaissance Squadron were based in Newfoundland. During the first week of December, eight B-17Bs and nineteen B-18s were delivered to the 6th Bomb Group, which had arrived at Rio Hato, Panama, on 9 December, to defend the Panama Canal.

Brig Gen Martin F. Scanlon, second from right, gets a first-hand report from Lt R.W. Elliott of the 19th Bomb Group on what happened to a Japanese ship that attacked his B-17 over enemy territory. USAF

In the Philippines, the Far East Air Force units there were mostly caught on the ground, just as the units at Hawaii had been. Constituted as the Philippine Department Air Force on 16 August 1941 and activated in the Philippines on 20 September, on 28 October 1941 it was re-designated the Far East Air Force. Fifth Bomber Command, constituted the same day, had only one heavy bombardment group, the 19th. The first word the FEAF had of the Japanese attack on Pearl Harbor was received on Luzon by commercial radio between 03:00–03:30 local time. Within thirty minutes, radar at Iba Field

plotted a formation of aircraft 75 miles (120km) offshore, heading for Corregidor. P-40s were ordered off to intercept but failed to make contact. Shortly before 09:30, after aircraft were detected over Lingayen Gulf heading toward Manila, B-17s at Clark Field, Luzon, were ordered airborne to prevent them being caught on the ground. A composite squadron of nine B-17Ds from the 5th and 11th Bomb Groups of the Hawaiian Air Force (later, 7th Air Force) led by Major (later General) Emmett 'Rosie' O'Donnell, had arrived at Clark Field from Hawaii on 10 September 1941. As the 14th Squadron it had become part of the 19th Bomb Group on 1 November. In October–November, twenty-six B-17Cs and B-17Ds, led by Col Eugene L. Eubank, the CO, had also flown in to Clark from California via Hawaii, Midway, Wake, Port Moresby and Darwin.

By 11:30 the B-17s and P-40s sent into the air earlier had landed at Clark and Iba for refuelling, when radar revealed another formation of aircraft 70 miles (113km) west of Lingayen Gulf and heading south.

At about 11:45 fighters were ordered off from Del Carmen to patrol Clark Field, but they failed to arrive before the Japanese attack, which commenced shortly after noon. Eighteen Fortresses were destroyed. Only one Fortress at Clark Field, and sixteen B-17Cs of the 14th Bomb Squadron escaped; the latter had been transferred to Del Monte, a small satellite field on Mindanao, some 600 miles (965km) to the south of Clark. During the morning and afternoon of 9 December, the 19th Bomb Group mounted a limited reconnaissance mission in search of the Japanese invasion force, and landed on Clark and San Marcelino.

Next day five B-17Cs mounted the first American bombing raid of the war when they attacked a Japanese convoy landing troops and equipment at Vigan and at Aparri in northern Luzon. Maj 'Rosie' O'Donnell, 14th Squadron CO, made five runs over his targets before the bombs would release, while Capt Elmer L. Parsel's crew claimed a hit on a transport. Three other 14th Squadron crews dropped 100lb (45kg) bombs on the transports at Vigan or targets of opportunity at Aparri. There had only been time to load one 600lb (270kg) bomb aboard Lt G.R. Montgomery's B-17: this was dropped on the Japanese transports, and then Montgomery returned to Clark for another bomb-load. Armed with twenty 100-pounders this time, Montgomery returned to the target area and dropped them before returning alone. He was forced to ditch four miles off Del Monte, but all the crew were rescued. Lt George E. Schaetzel's B-17, which carried eight 600-pounders, was attacked by Zeros and was badly hit. Schaetzel managed to lose the fighters in cloud and landed the badly damaged Fortress at San Marcelino between Clark and Del Monte with one engine out.

The third B-17C, piloted by Capt Colin P. Kelly Jr, carried only three 600lb bombs. Kelly ignored the Japanese landing operations under way at Vigan, and carried on to Aparri in search of an enemy aircraft carrier which had been reported. Finding no sign of the carrier, Kelly returned to Vigan and proceeded to attack a heavy cruiser (the *Ashigara*) from 22,000 ft (6,700m). One of the three bombs hit the aft gun turret and the ship caught fire. A group of Zeros gave chase, and about fifty miles from Clark Field they caught up with the B-17. Successive attacks destroyed parts of the aircraft, which then caught fire in the bomb-bay area. Sgt Delhany, waist gunner,

Tail-gun station on a B-17E pictured on 1 October 1941 showing the early style ring-and-bead sight mounted outside the window, which was replaced on late model Fortresses two years later by an internal reflector sight. In the Pacific, Japanese fighter pilots, who had grown accustomed to attacking the Fortress from the rear, received an unpleasant shock when they came up against the rear gun installation fitted to B-17Es for the first time. Prior to this, B-17 pilots had learned to compensate somewhat for this weakness by jinking their aircraft back and forth when attacked from the rear, giving the left and right waist gunners alternatively a shot at the approaching fighters. Boeing

(Below) **Early tail-gun station.**

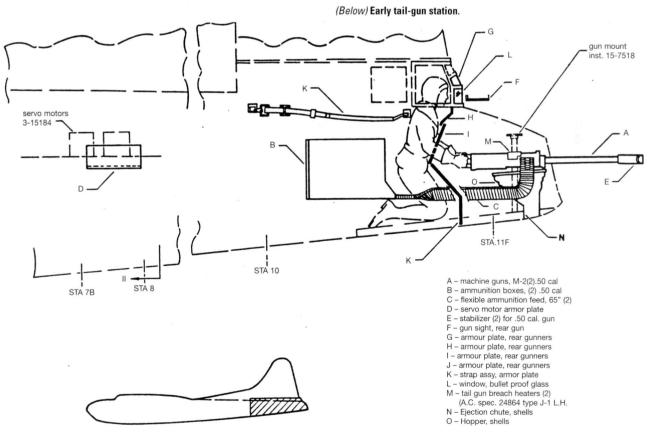

A – machine guns, M-2(2).50 cal
B – ammunition boxes, (2) .50 cal
C – flexible ammunition feed, 65" (2)
D – servo motor armor plate
E – stabilizer (2) for .50 cal. gun
F – gun sight, rear gun
G – armour plate, rear gunners
H – armour plate, rear gunners
I – armour plate, rear gunners
J – armour plate, rear gunners
K – strap assy, armor plate
L – window, bullet proof glass
M – tail gun breach heaters (2)
    (A.C. spec. 24864 type J-1 L.H.
N – Ejection chute, shells
O – Hopper, shells

shaded area shown

B-17Es on the line at Boeing. The nearest aircraft is B-17E 41-2393, which was delivered to Wright Field on 3 October 1941 and went on to serve in Newfoundland. Starting with the 113th B-17E, the remotely controlled Bendix belly turret which the gunner operated using a periscope sight, was replaced by a Sperry ball turret. Boeing

(Below) A .30-calibre machine gun could be mounted in sockets in the nose of the E and F models of the Fortress for operation by the bombardier and navigator. Three sockets, including one non-standard fitting in the roof, can be seen in this B-17E pictured in the US. Note also the early ring-and-bead sight atop the Browning and the empty side magazine. USAF

was decapitated by a burst of machine gun fire, and Pte Altman was wounded. Kelly bravely battled to keep the Fortress straight and level while his co-pilot, Lt Donald Robbins, and four other crew evacuated the stricken aircraft. Despite being fired on by the circling Zeros, they all landed safely on Clark, but the Fortress finally exploded before Kelly could escape.

America badly needed a hero, and Kelly was later posthumously awarded the DSC and was later recommended for the Medal of Honor, for 'sinking' the Japanese battleship *Haruna*. This story was given out to boost morale at home, but Kelly's bravery in attacking a Japanese ship against such overwhelming odds and staying at the controls of his doomed aircraft while his crew escaped, was unquestioned.

Maj David R. Gibbs assumed command of the 19th Bomb Group on 10 December from Col Eubank, who moved to HQ, V Bomber Command in Manila. Two days later, Gibbs took off in a B-18 for Mindanao and was never seen again; he was presumed killed in action. Rosie O'Donnell took command of the group. By now the Japanese had successfully established a bridgehead at Legaspi on southern Luzon. Six B-17Cs from Del Monte tried to go after a Japanese carrier at Legaspi on 14 December, but only three reached the target area because of aborts. There was no carrier to be seen, but there were many shipping targets to be had. Lt Jack Adams, who unloaded all his bombs during the first pass, was attacked by six Zeros and crashlanded on the beach on the island of Masbate, just south of Luzon. The crew were fired on as they left the aircraft but they escaped, and most eventually returned to Del Monte with the help of Filipino guerrillas. Lt Elliott Vandevanter made three runs over Legaspi and returned safely to Del Monte.

The third B-17, piloted by 1st Lt Hewitt T. 'Shorty' Wheless, dropped all eight 600-pounders on shipping while confronted by eighteen Zero fighters. They attacked and sprayed the B-17 with gunfire, killing Pfc W.G. Killin, belly gunner, and badly

wounding three of the crew. Wheless kept the B-17 in the air with a series of violent evasive manoeuvres, but the aircraft was badly shot up and losing fuel so he knew Del Monte was out of the question. He headed for a small strip at Cagayan, twenty miles north-west of Del Monte. On the approach Wheless could see that the strip was covered with obstacles, but he had to put down. The B-17 smashed its way along the strip until the brakes locked and the bomber stood on its nose before falling back on its tail. Shaken, the wounded crew scrambled out of the bomber safely. The Fort was punctured by 1,200 bullet holes, and Wheless was later awarded the DSC.

The decision was taken to move the surviving Fortresses of the 19th Bomb Group further south, out of range of Japanese aircraft. On 17 December 1941 some of the B-17s began evacuating Del Monte to fly 1,500 miles (2,400km) south to Batchelor Field, Darwin, on the northern tip of Australia. Two days later the Japanese bombed Del Monte, but the B-17s remaining escaped damage. On 22 December nine B-17s from Batchelor Field bombed the docks and Japanese shipping at Davao Bay, Mindanao, and claimed to have sunk a tanker, before they landed at Del Monte – which fortunately was still in American hands – to

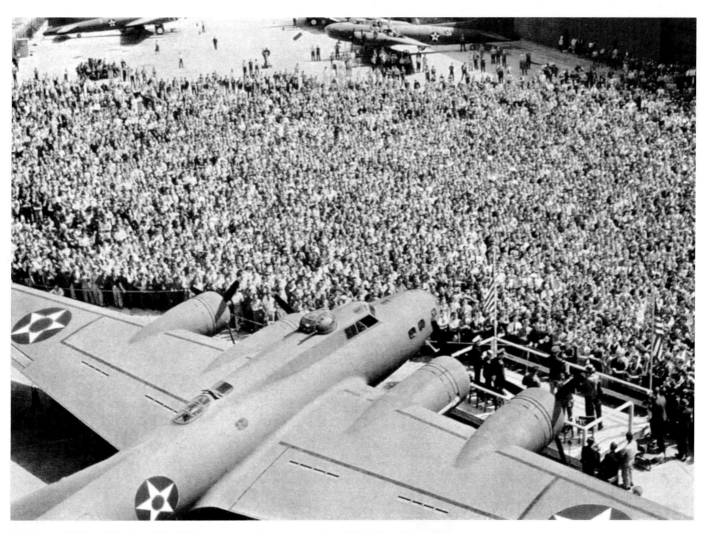

1st Lt Hewitt T. 'Shorty' Wheless of the 19th Bomb Group tells Boeing workers of his battle with eighteen Zero fighters at Legaspi on 14 December 1941. Wheless kept the B-17C in the air with a series of violent evasive manoeuvres, but the aircraft was badly shot up and losing fuel so he put down at a small strip at Cagayan, 20 miles north-west of Del Monte. On the approach Wheless could see that the strip was covered with obstacles, but he had to put down. The B-17 smashed its way along the strip until the brakes locked and the bomber stood on its nose before falling back on its tail. Shaken, the wounded crew scrambled out of the bomber safely. Wheless, whose Fort was punctured by 1,200 bullet holes, was later awarded the DSC. National Geographic

refuel. Next day, four serviceable B-17s took off again shortly after midnight and bombed Japanese transports at Lingayen Gulf, Luzon. On 24 December three B-17s bombed the airfield and shipping at Davao, and landed at Batchelor Field. Two B-17s left Manila for Darwin with personnel of HQ FEAF. All AAF units on Luzon, as well as ground forces, began leaving for the Bataan Peninsula. With the abandonment of the air echelon in the Philippines on 24 December, Clark Field was evacuated and the ground echelon was re-designated as ground forces and trained as infantry. The group was now dispersed on Bataan, Luzon; Del Monte, Mindanao; Batchelor Field, Australia; and Singosari airdrome near Malang, Java.

On 30 December, 759 officers and men of the 19th Bomb Group were sent by boat from Bataan to Mindanao, where they were made part of the Bisayan-Mindanao force. On 1 January 1942 Maj Cecil Combs, who was commander of the 93rd Squadron, assumed command of the air echelon, which was transferred to Singosari. With them went remnants of the 7th Bomb Group, including the 9th Squadron, commanded by Capt Robert 'Pappy' Northcutt, at Madeoin on Java. Personnel who could be evacuated from the Philippines by air and submarine joined the force in Java. On 12 January Maj 'Rosie' O'Donnell, in an old B-18, with auxiliary fuel tanks made from fifty-gallon drums, flew to Australia with Lt Clyde Box as co-pilot and Lt Edwin S. Green as navigator.

On 5 January, eight B-17s from Malang led by Maj Combs staged through Samarinda on Borneo during 4/5 January and attacked Japanese shipping in Davao Bay. Crews had to fight their way through an equatorial storm, high winds and rain as well as Zeros and anti-aircraft fire. The Fortresses hit a large warship, damaged Japanese submarines and smaller craft. Flying blind through the storm, the crews returned to Borneo, almost out of fuel, and refuelled for another raid. Another strike was made on this target four days later by B-17s flying from Kendari, on the eastern side of Celebes, where in 1940 the Dutch had built the finest airfield in the Dutch East Indies. On the 11th, the B-17s from Malang attacked landing forces on the island of Tarakan.

On 16 January two B-17Es from the 11th Squadron, 7th Bomb Group, and three LB-30 Liberators, all of which staged through Kendari II, raided Japanese shipping in Manado Bay, the most northern point of the Celebes Islands, and Langoan aerodrome, 20 miles (32km) south, respectively. The mission was at the behest of Field Marshal Sir Archibald Wavell, the supreme commander of the Allied Forces in the area, who badly needed a morale boost for his beleaguered British troops on Singapore. At 19:15 hours the two B-17Es, piloted by Maj Conrad F. Necrason (41-2461), and Lt J.L. 'Duke' du Frane (41-2459), and the three LB-30s, took off from Kendari and headed for their targets. At 22:30 hours Necrason and du Frane began the first of two runs on four transports, and hits were scored on a large vessel, which sank, although six of the ten 220lb (100kg) bombs failed to drop. Two of the bombs were then dropped in the runway of Langoan aerodrome. Five minutes after the attack about fifteen Zeros made attacks on the rear of the two B-17Es which lasted for forty minutes – but the enemy pilots were in for a shock, as 2nd Lt Bernice 'Bernie' S. Barr, Necrason's co-pilot, recalls:

These were the first two B-17s that had ever gone into combat with tail-guns in them. None of the older B-17s had these guns, and the Japanese Zero pilots had learned to come up and slip in behind a B-17, fire, and with their faster speed would overtake, all without even being shot at. However, this time we were armed in this quarter, and of course the Zero pilots did not know it. As they came in to attack, Pte A.B. Hegdahl, our tail gunner, shot two of them down. Their approach – from below the airplane, from the tail, from the side and from the top – all took place at about 26,000ft (8000m). This fight resulted in our gunners shooting down five Zeros. We got quite a few holes in our planes, but not enough to knock us out of the air. Pte Hegdahl was seriously wounded in the knee by an explosive bullet.

In all, six Zeros were shot down during the air battle, five falling to Necrason's crew. Du Frane's Fort had two engines put out of action, but both he and Necrason managed to keep them airborne and they put down safely at Kendari II at 01:00 hours on 17 January. An hour later, when Bernie Barr was helping a Dutch doctor attend to Hegdahl's knee, the siren sounded, and five Zeros attacked the grass field. They badly damaged du Frane's B-17, although Necrason managed to get airborne; Barr continues:

As we got about five feet off the ground, bullets came roaring through the airplane all the way from the tail, and up, through the cockpit over the pilot's and my head. They hit the instrument panel and the windshield, knocking some of the instruments out; but the airplane still flew. We headed into a rainstorm about ten miles from Kendari, dodging and using evasive action low over the ground until we got into the thunderstorm. The fighters lost us. It then took us about six hours to fly back to Malang, where Hegdahl was immediately taken to the city hospital for treatment.

Meanwhile the Zeros returned to the other B-17 which had been unable to get off the ground, and burned it up with their gunfire. Du Frane's aircraft was later blown up during the US retreat, but 'Duke' and his crew escaped and were later evacuated to Java. Du Frane was awarded the DSC; his citation stated that his crew had sunk a transport, and had also shot down seven Zeros, although in fact they had claimed only one.

On 19 January, through another driving rainstorm and fog, six Fortresses, led by Lt James T. Connally, pushed their way through to a surprise raid on Japanese vessels off the island of Jolo. In the dark and the rain they landed later at Del Monte, and picked up twenty combat pilots who had struggled through from Clark Field; less than a day later, these twenty men were flying B-17s from Java. On 24 January a Japanese invasion force landed at Kendari. Ambon, an island to the east, was invaded on 30 January and the Japanese quickly overran the defenders.

From 22 January–3 February, the B-17s launched at least fifteen missions out of Malang against enemy shipping moving through the Makassar Strait. Four were aborted because of bad weather, six proved negative, and the other five resulted in heavy losses – but four ships were believed sunk. From now on, bad weather and effective Japanese fighter interceptions prevented the Fortresses from delivering any worthwhile strikes on the all-conquering Japanese forces. By the end of January the Japanese had landed at Lae and at several places on Borneo and Rabaul, where air bases for extending Japanese air operations were constructed. On 3 February Port Moresby, the capital of New Guinea, was bombed, but despite fears of a Japanese invasion, it managed to hold out. The situation on Java, however, was perilous. To save their precious B-17s, pilots and crews took almost any risk. In one raid the

Japanese caught one Fortress on the ground and it seemed doomed to destruction; but Capt Dean Hovet, a communications expert who had been brought from Bataan to Java in a submarine, dashed to the B-17 and took off with only two engines running. For twenty minutes he hedge-hopped trees and brush, twisting and banking the bomber like a fighter, and managed to evade the Japanese fighters until their ammunition was expended.

On 5 February the Japanese began moving their own aircraft into Ambon to strengthen their air superiority in the area. Nine B-17s from the hard-pressed 19th Group were despatched to Kendari, the formation climbing slowly through heavy clouds. At 15,000ft (4,570m) they broke out on top – and ran straight into a horde of Zeros. Duke du Frane's B-17 was shot down in flames. Another B-17, piloted by Lt W.T. Pritchard, swung around in a wild turn and almost crashed into a Zero; trac-

ers ripped into the bomber, which plunged into the clouds on fire from nose to tail. Lt Lindsey made a skidding turn and kicked his B-17 into the cloud top as tracers ripped into his Fortress; losing speed the half-crippled B-17 fell off into a tailspin, and at 9,000ft (2,750m) it was still spinning. The co-pilot and navigator scrambled aft and baled out through the open bomb-bay, and the rest of the crew were about to follow when Lindsey miraculously recovered from the spin and pulled the nose up. Circling down carefully, he looked out across the barren Java Sea. There was no sign of the two crew in the water. With his compass and other instruments shot away, Lindsey battled with the badly damaged Fortress through a tropical storm and landed back at base.

Practically all the 19th Bomb Group's ground crews were still in the Philippines, and the few ground mechanics in Java did heroic work, driving themselves until they

were exhausted. B-17s returning from bombing raids had to make forced landings miles away from their base. If wrecked beyond repair, crews tore out badly needed parts and carried them to their base, otherwise salvage crews went out by truck and brought back the priceless parts. 'Wrecker' pilots such as Lt Clare McPherson risked their lives to fly disabled B-17s out of clearings where their original pilots had barely been able to land.

When Palembang fell on 16 February, no replacements could get through to the beleaguered 19th Bomb Group: each pilot who had a Fortress was on his own. Lt Philip Mathewson was one of a few pilots who made lone attacks on Japanese targets. The Japanese were only 35 miles (56km) away, and with anti-aircraft fire along the coast, crews had to climb inland to 35,000ft (10,670m), if they could get that high, to avoid enemy fire. Col Eubank realized that resistance was futile, and on

B-17Es 41-2459 and 41-2461 caused immense interest among 90 Squadron crews, who were particularly interested in the new tail design aand rear armament, when they passed through the desert airstrip at Shallufa in December 1941, en route to join the 19th Bomb Group in the Pacific. The 19th fought a gallant, but losing battle in the Philippines after the Japanese invasion and were forced to retreat to Australia on Christamas Eve 1941, before returning, briefly, to Java late in the month. Within two days of their arrival on 16 January 1942 41-2459 and 41-2461 were despatched on a mission with three LB-30 Liberators. Lt. J. L. 'Duke' Du Frane's crew in 41-2459 force-landed at Kendari, Borneo, and were strafed by Zeros. The crew escaped and were later evacuated to Java. The aircraft was later blown up during the US retreat. 41-2461, piloted by Major C. R. Bacrasson, was hit but got away safely. Antony Barwood

24 February, with the Japanese only twenty minutes away, he ordered the few remaining B-17s on Java to Australia.

Meanwhile, the 19th Bomb Group received B-17E models and reinforcements to carry the war to the Japanese. On 11 February the remnants of the 88th Squadron, some crews out of the 19th and 11th Groups, one pick-up crew and about six crews out of the 22nd Squadron commanded by Maj Richard N. Carmichael, had left Hawaii for Australia. Lt John Fields, now assigned as co-pilot on Lt Harry Spieth's crew, recalls:

The first leg was to tropical Christmas Island. The strips that we landed on were made of crushed coral, rolled and packed by a group of engineers from Hawaii. It was here that I saw my first green coconut and learned that it would do very nicely in place of a laxative! We left Christmas Island on the 12th, and made an eight-hour flight to Canton Island, a small coral atoll in the Pacific which had only one tree and one landing strip. This landing strip had numerous goony birds on it. The personnel on Canton had everything underground.

We went on to Fiji and spent a weekend waiting for the Free French to chase the Vichy French in New Caledonia up into the hills before we could land at Plindegaig. We got in and refuelled, but we had to get off again because we were not particularly safe there. We flew on into Townsville, Australia, and arrived there around 8 o'clock in the evening. The Australians thought that their great saviours had arrived when we tooled in there in the first B-17Es that they had ever seen! Truthfully, they were afraid that the Japs were going to move in and take Australia, and this *was* a possibility for several months.

The B-17Es used Garbutt Field at Townsville and were then dispersed to Charters Towers about fifty miles away, and to Cloncurry, 300 miles from Townsville. There was little to entertain the crews, though kangaroo hunting became popular at remote Cloncurry. A number of crews got dengue fever, and at times there were parts of ten crews in the hospital at once. There were other drawbacks, too, as John Fields recalls: 'Mosquitoes would nearly carry you off. In addition, there were kangaroo rats which would come down and check us out at night – they would be likely to jump down on your mosquito netting at any time. You would think a possum had attacked you!'

There were not enough aircraft to stem the all-conquering Japanese tide, which had now consumed the entire Netherlands East Indies, as well as the Philippines. General Douglas MacArthur, the commander-in-chief in the Philippines, sought shelter in the Malinta Tunnel on Corregidor. On 22 February MacArthur received a signal from President Roosevelt ordering him to leave his position on Corregidor and proceed to Australia to assume command of all US troops.

The same day a grand total of nine B-17Es from the 7th Bomb Group (whose 28th Squadron now became the famous 435th 'Kangaroo' Squadron of the 19th Bomb Group) left Cloncurry for Townsville to mount an attack on Rabaul Harbour in New Britain. Rabaul was to be the jumping-off point for the Japanese invasion of New Guinea, and further, Australia and New Zealand. Two Fortresses, piloted by Deacon Rawls and Frank Bostrom, taxied into each other in the pre-dawn darkness, and a third suffered mechanical problems, leaving six airworthy B-17s. These newly minted B-17Es, led by Maj Richard N. Carmichael, left Townsville on 23 February for an early morning rendezvous over Magnetic Island, and then across the Coral Sea, New Guinea and the Solomon Sea to Rabaul. a return refuelling stop at Port Moresby, New Guinea, was to cap their hastily planned mission of some thirteen hours' duration.

Ninety miles out, the formation was broken up by severe weather – Harry Spieth's crew could not get through it and had to return after about nine hours. Captain Bill Lewis, who was leading the second echelon, and Lt Fred Eaton in 41-2446, were able to locate their target first. Eaton lingered over Rabaul Harbour for half an hour looking for an opening in the clouds through which to commence his bomb run; he was finally able to pick out several large Japanese troop transports and make his dive, but was unable to get his bombs away and a second run was made. This time the bombs salvoed, though he was unable to observe the result. While on the bomb run, a Japanese anti-aircraft shell came straight up through the right wing, near the outboard engine, not exploding until it was already through the wing. The concussion knocked the wing down violently but did not otherwise damage the aircraft.

By now, as many as twelve Zeros had reached altitude with the B-17, and they began a series of gunnery passes. At 07:45 hours the first Zero was hit and downed by the tail gunner Sgt J.V. Hall. A second Hinomaru-marked fighter was destroyed by Sgt Russell Crawford at a waist-gun position. Sgt Hall hit a third Zero, which was observed to lose altitude but not confirmed to crash. The air battle continued for over forty minutes, during which Eaton jockeyed the B-17 from cloud to cloud trying to evade enemy fire. They sustained 20mm cannon and machine-gun strikes in the vertical stabilizer and the radio operator's compartment.

The long wait over the target, the two bomb runs, all the evasive manoeuvres and the battle damage sustained, resulted in Eaton running short of fuel just over the eastern coast of New Guinea. He realized that he would never make Port Moresby, situated on the far coast and across the treacherous Owen Stanley Range, and elected to set the B-17 down in what appeared to be a level and verdant field some eight miles inland. He therefore feathered the two inboard engines, and all the crew except Eaton himself, co-pilot Henry 'Hotfoot' Harlow and Sgt Clarence Lemieux, the engineer, took up prescribed crash positions in the radio operator's compartment. The B-17 came in neatly, but as it levelled out Eaton was shocked to realize he was landing in a kunai grass-filled reservoir of water five to six feet deep: the Agiambo Swamp. The B-17 did a slow 90-degree turn to the right as it settled into its last resting place – where at the time of writing it still remains, more than fifty years later.

The crew was uninjured except for a cut to the head of the navigator George Munro, a pilot pressed into service as a result of a shortage of qualified navigators. They carefully removed the Norden bombsight, placed it on the right wing and destroyed it with .45 calibre pistol fire, then tossed it into the swamp. They then set out on a cruel trek out of the swamp, through water five to six feet deep and razor-sharp kunai grass. They encountered huge leeches and spiders and heard crocodiles thrashing about. Six weeks later, with the aid of Australian coast watchers, they returned to Port Moresby and went back to the war against the Japanese.

The war continued to go badly for the American forces, and on 27 February the evacuation of Java began. What was left of the 7th Bomb Group, who were awarded a DUC for their action against the enemy 14 January–1 March, was reorganized in India, where B-17s were retained by the

(Above) General Douglas MacArthur's B-17E-BO (XC-108) 41-2593 Bataan, one of four B-17E and F's specially converted into transports under the C-108 designation in 1943. Although an E, Bataan had a 'blown' B-17F style Plexiglas nose with a single .50-calibre gun with chromed barrel (the only armament carried), and a navigator's astrodome added to the aircraft. A five-man crew and up to eleven passengers could be carried on the XC-108. Boeing

Lt Fred Eaton's bullet-riddled B-17E 41-2446 in the 435th Bomb Squadron, 7th Bomb Group, which crashed in a grass-covered swamp known as the Agaiambo, Papua New Guinea, after a six-ship attack on Rabaul on 23 February 1942. The B-17E, based at Townsville, Australia, ran out of fuel before reaching Port Moresby, but the swamp ensured a smooth ditching and the crew, who were uninjured, were picked up by Australian coast watchers and returned to Port Moresby on 1 April. 41-2446 was located eight miles inland from the coast of New Guinea by a passing Royal Australian Air Force helicopter crew, and in 1986 the site was visited by surviving members of Eaton's crew, and officials of the Papuan Historical Museum. The Historical Society of Travis AFB became interested in returning the Swamp Ghost as it is called, to the USA, as it is the only B-17 left in the world in its original combat configuration. Kenneth W. Fields.

B-17F-25-BO 41-24554 Mustang **which flew missions with the 19th Bomb Group and the 43rd Bomb Group, completing 109 missions and claiming seventeen Japanese aircraft before being returned to the US as war-weary.** USAF

9th and 436th Squadrons until November, when the group converted to the B-24. Meanwhile, the next combat mission from Australia by the 19th Bomb Group, who were also awarded a DUC, was scheduled for the following day, 1 March; but it was called off and crews were sent to Cloncurry for dispersal. Two days later, on 3 March, the Japanese attacked the airfield and harbour at Broome, Australia, at 10:00, shortly after eight B-17s arrived, and wreaked havoc. Two B-17s were destroyed along with sixteen other aircraft, and forty-five Dutch civilians and twenty US airmen were killed.

At Cloncurry, six crews had immediately gone down with dengue fever. John Fields was one of them. After recovery he flew his second mission, early in March:

We left on 11 March from Cloncurry for Townsville, and on the 12th we left for Port Moresby, New Guinea, for a patrol mission on the 13th to Lae where we dropped our bombs.

When we flew out of Port Moresby, which was about a 2½-hour flight from Townsville, we lived in grass huts that the natives had built, and flew off a runway that was metal stripping placed on swampy ground. We had a grass hut mess-hall and had to do our own aircraft servicing. We serviced the aircraft from barrels of 'gas' that were dumped off the ships and floated onto the shore by the natives, and we had a little gasoline pump that we used to pump the 'gas' out of the barrel into the airplane. We could have used the fuel transfer pump from the aircraft itself, but we didn't like to do this because we knew we might need that fuel transfer pump in flight and we didn't want to wear it out, because some of these flights involved 2,400 gallons of 'gas'.

We would fly a mission, or two or three, out of Port Moresby, or occasionally out of Townsville, and then we would come back and go to the bottom of the list, and our turn would come up again later. In truth, it didn't always work out this way, though in principle it was supposed to. We found out early on that if you were married and had a family, well, the tougher

the mission the more reason they had for raising the younger, unmarried people up on the list. You would simply move up the list faster if you were single than you did if you were married.

On 18 March we flew a mission to Rabaul Harbour – there were only three aircraft and we flew at an altitude of 31,000ft [9,450m]. We didn't encounter any fighter aircraft. We didn't learn until next day how much damage we had inflicted, but we had hit a large Japanese cruiser from 600ft [180m], blowing the stern off it. Two days later I flew with Morrie Horgan to Lae, a stronghold on the north-eastern side of the mountains of New Guinea. We destroyed seventeen aircraft on the ground.

On 24 March I went to the theatre at Charter's Towers, but we were called out of the theatre to go back to Townsville, and the rumour was that we were going to the Philippines. We got to Townsville on 25 March, and sure enough, we had orders to go to the Philippines on an evacuation flight. We left Batchelor Field at Darwin on the 26th for Del Monte on the island of Mindanao. At the time, Mindanao was in Japanese hands with the exception of the airstrip adjacent to the Del Monte pineapple plantation. Our purpose was to bring out Manuel Quezon, President of the Philippines, and Generals Valdez and Romulo, and some of MacArthur's staff. [MacArthur and his family, Admiral Rockwell, Generals George and Sutherland and fourteen staff members, had been evacuated from Corregidor by four PT boats to Mindanao, where, on 12 March they were flown from Del Monte to Darwin by Frank P. Bostrom.] MacArthur didn't particularly go for the Air Force. He sent word ahead that he wanted an airliner to meet him at Darwin to take him to Alice Springs, and from Alice Springs he got on a train and went on to Melbourne. It took him four days to get there, when we could have had him there in eight hours!

The flight was long and tiring. We were scheduled to land during the hours of darkness at Del Monte, which we did. They had no lights on the runway, with the exception of smudge-pots which they lit for us to line up on, on the grass field in the direction that we were supposed to land. These were old highway markers that looked like a bomb, black smudge-pots that burned diesel fuel; they were extinguished just as soon as we had landed. We serviced our plane and ate wonderful pineapple and plenty of beer, but they didn't have any bread. Then they began to assign us the various people who were scheduled to go back with us. Those with priority were General MacArthur's staff, of which there were not very many; and President Quezon's family and nurse, also his chief of staff who was General Romulo, and one of his advisers, a General Valdez. A small staff went with the Philippine generals, and the next priority were the aircraft mechanics. So we filled our planes with people according to these priorities and for whom we had parachutes.

Others were crying, wanting to be smuggled aboard, but we had to tell them we couldn't take them, that we didn't have parachutes for them. Then they would say, 'Well, don't worry about a parachute; I don't need one; I won't use one' – anything to get on the plane and get off the island. We flew thirty-two hours out of the thirty-six on that flight: we flew back to Darwin, gassed up and went on to Alice Springs. On the way there Dubose ran out of gas; he had President Quezon's nurse on his ship. Luckily he was able to land safely out in the middle of the country. We searched for him for five hours before the other plane in the flight located him; they landed and pumped some fuel over into his plane.

We finished up the Philippine rescue flight in Melbourne. We had had engine trouble and had blown two cylinders, so they told us to stay there and change all four engines before we went back

to Townsville; we spent twenty-six days getting the engines changed out. Del Monte held out for another ten days after we left.

By mid-April 1942 the Japanese were well on the way to total domination in the New Guinea-New Britain-Solomon Islands area of the South Pacific. The turning point however, came when the Japanese invasion fleet heading for Port Moresby was defeated in the Battle of the Coral Sea on 7–9 May; the first battle in history in which the two naval forces did not exchange fire but which was decided by the two air fleets. John Fields recalls:

We could tell from the number of surface vessels that were coming into the area and congregating there that a big naval battle was shaping up. We flew missions out of Townsville on the 6th, 7th, 8th and 11th of May. On 6 May we found the Jap fleet – we sighted an aircraft carrier and made a run on it. We were in the same flight as 'Hotfoot' Harlow, and Harlow bombed a heavy cruiser. Wilbur Beezley was flying with us, too. We had heavy anti-aircraft fire, but not too many fighter planes because they were all carrier-based; their fighters were too busy with the Navy and the low-level stuff.

On one of our Coral Sea missions there was a bit of confusion. The Navy had told us that everything north of a certain parallel would be

friendly. We were north of this line, and there was a squadron of B-26s on the mission with us too. We came in at about 18,000ft (5,500m) and could see some planes flying below and diving at low level. We thought these were the B-26s, so we lined up on the battleship that they were bombing and dropped our bombs on it. It turned out to be the Australian flagship *Australia*, and the planes we saw diving were Jap bombers. Luckily we didn't hit the *Australia* and they didn't hit us.

The next major Pacific battle occurred on 3 June when the Japanese forces attacked Midway Island. Eight B-17Es of the 431st Squadron, 11th Bomb Group, led by Lt Col Walter C. Sweeney in *Knucklehead* had arrived on Midway from Hawaii on 29 May, and these were joined by nine more the following day. Six B-17Es returned to Oahu on 2 June. At 12:30 hours on 3 June, nine B-17s on Midway took off in search of the Japanese invasion fleet which had been sighted by a PBY an hour earlier only 700 miles (1,130km) distant. At 16:23 hours the fleet of twenty-six ships was sighted some 570 miles (900km) from Midway. Six B-17Es of the 431st, with three B-17Es of the 31st Squadron, 5th Bomb Group, attacked in three flights of three from altitudes of 8,000, 10,000 and 12,000ft (2,440, 3,000 and 3,660m) respectively. Sweeney

B-17E 41-2462 Tojo's Jinx, **guarded by an American soldier, in the 93rd Bomb Squadron, 19th Bomb Group, pictured at Longreach, Queensland, Australia, June 1942.** USAF

B-17E 41-2634 Tojo's Physic **and Captain Felix M. Hardison's eight-man crew in the 93rd Bomb Squadron, 19th Bomb Group, pictured at Longreach, Queensland, Australia, June 1942. Back row, L–R: Lt Albert Nice, navigator; Lt Ellsworth McRoberts, co-pilot; Captain Felix M. Hardison; M/Sgt David Semple, bombardier; S/Sgt William Bostwick, engineer; Cpl William Koon, gunner. Kneeling: Sgt Orville Kiger, radio; unknown (possibly National Geographic writer Howell Walker); Pte John Irons. Lt Col Hardison went on to command the 19th Bomb Group, 1 January–12 February 1943.** USAF

10,000ft [3,000m]. Home we came again, just dog-tired but happy. We had really done some good that day, and we all remembered December 7th. We worked all that night loading bombs, gassing the ships and trying to get No. 4 engine in shape because we knew we would really need it the next day.

(Although the B-17 crews claimed a total of five hits, and Lt Ed Steedman and Capt Willard Woodbury claimed near misses, they had been fooled by the Japanese smoke screens laid down by destroyers and had mistaken the smoke for burning ships. In fact, no hits were scored.)

That night seven more B-17Es from the 42nd Squadron, 11th Bomb Group, arrived at Midway to reinforce the small Fortress contingent. Thus at 04:15 hours on 4 June, fourteen B-17Es cleared Midway Island and assembled in the vicinity of Kure Island. Sweeney's crews then set out to attack the same main body they had bombed the previous afternoon; but en route to the target, word was received that another enemy task force, complete with carriers – namely *Soryu* and *Hiryu* – was approaching Midway and estimated to be only about 145 miles (230km) away. The B-17Es turned to intercept, climbing to 20,000ft (6,000m), but the carriers circled under broken cloud and the Fortress crews had to search for them. Capt Payne spotted the first carrier which was seen to break cloud cover; he directed the formation over his radio and went into the attack, followed by Capt Cecil Faulkner, and Capt Carl Wuertele in *Hel-En-Wings*. Col Sweeney continues:

The enemy started firing as soon as we opened our bomb-bays. The fire wasn't effective, but it was a bit disturbing. The fighters came up to attack, manoeuvring beautifully, but they failed to follow through. It appeared that their heart was not in their work, and in no case was their attack pressed home. We divided our ships into three groups: each group was instructed to take a carrier, and we bombed away. We are fairly certain we hit the first carrier, but we didn't claim it. The second group, under the command of Capt Cecil Faulkner, hit [sic] its carrier amidships. Lt Col Brooke Allen, commanding the last flight, secured hits [sic] on the third carrier. We didn't have time to wait and see them sink, but we left knowing they were badly crippled.

(In fact, none of the enemy carriers were hit.) Sgt Handrow in Capt Tokarz's ship wrote:

and his two other B-17Es in the first flight picked out a large ship and tried to bomb it. Sweeney wrote:

At the bomb-release line we encountered very heavy anti-aircraft fire. It continued throughout the attack and, as in the attacks that followed, was plenty heavy. My flight didn't claim any hits on this run; we hit all around the enemy but didn't see any evidence of damage.

Capt Clement P. Tokarz led the second element in *The Spider*. Sgt Horst Handrow, his tail gunner, wrote:

There below was a task force that spread all over the Pacific. We didn't have enough gas to look any farther so we picked out the biggest battlewagon we could find and started to make a run on it with the bomb-bay doors open. The anti-aircraft was coming up now and the sky was black with it. Bang! We had a hit in the No. 4

engine. On we went on our run. Bombs away! Two hits were scored with 500lb bombs. The battleship seemed to blow up in one spot, and black smoke was coming out of her in a black cloud. She stopped right there, and the cans were coming in to aid the burning ship which couldn't go anywhere under its own power.

The third element, led by Capt Cecil Faulkner, went after a cruiser and claimed to have hit it at the stern. One pilot in the second flight, Capt Paul Payne in *Yankee Doodle*, had two bombs hang up on the first trip so he made an additional individual run through the ack-ack and claimed a direct hit and one near miss on a large transport, setting it afire. Sgt Handrow continues:

As we left the area I could see another ship burning and a transport sinking. Not bad for nine Fortresses when it comes to moving targets! The bombing mission was made at

We started our run, but couldn't get in because the clouds covered up the target and the anti-aircraft was thick. No. 4 engine went out again, and we played around at 22,000ft [6,700m] with the clouds and the anti-aircraft. Then we saw a big *Kaga* carrier come out from under the clouds: the rising sun on it looked like a big bullseye, and we used it as such. Down went the bombs from three ships; the deck got three hits [sic], the waterline four; she was sinking and burning [sic] at the same time. Zero fighters attacked us on the way home, but wouldn't come in close enough so we could get a good shot at them.

We got a radio report that Midway was being bombed. What a funny feeling we got; what if we couldn't get in there, what the heck were we going to do? We didn't have enough gas to go back to Hawaii. As we drew closer we could see

back to Japan. Home we went again, still fooling around with No. 4 out; then No. 2 started giving us trouble. It looked like our little fun picnic was over, because we were ordered to go back to Hawaii. Take-off from Midway was made at 02:00 hours. It was a tired-out crew that landed at Hickam that night. All the men in the crew got the Silver Star for this battle.

Other B-17Es carried on the attack on 5 June. In the morning eight B-17Es attacked a task force 130 miles (209km) from Midway, and claimed hits on two large warships. During the afternoon six B-17Es claimed hits on a heavy cruiser 300 miles (480km) from Midway. The last strike, by 7th Air Force aircraft, in the Battle of Midway was by five B-17Es, which bombed a heavy cruiser 425 miles (685km) from Midway.

Air Forces. One of Kenney's first tasks was to clear the skies of Japanese over New Guinea and then New Britain , and to advance on the Admiralties.

Pease, Medal of Honor

The 19th Bomb Group helped considerably in this task. After a brief rest in Australia, the 19th had resumed combat operations, participating in the Battle of the Coral Sea 4–8 May, and raiding Japanese targets during the enemy's invasion of Papua. From 7–12 August the 19th Bomb Group attacked targets near Rabaul, New Britain, and were awarded a second DUC for these missions. For his actions during 6–7 August 1942, Capt Harl Pease Jr was

B-17E 41-2633 Sally **of the 19th Bomb Group after a crashlanding in Australia on 27 June 1944, following a raid on the Japanese airfield at Lae, New Guinea. Captain Wilbur Beezley struck a barrier on the runway at the advanced base at Mareeba in the dark and the impact blew out the left tyre. The plane dropped with such force that the landing gear ploughed up through the No. 2 engine.** Sally **was later stripped down and furnished with a table, a bunk and a few chairs, to become General George C. Kenney's personal aircraft until a couple of spars were cracked in a thunderhead and** Sally **had to be retired.** USAF

a cloud of black smoke hang over the island. Something was really burning there, and our hopes sunk with that sight. In we came, and to give us cheer we saw that the marine ack-ack batteries had kept the runways open, even if everything else seemed to be hit.

We landed and started to gas up and load bombs again for another run [in the late afternoon] on the Japs, who by then were only 90 miles (145km) away. Up again, and this time we picked out a big cruiser – but just as we started on the run, six Navy dive bombers dived down on him; at last we were getting help from the Navy. So we picked out a nice transport loaded with Japs. Two hits and the Japs were swimming

One B-17E was shot down at sea 15 miles (24km) from Midway: all except one of the crew were rescued. Another B-17E was lost due to fuel shortage.

The battle ended in victory for the US. Losses in aircraft and ships were heavy, but the Japanese had lost four valuable aircraft carriers. During 3–5 June the B-17Es flew sixteen attacks (fifty-five sorties) for the loss of two aircraft. In the wake of the Battle of Midway, a great shake-up of commands took place. Then on 4 August, Maj Gen George C. Kenney was officially placed in charge of MacArthur's air operations in the south-west Pacific, taking command of the Allied

posthumously awarded the Medal of Honor. On 6 August Pease was forced to return to Mareeba from a reconnaissance mission over New Britain when one engine of his B-17 failed. Pease was anxious to take part in the big raid planned for the 7th against Vunakanau airfield in the Bismarck Archipelago, so he and his crew worked for hours on 41-2429, a replacement plane. They finally arrived at Port Moresby after midnight.

On the morning of 7 August, sixteen B-17s of the 19th Bomb Group, led by Lt Col Richard H. Carmichael, took off for Vunakanau airfield where 150 bombers

Photo taken from 23,000ft (7,000m) of bombs dropped from B-17Es of the 19th Bomb Group on Japanese shipping in Rabaul Harbour, 12 August 1942. Hits were claimed on three vessels. Bernie Barr Collection

threatened the US Marine Corps' landings on Guadalcanal. One B-17 crashed on take-off and two aborted with mechanical malfunctions, but by skilful flying, Pease maintained his position in the formation, despite a still troublesome engine, and made it to the target. At this point the bad engine gave out. Pease feathered it and dropped his bombs on the target, but the lame duck was soon singled out by the Japanese fighters. In the air battle that continued after the bombers left the target, Pease's B-17 was hit in the bomb-bay tank, which burst into flames, and the bomber fell behind the formation and was lost. There were reports of two parachutes being seen, and some years

later it emerged that Pease and Sgt Czehowski, a gunner, did bale out and were taken prisoner. On 8 October 1942 Pease, Czehowski and four other prisoners were executed by the Japanese at Rabaul.

A New Group Enters the Fray

In August 1942 the 43rd Bomb Group (motto: Willing, able, ready') at Port Moresby joined the 5th Air Force. (The 5th had been re-designated from the FEAF in February, and did not function as an air force for some time after February 1942, the AAF organizations in the south-west Pacific

being under the control of American-British-Dutch-Australian command, and later, Allied Air Forces. HQ 5th Air Force was re-manned in September 1942.) The 43rd Bomb Group had been activated on 15 January 1941 and had moved to the south-west Pacific via Capetown, South Africa, during February–March 1942. During October, several daylight and night raids were made on Rabaul, eastern New Britain, the main Japanese base in the Pacific; some crews flew as low as 250ft (76m) to hit their targets. When the 19th left Australia for the USA on 1 November 1943 to serve as a replacement training unit, some of the group B-17s were transferred to the 43rd.

Raids on Rabaul continued during January and February 1943. During a raid on shipping in the harbour on 5 January, Brig Gen Kenneth Walker, commanding general of 5th Bomber Command, was killed aboard one of the two B-17s shot down. The 43rd Bomb Group also experimented with 'skip'-bombing, and used this method for some shipping strikes, including several decisive actions during the Battle of the Bismarck Sea, 2–4 March.

Two months later, on the morning of 16 June, Capt Jay Zeamer Jr, aged twenty-five, a pilot in the 65th Squadron, set off on an aerial mapping sortie over the Solomon Islands. It was his 47th combat mission. The night before, the crew, all of whom were volunteers, were told to include a reconnaissance over Buka passage, as 400 enemy planes had just landed there. Zeamer arrived at the mapping site before the sun had risen high enough to take photos, and proceeded to Buka first. With just forty-five seconds of the mapping mission rmaining, *Lucy*, their B-17E, was attacked by more than fifteen fighters. Although mortally wounded, 2nd Lt Joseph Sarnoski, bombardier, remained at his nose-guns and fired at the enemy attackers until he died at his post. Though seriously wounded by shrapnel in his legs and both arms, Zeamer manoeuvred *Lucy* for forty minutes during the combat until the enemy broke off their action, then directed the flight to a base more than 500 miles (800km) away. When Zeamer passed out from loss of blood, Sgt John Able, the top turret gunner, took over, as co-pilot Lt John Britten was also injured. Zeamer, who was barely conscious, put *Lucy* down at Dobodura on New Guinea, with one crewman dead and five wounded. Zeamer hovered on the edge of death for three days, and spent fifteen months in more than a dozen hospitals. He

(*Above*) **Field modifications to B-17E 41-2432** The Last Straw **in the 63rd Bomb Squadron, 43rd Bomb Group, shows an early attempt to improve the forward fire power of the Fortress in the Pacific by installing tail-guns in the nose.** USAF

B-17s of the 43rd Bomb Group at Seven Mile airfield, Port Moresby. By August 1942, the 43rd in Australia had become the fifth B-17E group to be deployed against Japan and this unit was later awarded a DUC for skip-bombing on shipping strikes in the South Pacific, including attacks on enemy vessels during the Battle of the Bismarck Sea, 2–4 March 1943. USAF

B-17E 41-24353 Cap'n & The Kids **flew eighty missions with the 43rd Bomb Group before joining the 69th Troop Carrier Squadron, 433rd Troop Carrier Group, 54th Troop Carrier Wing. Modified to drop supplies,** Cap'n & The Kids **was one of eight war-weary B-17Es that took part in essential operations to deliver weapons, ammunition and medical supplies to Momote Island during the invasion of the Admiralty Islands, 19 February– 4 March 1944. The aircraft participated in further supply drops during the invasion of Hollandia in April 1944.**
Boeing

and Sarnoski were both awarded the Medal of Honor. Radio operator, Bill Vaughan, who while severely wounded managed to pick up a distant radio signal that allowed them an approximate heading to get them home – the navigator had been critically wounded – was awarded the DSC.

Gen Kenney tried to obtain more B-17s, but they were needed for Europe and he got Liberators instead. In May the 43rd began converting to the B-24, and by the end of September had fully converted to the Liberator. Some of the surviving B-17Es served

as armed transports and troop carriers and were still in action as late as May 1944 during the Pacific island-hopping campaign. Operating from Australia, new Guinea and

Owi in the Schouten Islands until November 1944, the 43rd made numerous attacks on Japanese shipping in the Netherlands East Indies and the Bismarck Archipelago.

Captured B-17E in flight photographed from a B-17D that had also been captured. Altogether, the Japanese obtained three Fortresses, two B-17Ds and one early B-17E, which were flown to Japan and put on public display with other captured US aircraft. These captured Fortresses were carefully evaluated and were used to develop fighter tactics against them. USAF

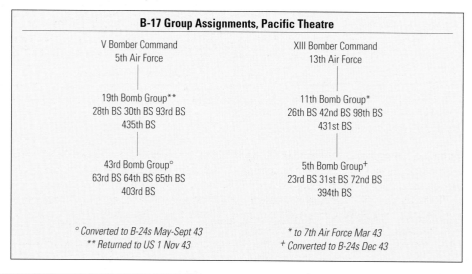

B-17 Group Assignments, Pacific Theatre	
V Bomber Command 5th Air Force	XIII Bomber Command 13th Air Force
19th Bomb Group** 28th BS 30th BS 93rd BS 435th BS	11th Bomb Group* 26th BS 42nd BS 98th BS 431st BS
43rd Bomb Group° 63rd BS 64th BS 65th BS 403rd BS	5th Bomb Group+ 23rd BS 31st BS 72nd BS 394th BS
° Converted to B-24s May-Sept 43 ** Returned to US 1 Nov 43	* to 7th Air Force Mar 43 + Converted to B-24s Dec 43

CHAPTER FOUR

The Cactus Air Force

War in the South Pacific, 1942–1943

In February 1942 the 11th Bomb Group (motto: *Progressio sine timore aut praejudicio*, 'Progress without fear or prejudice') was at Hickham Field, Hawaii, training with B-18s; it also received B-17s for operations with the newly constituted 7th Air Force. In March the group was commanded by Col la Verne G. 'Blondie' Saunders, so-named because of his coal-black hair. On 14 June Saunders took off from Hickam Field for an audacious moonlight raid on Wake Island. Horst Handrow wrote:

> We flew from Hawaii to Midway Island, loaded up with bombs and gas, and started back for Wake. The moon was bright and everything was perfect for the night raid. Over we roared at 4,000ft [1,200m] with the bomb-bay doors open. We cleaned that place up good. Fires were stared all over the island, and the anti-aircraft made the night look like the Fourth of July.

A B-17E pictured on 19 February 1942. The Japanese considered the B-17 a tough and well-armed adversary, and one that was very difficult to shoot down. It could absorb an incredible amount of damage and still remain flying. Boeing

Following the raid the 11th Bomb Group returned to Hawaii, and soon speculation was rife that they were to proceed to the South Pacific theatre of operations. Late in July 1942 the 11th Bomb Group left Hawaii and flew via Christmas Island, Canton Island and Fiji to Noumea, capital of New Caledonia, for operations against Guadalcanal, a hilly, tropical, jungle-covered island in the Solomon Islands group, where on 4 July the Japanese had started building an airfield on the Lunga Plain. With Lunga airfield complete, the Japanese could send land-based bombers on raids on the New Hebrides for a thrust southwards. Guadalcanal is enclosed by the small islands of Tulagi, Gavutu and Tanambogo.

As early as April 1942 Tulagi had been deemed the number one American objective in the Solomons; the deep and spacious harbour with air cover from Guadalcanal presented the Japanese with an excellent naval base to threaten the lifeline to Australia. The task of preventing this was given to Vice Admiral Robert L.

Ghormley, commander, South Pacific area (COMSOPAC). His air commander was Rear Admiral John S. McCain, who controlled all land-based aircraft in the South Pacific area, including those of the USAAF. Maj Gen Millard F. Harmon was charged with the training and administration of all US Army ground and air force units in the South Pacific.

To avoid overcrowding, Saunders decided to leave the eight 431st Squadron B-17s at Nandi on Viti Levu in the Fiji islands and take the remaining twenty-seven B-17s to Plaines des Gaiacs airfield on New Caledonia (the island already accommodated thirty-eight fighters of the 67th Fighter Squadron and ten B-26 Marauders). On arrival at Tontouta near Noumea, Saunders retained the 42nd Squadron but later despatched the 98th Squadron to Koumac on the north side of the island, and sent the 26th to Roses Field at Port Vila on Efate in the New Hebrides. The 11th Bomb Group had to be ready for a week of intensive bombing operations against 'Cactus' (the

code-name for Guadalcanal) as a prelude to the invasion of the island on 7 August by US Marines.

Although an advanced strip was ready on the island of Espiritu Santo, about 150 miles (240km) north of Efate, Saunders decided to open his attack from Efate, which possessed better servicing facilities. (The 11th Bomb Group's ground echelons did not arrive by sea until early September.) The first 900-mile (1,450km) round trip mission to Tulagi Harbour began on schedule on 30 July. The two 431st Squadron B-17s despatched were badly shot up by Zeros but returned safely with claims of two Zeros shot down. The following day it was the turn of two 98th Squadron B-17s to bomb Lunga airfield. Col Saunders flew with Lt Buie's crew. The second B-17, *The Blue Goose* (so called because it had acquired a light blue gloss paint scheme at the Hawaiian air depot), was flown by Lt Frank 'Fritz' Waskowitz, a former University of Washington football star, who had been badly burned in the attack on Pearl Harbor. He and his crew were nicknamed the 'USO Kids' because they had once landed at a forward strip and jokingly asked where the nearest USO club was located. Both crews achieved almost total surprise and only light and inaccurate flak met the Fortresses.

On 1 August the 431st Squadron moved up from Nandi Field to Efate and then to Espiritu Santo, but crews were left kicking their heels at Button Field, Bomber 1 as they awaited orders. On 3 August Horst Handrow, tail gunner in Capt Sullivan's crew, and his fellow crew members, were

Two Zeros hung over our formation but wouldn't come in to attack; they were sending our speed and altitude to the ack-ack guns below. We soon left them behind and headed back to our base at Santo. More planes were taking off for 'Canal when we landed. We loaded up again with twenty 100-pounders, but no orders came through that day so we waited for the next day. Rain set in that night, and us with planes out. What rotten luck. Death was in the air because the only landing lights we had were two trucks parked at the end of the runway. We stood there with cold sweat running down our faces. Who wasn't going to make it? We saw a

you could see the stuff fly up in the air. Seven Zeros were around that day and they would come in every once in a while and make a pass at you.

Eventually the Zeros came in too close and four were shot down. One of the crashing fighters plunged into a 26th Squadron Fortress flown by Lt R.E. McDonald and brought that down, too; all the crew were lost.

Raids continued on 5 and 6 August, and then the USMC landed on 7 August as scheduled. They met no opposition while the Fortresses conducted unproductive searches at sea for the Japanese fleet to the north of the Solomons. Casualties were Lt Robert B. Loder of the 98th Squadron who was thought to have crashed in mountains on New Caledonia; Maj Marion N. Pharr, the 431st Squadron CO, who also failed to return. Maj James V. Edmundson of the 26th Squadron assumed command and took the crew previously assigned to Capt Sullivan; the latter was sent to Fiji to pick up another crew.

On 8 August the American marines reached the Japanese airfield and discovered that the enemy had fled. The airstrip was named Henderson Field after the commander of the USMC dive bombers at Midway. Meanwhile the Forts continued their search at sea. They saw part of the Japanese Navy turning for home with two ships in the task force burning as a result of action in the Solomons area. On 11 August the Fortresses of the 11th Bomb Group went on a hair-raising low-level photo mission over a Japanese-held island. Horst Handrow wrote:

L–R Rear Admiral John S. McCain, who commanded all land-based aircraft in the South Pacific area; Col (later Brig Gen) Laverne G. 'Blondie' Saunders, CO, 11th Bomb Group; and Maj Gen Millard F. Harmon, commanding general US Army Forces in the South Pacific area. Sam Moses via Bill Cleveland

We came in at 40ft (12m) with guns going to keep the groundmen away from the ack-ack batteries. It was real fun. We laid it on the two freighters and one can which was unloading the stuff – we were so close I could see the glass coming down. But the second time through they opened up on us. We put it right back, having all the pictures we wanted, and tailed it for home. Happy day that was.

Next day we were called out of bed at 3am and we knew right away that something was up. Our crew jumped into the plane and in fifteen minutes we were on our way to Guadalcanal which was being shelled by three Jap cruisers. 'Get a cruiser': those were our orders, and we were out there to fulfil them. – all alone, too. As we came in sight of the island we saw one cruiser, but it looked like a light one so we passed it up and started looking for the heavy cruiser which was also in there; we saw it five minutes

told to get ready for their first crack at 'Canal with a raid on the airfield. Handrow wrote:

After four and a half hours of flight we saw our target. We were at 12,000ft [3,660m]. We made our run, and eight 500-pounders hit across the runway – two fires were burning very nicely when we left. The anti-aircraft wasn't very heavy because most of the ack-ack batteries had already been put out for keeps.

plane light going towards the jungle. 'That isn't the runway', I almost shouted. Too late, and with explosion of gas' tanks and falling of trees the B-17 went down and started to burn. Five men lost their lives; four got out okay. That was the beginning of our bad luck. We watched out there in the rain with our fingers crossed until they'd all landed.

We took off again for 'Canal on 4 August and this time did our bombing at 3,000ft (900m), hitting trucks and supplies; we were so low that

B-17E waist gunner maintains a watchful eye during a photo reconnaissance mission over New Guinea. The gun mount allowed him to swivel his machine gun inside and outside the window opening. USAF

later while we were flying at 9,000ft [2,740m]. We started to circle it, but it slowly circled us so we couldn't make a good run on it. Anti-aircraft was coming up, but then with the sun at our backs, down we came with bomb-bay doors open, down until we were at 5,000ft (1,500m) – mighty low to be fooling with anything but big. Out went the bombs: two hits and one close miss – not bad for four bombs. She was burning now and all she could do was go around in a circle. The cruiser threw everything at us but the boat. We watched for an hour and she was still burning and getting worse. She sank late that afternoon, so the marines said. It was a job well done even if we got grounded for three days for getting down that close. I still remembered December 7th.

On 20 August Henderson Field was repopulated with Wildcats and Dauntlesses. The Fortresses' daily action in support of the hard-pressed marines took its toll. By now the 11th Bomb Group had lost eleven B-17s, although only one as a result of combat. Some crews were sent to Fiji for a well earned rest. Three days later the US Navy received warning that the Japanese were moving on the Solomons from the north. US carrier task forces were despatched to meet them, and at 12:15 hours on 24 August Col Saunders was advised of a contact with the enemy task force 720 miles (1,160km) from Espiritu. Admiral McCain, aware that a B-17 strike would involve hazardous night landings, left the attack decision to Saunders. He accepted the risk, and two flights of Fortresses were despatched separately. Three B-17s of the 42nd Squadron, led by Maj Ernest R. Manierre, and four from the 26th Squadron led by Maj Allan J. Sewart, set out over the Pacific to the north-west of Santo. Manierre's flight made contact with the task force in the late afternoon, observing *Ryujo*, a crippled carrier, being

B-17F-10-BO 41- 24457 The Aztec's Curse of the 26th Bomb Squadron, 11th Bomb Group, over the Rendova Islands in the Solomons. US Navy via Bill Cleveland

Lt John H. Pitts' crew pose in front of their B-17E *San Antonio Rose* of the 98th Bomb Squadron, 11th Bomb Group, on Koomac, New Caledonia in August 1942. Mrs Pitts via Bill Cleveland

By 23 September 1942 the 'Cactus Air Force' was taking positive shape with the arrival, at Espiritu Santo, of B-17Es of the 72nd Squadron, 5th Bomb Group, commanded by Maj Don Ridings. At around this time the squadrons on Santo also began receiving replacement crews and new B-17G models with chin turrets; these surprised the Japanese fighter pilots who had been used to making head-on passes against the B-17Es and Ds. (In mid-October two additional squadrons from the 5th Bomb Group – motto: *Kiai o ka lewa*: 'Guardians of the upper regions' – arrived, commanded by Col Brooke E. Allen. All three squadrons were placed under the command of 'Blondie' Saunders.) Also on 23 September Lt Durbin and the crew of *Skipper* in the 98th Squadron bombed the Rekata Bay seaplane base with incendiaries. They were attacked by five 'Dave' reconnaissance aircraft, but shot down one and damaged the others.

The following day the 98th Squadron again tussled with Japanese reconnaissance aircraft. *Galloping Gus*, flown by Capt Walter Y. Lucas, and *Goonie* piloted by Lt Durbin, dropped their 500lb (227kg) demolition bombs on cargo vessels in Tonolei Harbour on Fauro Island off the south-eastern end of Bougainville. *The Blue Goose*, flown by Lt 'Fritz' Waskowitz, also dropped his bombs successfully, a direct hit being scored on one cargo vessel and near misses damaging another. Ten 'Rufes' and ten 'Daves' attacked while the Fortresses made their bombing runs: one 'Rufe' was shot down in flames, a 'Dave' was shot down streaming smoke, and several other enemy aircraft were hit. Lucas returned to Santo while the damaged *Goonie* and *The Blue Goose* were put down on Henderson Field. None of the crew was injured. The 42nd Squadron did not fare so well, however, and Lt Charles E. Norton's crew in 'Bessie the Jap Basher' failed to return from a search mission.

On 28 September the Fortresses of the 11th Bomb Group headed for Shortland Island Harbour at the southern end of Bougainville Island. Horst Handrow wrote:

I already had a funny feeling when we got into the plane. 'Today we are coming back with holes, and lots of them', I said to the mechanics. We got up to Shortland Harbour and it was closed in by a big stormcloud. There were three planes in our formation. Then out of the clouds the Zeros started coming; I counted thirty in all. Boy, we really were in for it, and I didn't mean maybe – the sky was full of the little sons of a

towed by a cruiser or large destroyer. On the first run the bombs overshot, and the B-17s went round for another try: this time four direct hits were claimed on the carrier. (The *Ryujo* was later sunk by USN dive and torpedo bombers.)

Sixty miles eastwards, Maj Sewart's four B-17s surprised a second Japanese armada at twilight, and two or more hits were claimed on one large battlewagon. Large numbers of Zeros pressed home attacks, and five were claimed shot down by the American gunners, with two probables. Two of the B-17s were damaged and all were dangerously low on fuel, but the flight returned to Efate safely. Manierre's B-17s were not so fortunate: they returned to Santo after dark, and during the landing the Fortress piloted by Lt Robert E. Guenther crashed into a hillside after his No. 4 engine failed; the pilot and four of the crew were killed.

On 2 September Horst Handrow and the rest of his crew returned from leave on Fiji. The tail gunner was re-assigned to Capt White's crew. The following day Capt Buie of the 98th Squadron, who was on a special photo mission in the Buka Passage, put *Hellzapoppin* down on Henderson Field

after encountering heavy but inaccurate flak at Kieta. On 12 September *Hellzapoppin* was ditched off Plaines de Galacs, New Caledonia, after the fuel supply ran out, although Maj Rasmussen and his crew survived the water landing.

Missions continued daily from Santo while the airstrip at Henderson Field was made longer for upcoming B-17 missions. On 12 September Japanese bombers attacked the field, and the following day enemy ground forces launched heavy attacks. The marines fought back, and the Japanese were forced to retreat with heavy losses. On this occasion *Typhoon McGoon* in the 98th Squadron and two B-17s in the 431st Squadron were lost. Lt Van Haur's *The Spider* and Lt Woodbury's Fortress were forced to ditch in the sea, the latter having been hit by anti-aircraft fire over New Guinea; one engine was knocked out and the left wing was badly damaged. The B-17 hit the water just after midnight, Tech Sgt Ray Storey suffering a badly broken leg in the crash. The crew was picked up the following day and Van Haur's crew were rescued on 19 September, though by then two men had died of exposure.

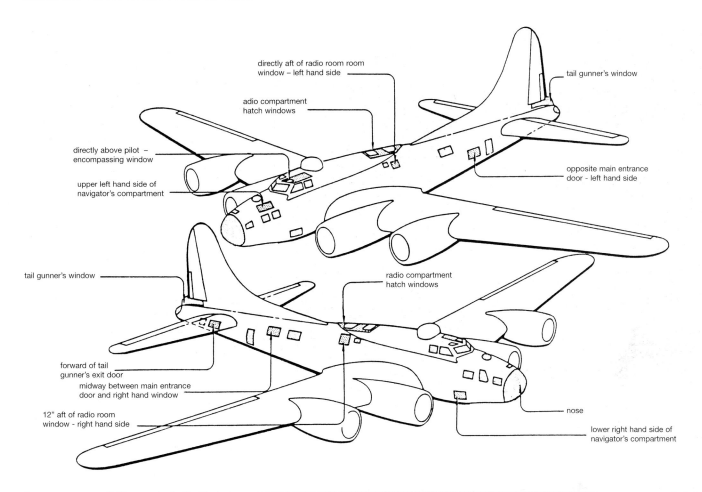

directly aft of radio room room
window – left hand side

tail gunner's window

adio compartment
hatch windows

directly above pilot –
encompassing window

opposite main entrance
door - left hand side

upper left hand side of
navigator's compartment

tail gunner's window

radio compartment
hatch windows

forward of tail
gunner's exit door

midway between main entrance
door and right hand window

nose

12" aft of radio room
window - right hand side

lower right hand side of
navigator's compartment

**Emergency egress. B-17 crews in the Pacific had
many water landings, but at least the Fortress
stayed afloat longer than a Liberator.**

(Right) **Maj Rasmussen, CO, 98th Bomb Squadron,
11th Bomb Group, stands beside B-17E** The Skipper,
**which was flown by Lt Durbin on the 23 September
1942 mission to the seaplane base at Rekata Bay
when it tussled with five Japanese** Daves**. The
Skipper** was credited with five enemy aircraft during
its first eight missions. USAF via Bill Cleveland

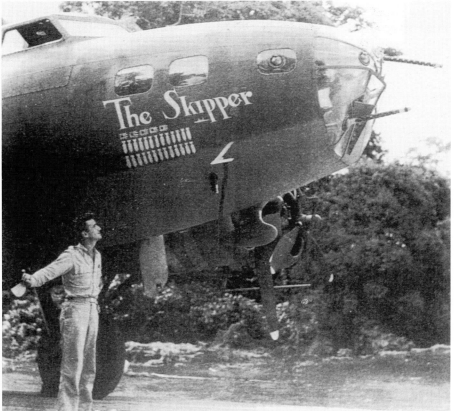

B-17E Galloping Gus **of the 98th Bomb Squadron, 11th Bomb Group, pictured at Santo in 1942. On 24 September Capt Walter Y. Lucas flew this aircraft on a bombing mission to Tonolei Harbour and returned to Santo safely.** Bill Cleveland

gun, and they started hitting us. One went past the tail and I gave him both barrels and down he went in flames. Good shooting, Handrow! Then they started to work my position over. A 20mm shell hit my section and pieces of steel went all over my position, through the seat I was sitting on, over my shoulder, just buzzing past my leg; it burned it more than anything else. 'That was close,' I thought. Once more the little sons of a gun sent bullets through my section, and this time a 7.7 went right through the oxygen line two inches from my heel. A little later again the stuff came through the tail, and this time it went through the door about three feet from me. Then another Zero went out past the tail and I gave him the works; that made two that day. Jim Orr and Pepe got one each, too, so four in one day; not bad shooting. After a twenty-minute air battle they went home – but not all thirty of them: thirteen were shot down that

day. We'll teach them to fool with our Flying Fortresses! We got a breather when we spotted a Jap cruiser, a nice heavy one. We started our run on it but couldn't get our bombs away, so we pulled out of formation to let another ship take our place.

The Blue Goose, flown by Handrow's old co-pilot 'Fritz' Waskowitz, pulled in to replace them. On the first run, Waskowitz's bombs failed to release; then as the B-17 came in on the second run it was attacked by Japanese Zeros. Fire in the cockpit of one Zero forced the pilot to rear back, and he pulled the stick with him; this turned his fighter straight up, and it collided with the underbelly of the B-17 – still loaded with bombs, it exploded in mid-air. Handrow observed: 'Nobody got out. It left me with a cold sweat, and I have feared anti-aircraft fire ever since.'

Fifteen Nagoya land-type Zeros carrying belly tanks attacked the returning Fortresses; in the ensuing battle the B-17s shot down eight Zeros, probably destroying two more and damaging others. *Goonie*, flown by Lt Durbin, was hit, and S/Sgt Eber J. Nealy, navigator, was wounded in the head and right thigh when 20mm cannon and 7.7 machine-gun fire explod-

B-17E 41-2523 Goonie **of the 98th Bomb Squadron, 11th Bomb Group; it was damaged by Japanese fighters on the 24 September 1942 mission to Tonolei Harbour, but Lt Walter Y. Lucas, the pilot, managed to land safely at Henderson Field, Guadalcanal.** Goonie **was badly damaged again on 29 September – piloted this time by Lt Durbin – returning from a raid on Bougainville, when fifteen Nagoya land-type Zeros attacked. S/Sgt Eber J. Nealy, navigator, was wounded in the head and right thigh by 20mm cannon and 7.7in machine-gun shells.** Goonie **was credited with seven Japanese aircraft destroyed in only fifteen missions, and carried a gold star on her nose denoting her participation in the Battle of Midway.** USAF via Bill Cleveland

B-17E Madame X **of the 98th Bomb Squadron, 11th Bomb Group, being repaired in the Solomons, 1942.** Madame X **named after a pre-war movie and flown by Lt Cope, was one of four 98th Squadron aircraft which participated in the mission to Bougainville on 29 September 1942 when** The Blue Goose **failed to return.** USAF via Bill Cleveland

ed in the navigator's compartment. *Flak* was heavy and accurate, and only two B-17s escaped damage. Handrow concludes:

We flew back to the 'Canal and landed there, on a flat tyre that bullets had hit; Capt White, our pilot, was really on the ball. We looked for more hits and found them all over the airplane: 450 in all. The rudder was all full, seventeen holes in my little tail section, one big one in the nose, a couple of hits in No. 3 engine. We had a close call, and we were really lucky that nobody got hit. The raid was therefore a flop – but he who runs away today, comes to fight again another day.

Further Japanese and US Marine reinforcements arrived on Guadalcanal in September and October. On 11–12 October the Battle of Cape Esperance was fought at sea off Guadalcanal. On the 12th, Col Saunders, flying with Maj Al Sewart, CO of the 26th Squadron, led a six-ship formation which took off from Henderson Field for a bombing raid on an airfield just north of the Buka Passage. Maj

James Edmundson led the second element with two wingmen from the 431st; he wrote:

We dropped 1,000-pounders on the runway. We could see fighters taking off as we were on our bombing run, and Zeros were soon at our altitude and continued to work us over as we proceeded south to our second target, a collection of ships at anchor in Buin Harbour at the south end of Bougainville Island. *Flak* was extremely heavy, and the Zeros stayed with us until we withdrew out of their range. Six Zeros were confirmed as destroyed. All six B-17s received battle damage, several engines were knocked out throughout the formation, several crew members were wounded, and Ed Lanigan, Al Sewart's navigator, was killed.

We arrived back over Henderson Field just as a bombardment was under way by about fifteen 'Bettys' with fighter escort, and the marine fighters were up after them. We were now low on fuel and out of ammunition, and by the time the field was clear for us to come in and land we were mighty glad to get on the ground.

That night, 12–13 October, will forever be known as 'the night of the big shelling' to all of us who were there. The Japanese had succeeded in getting a task force down 'The Slot', which included several cruisers and a couple of battleships. They proceeded to lob heavy artillery into Henderson Field throughout the night; several aircraft were hit, and fires were started in the ammunition and fuel dumps. The next morning there was only 2,000ft of usable runway available for those B-17s that were still flyable to take off from, to return to Espiritu Santo. Lt Hyland, a 42nd Squadron pilot in 'Yokohama Express', failed to return from another mission on the 12th.

Meanwhile the 431st Squadron had taken off from Button Field for the 'Canal; it had changed bomb-loads to 500-pounders and then 1,000-pounders for a heavy raid on the 13th. Horst Handrow wrote:

We took off from 'Canal and headed up the string of Solomon Islands, the target the airfield at Buka. The weather was bad and we got on the bomb run just as a storm was closing in on the place. Perfect bombing day. We made our run, four 1,000-pounders going right down the middle of the runway. The other formation dropped sixty 100-pounders through the parked airplanes – a nice couple of fires were started, and fourteen planes won't be flying any more.

Anti-aircraft were coming up, but it wasn't any too good. Three Zeros started in attacking us, and have two ships in our formation. Then they went after us, but we did okay on them: I got one as he went past the tail – he went down like a spin wheel on the Fourth of July! The other ship's gunner got one; he just blew up above us, and the pieces went right past the tail – it looked pretty good. Again we had some more holes. I got two more through my section. Back to Guadalcanal we went, and were grounded because of no oxygen system.

On 14 October we took off for Santo; 'peaceful Santo' we called it. That night was hell on Guadalcanal because the Japs came in with half their fleet and shelled the place all night. Five Fortresses were caught on the ground. Our plane was in the five, and so was our old ship. The gas works went up too, and there was only eighty-five gallons gas left for eighty-five planes, not enough to send up even a couple of dive bombers.

On 15 October we took off from Santo to bomb the Jap fleet shelling the 'Canal; our orders were to get the two transports unloading men and guns. We'd rather have gone after some bigger bait, but orders are orders. Twelve planes were in the formation. We went in in waves of threes, and we were in the second wave. I have never seen the ack-ack so thick. No.1 transport was already blown high, and she was burning. Down went our bombs, and four 500-pounders hit: blew it all to heck – what a sight! The water was full of swimming Japs. The third wave hit a battleship and left it burning.

Then seven Zeros attacked out of the sun. One went past, but I couldn't get in a very good shot. Then one started in on my tail. Was this guy nuts? They never do it because it's sure death, yet here he was coming, and getting closer. I started in firing with all I had, but he kept on coming – was he going to ram us? I kept on firing; two hundred rounds had already gone his way. Boy, I was sweating blood. He was only twenty-five yards away when he went down; ten more yards, and I would have got out of the tail: he was out to get us, and he almost did – what a life I lead! I really stuck my neck out when I got on combat. Back to Santo we went, me with more holes in the tail. One of these days they'll have more luck?

Zeros were not the only Japanese air menace in the Solomons. On 16 October, Lt Thompson and crew in the 72nd Squadron tussled with a Japanese four-engined flying boat while on a routine search mission east of Santa Isabel Island, about 60 miles (100km) from Rekata Bay. The battle lasted twenty minutes, at the end of which the flying boat was shot down after making a futile attempt at trying to escape into some scattered cloud. Sgt White, the engineer and ball turret operator, was hit in the eye by shattered glass when a 20mm shell hit the turret.

Next day a flight of six B-17s took off from Santo at around 14:30 hours to bomb Japanese supplies and installations in the vicinity of the Kokumbona River; they arrived at the target shortly before dark, and bombed in two elements on the target area. Some twelve tons of demolition bombs were laid squarely on some ammunition supplies and crews felt the concussion at their height of 10,000ft (3,000m). They returned to Santo at around 22:30 hours in the middle of a heavy rainstorm; despite this, all the Fortresses put down safely, although most had to make as many as three attempts.

On 18 October the 42nd Squadron moved up from Plaines des Galacs to Turtle Bay on the south-east corner of Santo, where the B-17s would be nearer their Japanese targets. By using Henderson Field as a staging post they could save on precious fuel, sent in by drums and poured into the tanks of the aircraft from buckets and cans. Fuel was consistently short during the entire campaign. *So Solly Please*, flown by Lt Williams, was packed 'from bombsight to tail' with an assortment of provisions, mess components and cooks, medical personnel and luggage so that a mess could be established on Santo. But crews were soon to discover that Turtle Bay was no paradise on earth: rain fell daily, and dengue fever and malaria were prevalent. Santo was also under constant threat from seaborne and aerial attack. The 98th Squadron's base was bombed four times, and twice during October it was shelled by off-shore submarines; however, the only damage occurred was when an 800lb (360kg) bomb felled a tree which crushed the wing of a B-17 attached to the 98th Squadron from the 424th Squadron.

New Blood

Santo soon became overcrowded, with the 98th Squadron, 11th Bomb Group, being joined by the 5th Bomb Group, commanded by Col Brooke E. Allen, and some New Zealand air and ground units. Even so, although taking off in formation from the one-way take-off and landing strips at the crowded bases was difficult, operations continued unabated against Japanese positions on Guadalcanal, and the neighbouring islands of Tulagi, Gavutu and Tanambogo. The 5th Bomb Group, with B-17 and B-24 aircraft, had left Hickam Field, Hawaii, in November, and since December 1941 had been engaged primarily in search and patrol missions from Hawaii. It joined the Allied drive from the Solomons to the Philippines, flying long patrol and photographic missions over the Solomon Islands and the Coral Sea, attacking Japanese shipping off Guadalcanal, and raiding airfields in the northern Solomons until August 1943.

November proved to be the decisive month in the six-month Guadalcanal campaign. The Japanese made several large-scale attempts during the month to land forces on the island and drive the US marines into the sea; the US naval forces were hard pressed, and the majority of the enemy fleet units were stopped by small numbers of ships and aircraft. By this time the squadrons of the 11th Bomb Group were operating regularly from Henderson Field. Japanese air raids were daily occurrences, and imperial naval forces shelled the field frequently. 'Pistol Pete', actually the name given to several Japanese gun

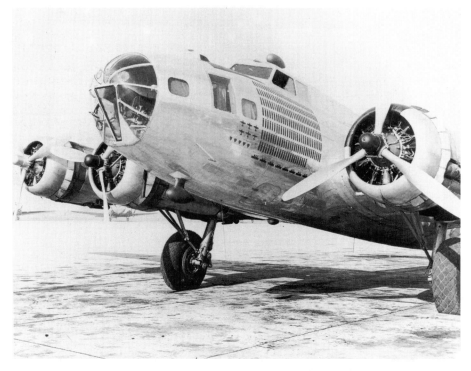

B-17E 41-2400 was built by Boeing and delivered to Douglas as the model for B-17F production. It was converted into a transport after many months of combat in the South Pacific. Oklahoma Gal **flew 203 bombing missions, sinking eight Japanese ships, and her gunners were credited with shooting down six enemy aircraft.** Douglas

B-17E Typhoon McGoon II **41-9211** (the first was lost on 13 September 1942) of the 98th Bomb Squadron, 11th Bomb Group, on New Caledonia in January 1943. Captain Joham's crew were flying this aircraft when they spotted a large Japanese task force north-west of Guadalcanal on 14 November 1942. Note the ASV (air-to surface-vessel) 'whisker brooms' search radar antennae protruding from the upper nose (two more of which were fitted under the wings) and six Japanese kills – all claimed shot down on the 14 November mission. USAF via Bill Cleveland

positions in the hills surrounding the field, also made life unpleasant for the air and ground crews.

Nevertheless, the Fortresses made life equally unpleasant for the Japanese army and naval forces. On 13 November the 11th Bomb Group despatched seventeen B-17s to bomb the damaged Japanese battleship *Hiei*, limping along north-west of Savo: one direct hit and five probables were scored, and the ship finally sank several days later. During a routine search the following day Capt Joham and his crew in *Typhoon McGoon II* in the 98th Squadron, spotted a large task force including two aircraft carriers north-west of Guadalcanal. Joham's radio operator notified Naval Command, while *Typhoon McGoon II* maintained a vigil high above the Japanese fleet. The Japanese ships opened up, and six Zeros and one 'Rufe', soon joined by others, attacked the lone B-17 through the *Flak*. Six fighters were claimed destroyed by the Fortress gunners before the aircraft limped back to Santos at 16:00 hours, riddled with

20mm cannon and 7.7 machine-gun fire. Projectiles had ripped the tail of the B-17 almost to shreds – yet the tail gunner had survived unharmed.

Thanks to Capt Joham and his crew, the 11th Bomb Group, naval surface vessels and aircraft, and the Marine Air Group at Guadalcanal, were able to find and attack the task force near Savo Island. The Fortresses, together with SBD Dauntlesses and TBF Avengers from Henderson Field, sank or severely damaged eight of the vessels. Next morning searches revealed many Japanese ships burning and sinking over a wide expanse of sea around Savo Island. Capt Lucas in *Buzz King* led four other 98th Squadron B-17s in attacks which scored direct hits and effective near misses on troop transports, and an American force of two battleships finished off the task force, sinking one battleship, two cruisers and several smaller ships.

On 18 November, Col 'Blondie' Saunders, in a 26th Squadron Fort piloted by Maj Al Sewart and Lt Jack Lee, led ten B-

17s, each loaded with cargoes of 1,000lb armour-piercing bombs, up the 'Slot' (the channel between New Georgia and Santa Isabel Islands north-west of Guadalcanal) against Japanese shipping at Tonolei Harbour on Buin. Capt Darby's B-17, from the 72nd Squadron, became stuck in a shell hole on Henderson Field but took off later. Darby's crew were to account for one Zero destroyed. Capt Lucas in *Buzz King*, Lt Durbin in *Omar Khayam*, and Lt Morgan in 'Galloping' Gus', all 98th Squadron pilots, scored direct hits on a cargo vessel and several misses. a 20mm shell shattered the glass and damaged the interior of the ball turret in Morgan's B-17, but no injuries were reported. Maj Whitaker and Lt Classen, both 72nd Squadron pilots, were attacked by Zeros, probably based at Buin airfield. Classen's crew claimed two Zeros destroyed.

After the bombing run was made, about twenty Zeros made head-on attacks at the formation. One fired a burst which raked Saunders' command ship, nicking Maj Sewart's arm and hitting Lt Lee in the ankle. Saunders went back to get a first-aid kit, and returned to the flight deck just as a Zero fired a second burst into the control cabin, sending a 7.7 through Sewart's heart, killing him instantly. Jack Lee was hit in the stomach; he fell back, and Saunders lifted him from the co-pilot's seat so he could take over the controls of the badly damaged B-17, which by now was flying with one engine out and another damaged. The left wing was blazing from escaping fuel from the wing tank. The only instrument still working was the clock, and Saunders told another B-17 to take over the lead. Col Saunders wrote:

From the co-pilot's seat I couldn't trim the tabs and handle the plane with those two dead engines on the left, so I got the pilot's body out and moved into the pilot's seat. I decided to make for some overcast and so we dived down. The left wing was red hot. The bank and turn indicator showed we were in a spin. We came out of the overcast at about 500ft, and I saw I'd have to put her down. This was about twenty minutes after the pilot and co-pilot had been hit. Other planes stayed around to protect us, but the Zeros didn't follow us that far. I told the other planes to take our position, and then headed for a little island in order to come down as close to land as possible.

Saunders successfully ditched the faltering bomber 1½ miles offshore at Vella Lavella on Ballale Island, although he cut his head when he banged into the windshield putting the B-17 down on the water at 95mph (150km/h); the wings hit and the bomber came to an abrupt stop. Saunders and Lt Donald G. O'Brien, navigator, slid through the cockpit window; the tail broke off, and the rest of the crew went out through the break. Lt Nelson Levi, bombardier, who had been badly wounded in the thigh, and Lt Lee, were carefully extricated from the wrecked bomber and placed in two life-rafts. Lee died as they paddled ashore. Natives found the airmen and took them to a village where the following afternoon a PBY Catalina, escorted by three Grumman Wildcats, picked up the men and returned them to Santo.

November witnessed the beginning of the end of Japanese attempts to retake Guadalcanal, and they withdrew to the islands in the north. Three major battles at sea took place off Guadalcanal, culminating in the Battle of Tassafaronga on 30 November. The B-17s were put on standby. Horst Handrow relates:

> We got word that Japs were out again, so every plane was on double alert. Lt Jacobs got shot down over the New Georgia islands; a Zero rammed them, and only one man got out. It was their first flight after Auckland [leave]. Hamalainen, my old radioman, went down in that ship.

Derailing The 'Tokyo Express'

Although many of the decisive battles for the control of Guadalcanal took place at sea, the 11th and 5th Bomb Groups flew support missions throughout, bombing Japanese ground forces and shipping. One of their frequent missions was against the 'Tokyo Express', the Japanese combat and transport ship task force that plied the 'slot' almost nightly to reinforce their hard-pressed ground troops on the embattled island. Meanwhile, the Japanese built a new airfield in a coconut grove on the New Georgia islands at Munda, leaving the coconut trees standing until the last minute, then felling them and filling in the holes so that the field was ready for Zeros the next morning.

On 1 December Capt Jake Jacobs of the 431st Squadron, 11th Bomb Group, failed to return from a search mission when his B-17 was brought down by an enemy aircraft which crashed into it in the vicinity of

Vella Lavella. Cpl Hartman, the tail gunner, managed to bale out and he was rescued later; he confirmed that the crew had shot down three enemy fighters. On 10 December the first escorts ever used in the area accompanied the B-17s to Munda Point. The twin-engined P-38 Lightnings were a welcome addition, since as many as forty Japanese fighters rose to meet the bomber formations. The fighters shot down five attacking Zeros while gunners aboard the B-17s claimed two more. Some of the Zeros flew between 1,500–4,000ft (460–1,220m) above the B-17s and dropped bombs with timed fuses on the Fortresses; crews reported approximately twenty bursts from these bombs. Maj Whitaker, the 72nd Squadron CO, returned alone to Guadalcanal and was attacked by Zeros. Four 20mm shells hit one wing, and one exploded in the other. Whitaker landed safely, but the main spar was damaged to such an extent that the B-17 had to be sent to the depot for major repairs. Another B-17, piloted by Maj Glober and Capt Carl Coleman, on routine search in the Bougainville sector, returned to base with one engine out and another badly damaged. Coleman lay dead in his seat, killed by a 7.7 bullet which had

entered the control cabin just below the windshield.

For three days running, 19–21 December, the B-17s attacked Munda again. Larger craters littered the sirstrip and prevented the Zeros from taking off. Meanwhile, pressure was applied to Kahili airfield on Bouganville's south-east tip. On the morning of the raid on the 19th, Capt Charters and his crew in the 98th loaded their B-17 'Skipper' with twenty 100lb and several 20lb fragmentation bombs, and two baskets of 'secret weapons' – in actuality beer bottles! For two hours in the dark early morning Skipper remained over Kahili, dropping bombs every fifteen minutes. Japanese searchlights probed the skies during the first bomb runs, but were suddenly and completely extinguished when the crew hurled out two of their 'secret weapons'!

On Christmas Eve the 11th Bomb Group took off from Guadalcanal between 21:00 and 23:00 hours for a strike against enemy shipping concentrating at Rabaul. Capt Durbin of the 98th Squadron in Buzz King was forced to return early after heavy fuel consumption, and a B-17 in the 431st Squadron also had to return early. Horst Handrow recalls:

B-17E Buzz King **41-2531 of the 98th Bomb Squadron, 11th Bomb Group, on Santo, 1942. During the Christmas Eve 1942 strike against enemy shipping off Rabaul, heavy fuel consumption forced Capt Durbin, the pilot, to return to Guadalcanal early. The aircraft had the best record of any B-17 in the group, with ten Japanese aircraft claimed shot down, and three hits on surface ships.** USAF via Bill Cleveland

We took off in #59, the worst ship in the 98th Bomb Squadron; we had twenty minutes gas' to spare if we made it up and back! It was a sweat mission. Fifteen minutes out of Rabaul, No. 4 engine went out, so we turned around and started back. Thirty minutes later No. 2 engine went out and thet left two. We dropped our bombs in the Pacific to make the load lighter. Then No. 1 started to act up, and it really looked like we were going to sit the plane down in the Pacific and Japs all around us. But luck was with us and we made it okay; we came in with ten minutes gas' left! It was #59's last flight.

The other B-17s dropped their 500lb armour-piercing bombs on fifty large ships in Rabaul harbour. Maj Lucas in *Typhoon McGoon* and Capt Crane in *Goonie*, both 98th Squadron pilots, made bombing runs together, scoring three direct hits on a large troop transport and damaging two other transports. The strike force returned to base and killed the tail gunner of a Japanese four-engined flying boat who 'was demonstrating a machine gun the emperor had given him for Christmas.

On 28 December Lt James Harp and his crew in the 42nd Squadron were lost when their B-17 was shot down. Capt Donald M. Hyland was also shot down, but he and his crew were rescued later by a US Navy PBY 'Dumbo'. Two days later Col Saunders handed over command of the 11th Bomb Group to Col Frank F. Everest. 'Blondie' was well respected by his men and had led them through many difficult air battles. He was promoted to brigadier general and was later chief of staff, B-29 operations, commanding the 58th Wing before sadly having to retire after losing a leg in an aircraft accident.

On 4 January 1943 the Japanese imperial staff finally issued orders for the evacuation of Guadalcanal to begin. On the 13th, the 5th and 11th Bomb Groups came under the control of XIII Bomber Command (Col Harlan T. McCormick), 13th Air Force (Maj Gen Nathan F. Twining), established on Espiritu Santo in New Caledonia. (The 5th would be destined to serve in the 13th Air Force until the end of hostilities, along with two B-24 groups, the 42nd and 307th.) January 1943 was occupied mainly by search missions, with a few bombing strikes at Bougainville and the Russell Islands, north of Guadalcanal. On 1 February the depleted 42nd Squadron, 11th Bomb Group, which was now down to just four B-17s, suffered a severe blow when three crews failed to return from a shipping strike in the Short-

land-Bougainville area. Capt Houx's B-17 was hit in the bomb-bay by *Flak* and disintegrated in the air. Shortly afterwards the other two B-17s, flown by captains Hall and Harold P. Hensley, were jumped by Zeros and shot down

By 9 February, the last remnants of the imperial army had been evacuated from 'Canal by sea. Two days earlier the official order relieving the 11th Bomb Group from duty was signed. In March 1943 the group returned to the Hawaiian Islands and was reassigned to 7th Air Force. (From May to November the 11th re-equipped with B-24 Liberators and then returned to the Pacific.)

The 5th Bomb Group Makes Its Mark

The 5th Bomb Group, now commanded by Col Marion D. Unruh, moved up to Henderson Field on 20 August 1943. A short time before, Lt Alfred B. Cohen, a 21-year-old navigator replacement fresh from the States, had joined the 23rd Bomb Squadron. He recalls:

The group had lost a lot of navigators in Japanese frontal attacks, and to malaria. I was one of fifteen volunteers who had put in for immediate duty, thinking that I would be posted to North Africa; I had always wanted to see Cairo. Imagine the shock when I opened my orders aboard a packed converted Liberator transport to learn that I was headed for 'APO 709-SOPAX-South Pacific'. Guadalcanal! I went cold and started to shake.

On arrival at Espiritu Santo I was assigned to the crew of Capt Tex Burns, soon to be the 23rd Bomb Squadron CO, whose navigator had been killed. The group had B-17Es and Fs, mostly battered Es, some of which were from Hickam at the time of the attack on Pearl Harbor. Burns, twenty-six, tall and lean and a wonderful pilot, asked if I had any gunnery training; I said I hadn't. 'Well,' he said, we're off to Guadalcanal tomorrow!' We landed in the morning during an air raid; our huts were situated in a coconut grove near the beach at Lunga Point. Another raid occurred the next night when the Japs bombed ships in the harbour; it was the most incredible fireworks. We used to scramble into our one-man foxholes, an oil-drum sunk in the sand – but on this occasion mine was already occupied! There was no pattern to the air raids; the Japs came over night and day in 'Bettys'.

There was no accommodation, and no preparations at Henderson Field. Our mess-kits were rusty and came in barrels, and discipline seemed lax. There was a big racket stealing drugs from

the emergency first-aid kits which were attached to the bulkheads aboard the planes at various points; these canvas packs were often raided at night. Once, two drunken pilots decided to fly back to the USA; they got a jeep out to a B-17 and took off, but they had forgotten to take the cover off the pitot tube and crashed nose down and were killed. By the time the Libs came in, discipline had been tightened up and we had to play volleyball and shave; then secondary duties came in. No one wore insignia. Living was very uncomfortable – we lived in tents, and there were no sheets or mattresses. It was hot and sticky by day, chilly at night. The wash-room was a bomb-bay tank on coconut poles, and the urinal a pipe hammered into the ground, which soon developed into a lake. Food was bad too; we depended on the Navy for supplies, and mostly it was spam, dehydrated potatoes, and grape juice which was known as 'battery acid', and dried eggs.

I flew my first mission, to an airbase east of Bougainville on New Britain, that first night. We had our briefing sitting on the ground – when I got there the crew were sitting around the place and it was more like a Boy Scout jamboree. Burns asked me the time: my throat was already constricted with fear – I was twenty-one and scared, and shrilled the reply. Burns, I was to discover, was brave and democratic, a great gambler from Texas University where he had graduated as an engineer. The ops officer decided bomb-bay loads, and said we must hit *something* tonight: 'Go up and hit targets of opportunity,' he said. The 5th Bomb Group had flown night missions and had run into night fighters, so they had then gone in during the day. A lot of the missions were designed to hit targets at dawn, leaving at 03:00. It was more like World War I, really.

To accompany me I had my tent-mate Sid Ingrams, a bombardier from North Carolina (they always sent someone along to accompany a new recruit on his first mission). We got off on the mission and over the target. As we approached, Ingrams said, 'It's just a milk-run – if you think this is bad, you should have been here when it was rough!' Then we were caught in some lights. Fireworks! Up came tracer – it looked like strings of pearls. I looked for Ingrams – he was crouched under the navigator's table! We dropped our bombs and came home.

My second and third missions were to New Georgia, but the weather closed in and we ended up dropping our bombs on the airfield at Kahili, a most dangerous target on the southernmost tip of Bougainville; we went there so many times that I soon became known as the 'Kahili Kid'. On my second mission I took along my 'oc-box', which contained my octant and map case, to the briefing; but then, as we were getting our supper before the 22:00 take-off, Lt Sylvan Einbinder, a smart-aleck type and a practical joker from the Bronx, New York, asked me what I was doing with the octant: 'Why, you don't need that, I never take one!' he said. I thought, 'Here's a seasoned vet, he must know,' so I took the octant

back and placed it under my bed. It was a stormy night, and in the tropics the shoreline is phosphorescent. It was broken cloud from the beaches on, and without an octant I was really nervous. Then the pilot got nervous: 'Where do you think we are?' he asked. I was sure I could match

the bays, wiggles and indentations, and I pointed to the spot. 'You sure? I don't agree,' he said. He put us at another spot, but I stuck to my guns. I was terrified, and then the weather closed in badly. We bombed Kahili blind.

As dawn broke I had the feeling that we were lost; there were no other planes in sight, and we couldn't see land. Then Tex said it looked like we'd have to make a water landing. (We had a lot of water landings. The B-17 stayed afloat longer than a B-24.) Then as it got light, there was a plane on each wing. Einbinder, who had got his octant, radioed to say that we were right on course! Sugar Loaf Island close to Guadalcanal came up. The sun was coming up too, but it had been an awful night.

Flying in the Pacific was totally different to Europe. We flew in shirt sleeves. We didn't wear chutes. One day we found out they were rotten (when you took your shoes off for bed, the next morning they would be green with mould). On searches we flew at under 1,000ft (300m), sometimes lower – even 100ft (30m). These searches were over ten hours, and all of them over water. It was easy to get lost. If we were bombing land targets, sometimes we flew at 20,000ft [6,000m], sometimes 3,000ft [900m] – it was never the same. We flew formations that were mixed. As navigator I often stood behind the pilots when I was not actually navigating, and as the Liberators opened their bomb-bay doors, I could see under them. B-17 pilots struggled to keep from sliding under the B-24s; throttles were always all the way back, and the warning horns - the landing gear warning - in our B-17s were always going non-stop!

We didn't do squadron bombing or squadron navigating. One night the intercom broke down and I had to pass notes to the pilots; this involved climbing through the tunnel to pass notes on changes of course. Every now and again tropical storms had to be avoided, and towering cumulus and lightning bolts on the props were common. We had a radio compass, but the radar was only good for picking up things in the distance. The B-17 was claustrophobic.

The most frightening thing I ever saw was a Jap night fighter over Kahili shooting down our B-17 wing man before we made our bomb run; I saw his exhaust and then the double lines of orange-red tracer – and suddenly that B-17 was a ball of fire and just dropped out of the sky. It was probably a Zero responsible. I said to pilot Dean Lucas, a mormon from Salt Lake City, 'Did you see that?' He said, 'Yes ... we go in.' The gunner said, 'Do we have to?'

There was no glamour in the Pacific, but at Christmas 1943, when our ten remaining B-17s were flown back to the US, it was beautiful, mist and sun streaking off their wings as they flew away.

The crew of Li'l Nell in the 5th Bomb Group at Henderson Field, Guadalcanal, 15 August 1943. *Back row, L–R:* S/Sgt Hildebrand, engineer; Capt A.D. Lucas, pilot; Lt W.L. Chestnut, co-pilot; Lt Alfred B. Cohen, navigator; Lt W.A. Hodges, bombardier. *Front row:* Cpl Waselowski, asst engineer; Cpl Granowski, asst radio man; Sgt Hamaker, tail gunner; Sgt Fredricks, radio operator (KIA Sept 1943). B-17s were last used in Alaska on the 13 February 1943 mission to Kiska Harbour and were redeployed to the South Pacific. By mid-1943, most B-17s had been withdrawn from the Pacific in favour of the longer-ranged B-24 Liberator which was better suited for operations in the Pacific, having a higher speed and bigger bomb-load at medium altitudes. The fuselage aerial has been obliterated by the censor. Alfred B. Cohen

The Big League

European Theatre of Operations, 1942–October 1943

The first of the B-17E groups to arrive in the United Kingdom was the 97th Bomb Group, based at Grafton Underwood, and Polebrook, Northamptonshire, the latter where earlier, RAF Fortress Is had taken off on raids over Germany. The 97th flew the first Fortress strike of the war on 17 August 1942, led by Col Frank Armstrong and Maj Paul Tibbets in 41-2578 Butcher Shop in the 340th Bomb Squadron, seen here leading the 97th out at Grafton Underwood. Butcher Shop was later transferred to the 92nd Bomb Group, being renamed Big Tin Bird and used as a hack by Lt Col Cy Wilson, CO 20th Fighter Group. USAF

Although the United States could not prevent the Japanese attack on Pearl Harbor on 7 December 1941, far-reaching decisions had been made in the event that America should become involved in the conflict with the Axis powers. Between 27 January and 27 March 1941, agreements between the United States and Great Britain were made for the provision of naval, ground and air support for the campaign against Germany. During late 1941 several tentative sites for USAAF installations were explored, including Prestwick in Scotland, and Warton near Liverpool, the proposed site for a repair depot. Others, like Polebrook, Grafton Underwood, Kimbolton, Molesworth, Chelveston, Podington and Thurleigh, all in the Huntingdon area, would soon become familiar to B-17 groups of the 8th Air Force.

On 2nd January 1942 the order activating the 8th Air Force was signed by Major General Henry 'Hap' Arnold, the commanding general Army Air Forces, and the headquarters was formed at Savannah, Georgia, twenty-six days later. On 8 January it was announced that a bomber command was to be established in England. Arnold designated Brigadier General Ira C. Eaker as commanding general of VIII Bomber Command, and his duties were to help prepare airfields and installations and to understudy the methods of RAF Bomber Command. Initially Eaker's headquarters were established at RAF Bomber Command headquarters at High Wycombe, Buckinghamshire. It was here, on 22 February, that VIII Bomber Command was formally activated. Almost six months were to elapse before the 8th mounted its first all-American bombing mission on German-held territory. Between 31 March 1942 and 3 April 1942, Eaker and his staff officers made a more detailed reconnaissance of the Huntingdon area, and the seeds of the future American presence were thus sown. Meanwhile in America, B-17 and B-24 heavy bombardment groups were activated for deployment to Britain.

The first of the B-17E groups activated was the 34th, at Langley Field, Virginia, on 15 January 1942; but in fact it was used to train other groups, and remained in America until late March 1944. On 3 February 1942 three more B-17E groups – the 97th, the 301st and the 303rd – were formally activated. It fell to these three groups, together with the 92nd, activated on 1 March 1942, and two B-24D groups, to establish the nucleus of the 8th's heavy bombardment force in England.

First to arrive in the United Kingdom was the ground echelon of the 97th Bomb Group, which disembarked on 9 June and entrained for their Polebrook base in

Northamptonshire where earlier, RAF Fortress Is had taken off on raids over Germany. In August 1942 the 92nd and 301st Bomb Groups arrived to join Eaker's rapidly increasing air force. The 92nd was the first heavy bombardment group to make a non-stop flight from Newfoundland to Scotland successfully. It took time to get the new groups ready for combat, however, and training was lacking in many areas. Colonel Frank A. Armstrong, one of Eaker's original HQ staff, was appointed CO of the 97th Bomb Group at Grafton Underwood at the end of July in place of Lt Colonel Cousland, and he set about reshaping the group. By mid-August he had twenty-four crews ready for combat. Meanwhile, as arguments went on behind the scenes about whether bombing in daylight was possible over heavily defended targets in Europe, or even that the B-17s' and B-24s' bomb-carrying capacity and armament would be enough, the first Fortress strike of the war was scheduled for 17 August 1942.

'Yankee Doodle' Goes To Town

General Carl 'Tooey' Spaatz, the American air commander in Europe, and members of his staff attended the briefing at Grafton Underwood. At 15:00 hours, six B-17Es took off from Polebrook and flew a diversionary raid on St Omer. Briefing over at Grafton Underwood, Frank Armstrong boarded *Butcher Shop* which was piloted by Major Paul Tibbets and led eleven B-17s to the marshalling yards at Rouen Sotteville in north-western France. Spaatz had felt confident enough to allow Brigadier General Ira C. Eaker to fly on the mission. He joined the crew of *Yankee Doodle*, lead aircraft of the second flight of six.

Over the Channel, the Fortresses were joined by their RAF escort of Spitfire Vs. Visibility over the target was good and bombing was made from 23,000ft (7,000m). A few bombs hit a mile short of the target, and one burst hit about a mile west in some woods, but the majority landed in the assigned area. Several repair and mainte-

nance workshops were badly damaged which put the German state railway out of temporary action. First of the congratulatory messages to arrive came from Air Marshal Sir Arthur Harris, chief of RAF Bomber Command: 'Congratulations from all ranks of Bomber Command on the highly successful completion of the first all-American raid by the big fellows on German-occupied territory in Europe. *Yankee Doodle* certainly went to town, and can stick yet another well deserved feather in his cap.'

Unfortunately for Eaker, his ability to wage a bombing offensive was hampered by the more pressing needs of Brigadier General James H. Doolittle's 12th Air Force which would have to be equipped and trained to support the *Torch* invasion of north-west Africa in November 1942. The 8th Air Force was thus denied valuable replacement men and machines, while new and existing groups were earmarked for the 12th. On 14 September both the 97th and 301st Bomb Groups were among those from the 8th which were assigned, on paper, to

B-17E 41-9023 Yankee Doodle in the 414th Bomb Squadron, 97th Bomb Group, was one of twelve Fortresses that took part in the first B-17 mission of the war, on 17 August 1942; it carried Brig Gen Ira C. Eaker to Rouen. Note the RAF-style camouflage. From 24 August 1942 this famous aircraft served with the 92nd Bomb Group, and later joined the 91st Bomb Group. USAF

With the F Model came production block numbers, which were allocated to the three companies in the BVD pool. This close-up shows B-17F-45-BO 42-5290 with B-17F-45-BO 42-5291 behind. The window containing the gun on the left-hand side was mounted further back than the one on the right-hand side so as to permit greater operating space for the navigator and bombardier when both were firing their guns. The F heralded a series of modifications and changes, including increased bomb-load, redesigned bomb-racks and additional armour plate, particularly at the waist-gun positions. USAF

the new air force, although they continued flying missions from England until October. On 5 September Eaker sent thirty-seven B-17s from the 97th and 301st Bomb Groups on missions to shipyards and airfields on the continent. The next day the 92nd helped swell the ranks to fifty-four Fortresses. Despite a Spitfire escort, two B-17s were shot down, the first US heavy bombers to be lost in the ETO. Eaker was shortly to 'lose' his only other B-17 group; the 92nd was needed to form the first combat crew replacement centre in the ETO. However, during September–November, VIIIth Bomber Command received four new Fortress groups – the 91st, 303rd, 305th and 306th – and they were equipped (approximately 200 aircraft) with a new Fortress model, the B-17F.

Large-Scale Production Begins With The B-17F

The first B-17F-1-BO was delivered to the Army Air Force on 30 May 1942, the B-17F being the first Fortress model to enter really large-scale production. The BVD pool was created when Boeing agreed to let Lockheed-Vega at Burbank, California and Douglas Aircraft at Long Beach build the B-17F under licence. Lockheed had first approached Boeing about building the B-17 under licence in April 1941 when it feared that gathering war clouds would severely limit the need for passenger transport aircraft.

The 'F' appeared to be similar to the B-17E, save for a frameless Plexiglas nose which gave the bombardier better all-round visibility. However, no fewer than 400 changes and modifications were made to the B-17 design, most of them being carried out on the production line itself. They included a new ball turret; dual brake system; external bomb racks; wider, 'paddle'-bladed propellers made by Hamilton Standard (the leading edge of the engine cowlings had to be reshaped and shortened so that the blades could clear the cowling when feathered); an improved oxygen system; carburettor intake dust filters; stronger landing gear; more photographic equipment; AFCE (automatic flight control equipment), which when used on the bomb run gave the bombardier lateral control of the aircraft through the Norden Bombsight's connections to the auto-pilot; additional ball-and-socket machine-gun mounts in the nose; and increased fuel capacity with the installation of 'Tokyo tanks' in the wings and an 820-gallon (3,728l) tank in the bomb-bay, which raised the total tankage to 3,630 gallons (16,500l). New Wright R-1820-97 Cyclones in place of R-1820-60s meant that the standard 1,200hp could be raised to 1,380hp ('war emergency' power) to give a top speed of 325mph (523km/h). Maximum bomb-load was 9,600lb (4,355kg) but the normal combat load was nearer 4,000lb (1,814kg).

Altogether, B-17F production totalled 3,400. Boeing built 2,300, and starting in July 1942, 600 and 500 each were delivered by Douglas and Lockheed-Vega respectively, in new factories built specially for the purpose. Many modifications were phased in during assembly and considerable confusion developed in the war zones when it was discovered that

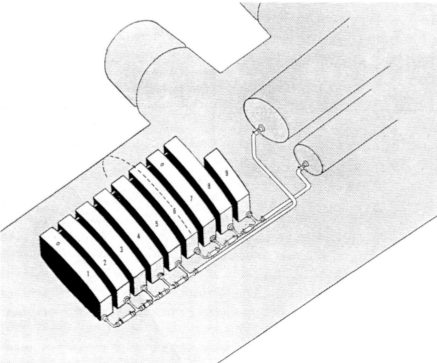

(Above) **B-17F-95-BO 42-30243, seen here on a test flight in the US with external bomb-racks. External racks were first fitted to B-17F-30-BO 42-5050, and controls were installed to permit them to be dropped in train with internal bombs. Starting with -55-BO, B-17Fs were built with revised bomb-rack controls which permitted the external bombs to be dropped with bomb doors closed. External bombs increased weight, caused drag, and cut down performance, and proved very unpopular with combat crews; as a result they were soon deleted. 42-30243 was assigned to the 331st Bomb Squadron, 94th Bomb Group, on 15 June 1943, where it became** Nip 'N Tuck. **Re-named** Good Time Cholly II, **it went MIA with Capt Willis T. Frank's crew on the mission to Le Bourget, 14 July 1943.** Boeing

The long range needed for operations in the Pacific led to extra fuel compartments called 'Tokyo tanks' being fitted to the Flying Fortress. They were flight-tested by Boeing test pilot, A. Elliott Merill and became standard, beginning with the B-17F-55-BO. The 'Tokyo tanks' increased fuel capacity by 1,100 gallons (5,000 litres), and were vented to allow for variations in the air pressure with changes in altitude. Boeing

although each manufacturer used the same block numbers in production, not all aircraft were similarly equipped. Differences often occurred in nose armament – but generally the BVD pool was a considerable success, and greatly speeded the flow of Fortresses to the war zones.

New-Found Offensive

The four new B-17F groups (and two B-24 groups) in eastern England had the task of proving conclusively that daylight precision bombing could succeed in the well defended skies over the Reich; but the RAF remained unconvinced, and even American instructors doubted their crews' ability to survive against the *Luftwaffe*. Eaker needed numbers, and on 9 October he was able to despatch over 100 bombers for the first time. In all, 108 heavies (including B-17Fs of the 306th, which was making its bombing debut) went to Lille, accompanied by a strong P-38 and RAF Spitfire escort. This first full-scale mission created many problems, which coupled with bad weather, saw only sixty-nine bombers drop their bombs on the target area. Claims by the American gunners far exceeded the number of attacking enemy fighters, and in fact the *Luftwaffe* lost just two aircraft.

Allied shipping losses rose dramatically in October, and November was to be even worse. On 20 October, Brigadier General Asa N. Duncan, Chief of Air Staff, issued a revised set of objectives to be carried out by VIII Bomber Command. In part it stated '... until further orders, every effort of the VIII Bomber Command will be directed to obtaining the maximum destruction of the submarine bases in the Bay of Biscay ...'. The limited number of Fortresses available prevented VIIIth Bomber Command hitting submarine yards inside Germany.

Losses throughout the remainder of 1942 during missions to the U-boat pens were high, although the planners still

Specification – B-17F (Model 299-O)	
Crew:	10
Powerplant:	Wright Cyclone R-1820-97 of 1,200hp @ 25,000ft (7,620m)
Performance:	Maximum speed 299mph (481km/h) @ 25,000ft (7,620m) Cruise speed 160mph (257km/h) @ 5,000ft (1,524m) Rate of climb 25 mins 42 sec to 20,000ft (6,096m) Ceiling 37,500 ft (11,430m) Range 1,300 miles (2,090km) with 6,000lb (2,722kg) bombs
Weights:	Empty weight 34,000lb (15,422kg); gross weight 56,500lb (25,628kg)
Dimensions:	Length 74ft 9in (22m 78cm); height 19ft 2in (5m 84cm); wingspan 103ft 9in (31m 62cm) wing area 1,420sq ft (132sq m)
Armament:	10 × .50 cal. machine guns; maximum bomb-load 6,000lb (2,722kg)

Sometimes B-17s like this 'F' were lucky to get back at all. via Robert M. Foose

believed that the bombers could fight their way through to their objectives without fighter escort. The theory was given further credence on 20 December when only six B-17s from the attacking force of 101 bombers were lost on the mission to Romilly near Paris, despite widespread *Luftwaffe* fighter activity in France. Romilly was a turning-point in the daylight aerial war, because for the first time the Fortresses had penetrated 100 miles (160km) into enemy territory and had successfully kept the *Luftwaffe* interceptors at bay (despite high claims, the American gunners actually shot down three and damaged one more). One fact alarmed Eaker and his staff: only seventy-two of the attacking bombers had hit the target, and these caused only minimal damage.

'Pickle-Barrel' Bombing

Senior officers worked on methods for improving bombing and aerial gunnery. Colonel Curtis E. LeMay, CO of the 305th Bomb Group, was destined to figure promi-nently in the shaping of bombing doctrine both in the ETO, and later in the Pacific. He was a committed disciple of the B-17; as he said: '...The Air Force kind of grew up with the B-17. It was as tough an airplane as was ever built. It did everything we asked it to do, and did it well.' LeMay did more than most to find the best method of defence against fighter interceptions without compromising bombing accuracy, and vice-versa. He had faith in tight-knit group formations, and trained his men hard in very close formation flying.

At first LeMay experimented with 'stacked up' formations of eighteen aircraft, before he finally adopted staggered three-plane elements within a squadron, and staggered squadrons within a group. At the same time he discarded the traditional techniques of individual bombing, and replaced it with that of 'lead crews', the most expert bombardiers being placed in these crews: the idea was that when the lead bombardier dropped his bombs, so did everyone else. Providing he was on target, all bombs landed near the MPI (mean point of impact), and the target could be successfully destroyed instead of damaged. LeMay's tactics were encouraged by Brig Gen Larry Kuter and later, Brig Gen Hayward 'Possum' Hansell. Eventually lead crews consisting of highly trained pilots, bombardiers and navigators, became 'standard operating procedure' (SOP).

Group bombing was first tried on 3 January 1943 when the 8th Air Force visited St Nazaire for the sixth time. A total of 107 bombers, with the 305th Bomb Group in the lead, was despatched – but only eight B-24s and sixty-eight B-17s found the target. LeMay's tactics also called for a straight and level bomb run to ensure accuracy. Seven bombers were shot down and forty-seven damaged, two so seriously that they were written off after landing in Wales. However, the majority of the bomb-loads fell on the pens.

If anyone needed further proof regarding the new bombing tactics, it came on 13 January when 8th Bomber Command completed an effective raid on Lille. The 305th Bomb Group again flew lead, and Brig Gen Hansell, commander of the 1st Bomb Wing, flew in the lead ship to witness the results for himself. Despite strong fighter opposition only three B-17s were lost, and gunners claimed six fighters destroyed and thirteen probably destroyed. But despite these successes the future of the 8th Bomber Command as a daylight bombing force was still in doubt. Losses had continued to rise, and in some quarters (particularly the RAF) senior officers believed that the American bombers should join the RAF night offensive. General Arnold, chief of the American Air Staff, was under pressure from his superiors to mount more missions, and in particular, to aim them at German targets.

In January 1943 Maj Gen Ira C. Eaker, who since November 1942 had been acting commanding general of the 8th Air Force in the absence of General Carl 'Toohey' Spaatz, met General 'Hap' Arnold at the Casablanca summit in North Africa attended by President Roosevelt, Prime Minister Winston Churchill and the combined heads of staff, to make a case for continued daylight bombing. Churchill had obtained an agreement from Roosevelt for the 8th Air Force to cease daylight bombing and join the RAF in night bombing. However, Eaker saw Churchill and managed to convince him otherwise: Churchill was most impressed with Eaker's brief memorandum, which skilfully summarized the reasons why the US daylight bombing

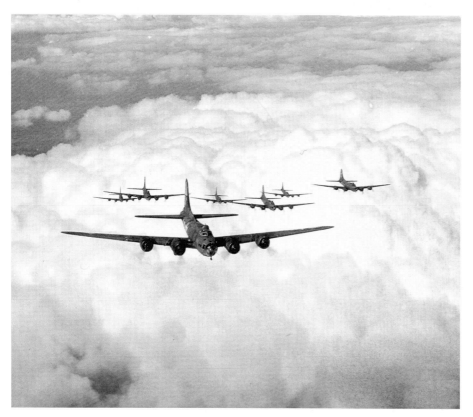

B-17Fs of the 91st Bomb Group in formation. In the period 1 January 1943–1 October 1943, only 24 per cent of bombs dropped by the 8th Air Force fell within 1,000ft (300m) of the MPI. From 1 October 1943–1 March 1944 it had risen to 40 per cent. The USAAF expected to get 40 per cent of its bombs dropped within 500yd (457m). USAF

smoke-screen, and two others bombed Emden. Despite heavy fighter opposition only three bombers (one B-17 and two B-24s) were shot down. The bombing was described as 'fair' – but the press went wild.

Yanks at the Court of King Arthur

Eaker attempted to pile on the pressure, but bad weather fronts restricted operations to only three full-scale missions in February. On the 4th, after a series of cancelled starts, eighty-six bombers bombed the marshalling yards at Hamm in the Ruhr Valley; this was the deepest penetration into enemy territory thus far.

Fighter attacks were intense, and five bombers were lost; moreover four more were lost on a follow-up raid on 4 March. In fact losses might have been higher but for the introduction of new, armoured *Flak* vests, developed by Col Malcolm C. Grow, chief surgeon of the 8th Air Force, in association with the Wilkinson Sword Company of Great Britain. They were worn by ten crews in the 91st Bomb Group on that day, and certainly saved the life of a radio-operator aboard one ship when a 20mm shell fragment struck his vest just above the hip. The armoured vest consisted of heavy canvas covered with overlapping plates of manganese steel, and it protected the chest and back from low velocity shrapnel and ricocheting missiles; on this occasion it was only dented. The whole suit weighed 20lb (9kg) and was cumbersome in the aircraft, but one other life at least was saved by the suit on a later raid when a 20mm shell exploded just two feet from one particular bombardier's chest: it peppered the vest, but the bombardier was unhurt. Each suit had a quick-release mechanism.

In all, 300 suits were ordered from Wilkinsons. The New York Times was quick to report in September 1943 that:

A London firm, specializing since 1772 in the manufacture of swords, is now beating its products into something much more useful at the moment. It is making suits of mail for American airmen ...Thus the cycle rolls around again, and the American fighters, like the Yankee at King Arthur's Court, find themselves back in medieval armor ...'

On 8 March Brig Gen Hansell flew in the 305th BG formation for the raid on the marshalling yards at Rennes to see for him-

'Pickle Barrel': this bombardier seems pleased with his strike efforts. Col Curtis E. LeMay in particular, 305th Bomb Group CO, worked hard to find the best method of combating fighter attacks without compromising bombing accuracy, and vice versa. LeMay discarded individual bombing, which had been standard operating procedure (SOP) from the outset, and introduced 'lead crews', whose expert bombardiers signalled to the rest of the formation when to bomb so that all bombs were released simultaneously no matter what position the aircraft were flying. Gradually lead crews, comprising highly trained pilots, bombardiers and navigators, became SOP. USAF

should continue. He particularly liked the phrase 'round-the-clock bombing' and although not totally convinced, was persuaded that day and night bombing should be continued for a time.

To demonstrate that daylight precision bombing could triumph over area bombing by night, Eaker decided to bomb the U-boat construction yards at Wilhelmshaven. On 27 January, ninety-one B-17s and B-24s were despatched to the U-boat yards in the port. Unfortunately bad weather conditions reduced the attacking force to fifty-three B-17s; these dropped their bombs on the shipyards from 25,000ft (7,620m) through a German

self if the success gained four days earlier could be repeated. He was not disappointed. Fifty B-17Fs plastered the marshalling yards from end to end and effectively stopped any supplies reaching German bases in Brittany for up to four days. Within the next five days two more marshalling yards in France were bombed, and without loss to the attackers.

With morale high, on 18 March Eaker sent seventy-three Fortresses and twenty-three Liberators – the highest number of heavies yet – to bomb the Vulcan U-boat yards on the Weser, a few miles north of Bremen. Near Heligoland the B-17s came under attack from the *Luftwaffe*, and during the bomb run the leading 303rd Bomb Group formation of twenty-two aircraft came in for some concentrated and accurate *Flak*. Capt Harold Stouse in the 359th Bomb Squadron, 303rd Bomb Group, brought the badly damaged *Duchess* back to Molesworth with the dead body of lead bombardier Lt Jack Mathis in the nose. Though mortally wounded over the target, Mathis, who was doing the aiming for all the other B-17s in the squadron, got his bombs away, and enabled the rest of the squadron to do likewise. he was posthumously awarded the Medal of Honor for 'conspicuous gallantry and intrepidity above and beyond the call of duty'.

Vegasack was officially described as 'extremely heavily damaged'. The bombers had dropped 268 tons of high explosive smack on the target, and later, photographic reconnaissance revealed that seven U-boats had been severely damaged and two-thirds of the shipyards destroyed. British Prime Minister Winston Churchill and Sir Charles Portal, chief of Air Staff, recognized the importance of the success achieved on the mission and sent congratulatory messages to Eaker. The next three missions did not go quite as well, however, and eight bombers were lost. Furthermore, on the last of these, on 31 March, to the E-boat pens at Rotterdam, the B-17s missed the target completely and caused 300 Dutch casualties.

On Sunday 4 April, Eaker switched to targets in France, and that morning Fortresses throughout the Bedford area took off for a raid on the Renault factory in the Billancourt district of Paris. Before the war the Renault works had been the largest producer of vehicles in France, and now the Germans were using it to turn out military trucks and tanks; their output was estimated at 1,000 trucks, tanks and

Capt Allen V. Martini of the 364th Bomb Squadron, 305th Bomb Group, pictured at Chelveston, on 20 May 1943, in front of Dry Martini 4th. USAF via Bill Donald

armoured cars a month. On the night of 3/4 March 1942 the RAF had destroyed the plant, but the Germans had rebuilt it in nine months by using slave labour; they had even managed to increase production to 1,500 vehicles a month.

It took two hours for the four B-17 groups to complete assembly; then ninety-seven Fortresses departed the rendezvous point at Beachy Head. However, when landfall was made at Dieppe, only eighty-five Fortresses remained, twelve having aborted through malfunctions. For once the sky was clear and blue, and many of the Spitfire escort fighters could be seen quite plainly; others were simply vapour trails in the upper reaches of the atmosphere. From their altitude of 25,000ft (7,620m) crews could see the black mass of Paris apparently cradled by the long, curved arm of the River Seine, 95 miles (153km) in the distance. Capt Allen Martini, pilot of *Dry Martini III* in the 364th Bomb Squadron, 305th Bomb Group (lead ship in the bottom-most squadron), wrote:

Up to that time, and for a little beyond, the day was strictly G.I: the sky was deep and blue, it was spring, and the Seine valley reminded me of the green Illinois river valley over which I had trained at Chanute Field. For some reason, the *Luftwaffe* hadn't welcomed us to France when we crossed the Channel at Dieppe. It was the first trip to Paris for the Cocktail Kids – they gave themselves that name – and they were plenty elated by their Cook's-tour, bird's-eye view of the Eiffel Tower and Notre Dame as well as the absence of opposition. We had been regularly making the milk run over the St Nazaire U-boat pens, where the 'black cumulus' was pretty deadly, and the contrast caused us no pain.

At 14:14 hours the Fortresses were over their target and 251 tons of high explosive rained down on Paris. Flak was moderate and not too accurate, and crews were able to pick out the Renault works despite the industrial haze which covered much of the city. Most of the eighty-one tons that landed square on the factory were released by eighteen B-17s of the leading 305th formation, and before the last group had left the target the whole area was blotted out by a thick pall of smoke reaching to 4,000ft (1,220m). Unfortunately the groups in the rear of the formation were not as accurate as the 305th had been, and many bombs fell outside the target area causing a number of civilian casualties. Capt Allen Martini continues:

Whenever the *Luftwaffe* gave us a break, which was seldom, we were likely to sing our way home, all ten voices roaring into the interphones in unison. We were a bit lulled now, and S/Sgt Dick Willis of Brocton in Massachusetts, a waist-gunner but a master of ceremonies and a band leader in civil life, was just giving out with 'The Last Time I Saw Paris' when the word came of enemy aircraft.

Lt James A. Moberly, navigator, was the first to see them. He caught a flash in the sun ahead, his experienced eye told him that it was a horde of Kraut fighters queuing for an attack, and he gave the alarm, adding, 'It had been such a lovely day!' I have seen that sight many times, enemy fighters queuing up like Londoners lining up for buses, and each time my stomach muscles tightened up hard as a rock. My stomach stays tight during an action and for some time afterward. A reflex act, it probably comes from fear of being hit in the vitals, and it braces you so that, once tied up, you wouldn't be taken by surprise if hit.

Having alerted the crew, telling them the enemy was massing ahead and off to the left, there was nothing I could do but stay in formation and watch the hostile queue. The pilots, having no guns, are the most helpless men on the bomber; moreover, their spot is the most exposed. There is a certain fascination bout watching Jerry get ready for the attack. He is fast but methodical, and he awaits his turn with no apparent impatience. In a matter of seconds he will be rolling over and coming at you with cannons blazing, but now you can only sit, knowing that every rpm takes you nearer gunfire. My co-pilot, Lt Joseph Boyle, had picked up his movie camera when Moberly spoke. A camera hound, Joe got some excellent shots of the ensuing battle which proved to be of interest to Bomber Command. A red-moustached kid from Teaneck, New Jersey, who had been a rug salesman, Joe earned his DFC on a raid over the locomotive works at Fives-Lille in January, bringing my ship home after my substitute, Major Tom Taylor, was killed. [On the 13 January raid the 305th had led, with Brig Gen Hansell, commander of the 1st Bomb Wing, flying in the lead ship, *Dry Martini II*. Capt Martini had missed the mission because of illness, and the pilot's seat had been taken by Maj T.H. Taylor, CO of the 364th Squadron. Taylor was killed by a cannon shot in the chest, and Boyle was wounded.]

I was squadron leader of the low squadron in our group. That is to say, *Dry Martini III* occupied the most vulnerable position, with nothing beneath us but air, the formation stacked up overhead, and only the guns of my squadron, five ships, bearing on the enemy if he attacked at that level. And he did. As he squared away for the assault, I warned the crew, 'Here they come, 11 o'clock, level!' That meant he was approaching from a little to the left of our nose.

A dozen to fifteen Fw 190s swarmed in, peeling off and turning upside down, their 20mm cannon making a red line of fire along their wings as they got us in their sights. Capt Bruce A. 'Curly' Gardner, our bombardier, of St John's, Arizona, and Moberly down in the nose, had to bear their brunt. Their .50 calibre machine guns replied furiously as the Focke Wulfs came into range at about 800 yards. The tracers were criss-crossing, the ship shuddering with the chain of recoil, as it always did during action, and fighters began to fall. Two Fw's went down in the first brush, one bursting into flame and twisting away, a red comet, the second disintegrating as a wing collapsed. Gardner got one, and during the action he destroyed two. Having fired, this first flight swept past us at 600 to 700mph [965 to 1,125km/h], our combined speeds, and rolled away to come around for a new swipe.

Their fire had been plenty effective. This type of formation had served us well, but I could see its number was up today – the *Luftwaffe* had solved it, and they were coming in low to get to the bottom layer, where the guns from above couldn't conveniently reach them. Three planes in my squadron went down before the first assault. Only one other was lost out of the whole mission in the subsequent fighting. Four cannon shells smashed through my windshield, shattering its plastic glass into small fragments, a piece of one shell striking Boyle in the jaw and knocking him out. I was blinded and so profusely powdered that I picked tiny granules out of my face for days afterward. Otherwise I was unhurt.

I lost control momentarily, and the *Dry Martini* dived out of formation; when I could see again, we were 1,000ft [300m] down. I at once attempted to rejoin the formation. The secret of the Flying Fortresses' defensive strength over Europe lies in their tight formations, which multiply the gun-power of the individual planes. However, I found that one of my engines had been shot out, reducing speed to the point where I could not hope to climb back. Moreover the enemy saw my predicament almost as soon as I realized it. I was now a straggler, and hence, as far as Jerry was concerned, his meat.

It was the *Luftwaffe's* pleasant custom to concentrate on cripples. Already they were picking on us, breaking off action with the formation and swarming in front, above, below, beside and behind us like big malicious wasps. The air was getting congested with twisting, flashing, yellow-nosed Focke Wulfs, Herr Göring's crack spitefuls, and they were really eating us up. Some pressed the attack home, and I mean it, coming in to within ten or fifteen yards before falling away. I was plenty bitter. In the 8th, the word 'bitter' is generic, covering any untoward situation from powdered eggs to being caught, as I was, on my own with three engines. The bomber's job is to bomb, not dogfight.

But there seemed nothing else for it, so I addressed all hands, giving this order: 'We're going to fight her home as long as she'll stay in one piece. Don't bale out, give 'em hell, and save your ammunition, because you're going to have to sweat this one out.' Back in the States, when our crew was first formed, the men had agreed to accept my judgement on when to stick it out and fight, and when to bale out. They now cheered the order to fight. With the skies alive with targets, the command to save ammunition may have seemed silly, but as it turned out, we barely had enough to get through.

I next revived Joe Boyle, prodding and slapping him until he came to. A 30° below-zero blast was rushing past us from the broken windshield, and Joe and I stuffed helmets, gloves and other detached objects into the jagged holes to break the draught. Joe could then photograph in greater comfort.

The only other surviving ship in my squadron dropped down to help us, but he stayed only briefly, the Focke Wulfs seriously wounding two of his men. He rejoined the formation, and that was the end of any assistance for *Dry Martini*. Our guns were pouring it on. The fire on the top turret blackened the upper windows over the cockpit. Our lads kept calling attacks as they developed in their quarters, and claiming hits. The pilot is the bird dog for attacks coming in from the front, and I was pretty busy warning the gunners. At first I could specify single attacks, but as the action heated up, all I could manage was, 'They're coming from nine, ten, eleven, twelve, one, two, three, high, lowlevel! Shoot 'em down!' Between times I called for an estimate of the enemy's numbers. The consensus reached sixty, a total being rapidly depleted.

Every now and then I could see one of the swarm give over, mortally wounded, and roll away out of action. That is a sight for sore eyes ... Part of my left aileron was now gone, and when I trimmed the ship to counteract the loss of control on that side, she took a skidding action. She was holding altitude, however ... Even so, the going got more rugged by the minute; there were brief respites, but the enemy kept coming in and we learned later that he had us marked for the kill and he sure wasn't sparing the horses! Just once, S/Sgt Mitchell reported no yellow noses in sight, but even while he was talking a new flight zoomed in on him, and he put a period to his report with a burst of .50 calibre fire. That little fellow in the tail had a vengeance against the Axis. He was part Filipino, and partly of Irish descent; he lived in the Philippines, and his mother, sister, wife and probably – as far as he knew – his daughter too, were either dead at the hands of the Japanese or prisoners. His father was also on the Axis trail, being a lieutenant colonel on General MacArthur's staff.

Dry Martini was still plugging along, but making heavy work of it. We kept moving down the Seine valley toward Rouen; our formation had passed almost out of view ahead and above us. It was becoming increasingly hard to manoeuvre the ship – the wings and fuselage had been punctured many times, and gaping holes showed everywhere. The fine ship was sluggish and cranky, and I began to have doubts that I could take her home. Apart from that, I feared that the guns and ammunition might not hold out. A gun can stand only so much firing before it burns out, and these guns were having no rest.

Still we pushed on. It began to seem a miracle that we were still afloat and none of us out of action. At about this time I became a true believer. I checked my time and found we had been passing through this *Luftwaffe* hell for only fifteen minutes – it seemed hours, when I thought of it. I had a brief weariness, and caught myself thinking of my father and mother back in Michigan, and a moonlight night on Lake Tahoe, where they had a summer cottage. I shrugged out of that and then, considering my predicament, it dawned on me that there must be a greater power up here in the sky carrying us through this one than just ourselves alone and the ship, staunch as she was. I had gone to Sunday school and church and thought myself to be a Christian, but I had never before experienced any real dependence on God. This time I prayed, not in any set form, but just a kind of whispered gratitude. What I really was saying was something like 'Thanks Lord, for giving us a hand'.

The city of Rouen showed up ahead, and a moment later and just beyond, a flight of Spitfires. I've seen the Spits appear out of nowhere to pick us up returning from a target a good many times; they are reliable Joes, and never did they look so good. Jerry saw them too, and began to peel out of action. The relief had come just in time: six of our guns were burned out and useless and out of the several thousand rounds of ammunition with which we had started to fight, only twelve were left. In another split second *Dry Martini III* would have been helpless, a sitting duck above the Seine. The gunners stayed at their posts, on the lookout for possible sneak attacks, but the main bout was at last over.

I decided to take the shortest cut home, ordering Moberly to put down his gun and chart

me a straight course. I then checked the wounded. Besides Boyle and Mitchell, three others had been hurt, but none seriously. Next I asked T/Sgt William Beach, of Lordsburg, New Mexico, the engineer, to inspect the ship for damage. He reported that as well as the aileron damage, the landing flaps under the wings had been shot away, the nose had been badly mauled, the tail was a mere fringe, and the second engine was ready to quit. Although the absence of flaps was a grave handicap, and the tail condition meant the loss of elevators and consequently lift, I decided to land the ship. First I instructed Ballew to get the crew into the radio compartment, in case I had to crashland her. Under those circumstances we crowded the men into the radio room, braced back to back, because it is at the centre of the ship's gravity and there is a large escape hatch overhead.

I came in high, keeping my airspeed up to avoid stalling. *Dry Martini III* was hot to handle, but with luck, I greased her in. I had fired a red flare to indicate that we had wounded aboard, and we were met at the hangar by a crowd of ground officers and men, including our commanding officer, Colonel Curtis E. LeMay. We were first in from the mission, and until they noticed the battered appearance of our ship, the men on the ground thought that we had been forced to turn back from the target. Shaking hands with the chaplain, Captain Gregory, I assured him fervently, and a bit to his surprise, that hereafter my crew and I would be in church every Sunday.

Dry Martini III was so battered that she would never fly again. Her gunners were credited with the destruction of ten enemy fighters, a record for a bomber crew on a single mission. In all, American gunners claimed forty-seven enemy fighters destroyed. After the raid, pictures smuggled back to England by the French resistance showed that the Renault works had been severely damaged. The next morning, 5 April, Martini was notified by Bomber Command that the *Luftwaffe* had challenged him by radio to an air duel: mentioning *Dry Martini* by name, Lord Haw Haw, on behalf of the *Luftwaffe*, had dared him to return. It raised a laugh everywhere in the 8th, and Colonel LeMay suggested that they letter *Dry Martini* on all the Fortresses 'and scare the hell out of them!' (*Dry Martini III* was followed by *Dry Martini IV* which served the Cocktail Kids until early in June: by then the crew had flown twenty-seven missions, and were disbanded and sent home.)

The German defences were constantly improving. Losses rose sharply on 17 April

when sixteen B-17s were lost from the attacking force of 106 that attacked the Focke Wulf plant at Bremen. Although *Flak* accounted for most of the battle damage sustained by the heavies, the *Luftwaffe* continued to inflict the heaviest losses despite having only 120 fighters based in France and the Low Countries. The 8th, on the other hand, increased in strength: in April, four new groups equipped with the B-17F (all but one group's aircraft were fitted with long-range 'Tokyo tanks') landed in England. A fifth 'new' B-17 group was added to the force when the 92nd Bomb Group resumed bombing operations.

'Snuffy' Smith MoH

In the absence of suitable escort fighters the Fortresses continued to defend themselves. Losses were mounting alarmingly, however, and to boost morale, acts of heroism were given centre stage in the press. S/Sgt Maynard 'Snuffy' Smith became the first enlisted man in the 8th Air Force to receive the Medal of Honor, for his actions in an attack on St Nazaire on May Day 1943. The 306th Bomb Group lost six B-17Fs, and Lt Lewis P. Johnson Jr's aircraft was hit several times, catching fire in the radio compartment and in the tail area. Smith, the ball turret gunner, on his first mission, hand-cranked his turret to get it back into the aircraft; however, when he climbed out he discovered that the waist gunners and the radio operator had baled out. He, nevertheless, remained in the aircraft and fought the fire with a hand extinguisher. Moreover the Fortress did not show any signs of leaving formation, so he assumed the pilots were still aboard and went to treat the badly wounded tail gunner. Then he jettisoned the oxygen bottles and ammunition in the radio compartment, and manned the waist guns during an attack by enemy fighters,m only stopping to dampen down the fires and treat the tail gunner. Johnson put the B-17 down at Predannack near Land's End after Smith had thrown out all expendable equipment.

Gaining Strength

On 4 May, six squadrons of P-47s and six RAF fighter squadrons accompanied seventy-nine B-17s to the Ford and General Motors plant at Antwerp. No bombers were lost. On 12 May, the 94th, 95th and 96th

B-17F-65-BO 42-29673 Old Bill in the 365th Bomb Squadron, 305th Bomb Group; pilot 1st Lt William Whitson, helped by gunner Albert Haymon and bombardier 1st Lt Robert W. Barrall, returned to Chelveston on 15 May 1943 after 20mm cannon fire from fighters over Heligoland had riddled the Fortress and shot out the Plexiglas nose, killing navigator 2nd Lt Douglas van Able and injuring Barrall. Whitson and Barrall were each awarded the DSC, and the rest of the eleven-man crew (which included a photographer) received eight Silver Stars and seven Purple Hearts. Old Bill was the creation of British artist and Stars and Stripes cartoonist Bruce Bairnsfather, who painted the nose of the aircraft with the World War I soldier, and was responsible for several marvellous murals at Chelveston. via Bill Donald

Bomb Groups – all equipped with the B-17F – formed a new 4th Bomb Wing in Essex and Suffolk under the command of Brigadier General Fred L. Anderson. On 14 May, Eaker was able to muster in excess of 200 bombers for the first time when 224 B-17Fs, B-24Ds and B-26 Marauders attacked four separate targets: B-17s of the 1st Wing, flying without escort, bombed the shipyards at Keil. Meanwhile, fifty B-17Fs from the

96th and 351st Bomb Groups bombed the airfield at Coutrai in France; and the 94th and 95th Bomb Groups led by General Anderson attacked the Ford and General Motors plant at Antwerp. RAF Spitfires and USAAF Thunderbolts gave excellent fighter cover on the Antwerp and Coutrai raids. Altogether, the four targets cost the Americans eleven aircraft (six of them B-24s). Not all the bombing was accurate, but for the

first time Eaker had demonstrated that he could mount several missions on one day.

On 17 May the Marauders made a second attempt to bomb Ijmuiden, but with even more disastrous results: all ten attacking B-26s failed to return. (After this débâcle the Marauders were transferred from the 3rd Bomb Wing to VIII Air Support Command for future medium-level bombing operations in a tactical role. Their Essex bases were taken over by the B-17 groups.) England was to continue the air war against Germany.

XB-40 'Destroyer-Escort'

During May 1943, an attempt was made to alleviate bomber losses with the introduction of a heavily armed B-17 'destroyer-escort'. This idea had first been proposed in August 1942. Since existing fighter escorts did not possess the range to accompany the bombers deep into Germany, the only logical step was a heavily armed B-17. In November 1942 Boeing converted the second production B-17F-1 into the XB-40 'destroyer-escort': two additional gun turrets, a Martin in place of the radio compartment guns, and a Bendix chin turret were fitted, and the single waist guns were replaced by twin .50s, making a total of

B-17F-1-BO (41-24341) was modified as an escort aircraft by Vega and became known as the XB-40 (pictured at Burbank on the occasion of its first flight, 10 November 1942). XB-40s made their operational debut on 29 May 1943, when seven in the 92nd Bomb Group took part on a mission for the first time. Intended to provide extra firepower for the beleaguered bomber formations, the YB-40s, which weighed almost 5 tons more than the standard B-17, proved less than successful as multi-gunned destroyer-escorts. The additional machine guns on each YB-40 did not add materially to the combined firepower a group formation could provide. Only stragglers were regularly attacked by the Luftwaffe, and the YB-40s were unable to protect these from concentrated attacks. Losses were not made good, although the YB-40s continued flying missions until the end of July 1943. Vega received no order for its proposed V-140 production version, and twenty Vega-built B-17Fs were modified by Douglas as YB-40s service-test models. Boeing

fourteen guns. Both the waist and tail guns were hydraulically boosted for improved control. Although it was still capable of carrying a bomb-load, it seldom did because of the added weight of the guns, armour plate and 11,275 rounds of ammunition.

Some twenty-two YB-40s were built by Douglas (although they were identified as Vega-built aircraft) and twelve were flown to England in January 1943 for operation by the 92nd Bomb Group at Alconbury, England. The first raid involving YB-40s took place on 29 May 1943 when four accompanied the Fortresses to St Nazaire. However, it was evident after the first few weeks of operations that the YB-40 did not add materially to the combined firepower of a group, and it could not protect stragglers from a concentrated fighter attack. It was only used in very small numbers, and flew its final mission on 28 July.

First Tourists

Contrary to popular belief, *Memphis Belle* in the 91st Bomb Group at Bassingbourn was not the first heavy bomber to complete an 8th Air Force tour of twenty-five missions: this honour went to B-17F-25-BO 41-24577 in the 303rd Bomb Group, flown by Capt Irl E. Baldwin, as he relates:

In September of 1942 my crew and I picked up 41-24577 from the United Air Lines modification centre in Cheyenne, Wyoming. Originally I had proposed the name *Yakima Queen*, or something to that effect, after my home town of Yakima in Washington state. The crew were anything but enthusiastic, however, and while there many others suggested, the only thing we could agree upon was that nothing worked for the entire crew. On or about our fourth mission [3 January 1943, to St Nazaire], after forming up over East Anglia and once the formation was complete, we (the 303rd Bomb Group) started out over the Channel: I called the crew on intercom and asked them 'How about "Hell's Angels" after the World War I movie (I had been deeply impressed by the movie and 'Lilac Time'). The entire crew checked in one by one with an affirmative.

I flew twenty-three of my twenty-five missions in *Hell's Angels* [beginning with No.1 to St Nazaire on 17 November 1942]. On one occasion, while we (the crew) were on leave in London, information was received that our plane was scheduled to fly, and without us! We terminated our leave at once and returned to the base, where, upon arrival at headquarters, I and

B-17F-70-BO 42-29742 KY-M Barrel House Bessie "from Basin Street" **in the 366th Bomb Squadron, 305th Bomb Group, pictured with Lt McIntyre's crew at Chelveston; she was named after a New Orleans blues song. The bombsight has been removed and twin .50 machine guns installed in the nose so that the aircraft could be used to fly formation off the lead ship and help protect it against head-on attacks by enemy fighters. The 'blues' bomber was lost on 29 May 1943 with Lt James G. Stevenson's crew returning from St Nazaire, France. Stevenson was forced to ditch 45 miles (72km) off the coast of England, and all except the tail gunner – S/Sgt Ralph Erwin, who drowned – were rescued by ASR after the crew took to their dinghy. After eight days at a British naval hospital and ten at a Flak house at Moulsford Manor, the crew returned to Chelveston.** via Bill Donald

the operations officer got into a big argument over someone else using our airplane – and I lost! There would be a second time that another crew would be assigned to fly *Hell's Angels*, and yes, once again I voiced my displeasure, and once again I lost. On that mission, at the last minute, another aircraft was pronounced as flyable and my crew and I would be assigned to it.

The crew of *Hell's Angels* received the recognition they deserved due to the fact that we had finished the twenty-five missions without ever aborting. On one mission, two of my gunners (one waist, and the tail gunner) froze their hands while trying to unjam their guns (frozen .50 calibres were a common problem in the early part of the war); had I known this, I would have aborted immediately because they could have lost not only some fingers, but quite possibly their hands. Later I found out that they didn't want me to know because they didn't want to be the cause of us aborting the mission. The men were laid up in

the hospital for about two weeks, but fortunately experienced no permanent damage.

Hell's Angels and the crew must have had charmed lives. With hundreds of holes over the airplane (we replaced the horizontal stabilizers due to the weight from the tin food-can patches), not once did any member of the crew receive a 'purple heart'. It would take eight months for us to finish our twenty-five missions, the last one for the original crew and myself coming on 14 May 1943; the target was Kiel. This was an important mission for the 303rd Bomb Group and me, as I was to lead the group to the target. In my mission report I said: 'Sorry I have to quit. It was a swell trip. Rough, but worth it. There were more fighters than I have ever seen before. The general consensus of opinion of my crew is that we won't have to go back there again …' When we finished our twenty-five missions, the 303rd had only eight of the original thirty-five crews and planes left.

The losses were mostly new crews and planes which started arriving in March of 1943.

The *Hell's Angels* air- and groundcrews were a cohesive unit with a pride that could only have been felt by having been a part of that team – a team in which if there was any doubt as to the aircraft being ready for the next mission, the aicrew would be out at the airplane helping the groundcrew get it ready! While the aircrew received the usual awards (DFC, Air Medal, etc) one award that I know everyone connected with *Hell's Angels* was proud to see awarded was the Legion of Merit to our groundcrew chief, M/Sgt Fabian Folmer, a former bank clerk from Colorado Springs. This was the first award to this decoration to any ground personnel in the 8th Air Force, and it was because of his exceptional maintenance of the aircraft, *Hell's Angels*. *Hell's Angels* went on to complete forty-eight missions on 13 December 1943, and she

was in contention with *Knockout Dropper*, another 303rd Bomb Group B-17, to become the first to complete fifty missions. *Knockout Dropper* won the contest on 16 November, and added to her fame by being the first 8th Air Force B-17 to complete seventy-five missions. *Hell's Angels* was flown Stateside on 20 January 1944, having been autographed by hundreds of members of the group at Molesworth, and having joined up with her original pilot, Capt Irl Baldwin, for a tour of industrial war plants. After completion of the tour on 19 May, *Hell's Angels* was re-designated TB-17F and transferred to the Training Command of the AAF, where she served proudly, and trained many crews until the end of the war. On 7 August 1945, *Hell's Angels* was scrapped, thus ending almost to the day of her delivery (8 August 1942) a proud flight record of both actual combat and flight training.

Operation *Pointblank*

In June, Operation *Pointblank*, an intermediate priority objective aimed at the German fighter strength, was finally published. The first steps had been taken at the Casablanca conference when the Allied leaders had agreed a combined bomber offensive from England. The Primary objectives listed were the 'German submarine yards and bases, the remainder of the German aircraft industry, ball bearings and oil ...'; secondary objectives were 'synthetic rubber and tyres and military motor transport vehicles.' The objective concluded: 'It is emphasized that the reduction of the German fighter force is of primary importance: any delay in its prosecution will make the task progressively more difficult ...'.

Contrary to popular belief, Memphis Belle **was not the first heavy bomber to complete an 8th Air Force tour of twenty-five missions: the honour went in fact to B-17F-25-BO 41-24577 'Hell's Angels' in the 358th Bomb Squadron, 303rd Bomb Group on 14 May 1943. After completing its forty-eighth mission on 19 May, all without ever turning back, it was flown Stateside on 20 January 1944, having been autographed by hundreds of members of the group at Molesworth and joined up with its original pilot, Capt Irl Baldwin for a tour of industrial war plants.** Hell's Angels **survived the war only to be broken up for scrap at Stillwater, Oklahoma, in August 1945.** USAF

A badly holed B-17F-25-VE 42-5809 LF-D: Mary Jane of the 526th Bomb Squadron, 379th Bomb Group, which crashlanded at RAF Coltishall returning from Wilhelmshaven on 11 June 1943 when the group lost six Fortresses. She was salvaged six days later. The inscription below the open radio hatch says, 'The boys have a lot to learn about shooting dice'. USAF

Capt Robert K. Morgan and crew of B-17F-10-BO 41-24485 Memphis Belle in the 324th Bomb Squadron, 91st Bomb Group, bid farewell to generals Devers and Eaker on 13 June 1943 at Bassingbourn before flying home to begin a Bond Tour in the USA. The Belle featured in a documentary about 8th Air Force operations, principally for American cinema audiences, made in 1943 by Major William Wyler, the famous Hollywood director. Five combat photographers were lost aboard B-17s during filming. During crew training at Walla Walla, Washington, Morgan had met Miss Margaret Polk of Memphis, Tennessee ,and the romance between the pilot and the Memphis girl had flourished for a time. The Belle crew flew the twenty-fifth and final mission of their tour on 17 May 1943, to Lorient, and it was duly recorded (using a 'stand-in' B-17F) in 16mm colour and used with great effect in the documentary, which was finally screened in April 1945. USAF

The CBO plan called for 2,702 heavy bombers in fifty-one groups to be in place before the Allied invasion, earmarked for mid-1944. One of the first missions in the combined bomber offensive took place on 13 June when the 1st Wing went to Bremen and the 4th Wing visited U-boat construction yards at Kiel. The mission coincided with the transfer to new bases in Suffolk of three B-17 groups in the 4th Wing, while three B-26 Marauder groups which had sustained heavy losses, arrived in their place. This move would give the B-26s longer-range fighter cover. Unfortunately, the 94th, 95th and 96th Bomb Groups' last mission from their old bases was a disaster: the mission to Kiel claimed twenty-two 4th Wing B-17Fs, and four others were lost from the 1st Wing.

The new 4th Wing CO, Colonel (later Brigadier General) Curtis E. LeMay, moved into the former 3rd Wing headquarters at Elveden Hall near Thetford and began building up his force. Imminent arrivals of three new groups – the 100th, 385th and 388th – would increase the 4th Wing to six groups. LeMay also replaced the 94th and 95th Bomb Group Commanders (the 95th had lost eleven B-17s on the Kiel raid).

Eaker, in pursuit of the CBO *Pointblank* directive, sent his bombers on the first really deep penetration of Germany on 22 June, to the synthetic rubber plant at Huls. Huls produced approximately 29 per cent of Germany's synthetic rubber and 18 per cent of its total rubber supply. It was also heavily defended. Some 235 B-17Fs were despatched, and most of the route was flown without escort. Unfortunately, one of the three diversionary raids planned to draw enemy fighters away from the Huls force only succeeded in alerting them, and sixteen B-17s were lost and another 170 damaged. Even so, some 183 Fortresses bombed the plant so effectively that full production was not resumed for six months.

word for 'lightning war') as it became known. On the 24th, 324 B-17s from the 1st and 4th Wings bombed targets in Norway, with one force flying a 2,000-mile (3,220km) round trip to Bergen and Trondheim, the longest American mission over Europe so far. Some 167 bombers from the 1st Wing bombed Heroya and completely devastated a factory complex, while forty-one bombers bombed shipping

Werke aircraft factory at Kassel, while 120 Fortresses from the 4th Wing bombed the AGO Fw 190 assembly plant at Oschersleben near Magdeburg. P-47 Thunderbolts of the 56th and 78th Fighter Groups, carrying unpressurized 200-gallon (910-litre) ferry tanks below the centre fuselage for the first time, escorted the Kassel force and prevented heavy losses. Fifteen B-17s were lost on the Oschersleben raid, but

'Blitz Week' proved expensive. On 28 July, fifteen B-17s were lost during the raid by 120 Fortresses on the Focke Wulf 190 factory at Oschersleben, although production was stopped for a month. On 29 July the shipyards at Kiel and the Heinkel assembly plant at Warnemünde were bombed, and then on 30 July, VIII Bomber Command brought down the curtains on 'Blitz Week' when 186 Fortresses from the 1st and 4th Wings went to the Fieseler Werke aircraft factory at Kassel, a round trip of some 600 miles (965km). The weather was fine and P-47 Thunderbolts with long-range fuel tanks escorted the heavies almost to the target and back again. Without the 'Jugs' along, B-17 losses would have been alarming because the Fortress formations were hit by a ferocious onslaught of enemy fighters making pass after pass. Altogether, twelve Fortresses were lost. 'Blitz Week' cost Eaker almost a hundred aircraft and ninety combat crews. USAF

'Blitz Week'

Bad weather throughout the rest of June and early July restricted the 8th to short-haul missions to France. Then new groups arrived, and on 17 July a record 332 bombers were despatched to Hannover. A lengthy spell of good weather was predicted for late July, and Eaker was poised to launch a long-awaited all-out air offensive. It started on 24 July, and continued all week – 'Blitz Week' (after the German

at Trondheim. On 25 July, Kiel, Hamburg and Warnemünde were bombed, with the loss of nineteen Fortresses. There was no respite for the bomber crews, and on 26 July more than 300 heavies were despatched to Hannover and Hamburg.

Bomber crews were stood down for a much-needed rest on 27 July, but the battle was resumed on 28 July, when 182 bombers made an attack on the Fieseler

production was halted for a month.

On 29 July the 8th flew its fourth mission in five days. The 1st Wing bombed the shipyards at Kiel again, and the 4th Wing dealt Fw 190 production a heavy blow in its accurate bombing of the Heinkel assembly plant at Warnemünde. Next day, in a fitting finale, VIII Bomber Command despatched 186 Fortresses to the aircraft factories at Kassel, escorted

B-17F-30-BO 42-5077 DF-T **Delta Rebel No 2 of the 324th Bomb Squadron, 91st Bomb Group in flight. This aircraft and 2nd Lt Robert W. Thompson's crew was one of twenty-five bombers that failed to return on 12 August 1943 when 330 heavies bombed targets in the Ruhr.** USAF

almost to the target and back again by P-47 Thunderbolts fitted with long-range fuel tanks. Altogether, twelve Fortresses were lost, including some that were so badly damaged that they never flew again.

'Blitz Week' had dealt heavy blows to the German submarine, munitions and aircraft industries, but the 8th Air Force had lost about a hundred aircraft and ninety combat crews, which left under 200 heavies ready for combat. The survivors were exhausted, and many had become 'Flak-happy'. Even so, losses were gradually made good, and on 12 August 330 bombers were sent to bomb targets in the Ruhr; twenty-five bombers failed to return.

Double Strike Débâcle

Three days later, VIII Bomber Command participated in the *Starkey* deception plan, created to make the enemy believe that an invasion of the French coast was imminent. Raids continued on enemy airfields in France and the Low Countries on 16 August. It was a prelude to the field order for 17 August, which called for a simultaneous attack by 376 Fortresses on the air-

craft plants at Regensburg, and the ball-bearing plant at Schweinfurt. Regensburg was the second largest aircraft plant of its kind in Europe and its destruction would produce a nine-month delay in production. It was estimated to produce 200 Bf 109s a month, or about 30 per cent of Germany's single engine aircraft production.

On 17 August Brigadier General Robert Williams, commander of the 1st Wing, led his force to Schweinfurt, while Colonel Curtis E. LeMay led the 4th Wing to Regensburg. To minimize attacks from enemy fighters the master plan called for LeMay's force to fly on to North Africa after the target. The 1st Wing, meanwhile, would fly a parallel course to Schweinfurt to further confuse the enemy defences and return to England after the raid.

Unfortunately, the 1st Wing was delayed in England by ground mists, and for a time it looked as if the 147 B-17s of the 4th Wing would not be able to take off at all. They could not be delayed for more than ninety minutes if they were to reach North Africa in daylight. That they finally got off at all was due entirely to the fact that LeMay's groups had been practising take-offs on instruments for the past few weeks. Only one of four P-47 groups assigned to

the 4th Wing actually managed to rendezvous with B-17s, leaving the Fortresses in the rear of the 15-mile (24km) formation without protection at all. The 96th Bomb Group flew lead. Behind them came the 388th and 390th Bomb Groups, followed by the 94th and 385th Bomb Groups comprising the 2nd Combat Wing. Bringing up the rear of the formation were the 95th and 100th Bomb Groups, each carrying incendiaries to stoke up the fires created by the leading groups.

Lt Col Beirne Lay Jr flew with Lt Murphy in *Piccadilly Lily* in the 100th Bomb Group formation as an observer. Lay had been one of Eaker's original seven officers who established VIIIth Bomber Command in England and had spent the early part of the war 'flying a desk'. The *Luftwaffe* began their attacks as the B-17s entered enemy territory, and it was the 95th and 100th Bomb Groups who bore the brunt. Lay had a ringside seat in the action:

A gunner called, 'Fighters at two o'clock low!' I saw them climbing above the horizon ahead of us to the right, a pair of them. For a moment I hoped they were P-47 Thunderbolts, but I didn't hope long. The two Fw 190s turned and whizzed through the formation ahead of us in a frontal attack, nicking two B-17s in the wings and breaking away in half rolls right over our group. By craning neck and back, I glimpsed one of them through the roof glass in the cabin, flashing past at a 600-mile-an-hour [965km/h] rate of closure, his yellow nose smoking and small pieces flying off near the wing root – the guns of our group were in action. The pungent smell of burnt cordite filled the cockpit, and the B-17 trembled to the recoil of nose- and ball-turret guns. Smoke immediately trailed from the hit B-17s, but they held their stations.

... Three minutes later the gunners reported fighters climbing up from all around the clock, singly and in pairs, both Fw 190s and Me 109Gs. The fighters I could see on my side looked too many for sound health, and no friendly Thunderbolts were visible. From now on we were in mortal danger. My mouth dried up and my buttocks pulled together. A co-ordinated attack began, with the head-on fighters coming in from slightly above, the nine and three o'clock attackers approaching from about level, and the rear attackers from slightly below. The guns from every B-17 in our group and the group ahead were firing simultaneously, lashing the sky with ropes of orange tracers to match the chain-puff bursts squirting from the 20mm cannon muzzles in the wings of the Jerry single-seaters.

For more than an hour the enemy fighters ripped into the B-17 formation. Without escort, the Fortresses stood no chance against their nimble attackers, and so many B-17s went down that Lay described how he:

... almost disinterestedly ... observed a B-17 pull out of the group preceding us and drop back to a position about 200ft from our right wing tip. His right 'Tokyo tanks' were on fire, and had been for a half hour. Now the smoke was thicker. Flames were licking through the blackened skin of the wing. While the pilot held her steady, I saw four crew members drop out of the bomb-bay and execute delayed jumps. Another baled from the nose, opened his parachute prematurely and nearly fouled the tail. Another went out the left waist opening, delaying his opening for a safe interval. The tail gunner dropped out of his hatch, apparently pulling the ripcord before he was clear of the ship. His parachute opened instantaneously, barely missing the tail and jerked him so hard that both his shoes came off. He hung limp in the harness whereas the others had shown immediate signs of life, shifting around in their harness. The Fortress then dropped back in a medium spiral and I did not see the pilots leave. I saw the ship though, just before it trailed from view, belly to the sky, its wing a solid sheet of yellow flame ...

Lay was very lucky. Nine of the 100th's twenty-four bombers failed to make North Africa, the highest loss in the Regensburg force. In the one-and-a-half hours preceding the bomb run, seventeen Fortresses were shot down; by the time the 4th Wing touched down in North Africa, they had lost twenty-four B-17s. Meanwhile the 1st Wing force, which initially was delayed by thick inland mists in England, had taken off three-and-a-half hours after the 4th Wing had departed. The delay gave the *Luftwaffe* time to refuel and re-arm after attacking the Regensburg force, and to get airborne again. The 1st Wing fared worse, losing thirty-six B-17s to enemy fighters. Worst hit were the 381st and 91st Bomb Groups, who lost eleven and ten B-17Fs respectively.

The B-17Fs that bombed their targets had been remarkably accurate. Eighty hits were made on the factories at Schweinfurt, while at Regensburg, all six main workshops were destroyed or badly damaged. Air Marshal Slessor for the RAF called the mission 'outstandingly successful – probably the best concentration on target yet seen', but the official total of sixty B-17Fs lost in combat was almost three times as high as the previous highest, on 13 June, when twenty-six

B-17Fs of the 385th Bomb Group in the 4th Wing, cross the aircraft plant at Regensburg on 17 August 1943, part of an ambitious and daring strike to mark the anniversary mission of the 8th AF, which also saw the 1st Wing head for the ball-bearing plant at Schweinfurt led by Brig Gen Robert Williams. To minimize attacks from enemy fighters, Col Curtis E. LeMay's 4th Wing B-17s flew on to North Africa after the target. The 1st Wing, meanwhile, flew a parallel course to Schweinfurt to further confuse the enemy defences before returning to England after the raid. via Ian McLachlan

Lt Robert Wolf's B-17F-85-BO 42-30061 LD-Q Wolf Pack *(centre)* **of the 418th Bomb Squadron, and three other 100th Bomb Group B-17Fs, head for North Africa after the 17 August raid on Regensburg. Note the damage to Wolf's aircraft, which received 20mm cannon fire to the tail-fin, and a life-raft released hit the left tailplane. The top aircraft is B-17F-30-VE 42-5861 XR-J** Laden Maiden**, flown by Lt Owen D. 'Cowboy' Roane in the 349th Bomb Squadron. Below this is B-1F-40-VE 42-5957 XR-D** Horny**. These three B-17Fs managed to reach North Africa; nine other 100th Bomb Group Fortresses did not.** Laden Maiden **failed to return from a raid on 30 December 1943 with Lt Marvin Leininger's crew; only the bombardier and navigator survived, and these evaded capture successfully. The rest of the crew were KIA.** Horny **was salvaged on 9 May 1944.** Wolf Pack **which was recoded 'T' and renamed** Just-A-Snappin'**, returned to the ZOI on 28 June 1944.** Thorpe Abbotts Memorial Museum

B-17F-95-BO 42-30325 Miss Carry of the 570th Bomb Squadron, 390th Bomb Group, over the Alps on 17 August 1943. Some 376 Fortresses bombed the aircraft plants at Regensburg and the ball-bearing plant at Schweinfurt. Sixty B-17s were shot down, almost three times as high as the previous highest, on 13 June, when twenty-six bombers were lost. On 29 January 1944 Miss Carry was involved in a mid-air collision near Hamelin, Germany, with B-17F-100-BO 42-30334 Virgin Sturgeon; Lt William J. Harding's crew were all made POWs, but Miss Carry returned safely. After another mishap, it was salvaged on 2 May 1944. via Ian McLachlan

(Right) B-17F-100-BO 42-30372 Shack Rabbit III and B-17F-85-BO 42-30130 of the 96th Bomb Group crossing the Alps after bombing Regensburg on 17 August 1943. Brig Gen Curtis E. LeMay, who in July 1943 had been promoted 4th Wing CO, led the raid in Capt Tom Kenny's B-17F-100-BO 42-30366, Fertile Myrtle III, in the 338th Bomb Squadron, in the leading 96th Bomb Group. After the target the surviving 128 B-17s, some flying on three engines and many trailing smoke, were attacked by a few fighters on the way to the Alps. LeMay circled his formation over Lake Garda to try to give the cripples a chance to rejoin them. Although the Snetterton Heath group did not lose a single B-17, the 4th Wing lost twenty-four aircraft, while sixty Fortresses which made it to North Africa had to be left behind for repairs. Fertile Myrtle III was badly shot up over Bremen on 16 December 1943 and crashed at Taverham near Norwich after being abandoned by Kenney's crew. via Geoff Ward

bombers were lost. Actually the overall losses were far worse: the 8th had really lost 147 B-17Fs; twenty-seven Fortresses in the 1st Division were so badly damaged that they never flew again; while sixty Fortresses had to be left in North Africa pending repairs. The almost non-existent maintenance facilities ruled out any further shuttle missions.

Bitter Conclusion

In August 1943 the escort range of a P-47 based in East Anglia with a 108-gallon (490-litre) belly tank was only 375 miles (600km), while the P-38 Lightning, even with two wing-drop tanks, could manage only about 100 miles (160km) more. In 1943 this theoretically meant that the P-38 could escort the heavies to Stuttgart, and just about accompany them to Leipzig, while the P-47 could not. In effect, the fighters' restricted escort range dictated that if heavy bomber losses on the scale of Regensburg-Schweinfurt were not to be repeated, then heavy bomber raids should be shallow penetrations, to France and the Low Countries, rather than deep into Germany where the B-17Fs were on their own – and even then, the missions required a diversionary sweep by bombers over the North Sea or elsewhere, to try to split the attacking fighter force. Above all, if the weather in England was bad, then the fighters could not take off at all. This situation was never better illustrated than on 6 September, when 338 B-17Fs set out for Stuttgart. Bad weather grounded the fighter escort and forced the heavies to bomb targets of opportunity in France and Germany. Altogether, forty-five craft were lost and many crews missed their targets or returned with their bomb-loads intact. Yet the next day, when over a hundred heavies attacked targets in Belgium and when the fighter escort was described as 'excellent', no bombers were lost.

Débâcles such as Regensburg-Schweinfurt and now Stuttgart, surely must have made the US planners acutely aware that the strategy of using unescorted bombers in daylight precision attacks on enemy targets was untenable. The future of the B-17 as a weapon of war, both in terms of acceptable losses, and its ability to carry large bomb-loads long distances, was now revealed as severely limited. Despite this, the purists still firmly believed in their theory that the bomber could bludgeon its way through; all that was needed was improved armament, and in particular, frontal guns in a powered turret, to ward off the all-too-effective head-on attacks by the *Luftwaffe*.

The B-17G Emerges

During September, the B-17G (Model 299-O) duly appeared. Its most significant feature was a 'chin turret', which in fact had also been fitted to the last eighty-six Douglas-built B-17Fs, for forward defence. The B-17G, which had first flown on 21 May 1943, was, in nearly all respects, identical to the F. The early B-17G retained the nose-window configuration of the early B-17F; bulged cheek windows were added at various stages of production by Boeing, Douglas and Vega. Beginning with the Boeing B-17G-50-BO, the waist-gun positions were staggered to allow the gunners more freedom of movement in combat. An all-new tail turret with enlarged windows and a reflector gunsight in place of the ring-and-bead sight was designed by the United Air Lines Modification Centre at Cheyenne, Wyoming. The 'Cheyenne' turret provided greater gun elevation and a completely redesigned gunners' enclosure, and it was installed during various stages of production at all three B-17G plants.

The B-17G was not in itself a solution to the problem of defence against fighter attack; if anything, the additional drag and added weight, plus the attendant increase in ammunition (after Regensburg-Schweinfurt many crews carried more, and extra *Flak* vests and armour plate), only served to make the Fortress even more vulnerable. If they were to bomb targets and take 'acceptable' losses in the process, bomber crews desperately needed a long-range escort fighter to accompany them, not just *to* the target, but back again. In the meantime, all new B-17 groups would be equipped with the B-17G, and production that year reached 250 B-17s per month; however, B-17G-equipped bomb groups would not arrive in England until February 1944. By then, all B-17s leaving the factory were unpainted because the natural metal finish improved performance and cut down production time.

New Bombardment Divisions

On 13 September 1943, VIII Bomber Command was officially divided into three bombardment divisions. The nine groups of the 1st Bomb Wing formed the First Bomb Division, and the 4th Bomb Wing became the Third Bomb Division. The B-24 Liberator groups became the Second Bomb Division and continued to fly missions separate from the two Fortress divisions.

On 8 October the First and Third Bomb Divisions were assigned the port at Bremen. The area was noted for its *Flak* defences, and much of north-western Germany's fighter strength was concentrated nearby. In order to try to split the enemy fighter force, the First Division approached the target from Holland, while the Second Bomb Division flew a long, curving route over the North Sea to attack Vegasack. The Third Division crossed the North Sea and approached the target from the north-west. Unfortunately, after the P-47 escort had withdrawn, low on fuel, the B-17s were met in strength. The unfortunate 381st Bomb Group, flying as low group in the First Division formation, lost seven of its eighteen bombers, including the lead ship. Altogether, the 8th lost twenty-six bombers. Fourteen were lost in the Third Division, seven of them belonging to the 100th Bomb Group. If it had not been for the installation of 'Carpet' RCM blinkers aboard some 96th and 388th Bomb Group B-17s, losses might well have been much higher. 'Carpet' was a British invention in which radio signals were used to interfere with radar-directed *Flak* guns.

Over the next few months 'Carpet' devices were fitted to all Fortresses.

A Classic Example of Precision Bombing

On 9 October, 115 B-17s were despatched to the Arado aircraft component plant at Anklam near Peenemunde, while 263 bombers attacked the port of Gydnia and the Focke Wulf plant at Marienburg. General Travis, the First Bomb Division commander, led his force to Anklam in *The Eightball*, a 303rd Bomb Group B-17 flown by Captain Claude Campbell. Fighter opposition was heavy, and fourteen B-17s, all from the 1st Combat Wing, failed to return. The Gydnia force, led by Lt Colonel Henry G. MacDonald, 40th Combat Wing operations officer, bombed ships and installations. Again, fighter opposition was heavy. The third force of B-17s, which bombed Marienburg, achieved the greatest success of the day. Anti-aircraft defences, thought unnecessary at a target so far from England, meant that the force could bomb from between 11,000 and 13,000ft (3,350 and 3,960m). At such heights accuracy was almost guaranteed, and 60 per cent of the bombs dropped by the ninety-six Fortresses exploded within 1,000ft (300m) of the MPI and 83 per cent fell within 2,000ft (600m).

Before the raid the Marienburg plant had been turning out almost 50 per cent of the *Luftwaffe*'s Fw 190 production. Results were devastating, and General Eaker called it '... a classic example of precision

One significant outcome of the XB-40 gunship was the adoption of the chin turret on B-17G models, and also Douglas-built F models from -70-DL on. At Boeing it was intended to fit chin turrets to B-17F-135-BO, but this block was re-designated B-17G-1-BO, and no Boeing-built Fs received chin turrets on the production line – although many Fs acquired them at modification centres in the US and in the ETO. B-17F-75-DL 42-3522 Gremlin's Delite of the 533rd Bomb Squadron, 381st Bomb Group, was one such late model 'F' with a chin turret. This aircraft, which at first was assigned to the 96th Bomb Group on 27 September 1943, finished her days at Walnut Ridge, Arkansas, in 1946. USAF via Ron Mackay

B-17Fs of the 570th Bomb Squadron, 390th Bomb Group, escorted by high-flying P-47s leaving contrails, en route to Emden on 27 September 1943. They were photographed by S/Sgt Stan Smith, waist gunner, aboard B-17F-120-BO 42-30783 DI-M Stork Club, flown by Capt Keith Harris. In the foreground is B-17F-45-DL DI-F 42-3329 Skippy, whose pilot, 2nd Lt George W. Harmon, was first to complete twenty-five missions in November 1943. Stork Club and 2nd Lt Vincent F. DeMayo's crew failed to return on 16 March 1943. On 5 February 1944 Skippy took off for a mission to bomb an airfield at Villacoublay, France, but whilst departing England the No. 2 engine exploded. Lt Thomas J. Sutters, pilot, was unable to feather the windmilling prop and he decided to return to base, but the engine set the wing on fire and they only made it as far as the River Thames where Sutters pointed the B-17 towards the Channel before all ten crew baled out safely.
USAF

bombing'. After bombing their targets the three formations of B-17s regrouped and headed for England. The flight back was long (ten hours and thirty minutes) and tiring. When they got back to England some groups had to let down by squadrons because of a heavy haze.

Thunderbolt escort, while B-24s flew a diversionary sweep over the North Sea. Aborts reduced the B-17 formations and German fighters wrought havoc among the remaining formations. Altogether, some thirty B-17s were shot down, including

twenty-five from the unlucky 13th Wing where the 100th lost twelve Fortresses. In all, 88 American bombers were lost on three successive days, from 8 to 10 October 1943. In the same period the 'Bloody Hundredth' alone had lost twenty Fortresses.

The 'Bloody Hundredth' Falter

Marienburg had been the epitome of precision bombing, but the raid which followed, on Sunday 10 October, was an all-out area bombing raid on residential areas of Munster. The raid, by 264 B-17s, was designed to deprive the Germans of its railworkers, practically all of whom were based in Munster, and to disrupt rail traffic which had to pass through to get to and from the Ruhr. About 245 single-engined and 290 twin-engined fighters were expected to oppose the mission, so the Fortresses were given a strong

Specification – B-17G (Model 299-O)	
Crew:	10
Powerplant:	Wright Cyclone R-1820-97 of 1,200hp @ 25,000ft (7,620m)
Performance:	Maximum speed 287mph (462km/h) @ 25,000ft (7,620m) Cruise speed 150mph (241km/h) @ 5,000ft (1,524m) Rate of climb 37 mins to 20,000ft (6,096m) Ceiling 35,600ft (10,850m) Range 2,000 miles (3,218km) with 6,000lb (2,722kg) bombs
Weights:	Empty weight 36,135lb (16,390kg); gross weight 65,500lb (29,710kg)
Dimensions:	Length 74ft 9in (22m 78cm); height 19ft 2in (5m 84cm); wingspan 103ft 4in (31m 50cm); wing area 1,420sq ft (132sq m)
Armament:	11–13 .50 cal. machine guns; maximum bomb-load 9,600lb (4,355kg)

B-17F-50-DL 42-3352 Virgin's Delight **of the 94th Bomb Group, piloted by Lt R.F. 'Dick' LePore of the 410th Lead Squadron, photographed by Capt Ray D. Miller, the squadron flight surgeon, leaving the burning Fw 190 factory at Marienburg on 9 October 1943. On the bomb run LePore was not using oxygen, and was in fact eating a Mars Bar from his PX rations! The target was completely demolished. Anti-aircraft defences had been thought unnecessary to defend a target so far from England, and so the heavies were able to bomb from between 11,000 and 13,000ft (3,350 and 3,960m). At these heights accuracy was almost guaranteed, and 60 per cent of the bombs dropped by the ninety-six Fortresses exploded within 1,000ft (300m) of the MPI, and 83 per cent fell within 2,000ft (600m). Before the raid the Marienburg plant had been turning out almost 50 per cent of the Luftwaffe's Fw 190 production. Gen Eaker called it a 'classic example of precision bombing'.** Virgin's Delight **and 2nd Lt Walter Chyle's crew failed to return on 29 November 1943 when the aircraft was ditched in the North Sea with the loss of all the crew.** USAF

'Black Thursday'

Despite the round-the-clock bombing of aircraft factories and component plants, British and American Intelligence sources estimated that the *Luftwaffe* had a first-line strength of between 1,525 and 1,100 single- and twin-engined fighters respectively (in fact it had 1,646 single- and twin-engined fighters). Eaker decided to send 291 B-17s to the ball-bearing plants at Schweinfurt on 14 October in the hope that VIII Bomber Command could deliver a single, decisive blow to the German aircraft industry and stem the flow of fighters to *Luftwaffe* units. On 17 August 1943 the 8th had failed to knock out the plants completely and had lost sixty Fortresses in the attempt; it had been a disaster, and the lesson was not lost on the young B-17 crews. They knew that despite escorting RAF and 8th Air Force fighter forces, 370 miles (595km) of the 923-mile (1,485km) round trip would be without friendly fighter cover.

B-17F-115-BO 42-30727 of the 367th 'Clay Pigeons' Bomb Squadron, 306th Bomb Group taking off from Thurleigh. White rectangles were first added to each side of the star on 28 June 1943 and at first the whole device was outlined in red, although experience in the Pacific led to this being changed to blue on 4 September 1943 to avoid any confusion with Japanese markings. 42-30727 was piloted by Lt William C. Bisson, and was one of ten Fortresses the Thurleigh group lost on 14 October 1943 when Brig Gen Orvil Anderson, commanding general of VIII Bomber Command, sent his bombers to Schweinfurt. Bad weather wrecked the timetable and losses were heavy. Flak knocked out two of Bisson's engines and fighters riddled the rear fuselage, killing S/Sgt Thompson E. Wilson, tail gunner. Only 2nd Lt Charles R. Stafford, co-pilot, who exited through the side cockpit window, and four crewmen in the aft section, escaped death. Richards Collection

crashed in England as a result of their battle-damaged condition, and twelve more were destroyed in crashlandings or so badly damaged that they had to be written off.

The losses were softened by press proclamations that 104 enemy fighters had been shot down, though the claims were whittled down to ninety-nine, or 33 per cent loss; according to official German records, however, only fifty fighters were lost. Despite this, the press and planners alike were carried away on a tidal wave of optimism. Even the British chief of the Air Staff, Air Marshal Sir Charles Portal said: 'The Schweinfurt raid may well go down in history as one of the decisive air actions of the war, and it may prove to have saved countless lives by depriving the enemy of a great part of his means of resistance.' Later, Brig Gen Orvil Anderson publicly stated: 'The entire works are now inactive. It may be possible for the Germans eventually to restore 25 per cent of normal capacity, but even that will require some time.'

Brig Gen Orvil Anderson, commanding officer 8th Bomber Command, and his senior staff officers at High Wycombe, were informed that good weather was expected for the following day. It was the signal for Anderson to alert his three bomb divisions throughout eastern england, and the spark that sent groundcrews out to their waiting Liberators and Fortresses to prepare them for 'Mission 115: Schweinfurt'. During the evening of 13 October and the early hours of 14 October, all the necessary information for the raid was teletaped to all 8th Air Force bases. At fog-shrouded bases throughout East Anglia flight crews were awakened early for briefings. At nearly all the briefing rooms, the pulling of the curtain covering the wall map shocked the aircrews into silence. Crewmen who had flown only a few missions noticed that even the veteran crews appeared to be in a state of shock, and there were few who did not at least have 'butterflies' in their stomachs despite some officers' platitudes that Schweinfurt was going to be a 'milk run'. Briefing officers spoke of routes where the flak was minimum, and areas where fighters were not expected, and they spoke in glowing terms of the friendly fighter cover – but the majority of crews were not fooled.

Gen Anderson had hoped to send 460 B-17s and B-24s into Germany in three task forces, the Fortress groups of the First and

Third Bomb Divisions flying 30 miles (48km) apart, while the sixty B-24 Liberators of the Second Bomb Division brought up the rear, flying to the south on a parallel course to the B-17s. Unfortunately, unpredictable weather intervened before take-off and effectively ended the Liberators' participation in the mission, and after the escorting P-47 Thunderbolts departed, most of the First Division groups were torn to shreds in attacks by well over 300 Luftwaffe fighters. By the time the target area was reached the 1st Bomb Division had lost thirty-six bombers and twenty had turned back. The Third Division came through relatively unscathed, and lost only two bombers; however, for them it was after the target that they met their stiffest opposition. To make matters worse, the Fortresses' return to England was hampered by the same soupy weather that had dogged their departure.

In all, the First Division had lost forty-five Fortresses, and the Third Division, fifteen. The 305th Bomb Group came off worst, with sixteen of its eighteen B-17s lost. The second highest loss in the First Division went to the 306th Bomb Group with ten; the 96th in the Third Division lost seven. Thus sixty Fortresses (or 19 per cent of its force) and 600 men had been lost. Of the 231 bombers that returned to England, 142 were damaged and another five fatal casualties and forty-three wounded crewmen were removed from the aircraft. Five B-17s had

Fortress Finale?

The losses sustained on 17 August had come back to haunt the planners, and 'Black Thursday' made it abundantly clear that a long-range escort fighter was desperately needed. Inexplicably, the first deliveries of the P-51B Mustang to England in November were assigned to three groups in the 9th Air Force for tactical operations only, and the first Mustang escort mission was not flown until 5 December. Finally, the first 8th Air Force group to receive P-51Bs was the 357th Fighter Group, but they would not fly their first escort mission until 11 February 1944. In the meantime, the P-47s and P-38s carrying drop tanks in addition to their normal internal fuel were the best that were on offer, but they would never be the answer. In November 1943 P-38 Lightnings based in East Anglia could manage 520 miles (840km) when fitted with two 75-gallon (340-litre) wing tanks; by February 1944 this had risen to 585 miles (940km) when carrying two 108-gallon (490-litre) wing tanks. By then the escort range of a P-47 based in East Anglia with two 108-gallon wing tanks was 475 miles (765km).

Until the Mustangs could operate in large numbers under 8th Air Force control deep into Germany, Eaker and his senior staff boldly persisted with large-scale raids, most of which were made at the expense of many valuable Forts and their crews.

CHAPTER SIX

Mediterranean Missions

15th Air Force Operations, Italy, October 1943–May 1945

Maj Paul Tibbets of the 97th Bomb Group in November 1942 at Biskra in North Africa. The 97th and the 301st Bomb Groups transferred from the 8th Air Force in England in 1942 to help form the 12th Air Force for the *Torch* invasion operation in North Africa, November 1942, and later became two of the six B-17 groups in the 5th Wing of the 15th Air Force in Italy. Tibbets

Between 14 September and 16 October 1942 the 8th Air Force in England was called upon to transfer fourteen fighter, bomber and troop carrier units, or about half its available air strength, to the 12th Air Force. The 12th, or 'Junior' as it was sarcastically referred to in conversation, was about to be used in the *Torch* invasion of North Africa, and so the embryonic air force assumed the highest priority when it came to allocations of equipment. Requests from 8th Air Force units for materials were denied: it was a case of, 'You can't have that, it's for 'Junior''.

The *Torch* operation went ahead on 8 November, with landings at Casablanca, Oran and Algiers. The two bomb groups chosen to transfer to the 5th Wing, 12th Air Force, were the 97th and the 301st, who by 8 November had flown twenty-one and nine B-17 missions respectively, from East Anglia. Joining the B-17s in the 5th Wing were the 1st, 14th and 68th Fighter Groups. Eight more groups, seven equipped with A-20 or B-26 bombers, and one fighter unit, joined the 12th directly from the US. On 16 November 1942 the 97th Bomb Group, which had flown the

first 8th Air Force B-17 mission from England on 17 August 1942, flew the first mission by the 12th, when six of its B-17s raided Sidi Ahmed airfield at Bizerte, Tunisia. On 22 November the B-17s were moved back from Maison Blanche near Algiers, to Tafaraoui, Algeria, because of Axis bombing raids on their airfield. The P-38 fighter escorts moved back also, to Youks-les-Bains. On 28 November, the 97th were joined by the 301st Bomb Group for the first time, when thirty-five Fortresses attacked Bizerte airfield and dock area. Because of mud, no Lightning escort could be provided and two B-17s were shot down by enemy fighters.

Throughout December 1942 and January 1943, bombing raids were made almost daily on key Axis targets in Tunisia and Tripolitania as Rommel's retreating *Afrika Korps* were pushed further into southern Tunisia. Then in February the decisive battle of the Kasserine Pass saw the German and Italian forces routed. In February 1943 also, the 5th Wing was reinforced with the arrival of the 99th Bomb Group, and in March they were joined by the 2nd Bomb Group. One of the oldest established groups in the AAF, the 2nd had served on anti-submarine duty for several months after the US entered World War II.

During February 1943, the unification of Allied air units under the newly activated Mediterranean Air Command took place, and the B-17s were assigned to the North-West African Strategic Air Force (NASAF). In July 1943 the heavies took part in Operation *Husky*, the invasion of Sicily. The 99th Bomb Group received a DUC for its performance on 5 July when the group helped neutralize fighter opposition prior to the invasion by penetrating enemy air defences to bomb Gerbani airfield.

One of the 97th Bomb Group pilots, who had been with the group since May 1943 and had taken part in the 12th Air Force bombing campaign in North Africa

B-17F-75-BO 42-29856 Patches **of the 346th Bomb Squadron, 99th Bomb Group, 12th Air Force, running up at Oudna, Tunisia, in 1943. The 99th Bomb Group's first DUC came for their part in a mission on Gerbani airfield on 5 July 1943 just before the invasion of Sicily.** Patches **joined the 815th Bomb Squadron, 483rd Bomb Group, at Tortorella on 31 March 1944, failing to return from a mission to Wiener Neustadt on 10 May 1944.** via Bernie Barr

and then raids on Italy, was Ped G. Magness in the 341st Squadron. These raids were far from being 'milk runs', and furthermore supplies and munitions were slow to filter through, as Magness recalls: 'Sometimes we had to wait on the ground until the bombs came in because the Germans were sinking our ships.' One one occasion he was shot down. 'On a mission to Bologna the *Flak* was extremely heavy, and we had a devil of a battle. The Germans lost about sixty-five fighters, and the USAAF about thirty-five fighters. We had two engines out and had to ditch in the Mediterranean.'

A French newspaperman was flying with Magness' crew. After ditching the B-17 the six-man crew and the reporter had to swim about 400 yards (360m) to the coast of Sardinia, which had just been vacated by the Germans. The reporter could not swim, and the crew could not get their rubber dinghy out of the aircraft; then a British one-man raft floated out of the aircraft, and the reporter was put in it. The bombardier dived thirty feet (9m) down to destroy the Norden bombsight. Everyone survived, although the crew nearly starved on Sardinia until they were rescued. The 12th Air Force began moving units to Sardinia in October 1943.

Magness had another close shave on 19 October 1943 during a raid on the airfield at Athens when an 88mm shell from a German anti-aircraft gun had crashed through the nose of his B-17. The shell, which had a time fuse, fortunately went through the nose without exploding but it caused the B-17's ammunition to explode. 'The navigator was badly hit, and the bombardier was trying to help him, as well as trying to keep from falling out of the bottom of the aircraft. The radio operator was badly injured too; he was begging for help, but we were at 30,000ft [9,000m] and couldn't go help him.'

After they got out of enemy territory, Magness decided to land on Sicily because the injured crew members would have bled to death before they reached Africa. Magness concludes: 'The anti-aircraft fire was so accurate that once we got home the airplane was all to pieces. They junked it.'

Meanwhile, General Henry H. Arnold's plan to create a Strategic Air Force in the Mediterranean was accepted: he proposed splitting the 12th in half, leaving the other half a tactical organization. On 1 November 1943, the 15th Air Force was officially activated under Maj General Jimmy Doolittle, with headquarters at Tunis. Doolittle took charge of two B-24 groups from the 9th Air Force (which was trans-

ferred to England to build up a tactical air force for the invasion of Europe planned for next spring), and from the 12th Air Force, he received four fighter and one recon group, and the four B-17 groups. The first 15th Air Force bombing raid of the war also took place on 1 November, when the 5th Wing based in Tunisia headed for Italy and bombed the La Spezia naval base and a communications target, and the Vezzano railway bridge nearby.

Next day, seventy-four B-17s of the 15th Air Force struck at Wiener Neustadt, in Austria, losing six Fortresses. Further raids were made by the 15th Air Force B-17s on targets in northern Italy, Greece, Bulgaria and France, though bad weather restricted operations during November–December. From December 1943–January 1944, the 97th and 301st Bomb Groups were based at Cerignola, Italy, while the 2nd Bomb Group were similarly based at Amendola for the remainder of the war. The 99th Bomb Group arrived at Tortorella airfield early in December 1943 and remained there until November 1945. Much of the strategic offensive in the Mediterranean, from Italy, was flown by fifteen B-24 bomb groups of the 15th Air Force, but the B-17s played their part. Early in 1944 the four B-17 groups in the 5th Wing were increased to six. On

16 March the 463rd Bomb Group, commanded by Col Frank A. Kurtz, was assigned, and on 12 April they were joined by the 483rd Bomb Group, commanded by Col Paul L. Barton.

Beginning of the Combined Bomber Offensive

New Year 1944 saw the 15th Air Force participate in combined bomber offensive missions in support of the *Pointblank* offensive mounted jointly from England and Italy against German aircraft plants, ball-bearing factories, oil refineries, and other

Horowitz, a pilot in the 348th Bomb Squadron, 99th Bomb Group, recalls:

I nearly crashed on take-off because part-way down the runway I found the horizontal stabilizer trim rolled all the way back. It was OK when I pre-flighted the plane earlier. I know that a B-17 wasn't made to take off at 50 knots ... anyway, we got off OK. On the way to the target we hit a heavy cloud layer, and when I broke through the top of the clouds I saw only one other plane from the 99th. Our new squadron CO, who was leading for the first time, was not following standard SOP. I saw the 2nd Bomb Group several miles ahead, and red-lined the power in order to catch up with them before I met with some undesirables.

on the alternative target, Maribor aircraft factory in Yugoslavia. When the group dropped their bombs, I followed suit. I stayed with the 2nd Bomb Group until we got back to the 5th Wing area, and then returned to our base.

A week later, in town, I met some buddies from the 2nd Bomb Group, and only then discovered how lucky I was: they had informed the lead plane of my place in the midst of their formation, but in fact they thought I might be an enemy B-17 – the Germans used captured B-17s to give ground batteries course, speed and height – so the CO told them to watch me, and if I didn't drop bombs when they did, to open fire and shoot me down! I'm glad I didn't know about it at the time!

The main thrust of the combined bomber offensive was scheduled for Operation *Argument*, a series of co-ordinated daylight precision raids by the 8th and 15th Air Forces, together with night area attacks by RAF Bomber Command, on enemy aircraft and airframe assembly plants in the Reich. After several cancellations because of bad weather, the plan was finally put into effect on 19 February when good weather conditions were predicted for several days.

The first in the concerted series of raids, which would become known as 'Big Week', began on the night of 19/20 February, when 823 aircraft of RAF Bomber Command raided Leipzig. It was a bad start, the RAF losing seventy-eight aircraft, and the 15th Air Force's effort against the Regensburg-Obertraubling Bf 109 assembly plant on the 20th having to be aborted when the 126 Fortresses despatched (the B-24s were needed at Anzio) were turned back because of severe icing condition over the Alps. On 21 February the 15th was completely grounded by bad weather in the Foggia area. On 22 February it was intended that the 15th Air Force strike at Regensburg, while the 8th struck at other targets in the Reich. Some sixty-five B-17s of the 15th Air Force were despatched to the Messerschmitt component plant at Regensburg-Prufening, while the B-24s went to the Regensburg-Obertraubling plant. In other bombing raids, one group of twenty-one B-17s dropped 42 tons of bombs on the marshalling yards at Peterhausen, while twenty-eight others bombed an airfield at Zagreb, Yugoslavia. Both were secondary targets. In all, fourteen B-24s and five B-17s were shot down.

On 23 February it was the turn of the 8th Air Force heavies to be grounded because of bad weather, while 15th Air Force B-24s

B-17F-95-BO 42-30267 Hustlin' Huzzy **of the 341st Bomb Squadron, 97th Bomb Group, en route to Sofia, Bulgaria, on 10 January 1944. The white tail triangle and white '1' have replaced the old black and tall T of the 49th Squadron, 2nd Bomb Group. In November 1943 the 2nd Bomb Group traded its B-17s equipped with 'Tokyo tanks' with the 301st Bomb Group, and then in March 1944 replaced its Fs with B-17Gs from the 99th Bomb Group.** Hustlin' Huzzy **was lost flying with the 341st Bomb Squadron, 97th Bomb Group, on the mission to Ploesti, on 23 June 1944..** USAF

targets. During January the 5th Wing carried the burden alone, while the B-24s were grounded for replacement and retraining, with four CBO raids, on northern Italy, Yugoslavia, and Wiener Neustadt. The strikes were small in number but effective nonetheless.

The 7 January mission by B-17s and their P-38 escort, to bomb Wiener Neustadt, is typical of the missions of this period. Jules

My bombardier wanted to salvo the bombs to lighten the load, but I forbade him to do it. Since I was a guest and didn't have a specific position in the formation (I didn't know what radio channel they were using so I wasn't privy to their excited radio chatter), I picked the safest spot to fly and positioned my new plane (which didn't have tail markings) behind and below the lead. When we got to their target it was covered with clouds so the group dropped

B-17Fs on the Boeing assembly line. In the F model the radio compartment hatch slid back, and a wind and rain deflector was fitted aft. Starting with blocks B-17G-45-DL, -55-VE and -85-BO, the radio compartment was enclosed with a frameless hatch with the gun located in a sill mounting. Boeing

The radio compartment gun position was only used in early production batches of the B-17G. Starting with blocks B-17G-45-DL, -55-VE and -85-BO, the compartment was enclosed with a frameless hatch with the gun located in a sill mounting. The gun was eliminated altogether on B-17G-105-BO and -110, B-17G-75-DL to -85, and B-17G-85-VE to -110. Boeing

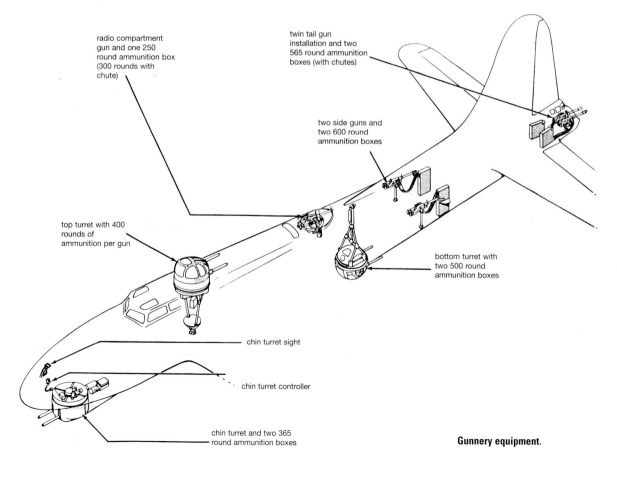

radio compartment gun and one 250 round ammunition box (300 rounds with chute)

twin tail gun installation and two 565 round ammunition boxes (with chutes)

two side guns and two 600 round ammunition boxes

top turret with 400 rounds of ammunition per gun

bottom turret with two 500 round ammunition boxes

chin turret sight

chin turret controller

chin turret and two 365 round ammunition boxes

Gunnery equipment.

bombed Steyr in Austria. Next day the 15th returned to Steyr when its B-17s, led by the 97th Bomb Group, set out again for the Steyr-Daimler-Puch aircraft plant. Despite a heavy escort of eighty-seven P-38s and fifty-nine P-47s, rocket-firing Bf 110s and single-engined fighters succeeded in shooting down ten B-17s in the 2nd Bomb Group, bringing up the rear, before the target was reached. The attacks continued after the target was bombed, and a further four 2nd Bomb Group B-17s were shot down. Two B-17s from the rest of the formation were also lost, bring the total B-17s lost to sixteen. Another smaller force of twenty-seven B-17s, which had become separated from the main force, bombed the oil refinery and torpedo works at Fiume for the loss of only one B-17.

On 25 February the USSTAF despatched some 1,154 bombers and 1,000 fighters to aircraft plants, ball-bearing works and components factories throughout the Reich. Very considerable damage was caused to the Bf 109 plants at Regensburg-Prufening by the 8th Air Force Third Bomb Division, and 149 bombers of the 15th Air Force. Some forty-six B-17s were despatched from Italy, led by a valiant ten Fortresses from the dec-imated 2nd Bomb Group. However, ten of the thirty-one B-17s of the 301st Bomb Group were forced to return shortly after take-off, leaving only thirty-six B-17s, which were unescorted, to continue to the target with the B-24s. Attacks by the *Luftwaffe* began near Fiume and continued to the target: for an hour and a half the German fighters made repeated and incessant attacks on the B-17s, stopping only briefly when heavy *Flak* bracketed the bombers on the bomb run over Regensburg. The twenty-one B-17s of the 301st bore the brunt of the attacks and lost eleven Fortresses shot down, while the 2nd Bomb Group lost three. The 15th's loss (altogether thirty-three B-17s and B-24s were shot down) was the 8th's gain, for it encountered only minor fighter opposition and lost just twelve of the 267 heavies that attacked.

Bad weather then grounded the 15th Air Force until 2 March, when almost 300 B-17s and B-24s, escorted by more than 150 fighters, made bombing strikes on troop concentrations in the Cisterna di Roma–La Villa area, and on several strong-points, including Stazione di Campoleone and Carroceto areas, in support of the beleagured US 5th Army troops at Anzio.

Next day about 200 Fortresses and B-24s set out for the marshalling yards in Rome, and the airfields and landing grounds at Viterbo, Canino and Fabrica di Roma; but eighty B-24s were forced to abort because of bad weather. Bad weather grounded the 15th Air Force until 7 March, when about 300 B-17s and B-24s bombed Toulon, and marshalling yards and airfields in Italy. Missions resumed again on the 11th after a spell of bad weather, and on the 15th more than 300 B-17s and B-24s bombed Monte Cassino which was proving an obstacle for the ground troops attempting to pierce the Gustav Line. The monastery atop the mountain was reduced to rubble, but the ground troops remained bogged down.

Three days later, on 18 March, 592 bombers and fighters – the largest 15th Air Force bomber formation hitherto despatched – bombed *Luftwaffe* airfields in the Udine, Gorizia, Lavariano and Maniago areas of Italy, with excellent results. On 30 March, 114 B-17s bombed the Sofia marshalling yards. The Fortress ranks were swelled by the addition of the 463rd Bomb Group based at Celone near Foggia. On 12 April the sixth and final B-17 group, the 483rd, joined the 5th Bomb Wing in Italy.

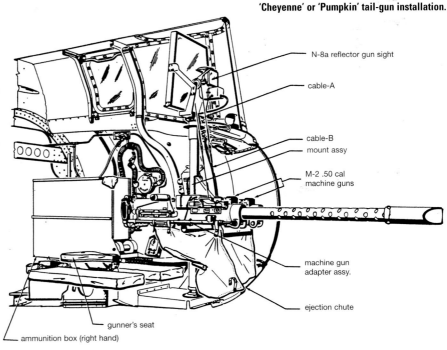

'Cheyenne' or 'Pumpkin' tail-gun installation.

N-8a reflector gun sight
cable-A
cable-B
mount assy
M-2 .50 cal machine guns
machine gun adapter assy.
ejection chute
gunner's seat
ammunition box (right hand)

Early models of the B-17G series had the conventional tail-gun installation as used in the F series. The United Air Lines modification centre at Cheyenne, Wyoming, developed a modified tail-gun arrangement, to give the twin fifties greatly increased elevation and azimuth range of the guns, while the old ring-and-bead sight outside the window was replaced with a new reflector sight inside the window. The 'Cheyenne', or 'Pumpkin' installation (which reduced the B-17's overall length by 5in (2.5cm)), also improved all-round visibility by using larger windows, and was used in the B-17G-80-BO (43-38473), -45-DL (44-6251), -55-VE (44-8287) and subsequent batches. Boeing

Tech Sgt Roy Baker, chief engineer and top turret gunner, and another crew member (white blobs in the radio room) in C.P. Lombard's crew in the 99th Bomb Group, prepare to jump from their stricken B-17 over northern Italy on 18 March 1944. Baker was on his 44th mission and was listed MIA for five months, but eventually rejoined his bomb group. via Frank Thomas

Group. The bombardier, Albert G. Willing, recalls:

The outboard right engine caught on fire and that spread to the wing. Then the engine started to run away. The pilot told us we could bale out, but he pointed out that we were only two minutes from bombs away. All the crewmen checked in and said they would stay aboard. We got off our bombs, but things were still hairy. We fell out of formation and started losing altitude. The fire was going strong and it felt like the engine would shake us to pieces. We were over Yugoslavia when the pilot told us to get out.

I'd left the bomb-bay doors open and went back to get the enlisted men out. After the last one, I jumped too. Just after that the pilot and co-pilot got things more under control, and they and the navigator and flight engineer flew that bird all the way back to base in Italy.

Willing and the five others who baled out were picked up by Yugoslavian partisans, and a few weeks later they were flown back to Italy in a C-47.

On 24 April, five B-17s in the 301st Bomb Group, equipped with Azon remotely guided bombs, made the first of two such attacks on the Ancona–Rimini railway line. A second raid was made on the same railway on 29 April. In April 1944, overall command of the combined bomber offensive had officially passed to General Dwight D. Eisenhower, newly appointed Supreme Allied Commander, Allied Expeditionary Forces (SHAEF). Eisenhower immediately ordered all-out attacks on German oil production centres as part of the overall plan for the invasion of Europe, scheduled for the summer of 1944.

The 15th Air Force had inadvertently opened the oil offensive on 5 April when some of the bombs dropped by 135 B-24s and ninety-five B-17s which were meant for the marshalling yards at Ploesti, cascaded onto the oil refineries nearby causing major damage and disruption. Thus began the oil offensive by the 15th Air Force, and with it an all-out attempt to destroy the Ploesti complex, the largest centre in the Reich. Ploesti was bombed again on 15 and 24 April, when 'incidental' damage was caused to the refineries. Four more heavy raids followed in May.

Tech Sgt Mike Johns, an engineer/top turret gunner in the 347th Bomb Squadron, 99th Bomb Group, was one who entered combat in May 1944, and missions for him came thick and fast. His first occurred on the 7th, when more than 420

By early April the Red Army had overrun German-occupied territory in the Crimea and the Ukraine, and had made inroads into Rumania. German relief supplies could only be transported to the front lines by using the Hungarian and Rumanian rail network. On 2 April the 15th Air Force carried out the first of twenty-six attacks on rail and transportation centres in the Balkans. Major marshalling yards at Bucharest, Budapest, Belgrade and Milan and others were all hit by the 15th Air Force. On 23 April 171 B-17s, led by thirty-six Fortresses of the 99th Bomb Group, attacked the Messerschmitt Bf 109 plant at Wiener Neustadt again. Thirty-one of the 99th Bomb Group's B-17s were damaged by *Flak* and fighter attacks and two 15th Air Force B-17s were shot down; one of these belonged to the 97th Bomb

B-17s and B-24s bombed the marshalling yards at Bucharest. Over sixty P-51s escorted the heavies to the target, and fifty-three provided withdrawal support. Johns recalls:

Being my first mission, I flew top turret gunner with a seasoned crew, whose pilot was Capt Schroeder. When about ten minutes from the target we got our first *Flak*. The first burst was about a hundred yards off the right wing and the second was behind the #3 engine and blew the Plexiglas dome off the top turret. What a way to start out fifty missions! We had to fly through a wall of *Flak* to hit the target, and after leaving the area we were attacked by several enemy fighters. Our escort had left us due to a shortage of fuel so we were on our own. I saw two B-17s go down, but our group got eight enemy fighters and several were seen trailing smoke.

Nish, and oil refineries at Ploesti, the 99th went to the Rumanian oilfields. Johns wrote: 'When we were about thirty minutes from the target, we were recalled due to bad weather, but two B-17s were hit in the wing tips. One went out of control and crashed – we saw only three chutes come out. Our waist gunner had a nervous breakdown and was grounded – he was assigned to a groundcrew.'

Attacks on oil and transportation targets, together with aircraft plants, remained the order of the day in the build-up to Operation *Overlord*, the invasion of occupied France, scheduled for June 1944. Although both the 8th and 15th Air Forces were heavily committed to pre-invasion attacks on enemy lines of communication, in an attempt to meet both

Frantic Joe

Amidst great secrecy on 2 June, the 15th Air Force flew its first 'shuttle' mission, codenamed *Frantic Joe*, in support of Russian operations in the Balkans. Crews were only given the details at the special 2 o'clock briefing attended by Major General Nathan F. Twining, C-in-C, 15th Air Force. After bombing the marshalling yards at Debreczen, Hungary, the 130 B-17s of the 2nd, 97th, 99th and 483rd Bomb Groups, led by Lt General Ira C. Eaker, would fly on to Russian bases at Poltava and Mirgorod. P-38 Lightnings would join the formation about 150 miles (240km) short of the target to fly top cover until the bombing was completed. At 07:00 hours, sixty-four P-51s of the 325th Fighter

Amid great secrecy on 2 June 1944, 130 B-17s of the 2nd, 97th, 99th and 483rd Bomb Groups, led by Lt Gen Ira C. Eaker, flew the first 15th Air Force 'shuttle' mission, codenamed Frantic Joe, in support of Russian operations in the Balkans. Here, on 11 June, B-17Gs of the 49th Bomb Squadron, 2nd Bomb Group, head for Foscani airfield in Rumania, during the return trip to Italy after taking off from Russia. USAF

Three days later we attacked Wiener Neustadt. *Flak* was very heavy over the target area, and accurate. After we dropped our bombs we were attacked by several Fw 190s. We fired hundreds of rounds at them, but the Fw 190 had a lot of armour plating and you could see the tracers bounce off them. We had ten holes in our plane.

Mike Johns flew missions to targets in Italy on 13 and 14 May, and then on the 18th, when almost 450 B-17s and B-24s attacked marshalling yards at Belgrade and

transportation and oil objectives they continued to bomb both types of target right up until D-Day. For three days, starting on 25 May, the B-17s and B-24s of the 15th Air Force bombed marshalling yards at Lyon, St Etienne, Avignon, Nîmes and Marseilles, and throughout the rest of May 1944 the 15th Air Force continued heavy raids on transportation and aircraft production targets, and bombed railway networks in south-east Europe in support of Russian military operations in Rumania.

Group would get airborne and rendezvous with the Fortresses near the Yugoslav border to escort them to the Dnieper river, before leaving them to set course for their base at Piryatin, near Kiev.

Major Bernie Barr, co-pilot in Major Morris' B-17 in the lead ship of the 416th Bomb Squadron, 99th Bomb Group, was flying his first mission in Europe. He recalls:

Having been on combat missions in the South Pacific with a single B-17, or no more than four or five B-17s, it certainly was a great sight to see all the airplanes from each squadron take off and gradually fly into position in the group formation. It also made one feel safe – though at the same time there was the apprehension of getting into an airplane that would easily become the target of someone shooting live ammunition at you, either from a fighter airplane, or from the anti-aircraft guns on the ground.

Twenty-year-old Joe C. Kenney, a radio operator in the 346th Bomb Squadron, 99th Bomb Group, flew in a B-17 flown by his CO, Colonel Ford J. Lauer, with Brig General Charles W. Lawrence of the 5th Wing in the co-pilot's seat. Kenney recalls:

We led the 5th Wing on this trip, and we hit the Debreczen marshalling yards with excellent results. The initial force from our bombs was so great that the entire red tile roof of the depot was seen to rise to a significant height before it disintegrated. We did have some *Flak* , but this was of little consequence. However, a B-17 from the 97th Bomb Group exploded just off target for unexplained reasons. We flew on to Poltava, a most interesting trip, to say the very least.

Bernie Barr adds:

After seven hours in the air we were all tired and eager for rest and food. The intelligence debriefing didn't take long since there was so little opposition from the enemy. Off we went to our assigned tents and canvas cots which had already been set up. After a quick wash in the large community bathroom, we stood in the mess chow line where we were fed American GI food by big, buxom Russian women.

The B-17 crews were met by representatives of the American and British press corps who had flown in from Moscow with the US ambassador, Averell Harriman, his daughter and secretary. Joe C. Kenney adds: 'Our experience in Russia was an education in itself. We were appalled by the incredible amount of destruction done to Poltava, and the plight of the citizens during the German occupation was horrible. The city itself was pretty much in rubble. I saw women off-loading bales of steel mat runway from railroad flat cars, and they were doing this impossible job by hand.' At Poltava (and Mirgorod), the runways had been lengthened from 3,000 to 6,000ft (914 to 1,830m) by Russian women, who laid steel mats under the direction of American engineers. The all-important steel

B-17G-30-DL 42-38201 2nd Patches, **an olive-drab Fortress in the 346th Bomb Squadron, 99th Bomb Group at Tortorella, was a worthy successor to the first Patches. Pilot Walter Moody brought her back from a raid on Wiener Neustadt on 23 April 1944 with 1,100 holes, as well as a machine-gun slug embedded in a blade of No. 2 propeller. She was so badly damaged that her outer right wing panel, flaps, rear entry door, rudder and fin, had to be replaced, and these were left in natural aluminium. For this mission the 99th received their second DUC, while Sweeney and his second element lead both received the DFC. It was after this miraculous escape that 42-38201 had her name painted on each side of the nose, and a shark mouth sketched over her chin turret. On 2 June 1944 2nd Patches was the fifth aircraft on the ground at Poltava on the first leg of the shuttle mission to Russia. Moody's crew bade her goodbye upon their return to Italy. Her luck held for over twenty missions, until this take-off crash on 24 August 1944 consigned her to the scrap heap.** Phil Sweeney, via Bernie Barr

matting, supplies, and fuel in steel drums (the latter from British sources in the Middle East) for the operation were transported using more than 2,100 freight cars in the move to Poltava.

While in Russia, the four B-17 groups flew a mission to Galati airfield, Rumania, on 6 June, escorted all the way by the P-51s. Joe C. Kenney in the 99th Group recalls:

Bombs plummet from the bomb-bay of B-17G 42-32053 of the 49th Bomb Squadron, 2nd Bomb Group, on Foscani airfield, Rumania, on 11 June, during the return trip to Italy. This aircraft was shot down by Flak **near Budapest on 27 June 1944.** USAF via Ron MacKay

This target was more easily reached from Russia than from our bases in Italy. Our bomb-load was of 'frags', and as always, I regarded this to be a 'hot' load. We achieved excellent coverage of the airfield, catching quite a number of German planes on the ground. However, at 'bombs away' we had a cluster hang up on the outer bomb-rack, and I watched helplessly as other clusters broke apart and cascaded over this hung-up cluster. The bombardier salvoed it out the instant I told him where our problem was, but fractions of seconds can seem like eternities under these circumstances! When we returned to Poltava I had the impression that the Russians thought our mission was mighty successful because they were so tremendously excited. But we learned when we had landed that the Normandy invasion had taken place, and that they were celebrating this.

On 11 June, the shuttle force took off from Poltava bound for Italy, bombing Foscani airfield in Rumania *en route*. Joe C. Kenney recalls:

We hit this target with good results, and ran into some fairly accurate *Flak* over the target. The 97th Bomb Group lost a B-17, probably from damage caused by *Flak* – we saw it drifting farther and farther behind, with fighters beginning to make passes on it as it drifted out of sight. It became a straggler, and this is always a bad situation. We arrived back in hot, dusty, sunny southern Italy, and what a contrast it was from the Ukraine!

Oil Again

On 23 June the 15th Air Force returned to the Ploesti oilfields which they had last bombed on 6 June. More than 400 B-17s and B-24s attacked oil storage at Giurgiu, two oil refineries at Ploesti, and marshalling yards at Nish. More than 100 aircraft were lost.

On 23 June, the 15th began a series of raids on marshalling yards and oil targets in the Balkans, with strikes by 335 heavies on targets at Craiova, Piatra and Ploesti. A total of 139 bombers arrived over the oil refineries at Ploesti and dropped over 280 tons of bombs on the target. One of the six aircraft lost on this day was B-17F-35-VE 42-5951 *Opissonya* in the 341st Bomb Squadron, 97th Bomb Group, whose bombardier, 2nd Lt David R. Kingsley – on his twentieth mission – was posthumously awarded the Medal of Honor for his heroism after the Fortress was badly damaged by *Flak* on the bomb run. Kingsley was still able to drop his bombs successfully. Then three Bf 109s attacked and damaged the B-17 still further, and the tail gunner, Sgt Michael J. Sullivan was badly wounded in the upper arm. Kingsley administered first aid. Meanwhile *eight* more 109s attacked and the ball gunner was hit by 20mm shell fragments and badly wounded. When the pilot gave the order to bale out, Kingsley immediately assisted the wounded gunners – he even gave Sullivan his own parachute harness when the gunner's could not be found. He helped the wounded men bale out of the doomed B-17, and stayed with the aircraft, which was on automatic pilot, until it crashed and burned. His body was later discovered in the wreckage.

Disaster at Memmingen

Losses in late June–early July began to rise steadily. On 26 June, 677 B-17s and B-24s attacked targets in the Vienna area: an estimated 150–175 fighters attacked the bombers, and thirty aircraft, mostly B-17s

B-17s of the 15th Air Force attack the Schwechat oil refinery at Vienna, Austria, through thick Flak. USAF

15th Air Force B-17s over the Messerschmitt factory at Wiener Neustadt near Vienna. USAF

(Below) B-17G-25-DL 42-38069 and other Gs of the 49th Bomb Squadron, 2nd Bomb Group, are seen returning to Italy from Blechhammer, Germany on 7 July 1944 accompanied by a P-38 Lightning which was hit by Flak over the target area and has its starboard engine feathered. 42-38069 was lost on the mission to Odertal, Germany, on 2 August 1944. USAF

and B-24s, were lost. Mike Johns, in the 347th Bomb Squadron, 99th Bomb Group, went to the Winterhafen oil depot in the Austrian capital:

The *Flak* was intense, heavy and accurate – it was the worst *Flak* I had ever seen. One B-24 went down over the target, and nine chutes were seen. Two B-17s went down over the target from *Flak*, and there were eight chutes from one, and none from the other. Capt Charles R. Katzenmeyer, the pilot, said 'They're throwing everything at us but the kitchen sink!' And N. Mosley, the tail gunner, remarked, 'Yeah, I see a guy down there with a pipe wrench!'

One target that could always be expected to be heavily defended were the oil refineries at Blechhammer and Ploesti. On 7 July, more than 560 B-17s and B-24s attacked two synthetic plants at Blechhammer. Mike Johns recalls:

Flak was heavy, intense and accurate over the target area. Worse, when the bombardier released the bombs, half of them did not drop, and I had to go into the bomb-bay on an eight-inch wide catwalk and trip the hangers with a screwdriver! The outside air temperature was about 40° below zero, and enemy fighters were everywhere – Ju 88s and Me 210s were firing rockets at us from 6 o'clock level, and there were about sixty fighters total with approximately twenty Me 210s attacking us from 12 o'clock high. All the top turret gunners were firing at them. I picked up one in my sights and started tracking. He wasn't firing so I assumed his guns were jammed, or the pilot was wounded. I was sure he was going to crash us. When he was about 1,000 yards out I opened up both .50 calibre guns and emptied both belts –

approximately 1,800 rounds. I could see the tracers going into the plane. When he was about 200 yards out, he exploded! I put in a credit for the kill, but since other gunners were firing at the same fighter, credit was denied. We had lost of *Flak* holes in our plane.

Joe C. Kenney in *Heaven Can Wait*, flown by Lt Janisch in the 346th Bomb Squadron, considered this mission to have been the worst up to that time:

We were deep into Austria when we were attacked by a large force of Me 210s escorted by Me 109s. The Me 210s remained just out of .50 calibre machine-gun range and launched

rockets into our formations. These rockets had that strange erratic trajectory indicating a certain instability, but there were enough of them to be quite effective. The 463rd Bomb Group close by to our right took the heaviest and most accurate part of the attacks, which came in waves of six with many continuous attacks being completed.

After the initial attack, two B-17s fell from formation from the 463rd, with a third compelled to salvo his bombs to remain with the group. One of the former simply went into a spiral, and went on into the ground with no survivors. The second, on fire, crossed behind us, and all ten men baled out. One of the 210s went in on these ten men, strafing them repeatedly, the puffs of machine-gun fire from the Me 210 clearly visible to us. We were, of course, unable to give any kind of help. This is where I learned to hate the Nazis and all they stood for. The enemy continued to press us enough to keep our position hot until our escort finally showed up. The P-51s were able to shoot down several enemy planes before they could clear the area.

We went on into the target area where the

Flak was heavy and accurate as predicted, and dropped our bombs on the spot very effectively, the smoke rising from the target to over 25,000ft [7,620m]. After making its pass, the B-17 that had run into trouble earlier pulled from formation, beginning a fairly rapid descent. The crew baled out before it went on in. I had no idea of how many planes the 15th lost in this rough – this roughest of missions.

(In all, eighteen aircraft were listed as destroyed, and a large number missing.)

Two days later, on 9 July, the 15th pounded the Ploesti refineries for the ninth time in the first Pathfinder-led mission from Italy. The 15th then returned to attacks on marshalling yards, and later, airfields and aircraft factories in Austria and Germany.

A – armour plate, pilot's
B – armour plate, copilot's
C – Bendix chin turret
D – machine gun, M-2 .50 cal
E – bombardier's stand
F – Bendix chin turret controller
G – Bendix chin turret sight
H – handle - emergency bomb release

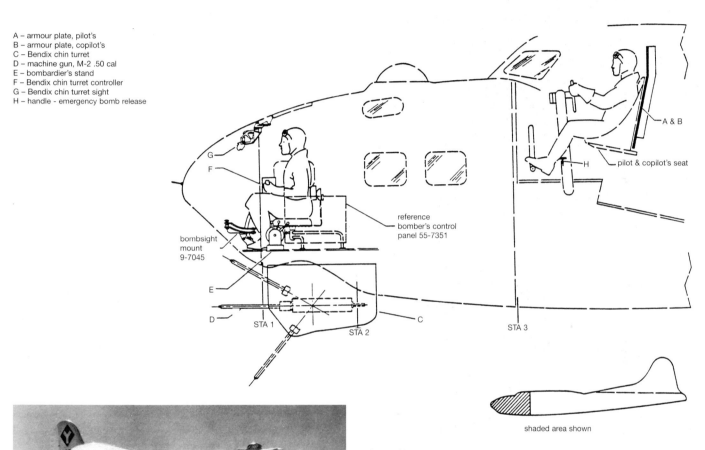

A & B

pilot & copilot's seat

H

reference bomber's control panel 55-7351

bombsight mount 9-7045

G

F

E

D

STA 1

STA 2

STA 3

C

shaded area shown

(Above) **B-17G chin turret**

A B-17G of the 347th Bomb Squadron, 99th Bomb Group, flies over a column of smoke which rose to a height of 23,000ft during a heavy raid on the Ploesti oilfields on 15 July 1944. The 'G' model, which was easily distinguishable because of the addition of a Bendix chin turret, originally configured for the XB-40 gun-ship, flew on 21 May 1943, and delivery of the first of 4,035 Boeing-built models to the USAAF began on 7 September 1943. The 15th Air Force adopted a new-style 'Y' 5th Wing design in April 1944, and the 99th used a black 'Y' on a white diamond on camouflaged aircraft, and the reverse on unpainted B-17Gs. USAF

Ball turret.

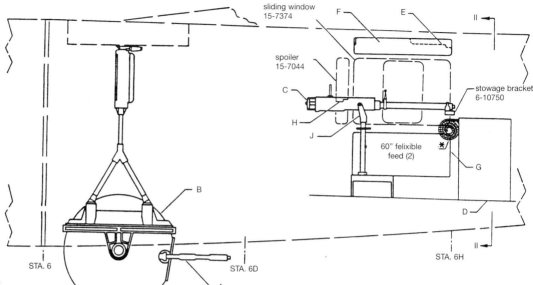

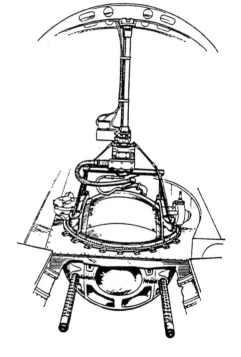

A – machine gun, M-2 .50cal (H39B5344) (2)
B – turret, lower spherical
C – machine gun, M-2 .50 cal. (H39B5344) (2)
D – ammunition box (2), side gun
E – armour, side gun
F – armour, side gun
G - armour, side gun (2)
H – side gun breech heater (2) A.C. spec.
    24864, type J-I)
J – yoke assy. (2)

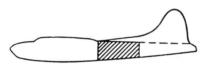

shaded area shown

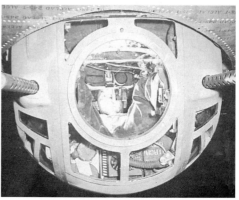

Perspex side panels which completed the spherical appearance of the Sperry ball turret on the E and F models, were deleted on the G model. Each gun had an ammunition box with a chute for feeding the guns and leading away the links and fired shells. The top box (maximum capacity 505 rounds) fed the left gun, the lower box (maximum capacity 425 rounds) fed the right gun. Controlled power drives gave tracing rates from 0° to 45° per second in azimuth and 0° to 30° per second in elevation. The gunner's hand controls and elevation limit stop were in a unit which regulated the amount of turret movement in azimuth or elevation. When the hand grips were released, they returned to their centre position. Gun-firing switches in parallel were at the end of each hand grip; either switch fired the guns. The gunner operated the range control with his foot. Foot pressure in the support increased the range up to 1,000 yards (914m). Boeing

On 18 July, a force of 167 B-17s of the 5th Wing was despatched to bomb Memmingen airfield, a Bf 110 and Me 410 repair and assembly installation in Germany. This high-priority counter-air target had recently seen an increase in operations, with up to seventy-five 110s and 410s being based there, and they were not too well dispersed. All six B-17 groups set out for the target, but over the Adriatic, flying through eight-tenths cumulus clouds, the groups in the combat wing formation became separated. Unable to penetrate the thick cloud, forty-four B-17s in two of the groups aborted,

unescorted. The formation crossed over the northern edge of Italy, over Austria and into the target area in south-western Germany. At the IP, about seventy-five single-engined fighters manoeuvered for their attack on the B-17s. As the fighters made a wide turn to attack the Fortresses from the rear, a much larger force of fighters fell in behind that first formation: the B-17s were now outnumbered by seventeen to one.

The Bf 109s and Fw 190s attacked in waves of five or six in close javelin formation on a level with the tails of the rearmost B-17s, and fired salvo after salvo of cannon

The twelve surviving B-17s fought their way to Memmingen and got their bombs away. As the depleted formation turned off the target, a dozen P-38s of the 1st Fighter Group appeared and took on the enemy fighters, thus preventing further losses. Post-mission reconnaissance revealed that of the 118 single- and twin-engined enemy fighters on the ground, seventeen were claimed destroyed, four probably destroyed, and fourteen damaged. Two and possibly three of the hangars were heavily hit and totally destroyed, while four other hangars suffered direct hits. The 483rd had

B-17G of the 15th Air Force opens it bomb doors over an enemy target. USAF

while twenty-seven Fortresses in another attacked an alternative target. Worse, the extremely bad weather prevented the fighter escort from rendezvousing with the Fortresses that were left.

Spurious messages were sent out by German radio stations instructing the groups that since the primary could not be attacked, they were to bomb alternatives. In the absence of a genuine recall signal, the twenty-six B-17s of the 483rd Bomb Group, which was being led by Captain Louis T. Seith, CO of the 840th Squadron, decided to press on to the primary, alone and

and rockets into the Fortresses. The last box, which consisted of seven B-17s of the 816th Bomb Squadron, was wiped out in the first attack. Next it was the turn of the 817th Squadron, flying number three box position, and five B-17s went down in rapid succession, some on fire and with their gunners firing to the end. The *Luftwaffe* then concentrated on the number two box, and two more B-17s were shot down. One broke apart from the impact of the concentrated firepower; the other was in flames, although the tail gunner was observed still firing until it disappeared from view.

paid for their accuracy with the loss of 143 officers and men, and fourteen out of the twenty-six B-17s failed to return.

Anvil

When the weather permitted, the 15th Air Force, together with the 12th Air Force, 'softened up' targets in southern France in preparation for the invasion, codenamed *Anvil*. On 13 August, 136 B-17s bombed gun positions and bridges around Toulon, and on the 14th, the 15th

Air Force repeated the raids with strikes by 540 B-17s and B-24s as the *Dragoon* invasion convoy headed for the French Mediterranean coast. John A. Plummer, a pilot in the 347th Bomb Squadron, 99th Bomb Group, was one who took part:

The missions of 13 and 14 August destroyed Nazi gun emplacements and lines of communications along the southern coast of France near Toulon. The mission of 15 August [the first 15th Air Force mass night raid, by 252 B-17s and B-24s] was in direct support of Allied troops who would be landing there. I was not aware that such an event was pending, but when we were scheduled for some night-flying practice, I knew something was cooking. After landing from the mission on 14 August, about 16:00 hours local time, our crew was informed that a special secret briefing for the invasion of southern France would be held at 01:30 hours, 15 August, thus only 9½ hours after landing from the mission on the 14th. All of the pilots who would fly on the invasion were given dark red goggles, which we were to wear constantly until we were lined up for take-off. The dark red glasses were to protect the rods in the retina of our eyes from the white light, so that our night vision would be protected for the 'blacked-out' night-formation flying that was to come during the early hours of the following morning – and this system really did work! These glasses were so dark, we could scarcely see anything!

Everyone on the crew was really very tired after two consecutive days' flying, so we were fed the evening meal and then went to bed to try and get as much sleep as possible. We were awakened at about 23:30 hours, got dressed and stumbled over to the mess-hall for breakfast, then up to Group HQ for the 01:30 briefing, with our take-off scheduled for around 03:00 hours. Our mission was to hit Beach Head #261, near Toulon, with thirty-eight 100lb GP bombs between the hours of 07:15 and 07:30. Our bombs were to start at the water's edge and walk right across the beach, and other aircraft following would pick up the bombing where we left off, continuing to walk the pattern bombing on inland. The objective was to destroy enemy land mines, ground personnel and their lines of communication. The bombing altitude was 13,500ft [4,115m]. The landing forces were to be 1,000ft (300m) off shore when we attacked from the air.

Those damn night glasses may have been fine for preserving our night vision, but in the dark of the night you couldn't see anything, and I had to be led everywhere! And when we got to the aircraft, for the first time *ever* I did not perform a visual inspection; the groundcrew chief

assured me that the big bird was ready, and I took his word for it. In the cockpit, neither Lt Todd or myself needed any light to start up the engines, and none of the aircraft had any lights showing. Since I couldn't see anything, Todd lifted his goggles and did the taxiing out to take-off position, than at take-off time, with the Fort lined up, I took off my goggles. It was amazing: I could see real well, better than on a night when the full moon was out, but on this night there was no moon. Moreover the cockpit instrument lights on the Fort were also red, so this blacked-out night formation flying, for the next 3½ hours, would be a piece of cake.

I was No. 5, and before No. 4 was off the ground I poured the coal to all four engines – and I never lost sight of my leader. Since the wind was calm, I hit the prop wash of the other aircraft that had taken off before me, but by now I was used to it, and ploughed right through it. Take-off and formation join-up was routine, and I could see the other ships in the formation, and the ground below. Our night vision would remain good until the rods in the retina of our eyes were subjected to white light.

Then it happened: to my right there was a tremendous explosion; it appeared to be very close and near our altitude, and the explosion's

B-17G-50-DL 44-6397 of the 416th Bomb Squadron, 99th Bomb Group, drops its bombs on the Szob railway bridge, north of Budapest on 30 March 1944. Initially, all the 463rd Bomb Group's B-17Gs which crews had flown into theatre, were given to the 99th Bomb Group in return for their older and many war-weary B-17Fs. After crews had flown in combat with other groups, the 463rd Bomb Group flew its first mission on 30 March 1944. 44-66397 was finally lost on 23 March 1945, on the mission to Ruhrland. USAF

white light completely destroyed Todd's and my night vision. After a few seconds I recognized the exhaust flame of the No. 4 engine of my lead, even though it was much subdued because flame arrestors had been installed, and I locked on to it. I had barely gotten back into formation when another explosion lit up the night sky. It was obvious that there had been a mishap of great proportions, probably a mid-air collision. About a minute later there was a third explosion. This really shook up the crew, and me. Would this happen to us in another minute? I found out later that the explosions were caused by three B-24s blowing up shortly after take-off. The unofficial reason was that it was the work of saboteurs, who had placed explosives within the wing root area of the aircraft, which were detonated by an aneroid (barometric) device. Thirty fine men died in those explosions. One of those aircraft could just as easily have been mine: remember, I had not been able to make a visual inspection of my aircraft, either, because of the red glasses.

As we continued, things quieted down, and the voices on the intercom became silent. Flying formation at night when all you can see is the muted exhaust flame from your leader's Nos. 3 and 4 engines is nerve-racking and very fatiguing. It had been at least 45 minutes since take off and I had done all of the piloting. I was hot, thirsty, tired and I needed a rest, but I couldn't take my eyes off the leader's exhaust flames or I would lose him; so, using the intercom, I called Todd to take the plane for a while. There was no response from him. I repeated the call several times with no response, so I called for the top turret gunner to tell Todd that I wanted to talk to him; there was no response from the top turret gunner either! This had never happened before. My calls on interphone were always answered immediately. I became a little cross, and shouted over the interphone, 'This is the pilot, respond to me immediately, tail to nose, over!' To my utter amazement, no one responded. I then took my eyes off the lead plane, and gave a quick glance at Lt Todd, my faithful friend and co-pilot. He was slumped over in his seat, fast asleep!

While flying with my left hand, I shook Todd gently with my right hand – then I shook the hell out of him, but to no avail! So I had to assume that the whole crew was sound asleep, and that I was the only one awake in the entire aircraft! It transpired that prior to take-off, the flight surgeons had given everyone pills to keep them awake. I took mine, but I found out after the mission that the rest of the crew had been given sleeping pills by mistake! So I hung in there, alone, for a solid three hours until the crew began to stir!

At dawn's first light, which was around 05:45, my sleeping crew awakened and seemed all refreshed. We were over Corsica in squadron formation and in rendezvous with the other three squadrons of the Group. We were early, so we circled the island and departed in group formation in sufficient time to reach the southern coast of France within our strike time of between 07:15 and 07:30. The air was full of bombers and the sea was filled with lots of surface ships. We hit our targets right on schedule, and the ground troops came ashore without a casualty, and moved inland with minimum resistance. What a great feeling it was to have been a part of such a great and noble undertaking! I observed the landing barges approaching the beaches, and tears of courage, pride and honour swelled my eyes. I wept.

The return flight back to Foggia and our home field lasted about 2½ hours, and as Todd set the big bird down on our PSP runway, it was a good sound. Rest was not far away. I was not physically able to attend the mission critique as I nearly collapsed when I got out of the aircraft. They took me to my quarters and I slept, and slept. Mission accomplished.

The heavies pounded the invasion beaches around Cannes and Toulon, while twenty-eight other fighter-escorted B-17s bombed road bridges over the Rhône. A proposed strike by B-17s on coastal gun positions had to be aborted because of poor visibility in the target area. On the 16th, 108 B-17s supporting *Dragoon* attacked railway bridges near the invasion beaches.

'Fight with Might'*

On 17 August, Joe C. Kenney prepared to fly his fiftieth and final mission of the war:

When we went into briefing, I saw that our scheduled mission was to be to Weiner Neustadt. While I sat there contemplating the prospects of finishing up on a rough one, a captain from headquarters came in, erased Weiner Neustadt, and then chalked in Nis, Yugoslavia. What a relief! The only problem was that we had another load of frags, and I certainly rated that a 'hot' load. We took off in *Wearie Willie* and had some interesting possibilities when the bombardier discovered that the armourers had failed to safety-wire this load – this meant that when the bomb-bay doors opened, the arming wires would turn in the wind, arming the bombs while they were still in the bomb-bay. As it turned out, we had no *Flak* or fighters, and even though I saw some of the arming props turn, our bombardier toggled these out in perfect sequence, and they all went out without a hitch. A radio operator appreciated a considerate bombardier since he has to watch 'em go. This was a genuine 'milk run' for my last mission.

On 19 August, the 15th Air Force bombed Ploesti for the twentieth (including one raid by P-38s) and final time. There were no bomber losses. Production at Ploesti had been reduced to just one-fifth of its potential capacity, almost 13,500 tons of

* *Motto of the 99th Bomb Group.*

B-17G-50-DL 44-6405 Big Yank **of the 817th Bomb Squadron, 2nd Bomb Group, lands at Tri Duby (Three Oaks) airfield in a pocket of liberated Czech territory in September 1944 to fly out American airmen evadees. The area was completely surrounded by German-occupied territory.** Hans Heiri-Stapfer

B-17G-25-DL 42-38078 Sweet Pea **of the 429th Bomb Squadron, 2nd Bomb Group, took a direct** Flak **hit over the Debreezen railway yards in Hungary, 21 September 1944, but flew back to its base in Italy safely. Upon landing the tail-wheel gave way, causing the aircraft to bend at the point where it had received the hit. The entire crew was unhurt.** Sweet Pea **was repaired, but crash-landed at Bari on 1 June 1945 and was destroyed by fire.** USAF

ing out in black, deadly puffs ahead of him. He and his pilot, George Kulp, a quiet introspective student from Harrisburg, Pa, spotted a large dark burst suddenly appear near the tail of the B-17 to their right:

> It was only our fifth mission, and the fire we saw on the other missions was more fascinating than frightening. The shells would burst and the smoke would float away and nothing would happen. It was interesting. But this time it was different – we could see a lot of *Flak* bursts, they were closer, and the bursts weren't black any more, they were red. Normally we bombed at 28,000 to 32,000ft [8,500 to 9,750m] but we were told we'd have to bomb from 20,000ft [6,000m] over the Yugoslavian target because it was smaller and our accuracy would be better from that height.
>
> When our flight got over the target it was obscured by smoke from the bombs dropped by the planes ahead of us. At that point our whole squadron made a 360-degree turn to go back over the target, and it was on that second time that the guns zeroed in on us.

As the turn was made, a massive, violent *Flak* burst struck the side of Haner's B-17; then another – the Fortress rocked and shuddered.

> It sounded like someone throwing nails into a metal pail, like someone outside tossing metal things at the side of the plane. You could smell the powder. Our outside engine on the right took a hit and caught fire, so we feathered it. Then our navigator yelled over the intercom that he'd been hit in the shoulder. The engineer went down to the nose section to help him.
>
> The *Flak* was bursting all around us. I looked behind me at the tunnel to the waist guns, and it was like someone had set off a huge blowtorch – it was a mass of flames, blue and white, like one big furnace. I guess the ruptured oxygen lines were feeding it. The radio operator grabbed a hand-fire extinguisher, but it didn't work. The alarm bells on the plane were going off: it was time to get out.

George Kulp set the B-17 on auto pilot, and with Haner, followed the rest out. One by one, with the flames consuming the plane around them, the crew jumped. In Haner's account:

> I went out head first. I pulled the ripcord on my chest 'chute right away and it snapped open. There was a tremendous wind at first. As I started down I could see our plane flying off; it was trailing smoke and finally I lost sight of it. At first

bombs having been dropped on the refinery complex at a cost of 223 aircraft. Ploesti was finally overrun by the Red Army on 30 August. Operation *Reunion* began on 31 August, when thirty-six B-17s, in the first of three airlifts, evacuated liberated American PoWs from Bucharest to Italy.

In early September, with the German army in headlong retreat, the 15th Air Force attacked the main withdrawal route across the Balkans. Attacks were made on airfields in Greece and the Aegean Islands too, when the *Luftwaffe* attempted to use 120 Ju 52s and other transports to airlift their forces. By the end of the month most of Rumania and Bulgaria were under Red Army control, and by the end of the year German forces in the Balkans held only parts of Hungary and north and central Yugoslavia. Raids were made during October and November on mainly oil and communications targets in Austria, Czechoslovakia, Germany, Hungary and Italy, and other targets were bombed too. By the end of November, the 15th Air Force B-17s and B-24s had dropped 27,000 tons of bombs on oil targets.

These raids were costly in aircraft and crews. Apart from the threat posed by enemy fighters and *Flak*, the inhospitable

Alps had to be crossed, and bad weather, too, could hamper or even curtail operations. For example, on a mission to railway marshalling yards in November, the Fortresses crossed the Adriatic and veered inland, 20,000ft (6,096m) above the Dinaric Alps, and flew on ever northwards across towering peaks and rugged plateaus. It was then that things began to go wrong, as Gene Haner, twenty-two-year-old co-pilot in the 353rd Bomb Squadron, 301st Bomb Group, recalls:

> Our airspeed was about 150mph [240km/h], but as we were coming north we were hitting 100mph [160km/h] headwinds so we were using a lot of fuel. When we got to a point over northern Yugoslavia the commander in the lead bomber decided we'd have to settle for the secondary target. That was the rail yards at Maribor, at the north-eastern tip of Yugoslavia. Our crews were glad, because Vienna was supposed to have 300–400 anti-aircraft batteries. Intelligence had told us that the Maribor target had only six batteries. We were all relieved.

Haner's B-17 was a 'tail-end Charlie'. As the squadron approached Maribor railyards, Haner could see from his co-pilot's seat the bursts of anti-aircraft fire blossom-

I counted three other parachutes, but then they vanished. I could see the smoke from the target billowing up. The wind kept blowing me, but except for the sound of the wind it was very quiet.

As he neared the ground, Haner saw a church on a hillside and moments later he was landing on the ground, in a pasture. An old man and a boy were standing near a flock of sheep. They hurried over to Haner while the flier was unbuckling his parachute and in broken English told him that a German patrol was ten minutes away, and that he should wait for partisans. Soon a ragged group of partisans appeared, young men and women, some carrying rifles, some with pistols in their belts. They told Haner to follow them, and for thirty-eight days they dodged German patrols as they headed for Allied territory. Along the way they picked up five more of the crew, including George Kulp; the other four had been captured. They finally reached Zadar on the Yugoslavian coast, and there they were put on a British cruiser for Italy. Haner returned to operations as a first pilot, and flew twenty-one more missions

(Above) B-17G-50-DL 44-6349, which joined the 804th Bomb Squadron, 483rd Bomb Group at Sterparone, Italy, on 2 August 1944, pictured at, of all places, Horsham St Faith, a B-24 base near Norwich, England, a B-24 base. Possibly this Fortress was in transit to or from one of the air depots in the north of England. 44-6349 was lost on the mission to Bleckhammer on 13 September 1944. via Jack Krause

B-17G-55-DL 44-6606 of the 2nd Bomb Group landed at Miskolc airfield, Hungary, early in December 1944 after being damaged during a raid on Vienna. Miskolc was in an area liberated by Soviet and Rumanian troops, and was the home base of the 8th Rumanian Assault Group equipped with Henschel Hs 129 aircraft. The B-17 was repaired by Rumanian groundcrews who fixed an Hs 129 main wheel to the Fortress to act as a tail-wheel so it could take off again. With the adoption of staggered waist guns on late B-17Gs like this one, the fuselage star was applied aft of the right waist gun. Hans Heiri-Stapfer

Fortresses of the 346th Bomb Squadron, 99th Bomb Group, late in 1944. D.R. Black via Bernie Barr

in another group. His opinion regarding 'rehabilitation' procedure was cynical:

It was a little ironic in that in those days, if you were shot down or taken prisoner and were missing for forty-five days before returning, you'd be sent back to the States. We were gone only thirty-eight days, so we missed by seven. But one of our crew was taken by the Yugoslavian partisans to the Russian border and then flown to Egypt, and was gone just a little over the forty-five day limit, and he was sent home.

January 1945 marked a low point in 15th Air Force operations, as bad weather scrubbed most of the missions planned that month. Conditions in February were much improved, however, and the heavies began a series of twenty consecutive missions starting on the 13th. There was no

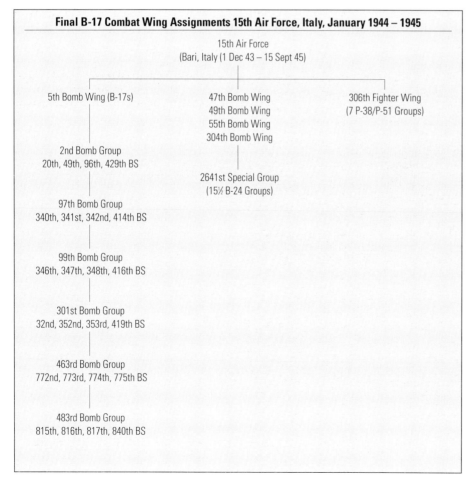

Final B-17 Combat Wing Assignments 15th Air Force, Italy, January 1944 – 1945

15th Air Force
(Bari, Italy (1 Dec 43 – 15 Sept 45)

5th Bomb Wing (B-17s)	47th Bomb Wing	306th Fighter Wing
	49th Bomb Wing	(7 P-38/P-51 Groups)
	55th Bomb Wing	
	304th Bomb Wing	

2nd Bomb Group
20th, 49th, 96th, 429th BS

2641st Special Group
(15½ B-24 Groups)

97th Bomb Group
340th, 341st, 342nd, 414th BS

99th Bomb Group
346th, 347th, 348th, 416th BS

301st Bomb Group
32nd, 352nd, 353rd, 419th BS

463rd Bomb Group
772nd, 773rd, 774th, 775th BS

483rd Bomb Group
815th, 816th, 817th, 840th BS

let-up during February and March, when attacks continued to be made on the enemy oil industry, but raids were mostly against German and Austrian lines of communication. The mission on 27 February was one of these, the target being the Augsburg railyards, an eight-hour trip. In a normal twenty-four-hour period, 2,000 box cars could be expected to pass through the yards, located on the south-west outskirts of the city, and briefing indicated that 920 units were in place. Bill Somers, top turret gunner in Bob Neeley's crew in the 348th Bomb Squadron, 99th Bomb Group, was one who took part; it was his seventeenth combat mission:

We rolled off the hardstand and into line for take-off. The weather was cold, and the early morning sun lent a sparkling brilliance to the ocean of six-man tents around the field. We were ready for take-off. I always dread the testy ride down the steel matted runway with the heavy bomb-load; it was always a scary beginning on every mission. We were carrying six 1,000lb [450kg] bombs. Brakes off, and we began our run. Slowly we built up speed. I began yelling when we reached 80mph [130km/h] – I stood between the pilots and called out '85, 90, 95, 100, 105 [170km/h] – come on, with this load we need another 5mph [8km/h] to get off the ground' – the weight was frightening, the engine noise

(Above) Fortresses of the 99th Bomb Group, B-17G-65-DL 44-46860 of the 347th Bomb Squadron, foreground, crossing the Alps. Two parallel black bands were applied to the rudder, fuselage and elevators of 99th Bomb Group aircraft, early in 1945.
D.R. Black via Bernie Barr

A 451st Bomb Group B-24 Liberator leads B-17G-60-DL 44-6643, a crippled 49th Bomb Squadron, 2nd Bomb Group, Fortress back from Linz, Austria, on 16 March 1945. USAF

deafening, and we needed to lift off, now. Would this lumbering giant ever get into the air? It would, and it did, and I breathed a sigh of relief as the aircraft began its laborious climb up into formation. After joining our squadron we rendezvoused with the twenty-one other planes in the group, and at a higher altitude joined other groups in the wing until we were all collected. We were now an armada of B-17s on the way to war.

The target was shaped like an inverted 'Y', 3,000 yards [2,740m] long and 600 yard [550m] across at its widest point. The word at the morning briefing was that there was the possibility of harassing attacks by fifteen to twenty enemy fighters and/or a few Me 262s from the Munich area. Any stragglers were warned to be on constant alert for north Italian-based fighters. The worst possible scenario was sixty-five to seventy enemy fighters. Enemy ground defences were estimated at eighty-eight heavy guns.

Over the target intense, heavy and accurate *Flak* peppered the 99th Bomb Group formation of twenty-eight planes. Bombing altitude was 23,500ft [7,160m] and we made a visual run. The *Flak* was predominantly of the tracking type, and it was tracking very accurately: it started over the target, and followed the formation off the target and during the rally; we were under extremely heavy fire for six to eight minutes. Eight of our aircraft sustained major *Flak* damage, and seven received minor damage; in all our group lost two planes to *Flak* and fifteen were damaged, and twenty-one men went missing. One of the losses took a direct hit to its right wing between the No. 3 and No. 4 engines; that ship caught fire, and I watched it veer off and go down in flames. There were six parachutes, and some were on fire. My friend Dwight Reigert was in one of those parachutes, and I watched in anguish from my top turret as he and his crew baled out. Dwight was captured in the very railroads we bombed, and he became a PoW.

The other B-17 just blew up – it evaporated in mid-air with pieces and parts all over the sky. Both of these aircraft belonged to the 346th Squadron. The 97th, flying near us, also lost two planes. My friend and tail gunner, Vic Fabiniak, flying in the 346th Squadron next to us, had his bomber disabled when hit by *Flak*; it seemed to be maintaining altitude, and was last seen over Austria when it left the formation and flew toward Switzerland. However, they lost their third engine and landed in Switzerland, where they were interned for the duration. In all, the Augsburg mission cost us plenty. Our raiding force lost at least four B-17s, four B-24s and a B-25. Some of the crews became PoWs, some were interned by neutral Switzerland, and others died. The two planes the 99th Bomb Group lost were the seventy-first and seventy-second of the war to date.

On 15 March, in the deepest penetration so far, 109 B-17s of the 5th Wing bombed the synthetic oil plant at Ruhland, just south of Berlin. Next day more than 720 heavies pounded oil refineries again, while some B-17s and B-24s parachuted supplies to northern Italy and Yugoslavia. Bad weather prevented heavy bombing missions for two days. Then on the 19th, transportation targets in and around Vienna were hit, as more than 800 B-17s and B-24s attacked marshalling yards at several strategic points. On 22 March, 136 B-17s – part of a force of more than 680 heavies in action this day – bombed the Ruhland oil refinery (and Lauta aluminium works to the north) and caused severe damage. Three B-17s were shot down by Me 262 jet fighters.

Venit Hora
('The Hour Has Come')*

On 24 March Berlin was bombed in the first 15th Air Force raid on the German capital, when more than 150 Fortresses set out for the Daimler-Benz tank engine plant, a 1,500-mile (2,400km) round trip. All went well until west of Brux, where the formation was taken completely by surprise when the leading elements came under an intense *Flak* barrage. In the van were twenty-eight B-17s of the 463rd Bomb Group, and they took the brunt of the very accurate and intense barrage. Four B-17s were shot down, and two more were so badly damaged that they had to return to base. Shortly after the *Flak* barrage had been cleared, the 463rd were bounced by fifteen Me 262s, which shot down one of the B-17s. They also shot down a B-17 in the 483rd Bomb Group. Further losses were only prevented by prompt action from P-51 escort fighters. Over the target the 463rd Bomb Group lost its sixth B-17, when it fell victim to *Flak*. Only fourteen B-17s in the 463rd returned to Italy. Six others were forced to put down in Yugoslavia with badly wounded crew and mechanical problems.

The biggest 15th Air Force operation of all occurred on 15 April when 1,142 heavy bombers, in support of US Fifth Army operations, bombed targets and dropped the largest bomb tonnage in a twenty-four

hour period. Some 830 B-17s and B-24s, escorted by 145 fighters, hit enemy gun positions, supply dumps, troop concentrations, maintenance installations and German headquarters, along roads at Wowser near Bologna. Another force of 312 B-17s and B-24s, escorted by 191 fighters, bombed railway bridges at Nervesa della Battaglia, Ponte di Piave and Casarsa della Delizia, and an ammunition factory and stores at Ghedi. Next day bad weather forced almost 700 B-17s and B-24s to abort the mission to the south-west of Bologna, but the strike went ahead on the 17th, when 751 heavies raided enemy positions immediately south and south-west of the city. Missions to the Bologna area continued on the 18th, and three days later Bologna was captured by ground forces. On the 21st, 240 B-17s and B-24s, with a P-51 escort, bombed marshalling yards at Rosenheim, Germany, and at Spital an der Drau, Vocklabruck and Attnang-Puchheim, Austria. Next day bad weather cancelled all heavy bomber operations, and on the 23rd, 719 B-17s and B-24s bombed bridges over the Brenta and Adige rivers. Rail and road bridges were bombed by about 700 heavies on 24 April.

On 25 April, the day delegates from fifty nations began a conference in San Francisco for the purpose of organizing the United Nations. On this same day a force of 467 B-17s and B-24s bombed marshalling yards and rail networks at Linz, Austria, as well as targets of opportunity. Everywhere, fighters patrolled the sky, strafing and dive-bombing targets on the ground if and when they presented themselves. Next day, the 26 April, bad weather caused the force of 117 B-17s and 196 B-24s to abort their mission to targets in northern Italy. The weather was also responsible for cancelled missions on the next four consecutive days. Finally, on 29 April, the German forces in Italy surrendered, and next day Hitler committed suicide in the bunker of his chancellery. The war went on, however, and on 1 May, despite bad weather, twenty-seven B-17s bombed marshalling yards at Salzburg. This was the final 15th Air Force bombing mission of the war. The 15th had dropped 303,842 tons of bombs on Axis targets in a dozen countries, including major installations in eight capital cities. Some 148,955 heavy bomber sorties were flown. The contribution made towards achieving the final victory in Europe was therefore of the highest importance.

* Motto of the 97th Bomb Group

CHAPTER SEVEN

'Higher, Stronger, Faster'*

Round-the-Clock Bombing, ETO, October 1943–Summer 1944

The day after the second Schweinfurt mission, 14 October 1943, all heavy bomb groups were stood down to lick their wounds. The losses and a spell of bad weather restricted the 8th to just two more missions in October – and then on 3 November, it was assigned Wilhelmshaven. Altogether, 555 bombers and H$_2$X ships from the 482nd Bomb Group were despatched to the port. H$_2$X, or 'Mickey Mouse' (later shortened to just 'Mickey'), was a recently developed American version of the British H$_2$S bombing aid. Some groups carried incendiaries to burn up the city. The P-38s which escorted them all the way to the target kept losses to a minimum, and crews were quick to praise their 'little friends'. The target was covered by clouds, and bombing results could not be determined.

On 5 November, 374 Fortresses led by five Oboe-equipped pathfinders, were assigned the iron foundry works, marshalling yards, and oil plants at Gelsenkirchen. Two days later, 112 B-17s bombed industrial areas at Wesel and Duren. Bad weather ruled out any more missions until the 11th, and then only fifty-eight heavies bombed Münster while 111 others were forced to abort because of bad weather over England during assembly. The 1st Bomb Division mission to Wesel by 175 B-17s had to be abandoned altogether.

First Fort to Fifty

On 16 November, a mission to Norway by 306 B-17s went ahead. H$_2$X and 'Oboe' sets had been proving troublesome, and the break in the weather would enable crews to bomb visually. The First Division's target was the molybdenum mines at Knaben, while the Third Division's objective was a generating plant at Vermark in the Rjukan valley about 75 miles (120km) due west of Oslo. The round trip to Knaben and Rjuken was slightly shorter than the 25 July 1943 1,800-mile (2,896km) circuit to Trondheim and the 1,600-mile (2,574km) round trip to Heroya. Both targets were connected with the German 'heavy-water' experiments

which would help give the Nazis the atomic bomb, but crews were not told this at the time. The raid on Rjukan by approximately 155 B-17s destroyed the power station in addition to other parts of the facility, and resulted in a complete stoppage of the entire manufacturing process. The Germans later decided to ship their remaining 'heavy-water' stockpile to Germany. However, all 546 tons of the heavy water were sent to the bottom of Lake Timm when the ferry boat being used to transport it was blown up by SOE agents over the deepest part of the lake. Lt John P. Manning in the 303rd Bomb Group brought *Knockout Dropper* back to Molesworth to make it the first B-17 to complete fifty missions in the ETO.

On 18 November, 127 heavies were despatched to Gelsenkirchen again. However, the Oboe sets aboard the leading Fortresses gave trouble, and directed the formation too far north of the target. After an unsuccessful battle with the elements the B-17s were forced to return to England. The bad weather continued over the next few days, but did not prevent RAF Bomber Command bombing Berlin on the night of 22 November. This led to rumours of an American follow-up raid being mounted on the capital the next day.

Heroism in the Air

On Friday 26 November, 633 bombers, the largest formation every assembled by the 8th, were directed against targets as far apart as Bremen and Paris. Two new B-17 groups, the 401st and 447th, had joined the 8th during November, and the 401st made its combat debut this day. Col

* Motto of the 92nd Bomb Group

8th Air Force B-17 Combat Bombardment Wing (CBW) Assignments 1 November 1943						
1st Bomb Division			**3rd Bomb Division**			
Group	*Wing*	*Base*	*Group*	*Wing*	*Base*	
91st	1st CBW	Bassingbourn	94th	4th CBW	B St E (Rougham)	
381st	1st CBW	Ridgewell	385th	4th CBW	Gt Ashfield	
			447th	4th CBW	Rattlesden	
401st	92nd CBW	Deenthorpe				
351st	92nd CBW	Polebrook	95th	13th CBW	Horham	
			100th	13th CBW	Thorpe Abbotts	
92nd	40th CBW	Podington	390th	13th CBW	Framlingham	
305th	40th CBW	Chelveston				
306th	40th CBW	Thurleigh	96th	45th CBW	Snetterton Heath	
			388th	45th CBW	Knettishall	
303rd	41st CBW	Molesworth				
379th	41st CBW	Kimbolton				
384th	41st CBW	Grafton Underwood				

(Above) B-17G-5-BO 42-31134/G of the 569th Bomb Squadron, 390th Bomb Group, en route to the secret German heavy water plant situated near the little Norwegian town of Rjukan, about 75 miles (120km) from Oslo, on 16 November 1943. Intelligence sources had learned that this, and the Fortresses' targets, the Molybdenum mines at Knaben, and a generating plant at Vermark in the Rjukan Valley, were all connected with the German heavy water experiments which would help give the Nazis the atomic bomb. In May 1944, 42-31134 was named Gung Ho and on 10 September 1944, this aircraft and Lt Charles F. McIntosh's crew failed to return from a mission when it crashed at Nürnburg; six crew were killed and three were taken prisoner. USAF

B-17F-27-BO 41-24605 BN-R Knock-Out Dropper of the 359th Bomb Squadron, 303rd Bomb Group, the first 8th Air Force B-17 to complete fifty combat missions, on 16 November 1943, and seventy-five combat missions on 27 March 1944. Knock-Out Dropper finished her days at Stillwater, Oklahoma, in July 1945. Lt Col Harry D. Gobrecht

B-17F-70-BO 42-29733 SU-L Louisiana Purchase of the 544th Bomb Squadron, 384th Bomb Group, overshot when Lt George Cosentine tried to make an emergency landing at RAF Coltishall, Norfolk, on 16 December 1943, on the return from Bremen, and ended up in the revetments; it was salvaged on 4 January 1944. The aircraft had previously served with the 91st Bomb Group at Bassingbourn and the 305th Bomb Group at Chelveston from 14 July 1943, before transferring to the 384th Bomb Group at Grafton Underwood on 6 November 1943, where it acquired its name. USAF

Harold W. Bowman's outfit would swell the First Division stream to 505 bombers briefed for the port area of Bremen, while 128 B-17s of the Third Division would head for Paris where skies were expected to be clear. Unfortunately the weather forecasters were proved wrong, and the Third Division was forced to return with their bomb-loads intact.

The First Division, *en route* to Bremen, encountered persistent fighter attacks by up to a hundred German fighters. Some eighty-six enemy fighters were claimed destroyed, twenty-six of them by B-17 gunners. However, twenty-nine Fortresses and five fighters were lost. These stark statistics do not include the death and destruction meted out to the B-17s that limped home to England with dead and wounded aboard. At Molesworth, thirty-five B-17s had taken off for Bremen. As the 303rd Bomb Group formation began its bomb run, *Star Dust* in the 358th Bomb Squadron, was seriously damaged by three German fighters attacking from the nose. 20mm shells knocked out the nose Plexiglas, killing the navigator instantly and seriously wounding 2nd Lt Charles Spencer, the bombardier. Spencer suffered serious cuts to his face, and his helmet and oxygen mask were ripped off. He lay in the windswept nose with the air tem-

perature at minus 67° until the flight engineer dragged him into the pilots' compartment; by this time his face was so swollen it was hard to see his nose, and it was difficult to give him oxygen. The flight engineer then left to attend to other wounded crew-members. Barely conscious and frozen, Spencer heard the enemy fighters attacking and struggled back to the nose guns, exposing himself to the blast of extremely cold air coming through the shattered nose, and the risk of being thrown out by violent manoeuvres of the Fortress. He continued to fire his guns until the enemy attacks ceased, and was found unconscious under his guns when the badly mangled B-17 and her crew managed to make an emergency landing at Docking. Although thought dead, Spencer survived, despite the loss of all his fingers, an eye, and months of operations to rebuild his face and a new nose and ears. He was awarded the United States' second highest award for heroism, the Distinguished Service Cross.

Three days later, on 29 November, the 303rd returned to Bremen. In the 303rd formation was *Dark Horse*, with the crew of Lt Carl Fyler aboard on their 25th and final mission before they finished their combat tour. *Dark Horse* was hit by *Flak* just after it dropped its bombs, losing its

right horizontal stabilizer, part of its right wing and two engines. Continuous fighter attacks inflicted massive additional damage to the Fortress, killing four crewmen and seriously wounding six, including the tail gunner, S/Sgt Joe Sawicki of Detroit, Michigan. Sawicki had fought with the Polish Air Force in 1942, and had been decorated with the Polish Cross of Valour; this was his thirteenth mission with the 303rd. During the attacks, S/Sgt Sawicki had his left arm severed completely, and he suffered serious abdominal injuries; but he still continued to fire his guns at the attacking fighters. Only when the crew was given the signal to bale out did he leave his position. Crawling to the waist compartment, he noticed the two waist gunners on the floor with serious injuries, each with a broken arm and serious facial wounds. Rather than depart the ship, he somehow managed to wrestle parachutes on both the gunners, and then push them out of the aircraft. Both men managed to pull the ripcords on their parachutes with their good arms; they survived the war as PoWs. Sawicki's body was found in the tail of the B-17 after it plunged to earth. He never received recognition for his actions, largely because the only witnesses were in PoW camps until after the war, and then because a recommendation for the Medal of Honor was lost in the bureaucracy.

On 30 November, seventy-eight Fortresses bombed Solingen, and also the next day; then ground haze over eastern England hampered missions again. On 3 December it was reported to the combined chiefs of staff that the *Pointblank* offensive was three months behind in relation to 1 May 1944, the tentative date for *Overlord* and the invasion of Europe. It could only place more pressure on the 8th Air Force to destroy German aircraft factories. Time and the weather seemed to be against them. On the 5th, about 550 heavies were despatched to airfield targets in France, but almost all the bomber sorties were frustrated by heavy cloud, and nine aircraft were lost. On 11 December the weather finally cleared sufficiently for 523 B-17s and B-24s to bomb Emden. Rocket-firing Bf 110s and Me 210s made persistent attacks on the bomber formations, and seventeen heavies were shot down.

Two days later, 710 B-17s and B-24s headed for Bremen for the first of three raids that month on the German port. This was the first time that P-51s escorting the bombers reached the limit of their

B-17Gs of the 390th Bomb Group in formation. Clockwise, starting at bottom left, is B-17G-90-BO 42-30223/S Rick-O-Shay (formerly Norma J) of the 568th Bomb Squadron, which failed to return with 2nd Lt Glenn E. Ryon's crew on 11 December 1943. Eight of the crew were killed. Next is B-17G-105-BO 42-30476/L Rovin' Romona of the 568th Bomb Squadron, which on 20 December 1943 failed to return, with the loss of 2nd Lt John R. Reeve's crew. Top left is B-17G-120-BO 42-30783 DI-M, The Stork Club, of the 570th Bomb Squadron, which failed to return with 2nd Lt Vincent F. DeMayo's crew, on 16 March 1944. Top right is B-17G-60-DL 42-3427/B Six Nights in Telergma of the 568th Bomb Squadron, which became Canadian Club in February 1944 and was salvaged on the 22 June 1945. Right is B-17G-15-DL 42-37818/D Dinah Might of the 568th Bomb Squadron, which failed to return with Lt Clyde J. Baugher's crew, 21 January 1944. Far right is B-17G-65-DL 42-3472/S Shoot a Pound of the 571st Bomb Squadron. This Fortress was subsequently named The Vulture and then The Paper Doll, and finished her days at Altus, Oklahoma, in October 1945. via Ian McLachlan

escort range, and the first occasion that more than 600 heavies (649) bombed a target. Another 535 heavies were despatched to Bremen on 16 December, and again on the 20th, when chaff was used for the first time on an 8th Air Force mission, a counter measure which 'snowed' the German radar screens; also nearly eighty P-51s and P-38s engaged arms with twin-engined rocket-firing fighters – but in spite of these measures, twenty-seven heavies were shot down.

On 22 December, 439 B-17s and B-24s attacked marshalling yards at Osnabruck and Munster, but effective bombing was prevented by a combination of bad weather and faulty PFF equipment. The B-17s were stood down on 23 December, but missions resumed on Christmas Eve when 670 heavies, including the B-17s of the 447th Bomb Group from Rattlesden which made its debut this day, bombed twenty-three mysterious missile sites in the Pas de Calais which went under the codename Noball. British intelligence revealed them to be sites for launching 'V'-weapons – pilotless rockets packed with a high explosive warhead in the nose and aimed at London.

On Christmas Day the 8th was stood down and missions did not resume until the 30th, when 658 heavies, escorted by P-51s and P-38s, bombed installations at Ludwigshafen near the German–Swiss border. Altogether, twenty-three bombers and twelve American fighters were lost on the raid, and twenty-three German fight-

ers were claimed destroyed. On New Year's Eve, VIII Bomber Command completed its second year in England with all-out raids on airfields in France. Missions of this nature were usually considered 'milk-runs' compared to those over heavily defended targets in Germany.

Strategic Air Forces, Europe

On 4 January 1944, B-17s of the 8th Air Force flew their last mission under the auspices of VIII Bomber Command. On 6 January both the 8th and 15th Air Force in Italy were placed under a unified headquarters called 'US Strategic Air Forces, Europe' (USSTAF – the overall USAAF command organization in Europe) at Bushey Hall, Teddington, Middlesex. Gen Carl 'Tooey' Spaatz returned to England to command the new organization, while Lt Gen James H. Doolittle took command of the 8th Air Force from Lt Gen Ira C. Eaker, who moved to the Mediterranean theatre to take command of the new MAAF (Mediterranean Allied Air Forces). Spaatz and Doolittle's plan was to use the US Strategic Air Forces in a series of co-ordinated raids, codenamed Operation Argument and supported by RAF night bombing, on the German aircraft industry at the earliest possible date. However, the winter weather cause a series of postponements, and the bombers were despatched to V1 rocket sites in northern France.

Big Week

Good weather was predicted for the week 20–25 February, and so Operation Argument – which quickly became known as Big Week – began in earnest. The opening shots were fired by the RAF which bombed Leipzig on the night of 19/20 February. Next day the 8th put up some 1,028 B-17s and B-24s and 832 fighters, while the RAF provided sixteen squadrons of Mustangs and Spitfires. In all, twelve aircraft plants were attacked on 20 February, with the B-17s of the First Division going to Leipzig, Bernburg and Oschersleben, while the unescorted Third Division bombed the Fw 190 plant at Tutow and the He 111 plant at Rostock.

The raids caused such widespread damage that it led Speer to order the immediate dispersement of the German aircraft industry to safer parts of the Reich. The 8th lost twenty-five bombers and four fighters. Three Medals of Honor were awarded to B-17 crewmen, the only instance in the 8th's history of more than one being issued on one day: 1t Lt William R. Lawley Jr, twenty-three years old, was a pilot in the 364th Bomb Squadron, 305th Bomb Group, which raided Brunswick; he was decorated for getting his badly crippled B-17 and his crew back to England, after suffering serious injuries at the target. And in the 351st Bomb Group, Sgt Archie Mathies, ball-turret gunner, and 2nd Lt Walter E. Truemper, navigator, valiantly brought Mizpah

(Above) **B-17G-35-VE 42-5918 ET-J** Heavenly Daze **of the 336th Bomb Squadron, 95th Bomb Group, over Norway. This Fortress flew its first sortie on 10 July 1943; it failed to return with 2nd Lt James E. Foley's crew on 11 January 1944 when it was attacked by two Bf 109s and Ju 88s and crashed at Osnabruck. All the crew, except the ball-turret gunner, W.S. Cadle, survived to become PoWs.** USAF

(Right) **A German fighter sets a B-17 on fire during the mission to Brunswick, 11 January 1944.** USAF

1st Lt William F. Cely, pilot, and 2nd Lt Jabez I. Churchill, co-pilot, in the 333rd Bomb Squadron, 94th Bomb Group, inspect their badly damaged B-17G-1-VE 42-39775/K Frenesi **which they brought home to Bury St Edmunds (Rougham) from Brunswick on 11 January 1944 with three wounded gunners after five crew and a cameraman had baled out over enemy territory (the interphones were out and they did not hear Cely's exhortation 'Poppa's gonna take you home'). Cely added the Silver Star to his DFC and Air Medal for bringing** Frenesi **back. In fact the aircraft was so badly damaged that it was scrapped, but five of the crew fought another day in** Frenesi II **(43-38834).** via Ian McLachlan

B-17G-30-DL 42-38109, in the 364th Bomb Squadron, 305th Bomb Group, which 1st Lt William R. Lawley Jr, helped by his bombardier, 1st Lt Harry G. Mason, brought back from Brunswick on 20 February 1944, to crashland at Redhill. Two gunners were so badly wounded that they could not have baled out. Lawley's was one of three Medals of Honor awarded to B-17 crewmen, the only instance in the 8th's history that more than one was issued on one day. via Bill Donald

Crew of B-17F-65-BO 42-29679 Ramblin' Wreck in the 401st Bomb Squadron, 91st Bomb Group at Bassingbourn. L–R, back row: 1st Lt Don 'Pop' Shea, navigator; 2nd Lt Clyde C. McCallum, co-pilot; 1st Lt William F. Gibbons, pilot; Wendy Q. Baum, bombardier. Front row: Tech Sgt William O. 'Blimp' Doupance, radio operator; S/Sgt Julius W. Edwards, left waist gunner; Bob Ginsburg, waist gunner; Stff Sgt Paul M. Goecke, tail gunner; Sgt Clarence R. 'Junior' Bateman, ball turret; Tech Sgt John R. Parsons, engineer top turret gunner. On 21 February 1944, this crew except Baum (replaced by 1st Lt Wilfred P. Conlon) and Bob Ginsburg (replaced by Sgt Jack S. Bowen) were shot down by fighters in B-17F-20-DL 42-3073 Lightning Strikes. via Walter A. Truax

back to Polebrook after their pilots were killed, but died attempting to land.

Next day, 21 February, 924 bombers and 679 fighters set out for the two M.I.A.G aircraft factories at Brunswick and other targets. H$_2$X blind-bombing equipment was used at Brunswick when heavy cloud prevented visual bombing, and some groups bombed targets of opportunity. This time the 8th lost nineteen bombers and five fighters, but sixty German fighters were claimed shot down. One of the bomber losses was *Lightning Strikes*, piloted by 1st Lt William F. Gibbons in the 401st Bomb Squadron, 91st Bomb Group, shot down by fighters just after the IP. Tech Sgt John R. Parsons, engineer top turret gunner, tells what happened:

We were doing exceptionally well, a good formation, a tight high box as we came to the target area. Since we were all a little bit to the south and to the east of the target, we were instructed to make a 180 and then drop. It sounded like a good idea, and it was, except the lead navigator, who was somewhat of a cowboy, turned too short, and of course it completely scattered the formation. We were in *Flak* like mad, a helluva lot of *Flak* – we were hanging out to dry, so to speak; there were nine airplanes behind ours, and I saw two of them blow up right off. I looked at the damnedest mess of fighters you ever saw – they swarmed in like bees. Of course, there were a lot of them shot down, but we wee in a position where we had to fight for our lives.

They would come in close and one would be attacking the rear, and another would be attacking the right or left side. Most of them came in from the left and, oh God, we had an Fw 190 come in right over the tail gunner, Paul M. Geocke. I told Paul to fight for his life. Everybody was shooting everything they had, and this guy comes in and I think he was the one that really hurt us – 20mm explosion in the No. 3 engine blew the whole cowling off, and three of the jugs in the engine were blown out; you could look down and see the guts just flying around in the engine. Of course you couldn't feather the darn thing, and when they all started going, it didn't help us at all. Also we had one helluva big hole in the No. 3 reserve tank, and burning gas was coming on board. The attacks kept coming. I saw tracers fly through the airplane, and I don't know how or why they didn't kill anybody, but they didn't.

I got down out of the top turret because the plane was going to go. Paul rang the 'bale-out' bell, and I felt air come up through the bottom so I knew that the bombardier and navigator were already out. I grabbed Clyde McCallum, co-pilot, and said, 'Mac – go!' We all went out of that airplane at about 20,000ft.

On 22 February, 101 heavies bombed aircraft production centres at Bernberg, Halberstadt, and Oschersleben in conjunction with a 15th Air Force raid on Regensburg. The majority of the 8th's bomb groups were forced to abort because of bad weather over England, and thirty-five bombers were shot down. Meanwhile, 154 more heavies bombed targets of opportunity, losing six aircraft. The 303rd Bomb Group was part of the formation which struck at the Junkers aircraft plant at Aschersleben. About an hour and a half before reaching the target, during heavy German fighter attacks, a 20mm shell seriously injured S/Sgt William T.L. Werner, from Lebanon, Pennsylvania, the tail gunner aboard *Luscious Lady* in the 427th Bomb Squadron. Realizing that survival of the B-17 depended upon him being able to defend it from rear attacks, Werner remained at his guns and continued firing without pause. About thirty minutes later, *Luscious Lady* was hit by *Flak* and Werner received wounds in the arms, abdominal area and leg. However, only after all fighter attacks had ceased did Werner, weakened by loss of blood, crawl to the waist gunners' compartment, where he collapsed. He had in fact survived because *Flak* had knocked out his heated suit and the freezing temperatures had lowered his body temperature, causing the blood from his wounds to coagulate quickly. Werner was awarded the DSC for his actions.

On 23 February, bad weather kept the 8th Air Force heavies on the ground. On 24 February, Doolittle despatched 231 B-17s of the First Division to Schweinfurt, losing eleven B-17s, while the Third Division struck at targets on the Baltic coast without loss. On the 25th, the USSTAF despatched some 1,154 bombers and 1,000 fighters, including 680 heavies from the 8th, to the ball-bearing works and components' factories at Regensburg, the Messerschmitt experimental and assembly plants at Augsburg, Furth, and the VFK ball-bearing plants at Stuttgart. Very considerable damage was caused to the Bf 109 plants at Regensburg-Prufening by the Third Bomb Division, which arrived over the target an hour after the 15th Air Force (who suffered high losses) and met only token fighter opposition. Bombing was highly effective, and fighter output at

Regensburg was severely reduced for four months following the raids.

Despite total losses during Big Week of some 226 bombers, Spaatz and Doolittle believed the USSTAF had dealt the German aircraft industry a really severe blow. However, the destruction was not as great as at first thought.

First American Bombs on 'Big B'

On 3 March 1944 the 8th failed to penetrate the bad weather over England and bomb Berlin. On 4 March it tried again, but only the 95th and 100th Bomb Groups managed to drop the first American bombs on 'Big B'. On 6 March, the 8th despatched 730 heavies and almost 800 escort fighters to targets in Berlin: a ball-bearing plant at Erkner in the suburbs of Berlin, the Robert Bosch electrical equipment factory and the Daimler Benz engine factory at Genshagen were all bombed. The American gunners claimed over 170 German fighters destroyed – but the 8th lost a record sixty-three bombers, with a further 102 seriously damaged, and eleven fighters.

On 8 March, the three divisions of the 8th Air Force contributed altogether 600 bombers and 200 escort fighters in the raid on the VKF ball-bearing plant at Erkner. The leading Third Division received the worst of the fighter attacks and lost thirty-seven Fortresses. Next day the *Luftwaffe* was notable for its absence, but nine bombers were lost to *Flak* as the 8th attempted to bomb Berlin through thick cloud. Altogether, the 8th Air Force dropped 4,800 tons of high explosive on Berlin during five raids in March 1944.

Any new 8th Air Force offensive was curtailed by the weather and it was not until 8 April that the heavies were able to assemble in force when 644 bombers were despatched to aircraft depots in western Germany. On Easter Sunday, 9 April, the Third Division attacked the Fw 190 plant at Marienburg, and despite the loss of one combat wing and some combat boxes from another, the Fortresses placed 71 per cent of their bombs within 1,000ft of the MPI.

After a raid on airfield targets in France and the low Countries on the 9 April, on the 11th more than 900 heavies hit the six Junkers and Focke Wulf assembly plants in eastern Germany. Some fifty-two Fortresses were lost. One who got back – just – was

1st Lt Edward S. Michael in the 364th Bomb Squadron, 305th Bomb Group, who brought *Bertie Lee* home to England after it had been devastated by cannon fire near Brunswick and had plummeted into a 3,000ft (900m) dive, its bomb-bay on fire. Michael was seriously wounded in the thigh and his instruments were shattered. He and co-pilot Lt Franklin Westberg finally got the B-17 out of the spin and

Michael ordered the crew to bale out. Sgt John Leiber, bombardier, had lost an arm and was pushed out with a 'chute by the engineer, Sgt Jewell Phillips. Phillips' parachute, meanwhile, had been shredded by shrapnel and he and the two pilots were too busy to decide who would use whose 'chute. 'If we can't all jump together,' Michael screamed at Westberg, 'then we'll all go down together!'

Against all the odds, Michael and Westberg reached an RAF airfield near Grimsby, where, fighting off unconsciousness, Michael performed a perfect belly landing, in spite of the fact that the undercarriage and flaps had been put out of operation, the ball turret was stuck in the lowered position with its guns pointing downwards, the airspeed indicator was dead, and the bomb-bay doors were jammed fully open. Michael was hospitalized for seven weeks. In November 1944, General Emory S. Adams, president of the War Department Decorations Board, turned down a submission for Michael to receive the Medal of Honor, *but* he was overruled, and the heroic twenty-six-year-old pilot became the second member of the 364th Bomb Squadron, 305th Bomb Group to receive an award.

On 13 April there was a mission to the ball-bearing plants at Schweinfurt: 2nd Lt Thomas F. Dello Buono, a native of New York City, was the bombardier aboard *Idaliza* in the 360th Bomb Squadron, the 303rd Bomb Group. During attacks by a swarm of fighters, a 20mm shell shattered the Plexiglas in the nose of the Fortress and exploded against Dello Bouno's *Flak* vest, seriously wounding him, and knocking him 12ft (4m) to the back of the compartment; a half-inch piece of shrapnel lodged in his chest near his heart, his left thumb was severed at the first joint, and fragments of the shattered Plexiglas lodged in his right shoulder. After regaining consciousness, Dello Buono crawled back to his nose gun, refused morphine and continued to fire at the enemy aircraft with the freezing winds all the while blowing through the shattered nose compartment. Forty minutes later, when the formation reached the target, he dropped his bombs squarely on the target. Refusing his crewmates' request to move back to the comparative warmth of the radio room, Dello Buono then continued to man his guns against the enemy fighters. Only when they crossed the enemy coast and England was in sight did he agree to move out of the

A Fortress could absorb a great deal of punishment, and this is never more graphically illustrated than in this picture of B-17G-5-BO 42-31227/Q *Dottie Jane* in the 447th Bomb Group, which 1st Lt Arthur R. Socolofsky of Chicago nursed back to Rattlesden on 6 March 1944 following a direct *Flak* hit under the floor of the radio room during a raid on Berlin. Cables, wires and tubing hang limp and frayed out of the gaping underbelly of the aircraft. Through this battered mass of machinery, the Fort's radio operator vanished into thin air five miles above Germany. The aircraft was salvaged the following day. USAF via Ron MacKay

B-17G-70-DL 42-3491 MI-G Chopstick G-George, a PFF ship in the 812th Bomb Squadron, 482nd Bomb Group, on fire in the bomb-bay on the mission to Berlin, 6 March 1944. This aircraft carried Brigadier General Russell Wilson, 4th Combat Bombardment Wing CO, and was flown by Major Fred A. Rabo and a mixed 385th Bomb Group and 482nd crew including 1st Lt John C. 'Red' Morgan, who had been awarded the MoH for his actions on 26 July 1943. Morgan and three others survived to become PoW, but eight of the twelve men aboard were killed. via Derek Smith

Bombs away! On 28 March 1944, Rheims Campagne was the target and these bombs were dropped by a B-17G of the 91st Bomb Group from 21,500ft (6,550m). via Walt Truax

(Left) B-17G-45-BO 42-97220 9Z-B Kickapoo Joy Juice of the 728th Bomb Squadron, 452nd Bomb Group, was lost with Lt Charles J. Robinson's crew on 28 March 1944. Six of the crew were killed, and three made prisoners of war. Mike Bailey

forward compartment, suffering from a painful case of frostbite. Dello Buono was awarded the DSC, the third 303rd Bomb Group airman to be so honoured.

May Day marked the opening of a series of all-out attacks on the enemy's rail network in France and Belgium, when 1,328 bombers struck at targets in France and Belgium. On 7 May, 1,000 8th Air Force heavies were despatched for the first time, and two days later 772 bombers attacked transportation targets. On 11 May, 973 bombers bombed marshalling yards in Germany and the Low Countries. On 12 May, the 8th Air Force was assigned oil targets at Brux, Böhlen, Leipzig, Merseburg, Lutzhendorf and Zeitz, while a smaller force was to attack the Fw 190 repair depot at Zwickau. Some 900 bombers, escorted by over 875 fighters, flew a common course to the Thuringen area where

B-17G-20-DL 42-37931 WF-D Bertie Lee, 364th Bomb Squadron, 305th Bomb Group, named after the wife of the pilot, 1st Lt Edward S. Michael; he belly-landed the plane near Grimsby on 11 April 1944 after it had been devastated by cannon fire near Brunswick and had plummeted into a 3,000ft (900m) dive, its bomb-bay on fire. Like 1st Lt William R. Lawley Jr in the same squadron on 20 February 1944, Michael refused to abandon his seemingly doomed B-17 because of wounded crew aboard who could not jump, and he was awarded the Medal of Honor. via Bill Donald

(Above) **Lt Thomas H. Gunn (fourth from right) of the 322nd Bomb Squadron, 91st Bomb Group, brought B-17G-20-DL 42-37938 OR-E** Betty Lou's Buggy **safely back to Bassingbourn on Sunday 19 April 1944** after sustaining heavy damage form Bf 109s at the Focke Wulf assembly plant at Eschwege near Kassel. Fighters holed the left wing fuel tank, put a turbo out, damaged an engine, knocked out the elevators and left aileron and exploded shells in the nose, cockpit, bomb-bay and fin. Gunn could only control direction by using the engines, and had to apply full right aileron to keep the B-17 level. Only the co-pilot and navigator were wounded. The rest of the crew view the damage with their groundcrew and reflect on how lucky they had been. USAF

Robert D. Smith, tail gunner of Betty Lou's Buggy, **inspects the cannon damage** which severed the rudder controls. The Fortress was repaired, re-assigned to the 324th Bomb Squadron (DF-E) and survived the war to be scrapped at Kingman, Arizona, in December 1945. USAF

the bomb divisions peeled off and attacked five targets: the big Leuna plant at Merseburg, 18 miles (929km) west of Leipzig; Lutzkendorf and Böhlen in the same general area; Zeitz, 25 miles (40km) south-west of Leipzig; and Brux, 42 miles (68km) north-west of Prague. This was the first time that the 8th had been assigned a target in Czechoslovakia, although Brux had been bombed before by the 15th Air Force.

One by one the B-17s took off and completed their complicated group and wing assembly patterns. Manningtree was the final assembly point, and crews carried on over the Channel in a bomber stream. The bombers crossed the enemy coast between Dunkirk and Ostend near the French–Belgian border. Altogether the *Luftwaffe* shot down forty-six bombers and ten fighters on 12 May, for the loss of almost 150 fighters.

Throughout the rest of May 1944 the 8th Air Force continued making heavy raids on transportation and aircraft production targets, being used as a tactical weapon to destroy lines of communication in France and the Low Countries preparatory to the invasion of France. To maintain the momentum brought about by the increase in missions, replacement crews arrived from the States at every opportunity. One of the new arrivals was 2nd Lt Richard R. 'Dick' Johnson, co-pilot in 2nd Lt Theodore 'Bud' Beiser's crew. Johnson recalls:

The last week of April found us on a bus headed for the bomb group to which we had been assigned – the famous 303rd, known as 'Hell's Angels'. As we drove past the little village of Molesworth and turned on to the base, a little over a mile from the village, we were greeted with some strange sights. There were so many B-17s that they couldn't be easily counted. The

B-17G-20-BO BX-D 42-31447 Cookie of the 338th Bomb Squadron, 96th Bomb Group, which was lost over the Baltic on 11 April 1944 with Lt Jack W. Splan's crew on the mission to Rostock; and B-17G-25-BO 42-31718 AW-T of the 337th Bomb Squadron, which crashed at Hartmannshein, Germany, on 12 May 1944 on the mission to Zwickau. Eight men in 2nd Lt Jerry T. Musser's crew were made PoW and two were KIA. USAF

B-17G of the 452nd Bomb Group crossing Berlin, 29 April 1944, with Templehof airfield beneath. A total of 579 B-17s and B-24s bombed 'Big B' this day, concentrating on the Friedrichstrasse section in the centre of the city. USAF

B-17G-40-BO 42-97167 QJ-N of the 339th Bomb Squadron, 96th Bomb Group at Snetterton Heath. This aircraft and Capt Jack E. Link's crew failed to return on 12 May 1944 when it crashed at Hahnsatten, Germany. Nine men were KIA and one made PoW. USAF

B-17G-30-DL 42-38213 (olive drab) and B-17G-35-DL 42-106984 (natural metal finish) at the Douglas Long
Beach factory. 42-106984 did not leave the US, while 42-38213 was assigned to the 20th Bomb Squadron,
2nd Bomb Group, 15th Air Force, and was lost on 7 July 1944 on the mission to Blechhammer. Douglas-built
G models were the first to become operational, the AAF receiving their first 'G' on 4 September 1943.
Leaving the bomber unpainted speeded up production and increased overall flight performance. Altogether,
Douglas built 2,395 'G' models. McDonnell Douglas

427th Bomb Squadron to which we had been assigned was on the base, while the other three squadrons' were just off the base. As we approached the barrack area of the 427th, some wag had hung a sign on the first billet area which said, 'Girls who visit on a weekend must be off the base by Tuesday.' Along the taxiway near the armament section were row upon row of bombs out in the open, some of the larger ones fitted with wings and empennage to be used as glide bombs. Once we were settled in, and after hearing 'You'll be sorry' a few times, we did the latest schooling.

After a few practice flights, Beiser's crew flew their first mission on 15 May, to bomb the two batteries of twenty-five guns each, at Mimoyecques, near Calais, Johnson filling in as co-pilot in 1st Lt Phillip W. O'Hare's crew in 42-97391, while 'Bud' Beiser and the rest of the crew flew with 1st Lt Steven Bastean, an experienced pilot. Each of the barrels of the guns at Mimoyecques were 416ft (127m) long and

capable of firing a 55lb (25kg) shell into the heart of London. Johnson recalls:

Lt O'Hare's position in the high squadron was number seven, 'Tail-End Charlie', one of the most vulnerable positions in the formation. 'Purple Heart Corner' is the next plane, on the outside of the formation. There was an undercast at the target, and we bombed by radar. The lead plane was equipped with this system, and all following planes dropped at first appearance of bombs from the lead plane. Just after 'bombs away' from about 25,000ft [7,620m] we encountered some *Flak*. However, it was light and inaccurate, the nearest burst being a quarter of a mile away. The German gunners may not have had their radar working, and so were shooting at the noise of our engines. None of our aircraft sustained damage, and all planes returned to base and landed before 10.30am. Total flight time was over four hours, and we were over enemy territory for barely seven minutes. My first combat mission was truly a 'milk run', so called because it was no more dangerous than delivering milk.

My second missions, on 19 May, was not so uneventful, as the target was 'Big B' – Berlin. Beister and I were reunited for our second mission. Each B-17 was loaded with 2,700 gallons [12,275 litres] of gas, and twelve 500lb [227kg] bombs. At 6lb [2.7kg] per gallon [4.5l], the weight of fuel for each plane was 16,200lb [7,348kg] and bombs weighed 12,000lb [5,443kg] for a total of over 14 tons. The B-17G carried over 5,000 rounds of ammunition for its thirteen machine guns. The weight of these .50 calibre guns, plus oil for the engines and oxygen for the crew, often brought the take-off weight of these aircraft to over 65,000lb [29,484kg]. Empty, they weighed about 35,000lb [15,876kg].

As we approached the target, the *Flak* was unbelievable – it was as if someone had painted a thin black line across the sky, and it was exactly at our altitude of 26,000ft [7,925m]. Berlin had large numbers of 88mm *Flak* guns all around the city, and many fixed guns of larger calibre were deployed in the area; many of these were 105mm, and some were 128mm. They were not as accurate as the 88s but made a larger explosion – when the target aircraft couldn't be seen, these guns fired a burst that would explode at, or above our altitude, thus forcing us to fly through a rain of shell fragments, or 'Flak'.

As we approached Berlin, clouds covered over half the earth below us, which made the target difficult to see. Many of our aircraft dropped 'chaff', bundles of tinfoil cut to the exact length of the German radar signal. This only helped during cloudy weather, as the German Flak gunners preferred a visual sighting.

Their 'final aimer' usually aimed for the left wing-root of the lead plane. The big disadvantage for the Flak gunners was the necessity to lead the target by two or more kilometres; that was how much they had to allow for the interval of travel by the target until the explosive shell arrived. Shortly after 'bombs away', 42-31386 Sky Duster, flown by Lt E.L. Roth in the No. 3 position in the high squadron, was hit by a direct burst, and went down. Only five parachutes were seen to emerge from the stricken

aircraft. We had heard rumours that some of our baled crew members were murdered by civilians, and this was confirmed after the war. So after leaving the hell in the air, many were faced with an equal hell on the ground.

Of the nineteen aircraft from our group which flew this day, one was shot down by Flak, three received major damage, eleven suffered less severe damage, and only four B-17s came back unscathed. Our aircraft had several Flak holes in the leading edges, and a few in the sides. Ours

B-17G-5-VE 42-39871, one of the Vega-built Fortresses from the 42-39858/39957 block, is hoisted above the others. 42-39871 was assigned to the 8th Air Force on 25 October 1943 and served in the 8th Weather Squadron (Provisional) before being used by the 652nd Bomb Squadron, 25th Bomb Group at Watton, Norfolk, from 22 April 1944. She was declared War Weary on 21 February 1945. 42-39878 went to the 305th Bomb Group at Chelveston, and was lost on 28 May 1944, while 42-39873 joined the 615th Bomb Squadron, 401st Bomb Group at Deenthorpe. Named Stormy Weather, this aircraft failed to return on 1 August 1944. 42-39869 (right) joined the 95th Bomb Group at Horham, where it became QW-R Heaven Can Wait in the 412th Bomb Squadron; it failed to return with Lt Richard P. Bannerman and crew on 11 April 1944. 42-39875 (off-centre) was assigned overseas on 14 January 1944 and joined the 303rd Bomb Group at Molesworth where it became Buzz Blonde, later Helen Highwater, and finally Through Hel'en Hiwater; it was lost on 15 January 1945. 42-39876 (centre) joined the 569th Bomb Squadron, 390th Bomb Group, 8th Air Force, on 21 October 1943 and was named Gloria Anne. She suffered battle damage over Berlin on 6 March 1944 and was salvaged two days later. 42-39892 was assigned to the 401st Bomb Group and went MIA on the mission to Berlin on March 1944. Altogether, Lockheed-Vega turned out 2,250 B-17Gs. Lockheed-California

The waist-gun positions on the F model were cramped and confined, and one of the eagerly awaited innovations were staggered waist-gun positions with permanently closed one-piece, flush-fitting windows. This arrangement gradually came to be fitted as standard on late G models, starting with the B-17G-50-BO (42-102379), -50-VE (44-8101)), and -25-DL (42-27989) (windows only). The two machine guns were also installed on the lower sill on a K-6 mount (on Douglas-built blocks from -40-DL (44-6001)), instead of on the older K-5 swivel post. USAF

followed on the 28th, in *Betty Jane*. The strange, winged 2,000lb (900kg) bombs which had greeted Johnson's arrival at Molesworth in late April were now loaded under the wings of the B-17s for a glide-bombing attack on the Eifeltor marshalling yards at Cologne. These bombs were actually GB-1 'grapefruit' bombs, produced by fitting small wings and empennage to a 2,000lb GP M34 bomb, and they were launched from the external wing-racks of B-17s. The 303rd, as well as the other two groups in the 41st Combat Wing, were expected to put two battle formations in the air. The 303rd put nineteen B-17s in the glide-bomb formation, and these departed Molesworth an hour earlier than the second element, which went to oil targets. Johnson recalls:

We crossed the French coast two miles south of Nieuport at 19,500ft [5,900m] and proceeded to Cologne. Our squadron, the 427th, went in first. Starting at 140mph [225km/h], we started a dive until we reached 208mph [335km/h]; at this point we levelled off for a few seconds, and released the bombs nearly 18 miles [30km] from the target. Unfortunately, our bombs, as well as those of the other two groups following, mostly spun in and exploded in fields 15 miles [24km] from the target. Of the fifty-nine B-17s of the 41st Combat Wing, 113 'grapefruit' glide bombs were released at the target and not one bomb came within a mile of that target! However, forty-two hits were scattered throughout Cologne, killing eighty-two people and injuring 1,500 others. The eleven-second delay in the fuse meant that this 2,000lb bomb would possibly skip through town for eleven seconds before exploding. The glide ratio of these bombs was an amazing five to one, which meant that if we dropped them from four miles [6km] high, they would travel twenty miles [32km] before striking the ground. Many of the bombs fell into sections of the city already bombed out by RAF night missions.

Later that evening, on German radio – which we always listened to – William Joyce, or 'Lord Haw-Haw' as he was called, reported that Cologne had been bombed by Allied bombers from an altitude of 40,000ft. [12,200m]. We had quite a laugh about that, since the B-17 wasn't designed to fly quite that high! Three nights later they had figured what really happened, and Lord Haw-Haw said that any airman shot down during such a mission would be executed the same day. He said that it was a terrorist raid, which it turned out to be, although this had not been our intent. This was not the reason that the attempt was never repeated, however. The failure of the system was evident from the results.

was listed as 'major damage', due to the fact that during the bomb drop, our B-17 was forced out of position by neighbouring aircraft. This put us directly behind the lead plane, flown by Lt Bordelon, with our group commander, Colonel Stevens leading the mission; when he dropped his bombs, his 'sky marker' bomb enveloped our plane with a white acid fog and this ruined all the Plexiglas in our plane – so flying home was difficult due to the milky-looking windshield.

Dive-Bombing Cologne

On 25 May, Dick Johnson completed his third mission, a raid on the marshalling yards at Blainville, France. He noted: 'Over enemy territory, almost exactly three hours. We did our part to damage the German war machine for the upcoming invasion.' Two days later he flew a mission to Mannheim in Germany, and another

B-17G-30-DL 42-38113 was the 1,000th Fortress built by the Douglas Aircraft Company at Long Beach, California; it was assigned to the 750th Bomb Squadron, 457th Bomb Group at Glatton, Hunts, and named René III in honour of the wife of the CO, Colonel James R. Luper. On 27 May 1944 he nursed the aircraft back to Glatton for a one-wheel landing after Flak had badly damaged it over Ludwigshafen. On 7 October, Luper led the 'Fireball Outfit' to Politz, whereupon René III was hit in two engines; the fires soon spread and engulfed the starboard wing, causing the outboard engine to fall away. Seven crew, including Luper, jumped from the doomed B-17, which crashed in Stettin Bay, the bomb-load exploding on impact. Luper became a PoW. He was killed in a B-26 crash in February 1953 while serving as deputy inspector general for security at Strategic Air Command. Douglas

(Right) Bombs fall from the bomb-bays of B-17G-35-DL 42-107091/D Forbidden Fruit of the 728th Bomb Squadron, 452nd Bomb Group, over Schwerte, Germany, on 31 May 1944. Capt Edward Skurka put the B-17 down at Rattlesden on 8 May 1944 after Flak had killed his rear gunner. Forbidden Fruit crashlanded on 17 February 1945 and was salvaged on 21 May 1945. Sam Young

The other mission of 28 May, to oil and transportation targets throughout Germany, was met by fierce resistance: upwards of 300 fighters intercepted the heavies, and thirty-two bombers and fourteen fighters were shot down.

Invasion Fever

Missions to Holland and France became the order of the day, and the aircrews who survived quickly notched up theirs. On 5 June, Robert Johnson flew his ninth, to the Cherbourg peninsular, to bomb heavy gun batteries on the coast. It was the eve of D-Day. By the time the Allies stepped ashore on Normandy on 6 June, the German rail and road systems in France and the Low Countries were in a chaotic state, and the sky overhead was clear of German fighters. Every airman, soldier and seaman who took part will never forget D-Day. Lt Beiser's crew in the 303rd was among many who flew, not one, but *two* missions on D-Day. His co-pilot, Dick Johnson, recalls the momentous occasion:

'Today is D-Day,' the briefing officer announced. 'The invasion has already started, and we are going to try to prevent the Germans from bringing up reinforcements. The weather is very bad, and we may bomb by radar,' he said.

Each B-17 was loaded with twelve 500lb [227kg], and two 1,000lb [450kg] bombs, and we wee off at 06:00 with thirty-four aircraft from the 303rd Bomb Group. Two aircraft aborted due to mechanical problems, Lt Bailie of the 358th Bomb Squadron, and Lt Fackler of the 359th Squadron. This was my tenth mission with the 427th Squadron, and Colonel Snyder, the CO, led the low flight. Walter Cronkite flew with Bob Sheets in *Shoo Shoo Baby* of our squadron. We were to bomb a bridge near the invasion coast, but the cloud cover at the target was total, so we were to bomb by PFF [radar]. Sixteen aircraft of the lead group dropped 192 500lb GP bombs, and thirty 1,000lb GP bombs on the target, with unobserved results. Our flight had a radar failure and dropped no bombs, so we flew with these back to base and made ready for our second mission of the day. (Since we tried to bomb, and went over enemy territory for thirty minutes, we got credit for the mission. By bringing our bombs back, we avoided 'Americide', which is the accidental killing of our own troops.)

Our target near the invasion coast in the afternoon was a bridge near Caen that we were unable to bomb because of an equipment failure

B-17G-65-BO 43-37544 **D-Day Doll** of the 710th Bomb Squadron, 447th Bomb Group, gets into the spirit of the occasion at Rattlesden, Suffolk. By the end of the war she had racked up seventy-nine missions, and was then flown back to the States to be cut up for scrap at Kingman, Arizona. USAF

of the lead aircraft. We saw *Flak* again, at a distance, but were not affected. The weather over the French coast was bad, with five-tenths cloud cover, but we could see bits of the inva-

sion activity. The number of wakes from ships and landing craft covered the entire English Channel for miles. We could see smoke on the French coast from all the artillery. To prevent

In the build-up to D-Day, thousands of B-17s, like these B-17Gs at a base air depot in the north-west of England, were stockpiled until they could be issued to the bomb groups. USAF

being fired upon by our own gunners, the fighters and medium bombers had wide, white stripes painted across the wings and fuselage. The heavies didn't bother with this, as we were too high to be seen. We had achieved the desired mastery of the air by this time, and the Germans had a bitter joke amongst themselves: 'If you see a camouflaged airplane, it's British; if you see a shiny, unpainted airplane, it's American; if you don't see any airplane at all, it's German.'

D-Day was the greatest invasion in the history of man. It ultimately established the United States as the premier superpower that it has remained. I feel that my own participation was important, but both my missions on that day were milk runs, as it was for most of the heavy bomber crews who flew that day. Penetrating the thick overcast over England and the Continent was a much greater danger than the Germans had to offer that day. The ground troops who did the fighting deserve the bulk of the credit. Our mission to neutralize the *Luftwaffe* had worked very well, although there would be a resurgence of their fighters in the missions to come.

Altogether, the 8th flew 2,362 bomber sorties, for the loss of only three bombers. The following day further missions were flown in support of the beach-head. Post-D-Day missions were flown to enemy airfields and troop concentrations in France and the Low Countries. Ominously, on 13 June, the first V1 pilotless bombs began falling in the London area, though of the four that were fired across the Channel, only one caused any damage, killing six people and injuring nine others. By 16 June the V1s were arriving at about 100 a day. Crews referred to the V1 sites in the Pas de Calais as *Noball* targets, but they quickly learned to give them a healthy respect, as the 'buzz bomb' sites were usually heavily defended. Bombing the small and easily hidden sites accurately was difficult, if well-nigh impossible, and almost 2,000 Allied airmen were killed in eighty days of assaults on the ski-ramp sites. Only when they were overrun by the Allied ground forces did the V1s cease to inflict destruction on southern England, but not before they had killed over 6,000 people and injured 18,000 more.

The B-17s returned to oil targets again, and on 20 June the Fortresses bombed refineries and oil storage dumps at Hamburg-Harburg. The 303rd Bomb Group went to the Rhenani-Ossag Minerallwerkes A.G. at Harburg, a suburb of Hamburg. It was Dick Johnson's eighteenth mission, and he recalls it well:

The *Flak* was so thick you couldn't see through it, and one of our aircraft was lost to *Flak* just after 'bombs away'. The Germans were determined to protect their oil supplies at any cost, and the *Flak* explosions were constant and unrelenting – the angry red centre of some of the explosions meant that they were very close. If you heard *Flak* explode, it meant it was within 50ft [15m] of our plane – the very loud engine noise would drown out the noise of any explosion farther away. Likewise, if you felt a jolt from a *Flak* explosion, it meant it was within 25ft [7.6m] or less of the plane. I saw plenty of red centres, and I heard several of them, too, during our 41mile [66km] (!) bomb run. Our groundspeed against the wind was barely over two miles [3km] per minute, allowing the German defenders a good chance to track us in the straight and level flight from the IP to the target.

Just before the IP, the B-17 flown by 1st Lt J.T. Parker, nearly dead ahead of us, suffered a double engine failure due to *Flak* damage; he was able to keep up for a short while and dropped his bombs with the formation, but couldn't keep up with the homeward-bound formation, and lost altitude though still under control. When we last saw him he was down near the ground, still under control, but he never made it back to base and all nine crew members became guests of the German government for the rest of the war.

We busted the target wide open. One group ahead of us had also hit it, and smoke was visible during the entire bomb run. There were

many great explosions among the oil storage tanks and on the cracking plant itself. From our vantage point at 26,500ft [8,000m] we could see clearly that the target was completely covered by bomb bursts. We hadn't bothered to carry any incendiary bombs on this trip, and undoubtedly they would have been redundant! However, only two of our B-17s escaped damage on this mission. Eleven suffered major damage, three crewmen were wounded by *Flak*, and one plane was lost. In fact it is remarkable that only one plane was shot down. Our plane suffered over 263 *Flak* holes of various sizes, and yet not one crew member was hit, and the plane flew as if nothing had happened to it. Several crew members each received an extra DFC for this mission. For my part, I lived through the mission and received an Oak Leaf Cluster to my previously awarded Air Medal (given to each crewman upon completion of six missions). This was my third Air Medal. Our seven-hour, two-minute flight had us over enemy territory for one hour and fifty minutes.

Frantic and *Cadillac*

On 21 June, the 8th flew the first of four *Frantic* shuttle missions to Russia during June–September 1944. The 4th Combat Wing and a composite from the Third Division led the 8th to Berlin with the First and Second Divisions behind. After bombing a synthetic oil refinery just south of Berlin, Fortresses of the 13th and 45th

B-17F-115-BO 42-30715 CC-Y Cincinnatti Queen **of the 569th Bomb Squadron, 390th Bomb Group, which in May 1944 became** Blues In The Night. **On 21 June 1944 she went MIA.** Mike Bailey

B-17Gs of the 96th Bomb Group pass the Alps en route to the Ain and Haute Savoie on 25 June 1944 to drop supplies to the FFI (Forces Françaises de l'Intériour, or the 'French Forces of the Interior') in Operation Zebra. The 96th Bomb Group contributed fourteen aircraft to the operation, including B-17G-60-BO 42-97556 MZ-G in the 413th Bomb Squadron. Some 2,088 supply containers were dropped by 176 B-17s of the Third Bomb Division, who were escorted by large formations of fighters, on the mission to five drop zones; only two B-17s were lost, and two others aborted with mechanical problems. Further large-scale drops were made in July, on 1 August and in September. In the early dawn of 11 April 1944 (a day when eleven of the 96th Bomb Group's B-17s failed to return from a raid on Rostock), 42-97556 was shot down by a Ju 88 intruder while en route to fly PFF for the 390th Bomb Group at Framlingham; it crashed at Great Glemham, Suffolk, killing one of Lt MacGreggor's crew and wounding two others. via Steve Adams

B-17G-35-DL 42-107073/J of the 730th Bomb Squadron, 452nd Bomb Group, crashlanded at Honington, Suffolk, on 30 July 1944. The Fortress was repaired, and it finished its days at Kingman, Arizona, in November 1945. via Ian McLachlan

Combat Wings, the Third Bomb Division, escorted all the way by sixty-four P-51s of the 4th and 352nd FGs, flew on to landing fields at Poltava and Mirgorod in the Ukraine, while the rest of the force returned to East Anglia. In all, 144 B-17s landed in Russia, seventy-three at Poltava, the remainder at Mirgorod. The P-51s landed at Piryatin. An audacious German raid on Poltava on 21/22 June destroyed forty-seven B-17s and damaged twenty-nine others. On 26 June, seventy-two Fortresses bombed an oil refinery target in Rumania; they then staged through Foggia, Italy, and on 5 July bombed a marshalling yard at Beziers, France, en route to England. The entire tour covered 6,000 miles (9,650km), ten countries, and 29¼ hours of operational flying.

On 14 July, during Operation *Cadillac*, 322 8th AF B-17s made a mass drop of 3,780 supply containers to the IFF (French Forces of the Interior) in the Ain and Haute-Savoie regions of south-east France. On 1 August, while heavy bomb groups struck at airfields in France, some B-17 groups again parachuted supplies to the French Underground movement.

On 6 August, the B-17s struck at Berlin and oil and manufacturing centres in the Reich, while seventy-six Fortresses in the 95th and 390th Bomb Groups, escorted by sixty-four P-51s, flew another shuttle mission to Russia, bombing the Focke Wulf plant at Rahmel in Poland en route. After the bombing the two groups flew on to their shuttle base at Mirgorod in Russia, scene of such devastation two months before. During their sojourn they flew a mission to the Trzebinia synthetic oil refinery and returned to Russia before flying to Italy on 8 August, bombing two Rumanian airfields en route. On 12 August the shuttle force flew back to Britain on the last stage of their journey, bombing Toulouse-Francaal airfield en route. Not a singe Fortress was lost during the entire shuttle operation.

The last of the *Frantic* shuttle missions was flown on 11 September, when seventy-five B-17s and sixty-four P-51s of the 8th AF attacked Chemnitz and flew on to the Soviet Union. On 13 September, the B-17s bombed a steel works at Diósygör, Hungary and landed in Italy. Five days later, on 18 September, 117 B-17s of the 8th Air Force in England dropped 1,284 containers of ammunition, guns and supplies to Poles in beleaguered Warsaw – but only 130 fell into the right hands.

B-17G-55-BO 42-102598 EP-F Super Rabbit **of the 351st Bomb Squadron, 100th Bomb Group, which crashlanded at Thorpe Abbotts on 28 July 1944. The aircraft was salvaged on 30 July.** via Mike Bailey

B-17F 42-6087 LD-Z Royal Flush **of the 418th Bomb Squadron, 100th Bomb Group, which was shot down on 11 August 1944 – its 75th mission – during a raid on the airfield at Villacoublay near Paris. Four of 2nd Lt Alfred Aske Jr's crew were killed, and five were made PoW.** Charles H. Nekvasil

B-17 Versus B-24 Controversy

During the last week of July, General Doolittle carried out the first stage of his plan to convert all five Liberator groups of the Third Bomb Division (which had arrived in England in April) to the B-17. The 486th Bomb Group at Sudbury and the 487th Bomb Group at Lavenham, which formed the 92nd Wing, were taken off operations for conversion to the B-17. Between the end of August and mid-September the three B-24 groups of the 93rd Combat Wing – the 34th, 490th and 493rd Bomb Groups – also changed over to the B-17.

The 493rd Bomb Group's conversion to Fortresses took place over one weekend with a quick flick through the 'handbook', a couple of briefings, and then straight into the 'practical'. 1st Lt Richard B. Lewis, one of the group's most experienced pilots, recalls:

Capt Earl Johnson took me on a guided tour of the 'new' aircraft; he pointed out what to look for on the pre-flight, and he also showed me the 'art' of climbing into the aircraft through the nose-hatch – difficult even for an acrobat, let alone an airman in full flight clothing! Taxi and take-off were uneventful, having overcome the difference in technique from a nose-wheel to a tail-wheel aircraft. The B-17 really was a dream to fly – you didn't have to fight it like the B-24. After an hour we feathered one engine, with hardly any difference noticed in the flight characteristics. Then Capt Johnson took his hands off the controls; he feathered the other engine on the same wing, and still she flew on with no variation in course! We finished off the conversion with three landings and then one more circuit, followed by a landing and taxi back to dispersal. I was now fully qualified, and the next day I commenced training the rest of the group's pilots!

1st Lt Gordon W. Weir, a navigator in 1st Lt Ellis M. Woodward's crew in the 861st Bomb Squadron, 493rd Bomb Group, had more to say:

Commanders of the Third Air Division found it difficult to coordinate an attack by a mixed armada of 24s and 17s. Standard procedure called for the 24s to fly about 10mph [16km] faster and a few thousand feet lower than the 17s. As for me, I appreciated the extra speed the 24 carried us through the *Flak*. Flyers of the 17s, on the other hand, claimed it was better to be higher, above the *Flak* batteries. Our B-24J had served us well, bringing us back from ten missions into France and Belgium, and three into Germany. I'd become used to seeing the slight flutter at the tips of the long silver wings; I was comfortable with my station and familiar with other positions in the plane.

The B-17 was aptly described as 'a plane big on the outside, small on the inside'. The wing was a few feet shorter than that of the B-24, but much wider. The fuselage was as round as a cigar, tapering to an end tipped with a broad tailpiece and capped by a lofty fin. The plane perched in the earth, nose in the air, tail to the ground, like a bird ready to soar.

Inside, arrangements were much like those of our Liberator, the chief difference being the absence of power turrets (with a gunner inside) at both nose and tail. Ours was the latest model Flying Fortress, the B-17G, armed with twin .50 calibre guns in a chin turret. Besides aiming our bombs, bombardier Mike Wright was to manipulate the turret with controls which resembled the handlebars of a bicycle. Mike's station was directly behind the large Plexiglas bubble capping the

nose; the Norden bombsight, by which he could fly the plane on the run to the target, was mounted in front of him. On either side of his seat were levers and panels of dials and switches feeding data to and from the Norden. I sat on the left, behind Mike, my charts, protractors, circular slide rules and log spread out on a shelf-like desk. An airspeed indicator, altimeter, radio compass, and driftmeter were at hand for dead reckoning. To my left was our trap-door entrance to the nose. It could also serve as our emergency exit; indeed, in common parlance it was the 'escape hatch'.

We could get to other parts of the plane through a passage around the bulkhead separating us from the cockpit. Behind the bulkhead,

Lt Gordon W. Weir, navigator, B-17G-80-BO 43-38253 Ole Rambler **in the 861st Bomb Squadron, 493rd Bomb Group. For protection he is wearing an M-3** Flak **helmet (the ear piece protection plates are raised), and a** Flak **vest.** Gordon Weir

above us on the left, sat 'Woody' at his command post; Bill assisted him from the right-hand seat. Mike and I could wave to them from the Plexiglas observation dome. The pilots were fronted by a complex array of instruments and controls, and looked out of windows that were none too large. Sgt Vales, as engineer, usually stood behind them monitoring the engine gauges; in combat he climbed into the top turret. Behind Vale's station was the bomb-bay, and a narrow catwalk led aft. Mike would balance on this catwalk as he removed cotter pins from the arming mechanisms of each bomb.

Stations for four airmen were in the rear of the plane. Sgt Sutton, no longer needed as a

gunner up front, worked the radio at a desk behind the bomb-bay; he also fired one of the two pivoting waist guns. Just aft of the radio desk, Sgt Archer climbed down into the powered ball turret, as he did on the B-24; farther back, Sergeant Spinney stood opposite Sutton at the other waist gun. In the narrow confines of the tapering fuselage Sgt Kenawell handled the twin 50s at the tail.

As for our feelings about the B-17 versus the B-24, we admired whatever plane we were flying. The 24 could carry more bombs farther and faster, and its front and rear power turrets meant that it was better armed than the 17. Nevertheless, we instantly liked our new Flying Fortress, amusingly named *Ramp Happy Pappy*. The pilots found it easier to fly, and Mike and I liked it for the increased visibility from the nose – we could make ground checks more easily. We all believed that the 17 was a rugged plane and that certainly proved true.

For a brief period the 493rd and other B-24 groups in the Third Bomb Division stood down – the war went on without us as we became familiar with our new machines. The transition went quickly, however, and the group was commended for it. Less than three weeks after receiving our Flying Fortress, we were riding it through the *Flak* on our fifteenth mission. [The 493rd flew its first B-17 mission on 8 September 1944, when the target was Mainz, Germany.]

The cold, grey dampness that was the English weather at times cast a cold grey dampness on our spirits. Perhaps this began as early as the murky days of September. The ground war was not going according to plan, certainly not our plan. In July and August our troops had swept across France and Belgium, over the border of Holland and into the Aachen corner of Germany. Hitler had barely survived a bomb planted in his bunker – and yet the war went on. Early in September our skies were filled with twin-engined Douglas Dakotas either carrying paratroops or towing gliders, part of an airborne and armoured thrust into the Netherlands which aimed to flank German defences and bring the war to an end. If it had succeeded, we'd have been home for Christmas, and Anne Frank and many an anonymous civilian and soldier would have survived the year. As it was, rain, clouds, and a refurbished German army snuffed the attack at Arnhem, and the war became truly a wasting grind.

CHAPTER EIGHT

An 'Abundance of Strength'*

8th Air Force Operations, August 1944–May 1945

The 15th Air Force in Italy helped deny Germany the precious oil it needed from Ploesti, but several large and important refining centres, many of them at the very limit of the B-17's range, were scattered throughout the Reich. The fact that they were dispersed throughout Germany made a concentrated and effective offensive extremely difficult. It fell to Fortresses of the 8th Air Force to strike at these targets, from Politz on the Baltic coast, to Brux in Czechoslovakia. In August, regardless of the fact that psychological breakdowns were closely related to the operational intensity of that time, the combat tour in England was extended to thirty-five missions on the ground that individual missions appeared less hazardous. Oil targets were the order of the day, and 8th Air Force attacks on oil-refinery targets in the ever-shrinking Reich continued in earnest. *Flak*

B-17G-30-DL 42-38091 in flight. The type A-2A ball turret was first introduced in this block (42-38084). Apart from changes in armament – starting with B-17G-25-DL (42-37989), enclosed waist guns were introduced on Douglas-built models – important improvements continued to be made throughout the G-model's life. One of these was the 'formation stick', an electric power boost arrangement for the control column activated by a pistol grip, which was introduced during -100-BO, -70-DL, and -80-VE blocks, early in 1945. via Mike Bailey

* Motto of the 306th Bomb Group

was an ever-present danger, and it could prey on the minds of most crews, as S/Sgt William C. Marshall 'Flaps' Brownlow, tail gunner in 2nd Lt William W. 'Woody' Bowden's crew in the 861st Bomb Squadron, 493rd Bomb Group, at Debach, recalls:

The missions we flew were exhausting and frightening. One of the most frightening experiences was the *Flak* that we had to fly through, with almost no manoeuvrability. The words 'Flak happy' were understood and experienced by most airmen. The *Flak* would tear into our planes, making loud noises and causing many ships to crash or blow up, and because of this continual exposure most of us would jump at any noise, even the dropping of a soap dish. We would laugh at ourselves and kid each other, but this reaction remained with most of us for months after completing our missions. Nevertheless our morale was excellent – we felt proud of American and British efforts to destroy Nazi Germany, and we knew that we would win the war. We also knew that our people at home were backing us 100 per cent!

Bloody Magdeburg

During September 1944, German oil production plummeted to only 7,000 tons and Draconian measures were called for. Reichminister Albert Speer was given 7,000 engineers from the army and unlimited 'slave labour' to reconstruct the synthetic oil-producing plants. Hundreds of additional *Flak* guns were erected around the *Hydriesfestungen*, as the plants became known, and the workers, who now came under the direct supervision of the SS, built deep shelters in which to take cover during air raids. (Plants quickly demonstrated a remarkable ability to regain full production quotas and between bombing raids were able to produce 19,000 tons during October, and 39,000 tons in November.)

12 September 1944 was the worst day in the short history of the 'Helton's Hellcats', as the 493rd Bomb Group was known, in honour of their first CO, Colonel Elbert Helton. A total of 217 B-17s of the Third Bomb Division attacked the Brabag synthetic oil refinery, Rothensee, and the ordnance depot at Friedrichstadt, in the old Hanse town of Magdeburg again. The Brabag synthetic oil plant, built in 1936, the Junkers aero engine factory at Magdeburg/Neustadt, the Krupp tank works at Buckau, and an ordnance depot at Friedrichsstadt, were among the main producers of war materials for Hitler's Germany. Magdeburg was defended by thirteen *Flak* batteries each comprising six, later eight, 88 or 105mm guns, and two railway-mounted *Flak* batteries comprising four 105mm guns. Despite the continual loss of young personnel to the fronts, Germany found it possible to double the numbers of *Grossbatterien* personnel, principally by decreasing the personnel per battery and using about 75,000 *Luftwaffenhelfer* (schoolboys). All schoolboys in Germany at the age of sixteen had to enter the *Flak* school in their neighbourhood. In addition, approximately 15,000 women and girls, 45,000 volunteer Russian PoWs, and 12,000 Croatian soldiers were drafted in to the air defence of the Reich.

Ellis M. Woodward's crew in the 861st Bomb Squadron, at Debach, were up for their first mission in *Ramp Happy Pappy* this day, as 1st Lt Gordon Weir, navigator, explains:

We were to lead the low squadron. In the briefing room the long red tape stretched to a city named Magdeburg, the target a munitions plant on the Elbe river; if we took it out, fewer shells might be thrown at us on future missions. The group made the now-familiar entry into Europe over Egmond-aan-Zee, and then along the edge of the north-west polder in the Zuiderzee of the Netherlands. Then zigging and zagging around known gun batteries, we followed a roundabout route into the heart of north-western Germany. The 493rd was to be the second group over the target. The skies were cloudless, a boon to the bombardiers aiming from above and to the AA gunners aiming from below. [A total of thirty-eight B-17s took off from Debach. Two aircraft aborted, leaving thirty-six to bomb the target.]

All went well until we neared the IP, the Initial Point, a ground feature over which the bomb run to the target would begin. We were then about 50 miles [80km] south-west of Berlin, and I fancied that from my 5-mile [8km] high seat in the sky, I could see the suburbs of the Nazi capital. At the turn over the IP, standard operating procedure was for each group to separate into

Lt Gordon W. Weir, navigator in the 861st Bomb Squadron, 493rd Bomb Group, examines the remains of B-17G *Ramp Happy Pappy* at Woodbridge a few days after Captain Ellis M. Woodward landed the badly shot-up plane on 12 September 1944 at the emergency airfield after suffering AA damage at Magdeburg. Flight engineer Joseph Vales, who manned the mid-upper turret, missed being severely wounded or even killed because on Woodward's orders, he had just come down to manually close the jammed bomb-bay doors; as he did so, a shell exploded in the gun sight. Shrapnel from Flak penetrated the nose compartment and wounded bombardier Mike Wright in the chest as he triggered the bomb release. Radioman-waist gunner T/Sgt Joseph Sutton was wounded by flying splinters when a cannon shell ripped up a piece of plywood flooring. S/Sgt Blair Archer also had a narrow escape when the swivel of his ball turret was shattered by enemy action. *Ramp Happy Pappy* was beyond repair and was pushed into the scrap pile at the base. Gordon W. Weir

three squadrons for the attack: the lead squadron goes in first, the high squadron then follows, and the low squadron heads in last. The group ahead of us had already shaken out into the bomb run, and our lead squadron was swinging toward the target. I heard Woody wonder aloud, 'Why don't they turn?' because the high squadron, impeded by winds or other troubles, seemed late in bending toward Magdeburg. Meanwhile our squadron had to veer off so the high squadron's bombs would not fall on us. When we could finally make our turn, our new course took us into a violent headwind that slowed our approach to the target to an agonizing crawl.

My job on the bomb run was to help Mike pick out the target, but he quickly identified the buildings near the river. Then for a while we had little to do but wait and watch. Up ahead the *Flak* was fierce: 'So thick you could walk on it!', we'd wise-crack after a mission – but not when we were flying into a blackening sky. The squadrons in front of us were being lashed by shrapnel. Suddenly, one of their B-17s burst into flames and then exploded; nothing was left but four thin black streaks as the burning engines plunged earthward. Off to the side another 17 was twisting down. I wondered how many men were struggling to get out, held back by the forces of the spin.

Our turn came. Around us flashes of red blossomed into black columns of smoke, and our plane bounced in the turbulent air. Then I felt a sharp thump, meaning that it was punctured. Mike was bent over the bombsight taking aim at the munitions plant; the plane rose a bit as the bomb racks emptied. Instead of calling out 'bombs away!' Mike yelled, 'I'm hit!' and began clawing away at his clothes to reveal the wound. I saw the hole in the Plexiglas and nervously relayed Mike's words on the interphone.

My message was drowned by an urgent call from Sergeant Kenawell, firing the tail guns. 'Fighters! Fighters!' Our plane shuddered from repeated hits, and a Focke Wulf 190 flashed by over our left wing. Our plane nosed steeply down. I grabbed my parachute and tore open the escape hatch. What a long, chilling way down! Mike, too, was busy fastening his parachute. I was still on the intercom expecting the command to bale out, when Woody let us know that our precipitous descent of thousands of feet was because much of our oxygen supply had been shot out (at 30,000ft [9,000m] an airman dies quickly from anoxia). We were going on. I looked around: of the eleven other planes in our squadron, only one remained.

The 493rd were savaged by enemy fighter attacks, and in just nine minutes – 11:09 to 11:20 hours – at an altitude of 23,000ft (7,000m), seven B-17s were shot down in repeated *Luftwaffe* fighter attacks. Four of

the Forts went down in flames and one exploded. 1st Lt Albert L. Tucker's crew were all killed except for S/Sgt Edward J. Borowy, who had been taken off the crew when the ball turrets were removed from the B-24s (then on B-17s the nose gunner went into the ball turret). It was their thirteenth mission. Gordon Weir continues:

Great strips of aluminium had been torn off our left wing – engines were leaking oil – the plane vibrated: one more blow from the fighters would surely finish us off. Where were they? Yet all these happenings were but a minute of a lifetime.

I returned to my desk to find out exactly where we were and to figure the heading to England. Could we get there? We learned that the elevators at the tail had been torn up. One of

the bounces on the bomb run had been from a shell that had ripped through the open bomb-bay, tearing out the rubber raft stowed above; so if we ditched in the sea, we'd have only our inflatable Mae Wests to keep us afloat. Fragments of 20mm shells from the fighter cannons had cut other holes in the fuselage, and splinters blasted from the plywood floor had cut Sergeant Sutton in the face. Over the intercom Sutton and Mike claimed their wounds were minor. And there was more good news, because Kenawell had destroyed an attacking Me 109.

The German fighters did not come back. Though at our lower flying level we were an easier target for anti-aircraft gunners, we escaped

further harassment by Flak. To lighten the load we tossed out all equipment we could spare, and the waist windows were chopped out to make for easier exits.

After eternal four hours, England lay before us. Woody, uncertain of the integrity of the plane, had Sergeant Vales relay the option of baling out. We all stayed. As Woody and Bill coaxed our riddled Fortress down to the long runway of the emergency landing field at Woodbridge, the rest of us huddled together on the plywood floor aft of the bomb-bay, heads down, clasping our knees, waiting for whatever was to happen. As the plane touched down, George Kenawell jumped to a waist window, but I hollered, 'Hold on!' because surely would have been hurt if he had leaped out while the plane bumped and lurched at high speed along the ground. George stayed, though

B-17Gs of the 452nd Bomb Group in flight. B-17G-25-VE 42-97697/Q, which is sporting 413th Bomb Squadron (96th Bomb Group) codes (MZ), went MIA on 2 October 1944. B-17G-45-BO 42-97308/P Hairless Joe **in the 728th Bomb Squadron went MIA on 31 March 1945.** via Robert M. Foose

he called back 'But what about fire?' He too had seen burning planes that day.

Finally, brakes and tyres gone, the plane slowed, swerved, and stumbled to a halt near an edge of the runway. We poured out, full of amazed gratitude at our survival. As for our oil-stained, *Flak*-lacerated Flying Fortress, *Ramp Happy Pappy* was happy no more, and the remains were for the scrap pile. But we owed much to the sturdiness of the B-17 – if similar damage had been done to us flying a thin-winged B-24, we'd have fallen.

In the 860th Bomb Squadron, 2nd Lt James P. Kittleson and Capt Wesley E. Carter and their crews were the two other B-17s that failed to return. Carter's ship was hit directly in the bomb-bay, and all ten men baled out. The fighter escort arrived just after 'bombs away'. Lt Brown only just managed to make it home, and his aircraft was so badly shot up it had to be salvaged. S/Sgt Hayward F. Deese Jr, engineer/left waist gunner in George M. Durgin's crew in the 863rd Bomb Squadron, recalls:

We were leading the high element of the 863rd Squadron in 43-38264 *Ulpy*. After the bomb run, Fw 190s with 20mm cannons hit us from the rear. On the first pass they shot down nine out of the twelve B-17s in the 863rd Squadron; our B-17 and two wing crews were left. Then they came after us and shot down the wing crews, and shot us up with 20mm cannon and 13mm MG. I got three pieces of 20mm in my back, and Don Gray, the right waist gunner, had a 20mm explode in his face and 13mm slugs in each leg. I was standing on two *Flak* jackets, and when I picked them up to return them after the mission there was a hole about 8in (20cm) in diameter under them, and a lot of 20mm shrapnel right where I had been standing. The *Flak* jackets were in shreds, but they surely saved my legs and my life.

Durgin called me to look at the left elevator damage, but I knew what was wrong because I had put a burst of 50 cal through it, shooting at an Me 109. We landed at Brussels and Gray, Ray H. Higginbotham Jr, tail gunner, and myself were put in the Canadian 1st Army Field Hospital. Gray died that night. When we flew back to Debach the next day we were the only crew out of twelve from the 863rd Squadron to make it back, and we were two men short.

Higginbotham was so badly wounded that he never flew again. Frank Deese was patched up, and he finished his tour of thirty-five missions with Durgin's crew. Gordon Weir has vivid memories of his war experiences at this time:

The 493rd never again suffered a downing of planes like that on 12 September, but commonly, one or two planes failed to return from a mission. As the months wore on, I noticed we didn't make any effort to guide or even to greet replacement crews – as veterans, our accumulated wisdom wasn't more than they could get from manuals and briefings; besides, we had enough emotional ties just with our old crews from McCook.

Two weeks after losing most of our squadron, we were again leading a formation into northwestern Germany; replacement crews filled the emptied slots. Our assignment was to destroy a tank factory at Bremen. The battle at Magdeburg was much on my mind, and because of this, the Bremen mission, number sixteen in our count, was a most difficult one for me and perhaps for the others in the crew. I was petrified as we headed into the thick *Flak* over the target, and exhausted by the time we rolled into the hard stand at Debach. After Bremen I was in better command of myself, and at least masked my fears. Fortunately my duties as a navigator kept me totally absorbed during much of our flights.

Mike also faced the Bremen mission with foreboding, and as an extra precaution rounded up extra *Flak* vests. This twentieth-century armour consisted of metal plates sewn into heavy cloth; each vest weighed a hefty 20lb [9kg] but it did offer some protection against shrapnel. Mike lined our compartment with them. I appreciated the extra shielding, but Woody and Bill found the added weight forward made the plane more difficult to fly.

Our squadron's bombing on this mission was not good. A strong tailwind made for hurried aiming, and our bombs fell far from the tank factory, probably farther from the target than on any mission before or after. Months later, after many more grim ventures over Germany, Mike and I were wryly amused when the Bremen mission was cited among the missions in which we earned the Distinguished Flying Cross for displaying 'courage', 'technical skill' and 'devotion to duty' in a 'devastating' attack 'destroying vital enemy installations'.

One dismally wet afternoon in late November I was splashing along toward the mess hall behind two airmen unknown to me, and I couldn't help but overhear part of their loud talk: 'We had to abort and come back over Germany alone. We thought about the rockets falling on London and decided to teach the Germans a lesson, so on every little village we passed over, we flipped a bomb smack in the middle of it!' Something to think about. War is brutal and brutalizing. If it went on long enough, we'd all be brutes.

All our final sixteen missions were against well-defended targets in Germany: nine times we disrupted the rail network; three times we burned oil installations; three times we blasted armament factories; once we aided our ground troops with a carpet bombing attack. To describe each of these missions would be tedious, and only a few stand out in my mind. Indeed, they were all much alike.

In the black hours of the morning a flashlight in my face and my name gruffly called would wake me from a fitful sleep. We'd all have hit the sack knowing we would be up the next day. After dressing, ablutions and a solemn breakfast, we'd walk through the darkness to the briefing. The crews flying took seats in one of the larger Nissen buildings. The front of the room had a raised platform not unlike a theatre stage, and we expected theatrics. The map covering the end wall was shrouded by a curtain, and gasps, sighs and muted wisecracks accompanied the revelations when the curtain was pulled back and we saw where we were to go. The prescribed route would be marked by a length of red tape, and we would then be told the nature of the target and the place of the 493rd in the 8th Air Force attack. A meteorologist spoke on the weather over England and Germany, his winter forecasts studded with probabilities.

After the weatherman had played his role, the assembled crews broke up for special briefings. Woody and Bill learned about the place of our plane in the formation, and the timing and mechanics of the assembly. Mike went off to get data on the bomb-load and to study the map and photos of the target. I and other navigators reviewed the details of group and wing assembly. We would be furnished with the charts for the day, given another weather scan with emphasis on the winds aloft, and told the stations to be used on our Gee boxes. Gee was a sophisticated electronics system given to all navigators in late 1944, developed by the British to help their flyers home in the dark. By moving markers on a fluorescent screen to line up on pulsed beams from designated stations, in theory, using special charts, you could pinpoint the plane's position. Alas, I never trusted this bit of modern technology: on my first use of this apparatus, outward-bound over the North Sea, readings from the yellow-green tube showed that we were in Sweden, then Spain – though we did receive a post-mission apology admitting to the blunder of giving us the wrong charts. However, unlike the night flyers of the RAF, we in daylight had little need for Gee over England. Over the Continent we found our screens snowed out by German jamming.

After our several briefings we drew our equipment for the flight. We especially appreciated the electric suits, which protected us from frostbite, or worse. Four to six miles up in the blue it was always cold, commonly 45° below in the summer, and 60° below in the winter. In the air I was constantly taking off the cumbersome gloves in order to write in the log, but I hurried to get my hands back in the warmth. The big decision in the equipment room was whether to indulge in the comfort of heated boots. But how far could a parachuted airman walk in felt shoes? Early on I favoured the electric comfort and just carried my leather boots aboard for emergency exits, but after 12 September I chose to suffer the cold and wear boots for walking.

Over our flight suit we pulled on a yellow life vest, a Mae West, to be inflated if we fell in the sea. Then we strapped on a parachute harness and stowed the clip-on parachute carefully near our seat. We heaved aboard our heavy *Flak* vest and helmet for the time of testing, and put in our pockets an escape kit that held a small nylon map of western Europe and a few French bills – just to remind us of the perils ahead.

A truck carried the crew to the hard stand where our plane was parked; each of us would be busy checking our equipment and going over the flight plan and our briefing notes. Then as the darkness thinned, we waited for signals. Three or four hours would have passed since the flashlight in my face. Then an arcing flare from the control tower, and the groundcrew pulled the chocks from the wheels: we trundled into our position in the take-off parade of thirty-six planes. Another flare, and in thirty-second intervals the 17s began moving down the runway and climbing into the air. Assembly would take another one or two hours before we headed for Germany.

Once on our way, at common operating altitudes of 15,000 to 30,999ft [4,750 to 9,450m], I and others of the crew were firmly tied to our plane. Wires from headphones and throat mike linked me to the intercom, and a tube from my oxygen mask pulled from the plane's life-giving supply. A cord from the electric suit was plugged into the wall. Moving around in the plane was awkward, and if encumbered with *Flak* vest and helmet, it was downright difficult.

Over Germany we always did what we had been ordered to do as best we could. Our mission duties did not end with our plane rolling again on the home runway, however, and after coming to a stop on the hard stand we would first clear our compartment of equipment and records. We then heaved our baggage on a waiting truck and climbed in for the trip back to the equipment room where we turned in our flight gear. Next we made our way back to where the mission began, the briefing room, where we would be debriefed – that is, an intelligence officer quizzed us about the *Flak*, fighters, and details of the flight. After we had answered his queries, he gave us a chit for a draught of government whiskey. This perk I usually passed up, giving my piece of paper to someone who would

B-17G-1-BO 42-31053 BX-W Stingy of the 338th Bomb Squadron, 96th Bomb Group, which was lost in a mid-air collision over Towcester, Northamptonshire, during a training flight on 9 October 1944. B-17F-75-DL 42-3510 AW-P, piloted by 2nd Lt Jack C. Core, in the 337th Bomb Squadron, rose straight up and hit B-17G-70-BO 43-37684 AW-E in the nose with its tail section, and 510 was sheared in two. Piloted by Lt Nick Jorgenson, Stingy (which had been named for General Frederick Anderson, 8th AF Commander Operation's young son), hit 684 with its rudder, and also broke in half. Core's crew of four were killed, as were all seven of Jorgensen's crew. via Mike Bailey

appreciate the beverage; frankly I was often too tired to enjoy anything but the release of sleep. Combat days were long: from the time we left our hut to our return was commonly twelve to sixteen hours. For one trip, to maintain alertness, I accepted the doctor's offer of a stimulant pill, but this was a mistake because the drug wound me up so tight I couldn't unwind for another twenty-four hours.

'Nothing can stop the Army Air Corps' … *Except*, our missions often didn't go off as planned because of weather. In the closing months of 1944, capricious winds off the North Atlantic brought sudden, unexpected changes in the English skies. All usually went well until after the briefing, and getting our equipment, and checking everything in the plane. Then we would wait with increasing impatience and boredom for signals from the control tower: the morning light might become a darker grey; fog become mists; mists become rain. Alternatively, skies might clear and still no signal would

come, and with bright blue overhead we could not understand why we were not up there and on our way. Most likely the fields of too many other groups were still closed in, or perhaps conditions had worsened over the target. If we hadn't taken off by late morning, the mission would be cancelled. 'Scrubbed' missions left us with mixed feelings, because as we retreated to our hut with the morning's efforts wasted, we knew the *Flak* we avoided this day must be faced on another – and only flights into Germany would lead to the flight home. More irritating and wasteful than missions scrubbed on the ground were those scrubbed in the air.

Yet the weather could offer protection as well as hazards. On nine of our last sixteen missions we attacked targets covered by clouds: gunners below were denied visual aiming and had to rely on radar tracking, and from the waist windows Spinney and Sutton eagerly tossed out chaff, metallic strips to fog the tracking screens. Nevertheless, the *Flak* was fierce enough. On these missions our plane flew alongside a Pathfinder plane, whose crews would use an array of radar instruments to pick out the target hidden beneath the winter clouds; Mike would toggle our bombs when the Pathfinder dropped his. However, we wouldn't learn the results of our work until a bold pilot in a stripped-down P-38 dashed under the muck to photograph the target.

Mercilessburg

Gordon Weir, in the 493rd Bomb Group, went to Merseburg, not far from Leipzig in central Germany, on 10 October, a clear day at Debach.

We set out for the continent without a PFF leader. 'Mercilessburg' was the most fearsome target in Europe, the oil refinery and chemical complex, vital to the Nazi war effort, being surrounded by more guns and more heavy guns than Berlin. These guns were grouped in large batteries, were aimed by radar, and fired in unison to batter the sky with clouds of shrapnel. The 8th had lost many planes over this target, and the 493rd had already been cut up there. We were well into Germany and had dodged some *Flak* when a radio message turned us around. Because we'd been under fire, we were credited with a combat mission, even though we had not flown through the maelstrom of steel waiting for us at Merseburg. Five weeks later no recall message came, and on the wing of a Pathfinder we were flying through the storm of steel over Merseburg.

The Merseburg refineries were bombed again on 2 November when the B-17s were assigned the vast I.G. *Farbenindustrie's* synthetic oil refinery at Leuna, 3 miles (5km) to the south of Merseburg. It was rated the number one priority target, and was estimated to be producing 10 per cent of all Germany's synthetic oil and a third of all the enemy's ammonia and other chemicals. At briefing, crews were warned that German fuel and replacement pilots were in such short supply that Hermann Goering, the *Luftwaffe* chief, was massing his forces to strike a telling blow on a single mission. All they needed was an opportunity.

The thirty-five aircraft in the 457th Bomb Group formation were blown 35 miles (56km) off course and away from the target by a 50-knot wind, so they flew on alone and sought the secondary target at Bernberg. The 'Fireballs' were therefore out on a limb and at the mercy of more than 400 fighters which were in the vicinity. At 12:48 hours the 'Fireballs' had still not joined the rest of the Divisional Bomber Stream, and came under attack from about forty German fighters.

Attacks were made on the low squadron from 6 to 8 o'clock low. The American gunners opened up on the Bf 109s and Fw 190s and some fighters did go down. But then one by one, the 'Fireballs' fell out of formation and hurtled down. *Lady Margaret* had its fin severed by the wing of a passing Fw 190, and several other hits sent it down in flames; it exploded shortly afterwards with only two men baling out in time. *Prop Wash* followed her down, and another seven B-17s exploded or crashed with a further nine being badly damaged. Only the timely intervention by Mustangs saved the group from total annihilation.

'Valor to Victory'*

It was for his actions on this day that Lt Robert Feymoyer, a navigator in the 447th Bomb Group, was posthumously awarded

* Motto of the 34th Bomb Group

the Medal of Honor. Feymoyer's B-17 was rocked by three *Flak* bursts, which showered the aircraft with shrapnel; Feymoyer himself was hit in the back and the side of his body, but he refused all aid despite his terrible wounds so that he might navigate the Fortress back to Rattlesden. He was propped up in his seat so he could read his charts, and the crew did what they could for him. It was not until they reached the North Sea that Feymoyer agreed to an injection of morphine. He died shortly after the aircraft landed at Rattlesden.

Losses were so bad on this mission – the 91st Bomb Group lost twelve Fortresses – that groups were stood down for two days following the raid. On 9 November, two more Medals of Honor were awarded to 8th Air Force B-17 crewmen; this day the heavies returned to tactical missions in support of General George Patton's Third Army, halted at the fortress city of Metz. The 8th was called in to bomb German lines of communication at Saarbrucken, and also enemy gun emplacements to the east and south of Metz to enable the advance through Belgium to continue. The mission was deemed top priority, and at bases throughout East Anglia, Fortresses taxied out in the mist and bad visibility. The conditions were instrumental in the loss of eight bombers during take-offs and landings, and further disasters befell some groups as the mission progressed.

While on the bomb run over Saarbrucken, the 452nd Bomb Group encountered an extremely accurate and intense *Flak* barrage. *Lady Janet*, flown by Lt Donald Gott and Lt William E. Metzger, had three engines badly damaged, and the number one engine set on fire; it began windmilling, and the number two engine was failing rapidly. Number four

showered flames back towards the tail assembly. Flares were ignited in the cockpit and the flames were fuelled by hydraulic fluid leaking from severed cables.

The engineer was wounded in the leg, and a shell fragment had severed the radio operator's arm below his elbow. Metzger left his seat and stumbled back to the radio room and applied a tourniquet to stop the bleeding; however, the radio operator was so weak from pain that he fell unconscious. The bombs were still aboard and Gott was faced with the prospect of the aircraft exploding at any moment. He therefore decided to fly the stricken Fortress to Allied territory a few miles distant and attempt a crashlanding. The bombs were salvoed over enemy territory and all excess equipment was thrown overboard. Lieutenant Metzger unselfishly gave his parachute to one of the gunners after his had been damaged in the fire. As *Lady Janet* neared friendly territory, Metzger went to the rear of the Fortress and told everyone to bale out. He then went back to his seat and the two pilots prepared for a crashlanding with only one engine still functioning and the other three on fire.

An open field was spotted and Gott brought *Lady Janet* in. At about a hundred feet the fire took hold of the fuel tanks and the bomber exploded, killing Gott, Letzer and the radio operator instantly. Both pilots were posthumously awarded the Medal of Honor.

Oil

On 21 November the 8th returned to Merseburg for the first of three more raids on the refineries in a week. Merseburg

B-17G-20-BO 42-31515 The Wild Hare of the 91st Bomb Group in formation. **Of the 8,680 G models built by the BVD pool factories, some 4,750, or more than one third of the total Fortress production, were lost on combat operations. The Wild Hare served as DF-J and N in the 324th Bomb Squadron, and as LL-M in the 401st Bomb Squadron; it failed to return with Lt Robert J. Flint and crew on 26 November 1944.** USAF

B-17Gs of the 835th Bomb Squadron, 486th Bomb Group, flying through Flak.
Clockwise are B-17G-75-BO 43-37966 H8-G – which failed to return when it force-landed on the Continent on 5 November 1944 – followed by a B-17G H8-K Red Raiders **(behind), and (top) B-17G-75-BO 43-37899 H8-T** Rack and Ruin, **which crashlanded at Sudbury on 6 December 1944.** USAF

had become synonymous with *Flak*, and crews hated all missions to the city. On 25 November the bombing was so poor that on 30 November the heavies were once again despatched to the oil plants. The plan called for the leading First Division force to attack the synthetic plant at Zeitz, while the Third Division was to strike at Merseburg itself, 20 miles (32km) to the north. Both the First and Third Bomb Divisions flew the route as briefed to Osnabruck, but the leading First Division formation flew on instead of turning for Zeitz. The Third Division wings were some 5 to 15 miles (8 to 24km) south of the briefed route. The error placed the Third Bomb Division within range of some ninety *Flak* batteries at Zeitz, and the Fortresses were subjected to an intense and accurate barrage. A strong headwind reduced their speed and aided the German defences, who succeeded in shooting down twenty-nine bombers and forty fighter planes on this bleak day.

Battle of the Bulge

On 16 December, using the appalling weather conditions to his advantage, Field Marshal Karl von Rundstedt and his Panzer formations attacked American positions in the forests of the Ardennes on the French-Belgian border, and opened up a salient, or 'bulge', in the Allied lines. In England the Allied air forces were grounded by fog, and it was not until 23 December that the heavies could offer bomber support in the 'Battle of the Bulge'.

On Christmas Eve a record 2,034 8th Air Force bombers and 500 RAF and 9th Air Force bombers took part in the largest single strike flown by the Allied air forces in World War II against German airfields and lines of communication leading to the 'Bulge'. The First Division made a direct tactical assault on airfields in the Frankfurt area and on lines of communication immediately behind the German 'bulge'. Crew were told that their route was specifically planned to go over the ground

troops' positions for morale purposes.

Brigadier General Fred Castle, commander of the Fourth Wing, led the Third Division on his thirtieth mission in a 487th Bomb Group Fortress. All went well until over Belgium, about 35 miles (56km) from Liège, when his right outboard engine burst into flames and the propeller had to be feathered. The deputy lead ship took over, and Castle dropped down to 20,000 ft (6,000m). At this height, however, the aircraft began vibrating badly and he was forced to take it down another 3,000ft (900m) before levelling out. The Fortress was now down to 180mph (290km/h) indicated air speed and being pursued by seven Bf 109s. They attacked and wounded the tail gunner, and left the radar navigator nursing bad wounds in his neck and shoulders. Castle could not carry out any evasive manoeuvres with the full bomb load still aboard, and he could not salvo them for fear of hitting Allied troops on the ground.

Successive attacks by the fighters put another two engines out of action and the B-17 lost altitude. As Castle fought the controls in a vain effort to keep the stricken bomber level, he ordered the crew to bale out. Some of them did so, and then the bomber was hit in the fuel tanks and oxygen systems, and this set the aircraft on fire. Castle attempted to land the flaming bomber in an open field near the Allied lines, but nearing the ground it went into a spin and exploded on impact. Brigadier General Castle was posthumously awarded the Medal of Honor, the highest ranking officer in the 8th Air Force to receive the award.

Gordon Weir, navigator in Ellis Woodward's crew in the 493rd Bomb Group has clear recollections of this time:

On Christmas 1944 we lifted off at dawn. Hitler was initiating his last attack, the Battle of the Bulge, and a week of foul weather had protected the advancing Germans. Skies had finally cleared the day before, and an immense armada of more than 2,000 aircraft had harried the Nazis. This holiday it was our crew's turn. The heavens were still moist. At fighting altitude our planes left long, thick and lasting contrails. We created the clouds we had to fly back through. On the flanks of the bomber stream we could see many dogfights. The *Luftwaffe* fighters tried to come in at us, but our P-51s kept them away. The 493rd was to zero in on a railroad tunnel near Arweiler, south of Bonn in south-western Germany. This was a strange mission to be assigned to a heavy bomb group –

(Left) **B-17G-60-VE 44-8355, a PFF ship in the 710th Bomb Squadron, 447th Bomb Group, flown by 2nd Lt Miles S. King, takes a direct Flak hit on the bomb run on 24 December 1944. The Fort crashed at Prum, Germany with the loss of eight crew; two more were made PoW.** via Derek Smith

B-17Gs of the 452nd Bomb Group in formation. B-17G-55-VE 44-8249 C- of the 729th Bomb Squadron, with H₂S radome extended, failed to return on 24 December 1944. B-17G-70-VE 44-8518 F- went MIA on 5 December 1944. USAF

such small targets were usually taken out by low-flying, twin-engined medium bombers or by swift, bomb-carrying fighters. The purpose of the attack was to cut off the rail transport feeding the German troops guarding lines south of the Battle of the Bulge. We accomplished little, because our bombs did not fall at the mouth of the tunnel.

Though, as usual, I was busy charting our path, and not unmindful of my personal safety with fighters off to the side and *Flak* ahead, my thoughts kept drifting back to Debach. The past few weeks we and our hut-mates had been stockpiling food and fuel, purloined, appropriated and liberated from mess-hall supplies. Added to the locker were special treats from home. Eggs were bought on the black market at a bargaining price of thruppence [1p] or ten cigarettes each. The raid on the Inverness distillery gave us a beverage to drink and booty to trade. All this economic activity was aimed at producing a party of holiday cheer beneath the curved, corrugated iron of our Nissen hut. My darker musings were that if we got shot down or were forced to land elsewhere than Debach, 'Doc' Conger and his crew and a few lucky guests would get to lap up all the goodies we'd long been scrounging for Christmas Day. As it turned out, we got back safely and on time. I for one enjoyed the hut party, especially the fancy eggnog concocted by Frank Littleton. However, I couldn't have partaken of the joy of that evening if I'd known that at the same time my brother Bob was lying on the straw of a Belgian farmhouse with his head cut open by Nazi shrapnel.

Overall, the Christmas Eve raids were effective, and severely hampered von Rundstedt's lines of communication. The cost in aircraft though, was high; many crashed during their return over England as drizzle and overcast' played havoc with landing patterns, and tired crews put down where they could. Only 150 aircraft were available for another strike on 26 December. Next day the wintry conditions were responsible for a succession of crashes during early morning take-offs. On 30 December the 8th again attacked lines of communication, and on the final day of the year the First Bomb Division kept up the attacks while Third Division crews returned to oil-production centres. This time they were assigned Hamburg, and it was the scene of yet another disaster for the 100th Bomb Group, which lost twelve Fortresses, half the total lost by the Third Division.

Gordon Weir in the 493rd has some heartfelt observations to make for 1944:

New Year came but we didn't celebrate 1945; we had three missions to go for a ticket home. On the second day of the year we turned in from liberated France to bomb the railyard at Bad Kreuznach, near Mainz. At this point, the supercharger on an inboard engine failed, and we flew into south-western Germany with only three engines. If this had been one of our earliest missions perhaps we'd have turned back, but by now the crew was with Woody in his determination to go on and get it over with.

Eight days later we attacked the heavily gunned railyards at Cologne; the 13th, an unlucky number, gave us lucky number thirty. We completed our tour by coming back safely from wrecking the railyard at Bischofsheim, north-east of Frankfurt; that day after briefing, I tossed down my shot of whiskey. Conger's crew tallied their thirtieth the next day, and in our shared hut that evening, the 14th, we truly celebrated 1945.

But was it, after all, worth it? The material and manpower given to making airplanes, the immense operational facilities, the months of training to convert a man from the street into an airman, and all the young men that we left out there in the empty air? Did the 8th Air Force strategy and tactics shorten the war? One thing is certain, and that is that future air battles would be different: the bomber armadas of World War II with their parade of squadrons in neatly stacked Vs were as obsolete as the Macedonian phalanx.

German production of fighter aircraft actually increased through 1944 into 1945, largely because the manufacturing plants were so well dispersed that it was beyond our power to damage them seriously. Therefore, some postwar surveys concluded that our bombing offensive was a failure. But our bombing was just good enough that the *Luftwaffe* fighters had to keep rising to attack us, and then they were mostly destroyed by our P-51s and P-47s. So in fact the *Luftwaffe* suffered a shortage of pilots rather than a lack of planes; and thanks to our efforts at such places as Misburg and Merseburg they ran out of fuel before they ran out of pilots. Thus we gained mastery of the skies, and from D-Day on our troops knew that their enemy was earthbound.

Military heroism is perhaps mostly a matter of getting used to combat as a way of life, to carrying on in a normal way in an abnormal environment. In our B-24s and B-17s we had no way of warding off the shrapnel fired at us – we had to sit there and take it. Some men of the 493rd could not function in combat and so they were sent home. What were the limits of personal endurance? What if all the missions had been like the one to Magdeburg? We could not know our breaking point. And yet I like to think that if our crew had been ordered to fly a fifty-mission tour, as did many bomber crews in the 15th Air Force out of Italy, we'd have done so with no more than the usual number of expletive-punctuated complaints.

In 1944–45 I didn't indulge in philosophical speculations on the turn-in from the IP; as we floated through the *Flak* in our aluminium fox-hole, I was trying to climb up into my helmet. Nevertheless, the lesson learned from combat is that there is a lot of luck, chance, and fortune in life. I've been lucky.

'Justice with Victory'*

January 1945 marked the 8th's third year of operations, and it seemed as if the end of the war was in sight. The Ardennes breakthrough was on the verge of failure, and Germany had no reserves left. In the east the Red Army prepared for the great winter offensive which would see the capture of Warsaw and Cracow, and the Soviets cross the German border. But there were signs that the *Luftwaffe*, at least, was far from defeated. On 1 January the First Air Division (this day the prefix 'Bomb' was officially changed to 'Air') encountered enemy fighters in some strength during raids on the tank factory at Kassel, an oil refinery at Magdeburg, and marshalling yards at Dillenburg; the Magdeburg force came under heavy fighter attack, while the Kassel force was badly hit by *Flak*.

Next day the B-17s once again pounded lines of communication, and raids of this nature continued for several days until the position in the Ardennes gradually swung in the Allies' favour. On 5 January the severe wintry weather over England was responsible for several fatal accidents during take-off for a mission to Frankfurt. Then a period of fine weather, beginning on 6 January, enabled the heavies to fly missions in support of the ground troops once more; these were mostly against lines of communication, airfields and marshalling yards. Finally the German advance in the Ardennes came to a halt, and ultimately it petered out. Hitler's last chance now lay in his so-called 'wonder weapons', the V1 and V2s. Missions were flown to tactical targets throughout the remaining days of January, but when the weather intervened, the 8th mounted shallow penetration raids on 'Noball' targets in France.

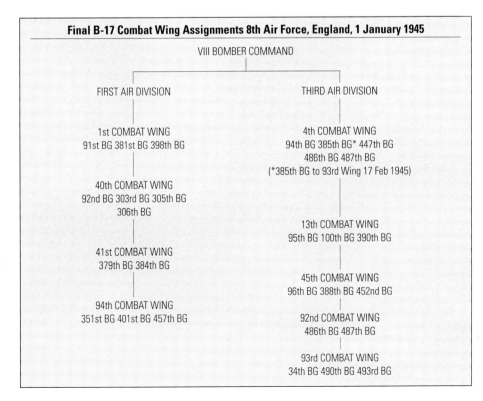

Final B-17 Combat Wing Assignments 8th Air Force, England, 1 January 1945

VIII BOMBER COMMAND

FIRST AIR DIVISION — THIRD AIR DIVISION

1st COMBAT WING
91st BG 381st BG 398th BG

40th COMBAT WING
92nd BG 303rd BG 305th BG
306th BG

41st COMBAT WING
379th BG 384th BG

94th COMBAT WING
351st BG 401st BG 457th BG

4th COMBAT WING
94th BG 385th BG* 447th BG
486th BG 487th BG
(*385th BG to 93rd Wing 17 Feb 1945)

13th COMBAT WING
95th BG 100th BG 390th BG

45th COMBAT WING
96th BG 388th BG 452nd BG

92nd COMBAT WING
486th BG 487th BG

93rd COMBAT WING
34th BG 490th BG 493rd BG

* Motto of the 95th Bomb Group

B-17G-70-BO 43-37797 CQ-Q American Beauty **of the 708th Bomb Squadron, 447th Bomb Group, which came to grief at Rattlesden, 9 January 1945. The aircraft was repaired and she finished her days at Kingman, Arizona, in December 1945.** via Ian McLachlan

(Below) **B-17G-50-BO 42-102490** Wicked Witch **of the 323rd Bomb Squadron, 91st Bomb Group, with the electrically driven Bendix Model 'D' chin turret, enclosed in a movable, aluminium alloy housing. The .50 calibre M-2 machine guns, whose barrels extend through zippered, fabric-covered slots, could be fired while rotating in elevation and in azimuth. Each gun had an ammunition box with a chute for feeding the guns and leading away the links and fired shells. The top box (maximum capacity 505 rounds) fed the left gun; the lower box (maximum capacity 425 rounds) fed the right gun.** Wicked Witch **received a direct** Flak **burst at Nürnberg, Germany on 20 February 1945 when it was being flown by 1st Lt Eddie R. Knight's crew. The pilots' compartment was hit and an explosion was observed, fire coming from the right side; a flash was also seen from the bomb-bay. The aircraft was last seen at 10,000ft (3,000m) approximately 25km (15 miles) south of Nürnberg/Fürth. Knight and five of his crew were killed, the other three were made PoW.** via Robert M. Foose

The 8th also attempted several tactical missions, but the weather was so bad that one mission after another was scrubbed, often just after take-off, with a consequent lowering in morale.

On 3 February 1945 Major Robert 'Rosie' Rosenthal, flying his fifty-second mission, led the 100th Bomb Group and the Third Division to Berlin. General Earle E. Partridge, Third Air Division commander, approved the selection of a squadron commander to lead the division. Marshal Zhukov's Red Army was only 35 miles (56km) from Berlin; the capital was jammed with refugees fleeing from the advancing Russians, and the raid was designed to cause the authorities as much havoc as possible. Just over 1,000 Fortresses were assembled for the raid. Although by this time the *Luftwaffe* was almost on its knees, the raid was still considered with apprehension because the *Flak* defences were as strong as ever.

A total of 2,267 tons of bombs reigned down into the *Mitte*, or central district of Berlin, killing an estimated 20,000 to 25,000 people. The German air ministry sustained considerable damage, the chancellery was hard hit and the Potsdamer and Anhalter railyards were badly hit. Reconnaissance photographs revealed than an area 1.5 miles (4 sq km) square, stretching across the southern half of the *Mitte*, had been devastated. The 8th lost twenty-one bombers over the capital, and another six crash-landed inside the Russian lines; among them was Major Rosenthal, who put his aircraft down in Soviet territory. He and two others were picked up by the Russians, while others were picked up by the Germans, one of whom was lynched by civilians. Of the bombers that returned, ninety-three had suffered varying forms of major *Flak* damage.

On 6 February the 8th resumed its oil offensive, with planned raids on synthetic oil refineries at Lutzkendorf and Meresburg, but bad weather forced all except one First Division Fortress to return to England while over the North Sea. Altogether, twenty-two bombers were lost in crash-landings in England. On 9 February the heavies returned to the oil refineries in the ever-diminishing Reich; bombing was made visually. Again the 8th turned its attention to missions in support of the Russian armies converging from the east. At the Yalta Conference early in February 1945, Josef Stalin, the Russian leader, and his army chiefs, asked that the RAF and 8th Air Force paralyse Berlin and Leipzig and prevent troops moving from the west to the eastern front. The British prime minister Winston Churchill and the American president Franklin D. Roosevelt agreed on a policy of massive air attacks on the German capital and other cities such as Dresden and Chemnitz: not only were these cities administrative centres controlling military and civilian movements, they were also the main communication centres through which the bulk of the enemy's war traffic flowed.

Spaatz had set the wheels in motion with a raid on Berlin on 3 February. Magdeburg and Chemnitz were bombed three days later, but the most devastating raids of all fell upon the old city of Dresden, famous for its pottery, in eastern Germany, starting with an 800-bomber raid by the RAF on the night of 13 February when two waves of heavy bombers produced firestorms and horrendous casualties among the civilian population. The following day, 400 bombers of the 8th Air Force ventured to the already devastated city to stoke up the fires created by RAF Bomber Command, and 8th Air Force crews were to return again in March and April 1945 on similar raids. However, the Allied air forces' top priority remained the oil-producing centres.

On 16 February the heavies hit the Hoesch coking plant at Dortmund, estimated to be producing 1,000 tons of benzol a month. Bombing was completed visually, and the *Luftwaffe* was noticeable by its virtual absence. But bomber losses continued to occur, mainly as a result of the bad weather which often affected forming up operations over England.

Clarion Call

On 22 February the 8th launched Operation *Clarion*, the systematic destruction of the German communications' network. More than 6,000 aircraft from seven different commands were airborne this day, and they struck at transportation targets throughout western Germany and northern Holland. All targets were selected with the object of preventing troops being transported to the Russian front, now only a few miles from Berlin. Despite the low altitudes flown, only five bombers were lost, including one to an Me 262 jet fighter.

Next day only two heavies failed to return from the 1,193 despatched; and on 26 February even the normally notorious *Flak* defences in Berlin could shoot down only five bombers. *Clarion* had ripped the heart out of a crumbling *Reich*, and the following two months would witness its bitter conclusion.

Replacement crews continued to pour into the ETO to fill the gaps left by crews who had completed their tours, or who had been lost. In February at Great Ash-

B-17G-35-DL 42-107117 IJ-O of the 710th Bomb Squadron, 447th Bomb Group, was involved in a collision at Rattlesden on 21 February 1945 with B-17G-35-DL 42-107003 *Bouncin' Baby* IJ-P. Derek Smith

B-17G-80-VE 44-8782 QW-R of the 412th Bomb Squadron, 95th Bomb Group, with H₂X radome extended. This aircraft flew its first sortie on 25 February 1945 and was assigned to the 100th Bomb Group on 25 May 1945, finishing her career at Walnut Ridge, Arkansas, in 1946.

(Below) B-17G-80-BO 43-38223 was delivered to the AAF on 12 July 1944. The cost of this bomber was about $300,000, and all of the 51,000 employees at the Hanford Engineering Works at Richland, Washington, gave a full day's pay to buy the aircraft. On 23 July the B-17 was flown to Hanford airport, where it was christened Day's Pay. The traditional breaking of a bottle over one of the propeller boxes was performed by Mrs K.B. Harris, a company employee, whose son, Lt J.E. Harris, was lost in action over Germany in April 1944. The B-17 was then flown to Kearney, Nebraska, and assigned to the crew of Nelson W. Warner. Upon arrival in England, Warner's crew were sent to the 94th Bomb group at Bury St Edmunds (Rougham), while Day's Pay was allocated to the 862nd Bomb Squadron, 493rd Bomb Group, at Debach, Suffolk, and assigned to Lt Arlys D. Wineinger's crew. The first mission flown by Day's Pay was to Düsseldorf, on 9 September, and it flew more than fifty missions in the 493rd Bomb Group. Then in February 1945, following the deactivation of the 862nd Bomb Squadron, it was transferred to the 94th Bomb Group, and had completed sixty-seven missions by the time it was returned to the ZOI, 10 July 1945. via Truett Woodall

field, Suffolk, 2nd Lt George H. Crow Jr's crew joined the 550th Bomb Squadron, 385th Bomb Group. 2nd Lt William W. Varnedoe Jr was the crew's navigator:

From arrival until right at the month's end we flew practice missions, getting familiar with the formations and the routine we would use in combat. In theory, the group would fly with three squadrons: a lead, a high and a low squadron, the high above and slightly left, so that it wasn't directly over the low. Then each squadron had a lead and low flight or a high flight if it was a high squadron. The flights were, in turn, made up of one or two elements of three planes each. These three B-17s formed the familiar 'V', of a lead and two wing men. In a tight formation their wingtips would almost – and sometimes did – overlap. The wing planes were supposed to be back only so far from the lead so the wings could overlap without touching, otherwise they were nearly abreast. Occasionally a fourth plane would be added to an element. He would then 'fill in the

diamond' and be slightly lower and trail the lead, unless it were the high squadron, high flight, then he would be above. If this happened in the low element of the low squadron, he was called 'tail-end Charlie', and this was a bad place to be because you were vulnerable to fighter attack.

The group would fly from thirty-six to thirty-eight Forts, though nominally it would fly thirty-six: three squadrons of twelve aircraft, each squadron consisting of two flights of six each, a two-element lead and a two-element low (high, if high squadron). Being in a tight formation gave maximum firepower, but only allowed us to carry two bombardiers in each squadron, in the lead and deputy lead: as he dropped his bombload, he'd also release a couple of smoke bombs, and at this signal, all of the other bombers in the squadron would release their bombs. A measure of the tightness and discipline of the squadron was the percentage of bombs that landed within 500, 1,000 and 2,000ft [150, 300 and 600m] of the MPI. The 385th Bomb Group finished tops in the 8th Air Force by this measure!

Close-formation flying like this had its drawbacks, not least the risk of collision, as Bill Varnedoe testifies:

On 1 March, my second mission, but first as a full crew, we headed for Ulm. We were left wing off Lt Ruseki's crew who were in the lead of the low element of the lead flight of the lead squadron. Left wing of the lead element was Lt

Chuck Armbruster's crew in a Fort named *Mr Lucky*; this put *Mr Lucky* above and to the right of us. Just as we passed into a hump of cloud, Rusecki suddenly came up out of it in a steep climb – he came up just over us and into Armbruster's Fort. *Mr Lucky* was hit by Rusecki's No. 1 and 2 engines, which cut into *Mr Lucky* about the rear of the radio room. Rusecki slid back, chewing up the waist section of Armbruster's plane, which was now in two separate pieces. I lost sight of Rusecki's Fort and the tail of *Mr Lucky* as I focused on the front half, which was sliding to the left and dropping, and was now mighty close to us on our level. I could quite clearly see Chuck Armbruster, looking back over his left shoulder, trying to see what was happening. As he continued to slide toward us, Crow pulled us left, out of formation, or there

would have been three planes in the collision. Armbruster's front half went into a flat spin and disappeared into the clouds, so near below. We then edged back into the lead slot, where Rusecki had been moments before. It *was* very eerie seeing all that metal ripping apart only yards away, but without making a sound, as if in a silent movie. Of course it *was* making a noise, but the constant, deafening roar of our own engines drowned out everything.

Another lasting image was the sight of the radio operator falling out of Armbruster's plane *without his parachute*. Seeing this incident, which was all over in fifteen seconds, and seeing that tumbling crewman, several of us wore our parachutes all the time while in the air, cumbersome or not. We later learned that there were only two survivors, the waist gunner of Rusecki's crew, who

baled out, and Joe Jones, the tail gunner of Rusecki's crew; Jones fell 10,000ft [3,000m] in the tail section and landed unhurt at a farm in Slijpe, Belgium, where a local cut him out with an axe!

Sometimes it seemed the assembly of the formations over England wasn't too well planned, but maybe it couldn't be helped that groups might have to cross each others' paths in going to their respective splashers (a splasher was a radio beacon, used as an assembly point). At this time practically the entire 8th Air Force was crowded into East Anglia, a space no bigger than Massachusetts, and air-traffic patterns were bound to interfere somewhat. On 5 March I saw a B-17 from another group pass close behind another; the propwash – the turbulence directly behind an aircraft – put the Fort into a spin. He managed to straighten it out, but at once went into a counter spin, and was by then too low to recover – he made quite a bang when he hit.

By March 1945 the Third Reich was on the brink of defeat, and the systematic destruction of German oil-production plants, airfields and communications centres, had virtually driven the *Luftwaffe* from German skies. Despite fuel and pilot shortages, Me 262 jet fighters could still be expected to put in rare attacks, and during March almost all enemy fighter interceptions of American heavy bombers were made by the *Jagdverband*. On 2 March, when the bombers were despatched to synthetic oil refineries at Leipzig, Me 262s attacked near Dresden. And on 3 March the largest formation of German jets ever seen made attacks on the 8th Air Force bomber formations heading for Dresden and oil targets at Ruhrland, and shot down three bombers.

On 18 March a record 1,327 8th Air Force bombers bombed the German capital. *Flak* was particularly hazardous, and thirty-

(Above) **B-17G-70-BO 43-37756** Milk Wagon **of the 708th Bomb Squadron, 447th Bomb Group, with 120 'milk-bottle mission symbols' on the forward fuselage. She survived the war and finished her days at Kingman, Arizona, in November 1945.**
via Derek Smith

B-17G-75-BO 43-38024 of the 490th Bomb Group, which was MIA on 9 March 1945 when the crew were forced to land on the Continent. via Mike Bailey

seven Me 262s of the I and II/*Jagdverband* 7 shot down sixteen bombers and five fighters – and another sixteen bombers were forced to land inside Russian territory – for the loss of only two jets. The jet menace became such a problem that, beginning on 21 March, the 8th flew a series of raids on airfields used by the *Jagdverband*. The raids also coincided with the build-up for the impending crossing of the Rhine by Allied troops. For four days the heavies bombed jet airfields and military installations.

On 22 March the 8th was requested by SHEAF headquarters to bomb the Bottrop

was the only remaining source of supply for the German war machine. On 23/24 March, under a 66-mile (106km)-long smoke-screen, and aided by 1,747 bombers from the 8th Air Force, Field Marshal Bernard Montgomery's 21st Army Group crossed the Rhine in the north, while further south simultaneous crossings were made by General Patton's 3rd Army. Groups flew two missions this day, hitting jet aircraft bases in Holland and Germany.

The mission to submarine pens at Hamburg on 30 March 1945, cost the 493rd three Fortresses, including one piloted by

aged but that no one was injured. Being so low on gas he waited until well on the final approach before lowering the flaps. When they were lowered, the right wing began to drop and the crew thought that the No. 3 engine had run out of gas (in fact the left flap had moved into position but the right flap did not, and later investigation revealed that the right flap cable had been cut by the *Flak* explosion). The right wing-tip struck the ground and the plane broke in half at the trailing edge of the wing; the tail section remained upright, but the front half of the plane

B-17G-50-VE 44-8200/L and B-17G-85-BO 43-38305/C of the 861st and 860th Bomb Squadrons, 493rd Bomb Group, respectively, letting their wheels down. 43-38305 caught fire on 11 March 1945 while being cleaned for nose art to be applied, and was scrapped. via Mike Bailey

military barracks and hutted areas directly behind the German lines, while 136 B-17s of the 15th Air Force attacked Ruhrland again and caused extensive damage to the plant. Forty Me 262s attacked the formation and shot down three of the Fortresses, while P-51s shot down one of the jets and damaged five others.

Next day the 8th struck at rail targets as part of the rail interdiction programme to isolate the Ruhr and cut off coal shipping. Since the loss of the Saar basin, the Ruhr

2nd Lt Russell A. Goodspeed, in the 861st Bomb Squadron, whose crew were on their first mission. Goodspeed returned from Hamburg with his No. 4 engine out after it took a *Flak* hit at the target. Debating whether or not to land at the emergency field at Woodbridge, the decision was made to try for the base at Little Walden. With the field in sight, and all fuel-warning lights blazing, Sgt Harry N. Davis, the engineer, fired the rocket to inform the tower that the plane was dam-

skidded to a halt upside down in a farmer's field. The four airmen in the radio-room were killed instantly, as well as the togglier in the nose; Goodspeed died six hours later. Only three crew survived.

Bomber crews were now hard pressed to find worthwhile targets, and the planners switched attacks form inland targets to coastal areas. Beginning on 5 April, the weather over the Continent improved dramatically, and the B-17s were despatched to U-boat pens on the Baltic coast. Every-

B-17Gs of the 447th Bomb Group in formation. B-17G-75-VE 44-8643/K, the nearest aircraft, survived the war and finished her days at Kingman, Arizona, in December 1945. via Derek Smith

Lt Marvin 'Mike' Wright, bombardier behind the N-6 Sight Unit for the Bendix chin turret aboard B-17G-80-BO 43-38253 Ole Rambler **in the 861st Bomb Squadron, 493rd Bomb Group.** Gordon W. Weir

where the Allies were victorious, but while the enemy kept on fighting, missions continued almost daily. Such was the 8th Air Force's superiority that the B-17s assembled over France on 5 April, before flying in formation for an attack on the marshalling yards at Nürnburg.

On 7 April the *Luftwaffe* employed converted Bf 109 fighters – called *Rammjägers* and flown by pilots from *Sonderkommando Elbe* – in the fight against American bomber streams attacking underground oil refineries in central Germany. During their ramming attacks the commandos were protected by Me 262s. The *Rammjägers* dived into the bomber formations from a height of 33,000ft (10,000m) and destroyed twenty-three aircraft.

One crewmen who experienced this frightening type of attack this day was Richard Spears, radio operator/right waist gunner aboard 'Stoopid Group' flown by Lt George A. Mance, in the 862nd Bomb Squadron, 493rd Bomb Group, whose target was an ordnance depot at Gustrom, northwest of Berlin. Spears recalls:

We were hit by fighters about thirty minutes before the IP. The first pass came at the tail, and I got off nine rounds at him; a '51 chased him off. A second attack came ten to fifteen minutes later. An Fw 190 hit our right wing, then the ship, and then peeled off on us. Three of us opened up, but he kept coming in and we were hitting him. He collided with our tail while I was still firing! I could see my tracers hitting his fuselage and cockpit. He knocked two feet off our horizontal stabilizer and went underneath us; three of the crew saw him going down in flames, so we claimed destruction. Just after this our No. 2 engine caught fire; we pulled out of formation and had a hard time avoiding other ships. We salvoed the bombs, but three hung up; I went forward to kick them out, but someone else got them out. We feathered No. 2 and got the fire out, and then trailed the formation in – and we really did sweat until we got to Allied territory! It's the first time I've ever prayed in the air!

Of the thirty-five missions we flew, that was unusually exciting. The fighter took about 20sq ft [2sq m] of the right horizontal stabilizer, slightly jamming the plane's controls. Sgt Spears shot 50s into the Fw from the prop to the tail as he went past; smoking and on fire, he rolled over and went down, and quite rightly Sgt Spears was given credit for the kill.

The *Stoopid Group* crew flew their final mission on 17 April 1945.

B-17G-90-BO 43-38513 QJ-M Never Had It So Good **of the 339th Bomb Squadron, 96th Bomb Group, in flight.** via Mike Bailey

(Below) **B-17G-50-VE 44-8200/L of the 861st Bomb Squadron, 493rd Bomb Group, dropping bombs. Note the H$_2$X scanner below the fuselage.** via Mike Bailey

Fame's Favoured Few

On 8 April, the 8th put up twenty-three groups of B-17s and ten groups of Mustangs to bomb targets in Germany and Czechoslovakia. On 9 and 10 April the German jet airfields were again bombed. On 16 April 'Orders of the Day' No. 2 from General Spaatz ended the strategic mission of the 8th Air Force, and only some tactical missions remained. On 17 April Dresden was again bombed. The German corridor was shrinking rapidly, and the American and Russian bomb lines now crossed at several points on briefing maps. During the week 18–25 April, missions were briefed and scrubbed almost simultaneously. General Patton's advance was so rapid that on one occasion at least crews were lining up for take-off when a message was received to say that General Patton's forces had captured the target the B-17s were to bomb!

The last major air battle took place on 18 April, when 305 B-17s and 906 B-24s of the 8th and 15th Air Forces, plus more than 1,200 fighters, attacked Berlin. Forty rocket-firing Me 262s tore into the 8th and 15th Air Force formations and shot down twenty-five bombers. Bill Varnedoe in the 385th Bomb Group flew his last mission, his twenty-sixth, on 20 April, and he could now reflect on the actions of the past two months and the role played by the Fortress in the air war in Europe:

> While we didn't have it as rough as crews flying in 1943 and 1944, enemy opposition had by no means disappeared. Twelve B-17s were lost from the 385th during my tour. The sporadic fighter opposition, such as that on my third mission to Dresden, was pressed by the Germans with just as much determination. And the nasty English weather, which made flying so hazardous, was exactly the same. If anything, weather was more deadly late in the war, since there were more of us milling around in the soup. We also flew more frequently than the early crews – I put in my twenty-six missions in only fifty-six days, an average of one every other day! I once flew on ten consecutive missions, eight of them on consecutive days.

The end came on 25 April 1945 when the 8th Air Force bombed the Skoda armaments factory at Pilsen in Czechoslovakia. To forty aircraft in the 92nd Bomb Group went the honour of leading the strike force. 'Fame's Favoured Few' was the oldest group in the 8th, and this was its 310th and final mission. The 303rd Bomb Group at Molesworth chalked up the command record this day, flying its 364th mission, while other groups came close to equalling it. The famed 'Hell's Angels' group had been the first in the 8th to complete 300 missions.

(Above) **B-17G-15-BO 42-31378 SG-M** Rum Dum **of the 550th Bomb Squadron, 385th Bomb Group, began operations in December 1943 with Jim Staber's crew, who had originally considered naming her** Smokey Stover **after a cartoon character. Someone called Charles Guffy, the ball gunner, a 'rum dum' and the name was adopted for their Fort.** Rum Dum **flew 105 missions without an abort, then took a Flak hit on 15 April 1945 on the 106th, and Howard A. Muchow had to put her down on the Continent. She was later flown back to England by a 'pick-up' crew, but made a wheels-up landing at Honington and was salvaged on 3 May 1945. Cpl Jimmy Lavin of the groundcrew painted the nose art and recorded her missions with bombs and fighter 'kills' with swastikas.** via Mike Bailey

At Molesworth the 303rd Bomb Group – Hell's Angels – had much to celebrate at the war's end. Here is the final tally, 25 April 1945. Lt Col Harry D. Gobrecht

Operation *Chowhound*

During the first week of May the German armies surrendered one by one, to Montgomery at Luneberg Heath, to Devers at Munich and to Alexander at Casserta, and finally to Eisenhower at Rheims in the early hours of 7 May. Starting on 1 May, even before the Germans had surrendered, Fortress crews flew mercy missions, called *Chowhound*, to starving Dutch civilians in Holland (together with RAF *Manna* operations, which had begun on 29 April) until the end of hostilities, carrying food. During the winter of 1944–45 15,000 Dutch civilians had died of starvation. Some of the deaths had been caused by the Germans in revenge for the help Dutch railway workers had given the Allies at the time of the Arnhem operation. Agricultural land had been flooded as an anti-invasion measure, and the invasion of Germany from the west had also left three-and-a-half million Dutch in western Holland living in a virtual island fortress.

Plywood doors were placed inside the B-17 bomb-bays, rigged to the bomb-release shackles, and the bomb-bays were then loaded with food packages. Formations flew in very low over an airfield, marked by white crosses, and dropped the food; one of the main drop-points was Amsterdam-Schiphol. Many Dutch waved at the Forts, and the pilots wagged their wings back at them. Altogether, six supply-drop missions were flown by the 8th Air Force. On 5 May the Germans in Holland finally surrendered. The Dutch cut out of flowers growing in a bulb field the words, 'THANK YOU BOYS' in large letters, and the words, 'MANY THANKS' could be seen from the air in other fields. The sixth and final 8th Air Force *Chowhound* mission was flown on 7 May 1945, the day before VE (Victory in Europe) Day.

(Above) **Six supply-drop missions were flown by the 8th Air Force. Starting on 1 May, before the Germans surrendered, the 8th Air Force mounted** Chowhound **missions (together with RAF** Manna **operations, which had begun on 29 April), dropping food supplies to starving Dutch civilians. During the winter of 1944–45, 15,000 Dutch civilians had died of starvation. Some of the deaths had been caused by the Germans in revenge for the help Dutch railway workers had given the Allies at the time of the Arnhem operation. Agricultural land had been flooded as an anti-invasion measure and the invasion of Germany from the west had also left three and a half million Dutch in western Holland living in a virtual island fortress. B-17G-70-DL, 44-6954 CC-F is from the 569th Bomb Squadron, 390th Bomb Group.** USAF

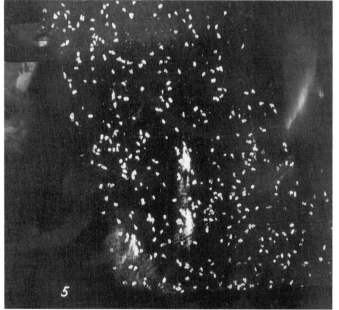

Sacks of flour being dropped over Amsterdam-Schiphol on 5 May 1945 by B-17Gs of the 493rd Bomb Group, the day the Germans in Holland surrendered. On 7 May the 8th flew its sixth and final Chowhound **mission to Holland. The missions cost three Fortresses, including two which collided soon after take-off.** via Truett Woodall

E Sempre L'Ora ('It is always the hour')*

The news of the Germans' final surrender was made known to the men at bases throughout eastern England on 8 May. B-17 groups then flew home Allied prisoners-of-war from their camps in eastern Europe to France, and airlifted displaced persons from Linz in Austria to their homes in France,

*Motto of the 96th Bomb Group.

Holland, Denmark and all other recently occupied countries. At war's end the heavies flew *Revival* missions, transporting Allied PoWs and displaced persons from holding camps on the continent. Lt Colonel Shepler W. Fitzgerald, CO, 493rd Bomb Group, recalls one such French PoW mission:

I led this mission into Linz, Austria after the end of hostilities, date unknown. The aircraft were

modified with platforms in the bomb-bays. The French prisoners had been working in the River Danube valley since early in the war and were to be taken back to Paris. We stuffed a max load into the aircraft, God knows how many, and we could hear them cheering when we circled the Eiffel Tower! While staying overnight in Linz we were taken to see the concentration camp nearby [probably Mauthausen]. Bodies were still stacked in boxcars on the siding, there were

Soon after the occupation of Linz, Austria, by US forces in May 1945, military government authorities organized the rapid repatriation from the district of Frenchmen and their families by US transport planes and Flying Fortresses, which made the journey from the Horching Flugplatz airfield at Linz to Le Bourget airfield near Paris in three hours. Here, B-17Gs of the 486th Bomb Group from Sudbury can be seen. B-17G-40-VE 42-98006/F is The Old Yard Dog, which finished her days at Kingman, Arizona, seven months later. Next in line are B-17G-50-DL 44-6477, B-17G-75-BO 43-37973 The Worry Bird, and B-17G-75-BO 43-37970. Some 38,000 Frenchmen and their families were thus transported by plane, 8,000 being carried in one day. Some of the French were 'voluntary' workers who were induced to work in Germany on the promise made by the Germans that their enrolment would release French prisoners of war. Others were slave workers and concentration camp victims. Many of the workers had their wives with them and several children were born in the work and concentration camps. OWI photo by F.H. Davies

B-17G OR-R Nine-O-Nine **in the 91st Bomb Group took its name from the last three digits of its serial number, 42-31909 when it was assigned to the 323rd Bomb Squadron at Bassingbourn in February 1944. When photographed on 18 June 1945, this famous Fortress had completed no less than 140 combat missions. It sits with other war wearies, waiting to be scrapped at the end of the year.** USAF via Tom Fitton

bodies in the ovens and the walking dead still in the camp. The US Army had just taken over the area. The Russians were just across the Elbe River bridge.

The B-17s airlifted troops from the United Kingdom to Casablanca where they continued on to the China-Burma-India theatre; they also acted as 'moving vans' for fighter groups going to Germany as part of the occupation forces there. In addition, *Trolley* or *Revival* missions were flown to bombed-out cities, the planes crammed with ground personnel to show

them what destruction their aircraft had wrought. The flights ranged from 1,000 to 3,000ft (300 to 900m) and the routes took passengers on what they described as a 'Cook's tour' of specially selected towns and cities which had been bombed by the 8th over the past four years.

What was the contribution made by the B-17 to winning the war? In the words of General Ira C. Eaker: 'The B-17 was, I think, the best combat airplane ever built. It could sustain more battle damage than any other, so much in fact that you wouldn't believe they could stay in the air.' And

General Carl A. Spaatz went as far as to say: 'Without the B-17, we might have lost the war.'

Final Allied Bomber Production Totals	
B-24 Liberator	18,188
B-17 Flying Fortress	12,731
Vickers Wellington	11,461
Avro Lancaster	7,374
Handley Page Halifax	6,176
B-29 Superfortress	3,970
Short Stirling	2,375

CHAPTER NINE

To Observe Unseen

RAF Coastal Command and 100 Group (Bomber Support)

Although the B-17 proved less than successful during its short career with No. 90 Squadron, the Fortress was supplied in large numbers to RAF Coastal Command, where it gave sterling service in the Atlantic and Bay of Biscay; a few were also sent to 100 Group, Bomber Command. Beginning in March 1942, forty-six Fortress IIA aircraft (sixteen B-17Cs and thirty B-17Es), and later, nineteen Fortress IIs (B-17Fs) and ninety-eight Fortress IIIs (B-17Gs), commencing HB761, were delivered to Great Britain for service with the RAF. The majority gave sterling service with RAF Coastal Command where they helped close the mid-Atlantic 'gap'.

In Service in Coastal Command

During March–July 1942, the first of forty-six B-17Es were delivered to the UK as the Fortress IIA (because they wre existing aircraft diverted, whereas the 'F' had yet to be built). One, FK185, was used as a test-bed for an experimental 40mm cannon in the nose intended for use against U-boats on the surface. After August 1942, nineteen B-17Fs went to RAF Coastal Command as the Fortress II (FA695/700 41-24594/24599 (B-17F-27-BO) and FA701/713 (B-17F-40-BO). Originally the British had signed a lend-lease contract in June 1941 for 300 Fortress IIs for the RAF, but these aircraft were diverted to the USAAF when Britain decided not to use the B-17s as bombers but only for maritime operations. Most were used by Coastal Command, although during 1944–1945, some served in two RCM squadrons in 100 Group.

Fortress Squadrons Coastal Command 1942–1945	
Squadron	History
59	Converted to Fortress II, December 1942. Used II/IIA on operations, January 1943–April 1943
206	Cvtd to Fortress II/IIAs August 1942. Used on ops, September 1942–April 1944.
220	Fortress I, December 1941–July 1942. II/IIA from July 1942–January 1945.
251 (Met)	Re-formed at Reykjavik, Iceland, 1 August 1944. Operated Fortress II/IIAs March 1945–October 1945
517 (Met)	Operated B-17F September–November 1943
519 (Met)	Operated Fortress II November 1944–September 1945
521 (Met)	Operated Fortress II/III August 1944–February 1946

N.B. Met: Meteorological calibration

B-17E 41-9141 in RAF-style camouflage scheme, and 41-9131 in US Army camouflage and markings, from the second production batch, in flight in America. The B-17E in the foreground was built for Great Britain with standard British camouflage, but was taken over by the US Army and flown in its original camouflage with US stars painted over the RAF roundels on both wings. Boeing

Line-up of Fortress IIIs (B-17Gs) for the RAF. The nearest aircraft is HB778 (42-97115), one of twenty-two (HB761/782) from block B-17G-40-BO 42-97098/97119. 42-97115 was transferred to the 333rd Bomb Squadron, 94th Bomb Group at Rougham on 24 February 1944 and finally to the 333rd Bomb Squadron, 96th Bomb Group that same year. The Fortress landed at Bulltofta, Sweden, on 11 April 1944 and was interned. In 1945 SAAB converted the plane to a fourteen-passenger airliner (SE-BAO) for SILA, who operated it for about three years. *Boeing via Mike Bailey*

Fortress IIA (B-17C) 'J' FL459, one of sixteen (FL449/464), of 220 Squadron RAF Coastal Command at Terceira, Azores, late in 1943. In 220 Squadron, 15 Group, Plt Off G. Roberson and crew and FL459 sank U-624, a Type-VIIC submarine, on 7 February 1943, and on 7 March 1943 Fg Off Bill Knowles and crew, again in FL459, sank U-633. Moving to 247 Group in the Azores, Flt Lt R.P. Drummond and crew flew 'J' and sank U-707 on 9 November 1943, and on 13 March 1944, Fg Off W.R. Travell shared in the sinking of U-575 with Fortress 'R' FA700 of 206 Squadron, and a Wellington of 172 Squadron. FL459 equipped 519 and 251 Squadrons, and was finally scrapped in 1945. *IWM*

RAF 15 Group and 247 Group (Azores) Fortress/U-Boat Actions

Date	Aircraft	Sqdn	Group	U-Boat	Remarks
27 Oct 42	FL457/F	206	15	U-627	Plt Off R.L. Cowey
15 Jan 43	FL452/G	206	15	U-337	Plt Off L.G. Clark
3 Feb 43	FL456/N	220	15	U-265	Plt Off K. Ramsden
7 Feb 43	FL459/J	220	15	U-624	Plt Off G. Roberson
9 Feb 43	FL195/L	206	15	U-614*	Sqn Ldr R.C. Patrick DFC
7 Mar 43	FL459/J	220	15	U-633	Fg Off W. Knowles
19 Mar 43	FK203/M	220	15	U-666*	Fg Off W. Knowles
19 Mar 43	FK208/B		15	U-384	P/t Off L.G. Clark
25 Mar 43	FK195/L	206	15	U-469	Flt Lt W. Roxburgh
27 Mar 43	FK195/L	206	15	U-169	Fg Off A.C.I. Samuel
24 Apr 43	FL451/D	206	15	U-710	Fg Off R.L. Cowey
6 Jne 43	FL458/A	220	15	U-450*	Sqn Ldr H. Warren
11 Jne 43	FA704/R	206	15	U-417	Wg Cdr R.B. Thomson
17 Jne 43	FL457/F	206	15	U-338	Plt Off L.G. Clark DFC
9 Nov 43	FL459/J	220	247	U-707	Flt Lt R.P. Drummond
6 Jan 44	FA705/U	206	247	U-270	Flt Lt A.J. Pinhorn DFC
13 Mar 44	FA700/R	206	247	U-575#	Flt Lt A.D. Beaty
13 Mar 44	FL459/J	206	247	U-575#	Fg Off W.R. Travell
26 Sep 44	FK191/P	220	247	U-871	Flt Lt A.F. Wallace (Capt)
					Fg Off E.C.W. Fields (pilot)

* Damaged
\# joint action with a Wellington of 172 Sqn

'Avenging in the Shadows'*

In November 1943, 100 (Special Duties) Group was formed at Bylaugh Hall, Norfolk, for the sole purpose of carrying out radio counter-measure tactics such as 'jamming' and 'spoof', tasks which were severely taxing the resources of conventional RAF bombers. In January 1944, 214 Squadron based at Downham Market, Norfolk, and commanded by Wg Cdr Desmond J. McGlinn DFC, and equipped with Stirlings, transferred from 3 Group to 100 Group at Sculthorpe, to retrain on the Fortress. In the spring this squadron received fourteen B-17s from the First Bomb Division, 8th Air Force. 214 Squadron were assisted by a small American RCM detachment commanded by Capt G.E. Paris, which arrived at Sculthorpe on 19 January to train the RAF crews in jamming using 'Jostle' equipment (which began arriving in May). Jostle and Window patrols would form the bulk of 214 Squadron's work, and for the ten months preceding the end of the war over 1,000 sorties were completed on 166 nights.

Meanwhile on the 10 February, six B-17Gs of the 96th Bomb Group, 8th Air Force, arrived from Snetterton Heath, and pending installation of Jostle equipment, were immediately fitted with 'Airborne Cigar' (or 'ABC'), plus exhaust flame dampers for night flying, and Gee navigation equipment. ABC was a device consisting of six scanning receivers and three transmitters designed to cover the VHF frequency band of the standard German R/T sets, and jamming 30–33 megacycles

Fortress IIA (B-17E) FK197, one of thirty (FK184/213), of 251 (Met) Squadron, RAF Coastal Command. 251 Squadron was re-formed on 1 August 1944 at Reykjavik, Iceland, for meteorological reconnaissance in the mid-Atlantic and Iceland area. IWM

* 'Ultor in Umbris', motto of the 214 Squadron

('ottokar') and later 38–42 megacycles (benito', R/T and 'beam').

214 Squadron moved to Oulton on 16 May, and there they were joined by the American 803rd Squadron (now re-designated the 36th Bomb Squadron), and equipped with six RCM Fortresses fitted with Mandrel and Carpet. By the end of the month, a total of twenty-two crews were fully converted on Fortress aircraft.

match against a German night-fighter with its bigger calibre armament. Also the ball turrets had been removed from 214's B-17s before I arrived on the squadron, so like all aircraft in RAF Bomber Command, we had little or no protection from the upward firing cannon (*Schrage Musik*) of the twin-engined German fighters.

After the Halifax, the Fortress was easy to fly, with few, if any vices. it was just like a four-engined Anson aircraft. It also had an excellent

crew failed to return. On 1 June Capt Paris, now relieved of his temporary command with the arrival of Capt C.A. Scott, took part in the first daylight operation from Oulton.

During June, 100 Group began its work of deceiving the enemy, using the airborne Mandrel screen and Window feint forces. On 5/6 June a Mandrel screen was formed to cover the approach of the Normandy

Fortress IIA (B-17E 41-2515) FK186 S for Sugar **of 220 Squadron RAF Coastal Command. This squadron, which was equipped with Lockheed Hudsons, had taken 90 Squadron's numberplate in December 1941 and moved to Polebrook on 1 January 1942, where 90 Squadron were based, to convert to the Fortress I. Operating from Northern Ireland, in April 1942, 220 began ASW operations with two Fortress Is, flying 308 operational hours in May. By July 220 Squadron was standardizing on Fortress IIAs and during the month flew 19 convoy escorts, one ASW patrol and four ASR sorties. IWM**

Sqn Ldr Bob Davies flew sixteen ops piloting Halifaxes before taking command of 'A' flight, and he flew ten ops on B-17s in 214 Squadron. He recalls:

As I had a Halifax crew (seven), I had to pick up three extra aircrew at Oulton – two waist gunners, and a special radio operator. My top and rear gunners were highly delighted, to have, at last, 'real' guns with which to fight. I personally though that, as in a Lanc or Halifax, no matter how many .303s the aircraft had, you were no

auto pilot. One second-tour crew even boasted that they selected the 'jink' position on the auto pilot and weaved all the way to the target and back! Something the poor old Fort didn't have, though, was speed, and we had to set course ahead of the main force to get to the target on time. Even when we left the target with the nose well down, Lancs and Halifaxes shot past us going very fast.

On 23/24 May, 214 Squadron lost its first crew when Plt Off Hockley RAAF and his

invasion fleet, and from subsequent information received, it appeared that considerable confusion was caused to the German early warning system. Sixteen Stirlings of 199 Squadron and four Fortresses of the American 803rd established a Mandrel screen in a line from Littlehampton to Portland Bill. Five Fortresses of 214 Squadron, flown by Wg Cdr McGlinn, Sqn Ldr Bill Day and Sqn Ldr Jeffery, the 'A'; and 'B' flight commanders respectively, and Flt Lt Murray Peden RCAF and Fg Off Cam Lye

RNZAF, also operated in support of the D-Day operation in their ABC role. A protective patrol lasting over five hours was flown at 27,000ft (8,230m), starting just north and east of Dieppe and running in an almost perpendicular line to the coastline carrying out jamming and Window-dropping manoeuvres in conjunction with twenty-four Lancasters of 101 Squadron of 1 Group. One Lancaster was shot down. Overall though, the patrol was outstandingly successful, and

Fortress Squadrons	
RAF Bomber Command 100 Group (Bomber Support) 1943-1945	
Date	*Remarks*
January 1944	214 Squadron reformed at Sculthorpe with Fortress II/IIIs
April 1944	First 214 Squadron Fortress sortie
23 Aug 1944	223 Squadron formed at Oulton, Norfolk (B-24s)
April 1945	223 Squadron converted to Fortress III
19/20 April	First 223 Squadron Fortress sortie
27 July 1945	214 and 223 Squadrons disbanded at Oulton

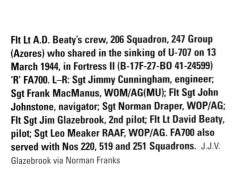

(*Above*) **Fortress IIA 'W' of 220 Squadron RAF Coastal Command. In November 1942, 220 Squadron operated from Ballykelly, Northern Ireland, and a met. flight detachment operated from St Eval. During the month Flt Lt Wright depth-charged a U-boat for the squadron's first attack on an enemy submarine.** IWM

Flt Lt A.D. Beaty's crew, 206 Squadron, 247 Group (Azores) who shared in the sinking of U-707 on 13 March 1944, in Fortress II (B-17F-27-BO 41-24599) 'R' FA700. L–R: Sgt Jimmy Cunningham, engineer; Sgt Frank MacManus, WOM/AG(MU); Flt Sgt John Johnstone, navigator; Sgt Norman Draper, WOP/AG; Flt Sgt Jim Glazebrook, 2nd pilot; Flt Lt David Beaty, pilot; Sgt Leo Meaker RAAF, WOP/AG. FA700 also served with Nos 220, 519 and 251 Squadrons. J.J.V. Glazebrook via Norman Franks

Flt Lt William Roxburgh DFC's crew in 206 Squadron, 15 Group, pictured sitting on a Liberator at Aldergrove, Northern Ireland, in July 1943. In Fortress IIA (B-17E) 'L' FK195 they sank U-469 south-east of Iceland on 25 March. L–R: Flt Sgt J. Griffith, Flt Sgt D. Eley, Flt Lt Roxburgh, Sgt J.K. Churchill, Flt Sgt R.E. Thomas, Sgt Rimmer, Sgt L.R. Meech RCAF (in cockpit) and Flt Sgt Simpson. R. Thomas via Norman Franks

(Below) A complete array of ECM jamming equipment which could be carried by the Fortresses of 100 Group at Oulton, Norfolk. Nos 214 and 223 Squadrons carried out spoofing and jamming operations from 1944–1945 using ABC (comprising six receiver/indicator units), 'Jostle' 'Big Ben' (installed in the bomb-bay because of its size), 'Airborne' 'Grocer', 'Dina', 'Piperack', and other devices. City of Norwich/100 Group Aviation Museum

earned a personal congratulation to all concerned by the C-in-C, Air Marshal Arthur Harris, in which he observed that 'the work carried out was of paramount importance in connection with the invasion forces'. In the course of this mission an Me 410 had the misfortune to choose to attack McGlinn's aircraft: it had Eric Phillips, the squadron gunnery leader, manning the tail turret, and he shot it down!

On 16/17th June, Bomber Command lost thirty-one bombers from 321 when it was despatched to the synthetic oil plant at Sterkrade/Holten in Germany. Six B-17s of the 36th Bomb Squadron joined sixteen Stirlings in routine Mandrel sorties to cover the attack. Then on 21/22 June, 214 Squadron were detailed to cover an attack on the Nordstern oil plant at Gelsenkirchen. Flt Lt Murray Peden, at a point approximately fifteen minutes from the target area *F-Fox*, was attacked by an Me 410. In the ensuing combat the Fortress was seriously damaged, the starboard inner engine being set on fire, and the intecom system put out of action. Both Flt Sgt Alfred 'Stan' Stanley, the wireless operator, and the special operator, were wounded in the attack, and Fg Off J.B. Waters, the air bomber, gave them some timely first aid; Waters also helped to restore the intercom. A few minutes later the Fortress was attacked by a Ju 88, but coolness and good shooting on the part of Flt Sgt Johnny Walker, the air gunner, drove off the night fighter. Strikes were obtained on both enemy machines.

With one engine still on fire, Murray Peden set course for home, and displaying great ability, successfully reached the long emergency airfield at Woodbridge. He made a spectacular arrival on two good and one partially serviceable engines, and came straight in. He was unable to acknowledge instructions because of the damaged equipment which rendered them almost unintelligible. The Fortress put down, but burst a tyre, causing it to swing violently off the runway towards a Lancaster of 61 Squadron which had just landed without hydraulics after an encounter with night fighters. Fortunately the Lan-

caster crew and the maintenance personnel milling around were able to get clear before the Fortress cut the bomber in two. Murray Peden recollects the occasion:

Years later, when I tracked down Dennis Copson, the only survivor of Butch Passant's crew he gave me a laugh. You have to understand that he had been wounded that night near Gelsenkirchen, and had had to be more or less chopped out of the turret when Passant landed; in fact as we were coming in he had just been assisted out of the turret by a ground crewman named Cpl Francis, who had been wielding the emergency axe from the aircraft to help free

Fortress BIII BU-A of 214 Squadron, 100 Group. This aircraft was the first B-17 in the squadron to be lost, on the night of 23/24 May 1944, when Plt Off Hockley RAAF and crew failed to return. Gerhard Heilig via Theo Boiten

him. They somehow managed to leave the scene at a handsome pace a few seconds before we arrived at a rate of knots and cut the Lancaster in half.

Four crashes occurred in all, in the space of thirteen minutes, but remarkably there were no injuries from any of them. Later, Peden was told that the Lanc' had a 12,000lb (5,500kg) bomb on board! Murray Peden, Waters and Walker were commended for their actions, and Stanley was awarded the DFM for continuing to carry out his duties after being wounded. Another Fortress, flown by Fg Off Johnny Cassan, failed to return from the Gelsenkirchen operation. W/O Doug Jennings, the bomb aimer, was the only survivor; he eventually returned to Oulton during August having first been signalled as 'killed', then reclassified as a PoW, and again reclassified as 'now in the UK'.

On 14 August, the 36th Bomb Squadron's eleven B-24H/J Liberators and

Photos of 214 Squadron Fortresses and especially 'Piperack', are rare. This close-up of the tail of Flt Lt Lile's Fortress BIII KH999 (B-17G-55-VE 44-8241 M-Mike shows to good advantage 'Piperack' ('Dina II', American-developed radar-jamming device, which replaced the 'Monica' tail warning installation when it was found that German night fighters were able to home in on 'Monica' transmissions from up to 45 miles (70km) away). Behind can be seen another BIII with plastic H$_2$S nose radome (fitted to all 214 Squadron aircraft during June–August 1944 to aid navigation). Geoff Liles via Murray Peden

Flt Lt Johnny Wynne of 214 Squadron in the cockpit of Fortress BIII E-Easy **at Oulton. On 16 November 1944, Wynne brought** E-Easy **back minus his crew who were ordered to bale out after an engine fire. Wynne then intended baling out himself, but his chute accidentally opened inside the aircraft and he had no choice but to try to fly it home. He made it to Bassingbourn. Five of his crew were beaten to death by German civilians.** Les Bostock

two B-17s left Oulton for Cheddington; where they continued to operate in 100 Group, principally on daylight missions, until January 1945. By the end of August, 214 Squadron, which shared the 24-hour watch on the V2 rocket launchings with 192 and 223 Squadrons, had completed 305 successful operational sorties as a counter-measure squadron with the loss of only three crews. It had achieved a record of no flying accidents for six months.

Although the crews were often unaware of the valuable contribution they were making, generally the spoofs and jamming operations undertaken by 100 Group aircraft were extremely effective. On one occasion a 214 Squadron crew took off from Oulton to join a Window force from Manston which failed to materialize owing to a last-minute recall; they, however, continued to 'press on' to the Ruhr, blissfully unaware of their isolation. They returned safely and were greeted with the news that the German defences had plotted them as a force of fifty aircraft!

Between 8 February and 22 March 1945, seven 214 Squadron crews failed to return to Oulton. In March 1945, 223 Squadron, which on 23 August 1944 had formed at Oulton, initially with a handful of B-24H/J Liberators from the 8th AF for Jostle jamming operations, learned that it would convert to the Fortress. On 15 April the first successful operation in a Fortress was completed.

The final operation of the war for Bomber Command took place on the night of 2/3 May, and RCM support for the night's operations, against Kiel, was provided by twenty-one Mandrel/Window Halifaxes, while eleven Fortresses of 214 Squadron, and four B-17s and five B-24s of 223 Squadron, flew Window/jamming sorties over the Kiel area. All told, a record 106 aircraft of 100 Group took part.

Miscellaneous RAF Fortress Units, March 1943 – June 1945	
Date	*Unit*
March–October 1943	No. 1 Operational Training Unit
October 1943–1945	No. 1674 Heavy Conversion Unit
April 1944–June 1945	No. 1699 (Fortrress Training) Flight
	Aeroplane & Armament Experimental Est
	Royal Aircraft Establishment
	Coastal Command Development Unit

B-17 Flying Fortress Units By Air Forces			
1st Air Force (ZOI)		*8th Air Force (ETO)*	
1st Photo Group		34th BG	381st BG
1st Search Attack Group		91st BG	384th BG
2nd Bomb Group		92nd BG	385th BG
		94th BG	388th BG
2nd Air Force (ZOI)		95th BG	390th BG
2nd Recon Gp		96th BG	398th BG
25th BG	383rd BG	97th BG	401st BG
39th BG	393rd BG	100th BG	447th BG
88th BG	395th BG	301st BG	452nd BG
304th BG	396th BG	303rd BG	457nd BG
331st BG	444th BG	305th BG	486th BG
333rd BG	469th BG	306th BG	487th BG
346th BG	488th BG	351st BG	490th BG
379th BG	493rd BG		
3rd Air Force (ZOI)			
2nd Recon Gp		*9th Air Force (MTO)*	
98th Recon Gp		9th BG	99th BG
88th BG		97th BG	301st BG
396th BG			
488th BG		*10th Air Force (CBI)*	
		7th BG	
4th Air Force (ZOI)			
34th BG	504th BG	*11th Air Force (Alaska)*	
444th BG	505th BG	28th Composite Group	
5th Air Force (Pacific)		*12th Air Force (MTO)*	
19th BG	43rd BG	2nd BG	99th BG
		97th BG	301st BG
6th Air Force (Caribbean)			
5th BG	11th BG	*13th Air Force (Pacific)*	
		5th BG	11th BG
7th Air Force (Pacific)			
5th BG	11th BG	*15th Air Force (MTO)*	
		2nd BG	301st MG
		97th BG	463rd BG
		99th BG	483rd BG

CHAPTER TEN

Post-War Postscript

B-17E 41-2401 was modified by Vega to include four Allison V-1710-89 liquid-cooled V-12 engines of 1,425hp each and redesignated XB-38. It flew for the first time on 19 May 1943 and proved faster than Wright-engined B-17s, but development was cut short when it crashed on 16 June after an engine caught fire.
Lockheed

On 29 July 1945 the last of 8,680 B-17Gs to roll off the production lines – a Vega-built aircraft at the Lockheed California plant – was accepted by the USAAF. It brought the grand total of Fortresses built by the B.V.D. (Boeing-Vega-Douglas) pool to 12,731, before Boeing production switched to the B-29 Superfortress. The B-17G was the most numerous Fortress model, altogether some 8,680 being built. At the peak of B-17 production in June 1944, Boeing was rolling out sixteen Fortresses every twenty-four hours. Boeing built 4,035 B-17Gs at Seattle, Washington; Douglas turned out 2,395 at Santa

Monica; and Lockheed-Vega built another 2,395 G models at Burbank.

The B-17G enjoyed a short but colourful post-war career as thousands of Fortresses surplus to military requirements became available. For instance, in 1946 a B-17G set the world's altitude record for a four-engined aircraft of 43,499ft (13,258.5m) and two more were modified to accept test turboprop engines. B-17G-110-VE 44-85813 was converted to an EB-17G for the USAAF at Boeing's Wichita Plant, early in 1946, and was then bailed to the Wright Aeronautical Co. to flight-test the nose-mounted 5,000hp

XT-35 'Typhoon' engine. For the next twenty years the plane was used to test other engines: in 1949, Wright used the EB-17G to flight-test the C-18 turbo-compound reciprocating engine, and during 1952–53 it was used to evaluate the J-65 turbojet powerplant. In 1955 the EB-17G was used again, to test the T-49 turboprop engine. In October 1956 the aircraft was re-designated JB-17G, and on 29 August 1957 it was sold to the Curtiss Wright Corporation of Wright Aeronautics, where it was registered as N6694C. During the year it was used to test the R-3350 turbo-compound engines.

B-17G-105-VE 44-85734 (N5111N), which early in 1948 became the second Fortress to be converted to Model 299Z standard for testing turboprop engines. In 1967, 44-85734 was acquired by the New England Air Museum at Bradley Locks, Connecticutt, where, on 3 October 1970, it was badly damaged by a tornado; the damage can clearly be seen in this photograph, taken in 1990. 44-85734 is being rebuilt using parts of B-17G-105-VE 44-85813 (N6694C), at Tom Reilly's in Kissimmee, Florida. Author

In post-war years PB-1Ws like XD1, BuNo77237 (B-17G-95-DL 44-83872), were used by the US Navy, fitted with an AN/APS-20 sea search radar, on anti-submarine and weather reconnaissance duties. XD1 was retired in July 1956, put on the civil register as N5236V, and was finally disposed of at Love Field in 1963. Boeing

B-17G-105-VE 44-85734 became the second Fortress to be converted to Model 299Z standard for testing turboprop engines, when it was modified by Boeing, Seattle, early in 1948. The aircraft had been a commercially owned test-bed from the start of its career, having been purchased by the Pratt & Whitney division of the United Aircraft Corporation from the Desperado Mining Co of Altus on 19 November 1947 for the modest sum of $2,700. The aircraft, registered N5111N, was used during the late 1940s and early 1950s to flight-test the Pratt & Whitney 5,700hp XT-34 engine, and the 3,750hp Allison T-56 turboprop powerplant. A third B-17G (BA 747B) was bailed to General Motors' Allison division for tests with the 3,750hp YT-56/501 turboprop engine. In 1967, 44-85734 was acquired by the New England Air Museum at Bradley Locks, Connecticut; where it was badly damaged by a tornado on 3 October 1970. It is being rebuilt using parts of 44-85813/N6694C, B-17G-105-VE, at Tom Reilly's in Kissimmee, Florida.

Civil and Military Transports

In World War II, sixty-eight B-17s had been forced to land in neutral Sweden during raids on the Continent of Europe, and in exchange for the repatriation of American crews, the Swedish government was given nine of these interned B-17s for $1.00. Seven were converted to fourteen-passenger transports, the nose of each being lengthened by 3ft (1m) and airline-type seats and fuselage windows installed;

4,400lb (1,996kg) of cargo could be carried in the bomb-bay.

The most famous of these transports is 42-32076, formerly *Shoo Shoo Shoo Baby* in the 91st Bomb Group at Bassingbourn, and named by Lt Paul McDuffee's crew after a popular song of the day; they completed twenty missions in this B-17. On 29 May 1944, *Shoo Shoo Shoo Baby* was interned at Bulltofta, near Malmö, with Lt Robert

task of restoration to flying condition was completed in 1988, and on 13 October the aircraft, now named *Shoo Shoo Shoo Baby*, was flown to the USAF Museum at Wright-Patterson AFB, Dayton, Ohio, by Dr William Hospers and Major Quinton Smith, for permanent display. *Shoo Shoo Shoo Baby* flew a farewell flight two days later before entering the museum. The tyres were injected with liquid rubber, and

in Korea where they were re-armed with the top turret and tail guns.

Captain Roy W. Owen was the pilot of VB-17 44-83661, the personal transport of Brig Gen Grills, on Guam in 1954–55. Owen recalls:

The airplane was plushed up with airline-type seats back in the waist area and a small kitchen on a cargo platform installed in the aft bomb-bay. In addition to monthly trips up to Far East HQ in Tokyo, I flew the general all over the Far East, to Hong Kong, Manila, Iwo Jima, Kwajelein, Okinawa, Saipan and Tinian. Early in December 1955 we got orders to deliver the airplane to Hickam AFB. The kitchen was removed, and a bomb-bay tank installed so it could fly to the west coast in January 1956, and then on to Tucson, Arizona to be converted to a target drone. We flew around the Hawaiian Islands for about three weeks, put a hundred hours on her, then made the big trip to Tucson via Sacramento. The last I saw of her was when I signed her over to the Storage Depot at Davis Monthan AFB. I expect she was later shot down over the Gulf of Mexico in some missile testing.

B-17s were used in a number of roles during 1945–48, some of them peaceful, others for more warlike operations. At the end of the war, B-17G-105-VE 44-85728 was purchased by Trans-World Airlines for conversion to an executive transport based on the CB-17 and XC-108. The aircraft, subsequently designated the Model 299AB and registered NX-4600 (later NL-1B), saw widespread use on survey and liaison work (as Fleet No. 242) prior to opening up postwar routes in the Near East. In April 1947 NL-1B was presented to the Shah of Iran, who had it registered as EP-HIM ('His Imperial Majesty'). The Institute Géographique Nationale purchased the aircraft on 12 May 1952, registered it F-BGOE, and used it on survey work until 22 August 1967. F-BGOE was scrapped at Creil in 1970.

Meanwhile in 1947, Universal Aviation of Tulsa, Oklahoma, became the first postwar operator to use the B-17 as a high-altitude camera platform. B-17G N5014N became the first aircraft to photograph and chart accurately much of the mid-western and south-eastern United States. A second B-17G was purchased on 10 July 1947. In the US, starting in late 1946, former military aircraft were issued only limited commercial licenses because they could not qualify for the standard licences of purely commercial types, and could not, therefore, carry paying passengers.

B-17G-5-BO 42-31163/T A Good Ship and a Happy Ship **in the 562nd Bomb Squadron, 388th Bomb Group, was one of sixty-eight B-17s interned after landing in neutral Sweden during World War II, and became one of seven converted to fourteen-passenger airliners. 2nd Lt Joseph F. Patterson landed 42-31163 at Rinkaby on 6 March 1944 when the group visited Berlin (losing seven B-17s). He and his crew were interned by the Swedish authorities, who after conversion by Svenska Aeroplan AB (SAAB), registered the aircraft as SE-BAM. After crashing at Mariefred on 4 December 1945, SE-BAM later became** Tom, **one of five B-17 transports operated in Denmark by A.B. Aerotransport, and soldiered on until 1948.** via Frank Thomas

Guenther's crew: they were on their twenty-fourth combat mission to Poznan, Poland, when engine problems forced them to abort.

After airline service with Swedish, and DDL Danish Airlines (as *Stig Viking*), and later, Danish military use, *Shoo Shoo Shoo Baby* was bought in 1955 by a New York company and sold to the Institute Géographique Nationale in Paris. In 1968 the aircraft was found abandoned at Creil Air Base in France with its engines missing; in 1971 the French government presented it to the USAF. In July 1978 it was transported by road to Frankfurt where a 512th Military Airlift Wing C-5 Galaxy flew it to Dover AFB, Delaware, for restoration by the volunteers of the 512th Antique Restoration Group. A massive ten-year

all the engine oil was drained, and replaced by preservative solution.

In the US, four B-17s were converted into transports under the C-108 designation, and CB-17 versions were converted for use as personnel transports: they first appeared in 1943. The CB-17s retained the defensive armament, but bombing equipment was deleted. Seating accommodation for up to sixty-four fully equipped troops was made in the nose, bomb-bay, radio compartment and aft fuselage. Some CB-17s had large cargo doors fitted to the left side of the waist area. By 1946 there were still twenty-six CB-17s in the USAAF inventory. VB-17 VIP transports, with customized interiors and fully equipped galleys in the radio compartment, also saw service

B-17G-35-BO 42-32076 Shoo Shoo Shoo Baby **of the 401st Bomb Squadron, 91st Bomb Group, 8th Air Force, which landed in Sweden following engine problems on the mission to Poznan, Poland, on 29 May 1944.** Shoo Shoo Shoo Baby's **nose was one of seven B-17s converted by the Swedes to commercial transport configuration, and was registered SE-BAP. After airline and military service in Sweden and Denmark in 1955, it was bought by a New York company and sold to the Institute Geographique National in Paris. In July 1978,** Shoo Shoo Shoo Baby **was flown by C-5 Galaxy to Dover AFB,Delaware, for restoration, and in 1988 was put on display at the USAF Museum at Wright-Patterson AFB , Dayton, Ohio.** via Frank Thomas/Air Force Museum

Fortresses saw widespread post-war use in South America as civil and military transports. In February 1947, the Fuerza Aérea Dominica took delivery of two B-17Gs to equip the Escuadrón de Caza-Bombardero. These two B-17s (and possibly a third) were kept in a guarded compound at Andrews Field, and they could only fly with presidential approval. They served until July 1954.

In 1956, eight B-17s were transferred to Bolivia directly from USAF surplus stocks, and assigned Bolivian civil registrations between CP-620 and CP-627. Hamilton Aircraft of Tucson, who received an additional seven B-17 airframes for scavenging for spare parts, prepared the Fortresses for delivery to the Bolivian government. In total, twenty-six B-17s, most of them acquired from the civil market, were used by Bolivian civil aviation fleet operators; at least nineteen of these were destroyed during 1955–65.

VB-17 (B-17G)-90-DL 44-83661, the personal transport of Brig Gen Grills, on Guam in 1954–55. In January 1956 it was flown by Captain Roy W. Owen to the west coast of America, and then on to the Storage Depot at Davis Monthan AFB, Tucson, Arizona, to be converted as a target drone. Roy Owen via Steve Adams

Clandestine Forts

In 1948 four civilian-owned B-17Gs in the US were purchased surreptitiously by the new state of Israel, at war with its neighbour Egypt. They were flown covertly across the Atlantic, but N7712M (44-83842) was interned when it landed in the Azores for refuelling. The other three – N5024N (44-83753), N5014N (44-83811), and N1098M (44-83851) – reached Czechoslovakia where two light Czech machine guns were mounted in the waist and two in the nose. Some of the crewmembers were armed with submachine guns. Only one of the B-17Gs was equipped with an oxygen system, and it was this one which was to be used to bomb Cairo en route to Ekron near Tel Aviv, the Fortresses' ultimate destination. The other two B-17Gs were to bomb an Egyptian military base at Rafah in the Sinai desert. A small artillery sight was installed in each of the Fortresses as the original bombsights had been deleted, and a few German 50kg (110lb) bombs were loaded aboard.

The three B-17Gs took off on the morning of 14 July and one of the crews manually bombed Cairo, accidentally missing King Farouk's palace. At Rafah the three B-17s came under anti-aircraft fire before they released their bombs; later, these were reported to have caused some damage to the base. On 17 July the Fortresses were bombing Syrian targets, including Damascus. Moving to Ramat-David, the B-17Gs were used to form 69 Squadron (the *Maccabeem*, meaning 'the hammers') and over the next few months they flew about 200 sorties against Egyptian and Syrian targets. They served the *Chel Ha'Avir* (Israeli Air Force) for ten years, including seeing action in the 1956 war. Finally they were scrapped during 1958–62.

A number of black-painted B-17s were operated over Red China by the nationalist Chinese from Formosa (now Taiwan) for some years.

In the US, the CIA also operated the B-17 on covert undercover missions: one of the most famous is B-17G 44-83785 (originally registered 44-85531), which was first sent to the Pacific theatre in July 1945. Three years later it was converted to a CB-17, and in 1949 it saw service as a VB-17. The B-17 was retired from the military in 1955 and sent to Kingman, Arizona for storage. 44-83785 was subsequently purchased by Intermountain Aviation of Marana, Arizona, an aircraft operation with heavy CIA ties. It was during this period that the Fulton 'Skyhook' personnel recovery system was developed using this aircraft. The 'Skyhook' system, designed by Bob Fulton, the great-grandson of the Robert Fulton of steamboat fame, was developed so that an aircraft could fly past a person and snatch him off the ground, after which he was winched up into the aircraft. The last time this system was used was for the James Bond movie *Thunderball*, when the aircraft was registered N809Z.

When its cover was exposed during the 1970s, Intermountain Aviation went quietly out of business and in 1975 ownership of N809Z was obtained by Evergreen Helicopters. That same year, Evergreen International bought the Marana base, now renamed Pinal Air Park, and in 1979 the B-17 was re-registered N207EV. Evergreen operated the B-17 until 1984, at which time it was placed in storage at Pinal. In 1987 its owner, Del Smith, asked Sandy Ellis to restore the aircraft to a state as close to the original as possible. The aircraft was completely rewired and an original design instrument panel fabricated and installed. All new glass and Plexiglas windows were fabricated and installed, while the hydraulic pack and the landing gear and actuators were overhauled. New flaps were fitted and new trailing edges for the wings fabricated and installed. The control surfaces were re-covered with Stits Polyfibre and the entire aircraft polished. After two years searching, all the required gun turrets were found and fitted. In deference to its background, the B-17 was renamed *Shady Lady* and painted in the colours of the 490th Bomb Group, which served in the 8th Air Force.

Early Warning, Recon, and ASR

Starting with a B-17F and a B-17G on 31 July 1945, a total of forty-eight B-17s, under the designation PB-1, were diverted

was the installation of the AN/APS-20B S-band search radar which was attached over the sealed bomb-bay doors (some aircraft had the large belly radome moved to a position on top of the fuselage). PB-1Ws began operation with VPB-101 (redesignated VX-4 on 15 May 1946) in the spring of 1946, and later equipped VP-1 at NAS Barber's Point, Oahu, Hawaii, and VP-51 at NAS San Diego. BuNo 83992 was later converted into an XPB-1W for use as an engine test-bed at the Cornell Aeronautical Laboratories.

One of the PB-1Ws flown to Johnsville was B-17G-95-DL 44-83872, which was assigned BuNo 77235. The PB-1W

Barely a year later, the aircraft was withdrawn from military service and flown to Litchfield Park, Arizona for open storage. In 1957 the PB-1W was purchased by Aero Service Corporation in Philadelphia for $17,510, registered N7227C, and used for survey work around the world. On 22 September 1967 the aircraft was purchased by the Confederate Air Force. In 1983 the Gulf Coast Wing at Houston, Texas carried out a complete rebuild, and the aircraft was resprayed as in the wartime colours of the 381st Bomb Group, 8th Air Force and called *Texas Raiders*.

Meanwhile in 1961, seven ex-WV-2 PB-1Ws at Dallas-Love Field, (WV-2 was

B-17G-95-DL 44-83872 (N7227C) Texas Raiders **in flight taken from B-17G-85-DL 44-83514 (N9323Z)**
Sentimental Journey **in October 1986. Prior to 1983, 44-83872 was painted in the colours of KY-D 41-24592 of the 366th Bomb Squadron, 305th Bomb Group; then the CAF's Gulf Coast Wing carried out a complete rebuild and repainted her** Texas Raiders**, with markings from 44-83872 VP-X of the 533rd Bomb Squadron, 381st Bomb Group, which was stationed at Ridgewell, Essex, in World War II.** Author

to the US Navy for anti-submarine and weather reconnaissance operations. In 1946, thirty-one of these aircraft were ferried from the USAAF supply pool to the NAMU (Naval Aircraft Modification Unit) at NAS Johnsville, Pennsylvania, for conversion to PB-1W airborne early warning aircraft. The major modification

received its first operational assignment in mid-1947, when it was delivered to NAS Quonset Point and VX-4. For almost seven years the aircraft operated with VX-4 and VW-2, and carried out many experiments for the Naval Aircraft Development Centre. In 1954, 77235 arrived at Atsugi, Japan to join VW-1, an early warning squadron.

the last Atlantic squadron to be equipped, while the other Pacific units were VBW-1 and VC-11) were snapped up by a local aircraft dealer. BuNos 77240 (N5232V), 77237 (N5236V) and 77243 (N5229V) were among those patched up and flown to England to participate in the movie *The War Love*.

Navigator's eye-view of the cockpit of B-17G-95-DL 44-83872 Texas Raiders. 44-83872 had been transferred in 1945 to the US Navy and redesignated PB-1W BuNo77235, assigned to VX-4 at Quonset Point. After a Navy career spanning almost ten years, it was retired in July 1956 and joined AeroServ Corporation in October 1957, registered N7227C. The Fortress was bought by the CAF in 1967 and restored to represent VP-X in the 533rd Bomb Squadron, 381st Bomb Group. Author

The starboard Wright R-1820-97 nine-cylinder, air-cooled Cyclones of B-17G-95-DL 44-83872 (N7227C) Texas Raiders roaring, and Hamilton Standard constant speed, three-bladed props whirring, just after take-off. These engines were designed to produce 1,200hp on take-off, and 1,380hp war emergency power. Normally the engines were operated at 1,000hp at 25,000ft (7,620m); they were even known to continue functioning with cylinders damaged by Flak. Author

Bombardier's eye-view from the nose of B-17G-95-DL 44-83872 (N7227C) Texas Raiders showing the bombsight, and overhead seat control and N-6 sight unit for the two Browning M-2 .50 calibre machine guns in the electrically operated Bendix chin turret. A cheek gun would normally be mounted top left and fired by the navigator during fighter attack. Author

SB-17G-95-DL 44-83706 of MATS (Military Air Transportation Service) pictured at Itazuke, Japan, without lifeboat during the Korean War 1953–54. USAF

VB-17G-95-DL 44-83798 of FEALF (Far East Air Logistics Force) pictured at Taegu, Japan, in 1953, during the Korean War 1953–54. USAF

Wartime reconnaissance versions, originally converted from B-17Fs and B-17Gs, were known as F-9/F-9A and F-9C respectively. All told, sixteen F-9s, twenty-nine F-9As, three F-9Bs (converted from F-9A) and ten F-9Cs were produced, all with cameras installed in the nose and the bomb-bay/radio compartment. In 1945, F-9s (B-17F) were re-designated FB-17F, and RB-17F in 1948. The F-9Cs (B-17Gs) were re-designated as FB-17Gs in 1945, and as RB-17Gs in 1948 also. The first mission flown during the Korean War took place on

became TB-17Hs). The B-17H was developed to carry a 3,000lb (1,360kg) 27ft (8m) long, droppable Higgins A-1 lifeboat, which had first been used in England in March 1945 by the 5th Emergency Rescue Squadron. Three parachutes were fitted to the lifeboat, which was a self-righting, self-baling type. Initially the 'H' retained the B-17G armament except the ball turret, but gradually all armament was deleted to save weight and to accommodate a radome in the former chin-turret position. In 1948, all ASR B-17s were re-armed and re-designat-

under the provisions of the 1947 Rio Pact, Brazil was supplied with the first six of thirteen SB-17Gs, these – five SB-17Gs and one RB-17G – arriving in May, and seven more during 1954–55. In 1955 the twelve surviving aircraft – 44-85579 having crashed in 1952 – were assigned Forca Aerea Brasiliera serial numbers between 5400 and 5411. The 1° and 2° Esquadrâos of 6° Grupo de Aviaçâo at Recifé operated these in the SAR, and photo survey-weather reconnaissance roles, respectively. Some of the SB-17Gs were converted to transports and

B-17G-110-BO 43-39457 was assigned to the 100th Bomb Group at Thorpe Abbotts in March 1945. When it returned to the ZOI at the end of the war it was redesignated B-17H and fitted with a droppable lifeboat for service with the 10th Emergency Rescue Squadron, based in Alaska. When Congress made the USAF a separate branch of the military in 1948 43-39457 became an SB-17G (for Search Bomber). Boeing

25 June 1950 by aerial mapping RB-17Gs of the 6204th Photo Mapping Flight based on Clark Field in the Philippines.

Search and Rescue

Starting in 1945, Boeing began specifically modifying approximately 130 B-17Gs to B-17H and TB-17H search and rescue aircraft (although in the event, only twelve received the B-17H designation, while five

ed SB-17G. At the outbreak of the Korean War (1950–53), SB-17Gs, refitted with cheek, waist and tail machine guns, were used in the search bomber role. The 2nd and 3rd Rescue Squadrons based in Japan, which were the only air rescue aircraft available to the Far East Air Force, used the SB-17 until it was quickly replaced by the SB-29 Dumbo as a result of the appearance by MiG-15 jet fighters in November 1950.

SB-17Gs were operated in small numbers by foreign air forces post-war also. In 1951,

were used as such until 1967. Five of the SB-17Gs were operated by the Forca Aérea Portugese at Lajes in the Azores, from 1947 to 1960 with the Esquadrilha de Busca e Salvamento on civil search and rescue duties. Three of the aircraft were lost in crashes and one, 44-83663 (FAB 5400), was returned to the US in 1968 and is now on display at Hill AFB. The other eight were withdrawn from service during 1965–1968.

Early in 1946 meanwhile, the US Coast Guard had acquired seventeen Vega-built

B-17G-90-DL 44-83663 N47780, formerly SB-17G 5400 of the Forca Aerea Braziliera up until 1968, was airlifted from Air International Inc, Clearwater, Florida to Hill AFB Heritage Museum, Utah, in 1986. It is painted as '44-83663 Short Bier', **to represent an aircraft in the 862nd Bomb Squadron, 493rd Bomb Group, 8th Air Force. However, the name was used only by the group's B-24J-160-CO 44-40442, which was subsequently transferred to the 490th Bomb Group before the 493rd converted to B-17Gs.** Hill AFB Museum

and one Douglas-built B-17Gs from navy storage depots, and re-designated them PB-1Gs. The chin-turret was replaced with a radome for the search radar, and quite often an A-1 airborne lifeboat was carried beneath the bomb-bay. Primarily, these aircraft were used for long-range ASR patrol, but they were also operated on iceberg patrol and high-altitude mapping operations. By 1953 the coast guard had eleven PB-1Gs based at five stations: five at Elizabeth City, North Carolina; one at Annette Isle, Alaska; two at Argentia, Newfoundland; two at San Francisco; and one at Port Angeles, Washington. One of these, PB-1G 44-77254, was the last military Fortress to operate in the US, and was retired at Elizabeth City on 14 October 1959.

B-17G-110-VE 44-85828/Bu No. 77254 served as a PB-1G photo-mapper on assignment to the US Coast and Goedetic Survey, 1946–59, and was the last Fortress to be operated by the US military. In 1960 77254 was registered N9323R, and was operated by Serv-Air Inc and Tropical Export Trading Co, before being converted to an air-tanker in December 1962 for Black Hills Aviation of Spearfish, South Dakota. Finally, in July 1978, N9323R was acquired by the 390th Memorial Museum at Pima Air Museum, Tucson, Arizona, in exchange for a C-54. The 390th Bomb Group, 8th Air Force, operated at least three B-17s called I'll Be Around, **and B-17G-30-BO 42-31892 DI-H** I'll Be Around Here, **in the 570th Bomb Squadron, which was salvaged on D-Day 1944.** Larry Goldstein

Drone Operations

In World War II, the only time the B-17s had been used as drones was in June 1944 when ten BQ-7s (war-weary B-17Fs and Gs) were used in Project *Aphrodite* and Project *Castor*, the follow-on operation, at Knettishall, England. The BQ-7s were pilotless radio-controlled aircraft filled with high explosives, designed to be controlled by a mother aircraft which steered the drone onto the target, normally a V1 or V2 weapons' site. The *Aphrodite* bombers were filled with 20,000lb (9,072kg) of Torpex or ten tons of RDX, while the *Castor* B-17s were filled with 18,425lb (8,358kg) of Torpex and were fitted with an RC-487 television transmitter. However, the projects proved both dangerous and unsuccessful. Remotely controlled 2,600lb (1,180kg) GB-4 glide-bombs launched from B-17s on two operational *Batty* missions to France in August 1944 were equally hazardous and inconclusive.

Post-war, the San Antonio air depot at Kelly Field, Texas converted a number of B-17Gs to radio-controlled QB-17L target drones – with TV cameras in addition to remote-control equipment – and to QB-17N remote-piloted drones. The latter had additional radio-control equipment, a different guidance system and the optical tracking equipment installed in detachable wing-tip pods equipped with explosive bolts and parachutes for recovery of test data in the event of the loss of the aircraft. Also, the TV transmitters were deleted. Initially the QB-17N drones were for use in Operation *Crossroads*, the Bikini atomic bomb tests which began in 1946, to collect date after the explosion. The director aircraft, or 'mother' ships, for the drones were designated DB-17. The Bikini test was flown by aircraft and crews from the 509th Composite Group, which had dropped the two atom bombs on Japan from B-29s in August 1945. Operation *Crossroads*, which went ahead on 1 July, involved eight B-29s, four QB-17 drones, five DB-17 director aircraft, and eleven SB-17Gs. Equipment fitted to the drones included AN/ARW-1 (control) to open and close the air sampler bag equipment, and an SCR-522 (VHF) set for transmitting a geiger counter warning, while the DB-17 drone control aircraft carried AN/ARW-18 (control) to activate the opening and closing of the air sampler bag on the drones.

In the spring of 1948, drones were used in Operation *Sandstone* at Kwajalein. During this operation, the drone were placed 2,000ft (600m) apart, starting at about 38,000ft (11,600m). They completed their task very well, although the top drone went out of control and into the water. The next series of tests was held under the codename *Ranger* in January 1951 when B-50 aircraft from the Special Weapons Centre at Kirkland AFB, New Mexico, were used for the drop, at Frenchman's Flats. Drones were not used because of the expense of using such aircraft. Instead, a radiological officer was aboard each sampling aircraft to monitor the radiation and to direct the aircraft to the spot where samples could be taken. This new technique proved successful on these low-yield shots and it was desired to try it out on large-yield weapons at Eniwetok Atoll in the Marshall islands.

In the spring and summer months, Operation *Greenhouse* was put into operation in the Marshalls. President Truman had ordered an acceleration in the development of the hydrogen thermonuclear bomb on 13 January and the *Greenhouse* detonations took place on 8 and 21 April, and 9 and 25 May 1951. Thirty-three QB-17s from the 3,250th Drone Group at Eglin AFB, Florida, were used to collect the radioactive fallout from a series of tests and to measure blast and thermal effects. Eleven were drones and twenty-two were director ships. Because of the length of time it took to have the QB-17s airborne, take-offs commenced at night. A single, huge searchlight at the end of the strip shone straight down the runway to aid take-off. One observer noted how incredibly strange it was to see and hear a Fortress come roaring along the runway in the black of night with the searchlight shining through the empty cockpit like a ghost ship.

About two hours after a detonation, six personnel in a director ship penetrated the cloud at the lower portion of the sheer. The operator noted that the cloud was still very radioactive since the radiological detection meter for gamma radiation went off scale, indicating an intensity of more than 500 roentgens. Good samples were obtained and proved that drones were not necessary to meet the Atomic Energy Commission requirements for samples of the bomb. Upon return to Eniwetok after the tests, the drones were decontaminated (they would be radioactive for several days). Special care had to be exercised when removing the containers of the fall-

out. After Project *Greenhouse* was completed, all thirty-three drones were flown back to Eglin, and some were then assigned to Point Magu Naval Air Station in Oxnard, California, flying drone missions for the US Navy.

QB-17Ls were used as targets for USAF fighter aircraft, and the drones were usually destroyed by early Nike Ajax surface-to-air missiles or Hughes Falcon AAMs. Normal procedure was for ground control to take off the drone, with the director or mother ship joining in formation shortly after lift-off. Control was then transferred to the 'beeper' pilot in the DB-17. The drone was flown to the range, with the director flying in loose formation. Once on the range, control was passed to the radar station for the 'dry' (practice) runs and the 'hot' (firing) runs. The director flew in formation to monitor the drone until the hot run, when it flew off-range for safety reasons. Being off-range did not always work, as, for instance, in 1952 when a fighter shot down a director, killing Colonel Audette, the commander, and several other drone group officers. Two sergeants in the rear managed to escape. Another director was shot up a couple of years later at Holloman AFB, but was not seriously damaged.

The directors had most of their combat equipment stripped out, and radio and television equipment installed. Until 1956, the VHF radio used to transmit commands to the drone was the AN/ARW40; the drone receiver was the AN/ARW41. A television receiver was installed i the director, and a camera and transmitter in the drone. A separate drone instrument panel was set up so that essential information could be transmitted to the director and the ground. The entire mission was monitored by the commander at a ground station.

In the winter of 1955–56, Sperry Corporation installed and tested a new system in both the B-17s and the F-80s. The radios were changed to UHF, AN/ARW-64 and AN/ARW-65, and the television was replaced by an FM/FM telemetering system. The retrofit of these new systems in 1956 may account for the change in designation from DB-17G to DB-17P. The programme was terminated in the late 1950s because there were not enough drones, but before that 107 QB-17s had been converted, and 1,025 missions had been flown. A number of the early conversions were carried out by Hayes International in Birmingham, Alabama. QB-17s were also used as target aircraft in missile tests. The final DB-17/QB-17 mission was flown on 6 August 1959, with 44-83727 being destroyed by a Falcon missile, fired by a F-101 Voodoo. The last B-17 in US military service, a QB-17L drone, was destroyed in 1960, ironically by a Boeing IM-99 Bomarc missile.

Retired drones were put into open storage in the scorching heat of Davis-Monthan AFB near Tuscon, Arizona in May 1959, but some soon found a new home. For instance in July 1960, B-17G 44-83684, a former DB-17G/DB-17P which was used from July 1950 until December 1951 as a drone aircraft, was acquired by the Heritage Museum Foundation; it was repainted in the colours of the 305th Bomb Group and named *Miss Liberty Belle*, and placed on static display at Grissom AFB, Indiana. In 1967, Tallmantz Aviation

– founded in 1961 when Paul Mantz, a Los Angeles-based charter operator, had merged with Frank Tallman – ever on the look-out for government surplus aircraft for movie use, acquired two ex-3205th Drone Squadron B-17s, 44-83525 and 44-83684. The latter came from the Maloney collection at Chino, and not long before had flown as *Picadilly Lilly* in the television series *Twelve o'Clock High*, filmed at Chino Airport between 1964 and 1967. Mantz, who once had a sealed bid of $55,000 for 475 surplus warplanes (including seventy-five B-17s) accepted, was killed in an accident during filming in 1966. *Picadilly Lilly* is now on permanent display at the Planes of Fame Museum at Chino Airport, California.

It took a very long time to restore 44-83525 to flying condition, but then it par-

ticipated successfully (as *Balls of Fire*) in *The 1,000 Plane Raid*, shot on location in January 1968. After filming was completed, Tallmantz did a deal with the owners, the Air Force Museum, swopping two aircraft and a missile for 44-83525. In 1973 Tallman sold 44-83525 to Junior Burchinal, curator and owner of the Flying Tiger Air Museum at Paris, Texas. After a cameo role in *MacArthur* in 1976 (as KY-LQ in the colours of the 93rd Bomb Squadron, 19th Bomb Group's *Suzy Q*), 44-83525 was put on display in museums in Arizona and Florida before being permanently displayed at Kermit Weeks' Air Museum at Tamiami Airport, Miami. In 1992, 44-83525 was picked up and damaged when the museum was destroyed by Hurricane Andrew.

B-17G-85-DL 44-83525 Suzy Q pictured at the Weeks Air Museum, Tamiami Airport, Florida in October 1989. The paint scheme (for a cameo role in MacArthur **in 1976**) is representative of the famous **B-17E** Suzy Q **(KY-L 41-2489)** which left Seattle on 1 January 1942 and was flown by Major Felix M. Hardison in the 93rd Bomb Squadron, 19th Bomb Group, early in the Pacific war, returning to San Francisco on 1 January 1943. 44-83525 was subsequently put on display in museums in Arizona and Florida before being permanently displayed at Kermit Weeks' Air Museum at Tamiami Airport, Miami. On 24 August 1992, 44-83525 was picked up and damaged when the museum was destroyed by Hurricane Andrew. The Indian head insignia was made official on 24 April 1942.
author/Graham Dinsdale

Fire Bombers and Flying Memorials

Some 105 B-17s have appeared on the civil register. Many were used as 'Borate' (a fire retardant) bombers, extinguishing forest fires for the US Forest Service. One of the first B-17s to be converted to tanker-cum-sprayer was B-17F-70-BO 42-29782, which brothers John and Max L. Biegert purchased in mid-1953 after a project to display the aircraft as a memorial in Stuttgart, Arkansas, fell through. The Biegerts registered the B-17F as N17W and installed seven tanks in the fuselage, along with two giant 450-gallon (2,046l) drop tanks from

vices and modified it as a sprayer; the aircraft also joined the Aviation Specialities fleet, on 19 March 1966. Three years earlier, on 23 February 1963, Aviation Specialities had bought B-17G-85-DL 44-83563 (N9563Z), and converted it to fire bomber 24E. In 1964 the company bought B-17G-85-DL 44-83575 (N93012) from the government and flew the aircraft to Mesa to begin a twelve-year rebuild. Previously, 44-83575 had been used in ASR work with the 1st Rescue Squadron in the Caribbean and then flown to Yucca Flats, Mercury, Nevada, to be used in atomic blast tests to determine the 'vulnerability of parked aircraft to atomic bombs'.

By 1977 the aircraft was fully restored: numbered *Tanker 99*, it was ready to fight fires. In October 1985 N93012 was sold to the Collings Foundation. Bob Collings sent the aircraft to Tom Reilly at Kissimmee for a complete rebuild, and the B-17 emerged two years later as pristine as the day it was built. Finished as *Nine-O-Nine* in 91st Bomb Group colours, the aircraft now flies the air-show circuit regularly each year with its B-24 stablemate, *All American*.

44-83563, meanwhile, had become something of a movie star herself. In 1961 she starred in *The War Lover*, and in 1969 went on to play a major role (with sister aircraft 44-85829 and 44-85840/N620L; the

One of the first B-17s to be converted to a tanker-cum-sprayer was B-17F-70-BO 42-29782, which brothers John and Max L. Biegert purchased in mid-1953 after a project to display the aircraft as a memorial in Stuttgart, Arkansas, fell through. The Biegerts registered the B-17F as N17W and installed seven tanks in the fuselage, along with two giant 450-gallon drop tanks from an F-94 under the wing, to give the plane a 3,100-gallon spraying capability. Late in 1961 N17W was sold to Abe Sellards, who converted the Fortress into a fire-bomber. It then joined the growing Aviation Specialities fleet in California (and later, Tucson, Arizona) as Tanker 04 and 84. N17W is now on display at the Museum of Flight in Seattle, Washington. Hugh R. McLaren Jr

an F-94 under the wing, to give the plane a 3,100-gallon (14,094l) spraying capability. Late in 1961, N17W was sold to Abe Sellards, who converted the Fortress into a fire-bomber. It then joined the growing Aviation Specialities fleet in California (and later, Tucson, Arizona) as *Tanker 04* and 84. In January 1968, 42-29782 was used in the filming of *The 1,000 Plane Raid*.

On 1 October 1965, meanwhile, the Biegert brothers had bought B-17G-110-VE 44-85829 (N3193G) from Aero Ser-

The B-17 was one of several staked out in the desert and subjected to above-ground atomic bomb detonations. In the first test the B-17 was parked just 10,000ft (3,000m) from a 1-kiloton explosion. In the second, a 31-kiloton bomb was exploded at the same distance away, and in the third, the B-17 was moved to within 8,000ft (2,440m) of a 19-kiloton blast. Thousands of repair man-hours of damage later, 44-83575 was declared suitably 'cool' in 1964 and sold to Aviation Specialities.

latter was lost later, on 12 July 1973, while fire-bombing near Elko, Nevada) in *Tora! Tora! Tora!* This old movie queen then reverted to a tanker again, with Globe Air Inc at Mesa, Arizona as *Tanker 89*; she was finally retired in 1985. In October that year she was purchased for $250,000 by the National Warplane Museum, Geneseo, New York, for restoration to flying condition as *Fuddy Duddy*. The original *Fuddy Duddy* flew ninety-six missions without an abort in the 708th Squadron, 447th Bomb

B-17G-85-DL 44-83575 (N93012) Nine-O-Nine flying in formation with two P-51D Mustangs. 44-83575 was
used in ASR work with the 1st Rescue Squadron in the Caribbean and later in atomic blast tests to
determine the 'vulnerability of parked aircraft to atomic bombs' at Yucca Flats, Mercury, Nevada, until 1964.
During the late 1970s and early 1980s the aircraft fought forest fires until, in October 1985, it was sold to the
Collings Foundation who had it completely restored by Tom Reilly at Kissimmee. Finished as Nine-O-Nine,
in honour of B-17G-30-BO 42-31909 in the wartime 323rd Bomb Squadron, 91st Bomb Group, 8th Air Force,
this Fort is now a regular on the US air-show circuit with its B-24 stablemate. Patrick Bunce/author

Group, from Rattlesden, England, before being destroyed in a collision over Mannheim, Germany, on 30 December 1944. *Fuddy Duddy* is now a regular performer on the US air-show circuit, along with 44-85829/N620L, which during its fire-fighting career was better known as *Tanker 54*.

44-85829 had been delivered to the US coastguard as a PB-1G on 27 July 1945;

then it served with the International Ice Patrol in Newfoundland with a home base in North Carolina. Later the B-17G flew ASR missions in San Francisco, and was finally surplused around 1960. It began a new career with the US Forestry Department, flying under restricted use as an insecticide- and fire-bomber. This career ended on 22 July 1985, its final flight

spraying grasshoppers in Oregon. The aircraft was offered at auction in 1986 but failed to reach the minimum bid, and was sold to the Yankee Air Museum at Ypsilanti, Michigan. Restoration to wartime flying condition began immediately, and in 1990 the aircraft, now named *Yankee Lady*, joined *Fuddy Duddy* and other restored B-17s on the US air-show circuit.

(Above) **B-17G/VB-17G-85-DL 44-83563 (N9563Z)** Fuddy Duddy **'closely' escorted by P-51D Mustang (painted to represent Capt Donald R. Emerson's aircraft in the 336th Fighter Squadron), near Buffalo, New York, in August 1995. The B-17, which is owned by the National Warplane Museum, is painted to represent B-17G-45-BO 44-297400/E in the 708th Bomb Squadron, 447th Bomb Group, which operated out of Rattlesden, Essex, until it was lost, with 2nd Lt Wylie W. Leverett and crew, on 30 December 1944.** Author

B-17G-110-VE 44-85829 (N3193G) Yankee Lady, **an ex-sprayer and tanker, owned by the Yankee Air Force Inc, at Willow Run, MI, pictured at the 'Wings of Eagles' air-show at Batavia, New York, in 1995.** Author

Another former fire-bomber and flyable performer in the US is B-17G-85-DL 44-83514, which in March 1945 was assigned to the 38th Reconnaissance Squadron, 13th Air Force, at Clark Field in the Philippines. Three years later it was used as a 'dumbo' aircraft by the US Navy with a lifeboat under its fuselage. In USAF service again, it was used as a DB-17 drone-controller aircraft until May 1959, when

across the US until it was sold by Aero Union to the Confederate Air Force on 24 February 1978. A radio competition was held to find it a suitable name and *Sentimental Journey* was the one suggested. The aircraft was at first operated by the Arizona Wing at Falcon Field, Mesa, Arizona, and then from September 1991, by the American Airpower Heritage Flying Museum at Midland, Texas.

then it was sold to Central Air Services, in whose service it operated as *Tanker 42*.

One of the most ingenious of B-17 fire-bombers was TB-17F-50-VE 42-6107 (N1340N), which in late 1953 was purchased by Bob Sturges in a sale of surplus military aircraft at Clarkston, Washington. In 1957 it was converted to a fire-bomber, and during the 1960s it was used by a number of companies, the last being Aero Flite Inc at Cody, Wyoming, who acquired it on 19 January 1968. Operator Ray Elgin numbered the aircraft *Tanker A34*. In 1970 a shortage of Wright Cyclone piston engines and spares led Elgin to replace the Wrights with four 1,670ehp Rolls-Royce Dart 510-65 turboprops from an ex-Capital/United Airlines Viscount.

During the summer of 1970 *Tanker A34* completed a few flights as a turboprop fire-bomber. In July, Frederick A. Johnsen, an aspiring University of Washington history major on a summer's outing to eastern Washington with his family, managed to include Wenatchee's Pangbourn Field, on the dry east side of the Cascade Mountains, in their weekend schedule, for he knew it was well served with air tankers:

B-17G-85-DL 44-83514 (N9323Z) Tanker 17 which operated with Aero Union Corporation of Chico, California, 1962-78, dropping retardant. This aircraft is now Sentimental Journey **and is operated by the Arizona Wing of the Confederate Air Force.** CAF

With conflagrations to the north, I figured on catching glimpses of *Moby Dick*, a majestic red-and-white PB4Y-2 Privateer fire bomber, in action as it lumbered out of Pangbourn Field loaded with retardant slurry. What unfolded at Pangbourn that weekend remains beyond the wildest dreams of most warbirds: like warplanes assembling for a battle, no fewer than *eight* warbird air tankers gathered at Pangbourn's US Forest Service base. A crosswind runway was blocked off to accommodate a diagonally parked line-up that included up to three B-17s, the Privateer, a tall-tail PBY-6A Catalina, an A-26, a PV-2 Harpoon, and at least one F7F Tigercat.

Persistent leaden overcast and stifling heat made the scene sombre as fire-bomber crews raced out on airdrop after airdrop. N1340N with its four Rolls-Royce Dart powerplants outperformed the conventional Forts dramatically in the pattern, and could be seen returning empty with two of its four engines shut down. From the west side of the Columbia River in downtown Wenatchee, the lumbering giants could be seen struggling for altitude as they left Pangbourn on the east side. It was methodical, hot work for aircrews and groundcrews alike. At day's end, the ramp became an incredible impromptu museum tableau of some of America's greatest warbirds.

Next day they were back in the air, bucking drafts over the flames as they repeatedly discharged dyed fire retardant. The dye helped

Acme Aircraft Parts acquired it and it was registered N9323Z. Late in 1960, Western Air Industries at Anderson, California, bought N9323Z for $8,000 and converted the B-17 into a fire-bomber with two 1,000-gallon (4,550l) tanks and associated plumbing. Operating as *Tanker 17*, the aircraft went on to fight major forest fires

In 1960 meanwhile, B-17G-105-VE 44-85778 (N3509G) was sold to Sonara Flying Service by Ace Smelting; in 1961 it was sold again, to Leo Demers, who converted the former bomber to a sprayer and fire-bomber, known as *Tanker 97*. Aero Union purchased the tanker, and it worked as *Tanker 16* from 1966 to 1972;

B-17G-85-DL 44-83514 (N9323Z) Sentimental Journey, **operated by the Arizona Wing of the Confederate Air Force, which was completely restored to World War II flying condition in 1981, the Sperry top turret and operational tail-turret 'pumpkin' coming from Art and Birdine Lacey's B-17G which sits atop their 'bomber gas station' in Milwaukee, near Portland, Oregon.** Sentimental Journey **takes the colours of the 457th 'Fireball Outfit', 8th Air Force.** Author

mark the places they had already bombed, to increase the efficiency of the crews in placing retardant strategically to block the spread of the blazes. The tarmac at Pangbourn Field ran red with the thick fire retardant, splashing from hoses and overflow valves on the air tankers; the clothing of the groundcrew members was stained with it, and the bellies of the bombers were smudged red where the slurry had spread into the slipstream on repeated drops.

My weekend came to a close, and I returned to a summer job at the University of Washington wind tunnel. The fire-bombers kept on, however, and a television documentary crew filmed their efforts that year, taking advantage of the intensity of the fire operations in Washington at that time.

On 18 August disaster struck the Dart-engined Fortress: on the aircraft's third run on a fire in Dry Creek, south-east of Yellowstone Park, Wyoming, it was caught in a down-draught: all four engines failed, and it crashed in the Elk Horn Mountains at Dubois, killing pilot Ray Elgin and his co-pilot. The reason for the total power failure is believed to have been the ingestion of smoke from the forest fire (virtually all forest fire-fighting aircraft are now powered by normal piston engines).

Fire-bombing is, of course, very hazardous work (*Moby Dick* succumbed to an onboard fire in 1972), and N1340N was not the only borate bomber to be lost. *Tanker E18* of Aero Union Corporation, built as B-17G 44-83542 and which also served as a DB-17G/P mother ship in the drone project, crashed while fire-bombing near Benson, Arizona, on 12 July 1971. A year later, on 12 July 1972, *Tanker B11* (B-17G 44-83864/N73648) belonging to Black Hills Aviation at Spearfish, South Dakota, crashed at Silver City, New Mexico. In 1969 N73648 was rebuilt at Spearfish using parts from several aircraft, including B-17G/PB-1W 44-83814/N66571, and was put on display at he USAFM at Eglin AFB in 1975. Four years later Blackhills Aviation lost another tanker. B-17G/TB-17G 42-102715 (N66573) had previously served Fairchild Aerial Surveys, where it had acquired the name *Batmobile 33* (because of its art-deco scalloping around the tail and nacelles), and then Ewing Aviation of Los Angeles, before becoming *Tanker 10*. The *Batmobile* was destroyed in July 1979 in a crash at Cayuse Saddle, about 45 miles (70km) south-west of Missoula, Montana, while fire-bombing. Pilot Joe LeRoux

In 1970 a shortage of Wright Cyclone piston engines and spares resulted in fire-bomber TB-17F-50-VE 42-6107 (N1340N) having all four engines replaced by 1,670ehp Rolls-Royce Dart 510-65 turboprops from an ex-Capital/United Airlines Viscount. The Dart-engined Fortress crashed fighting a fire in Dry Creek, south-east of Yellowstone Park, Wyoming, on 18 August 1970 after it was caught in a downdraught; following the failure of all four engines, it came down in the Elkhorn Mountains at Dubois, killing pilot Ray Elgin and his co-pilot. Fred A. Johnsen carried out three on-target and effective drops on the fire, but after the last drop he made a wrong turn in the box canyon, narrowly missing a spur ridge but catching one wing in the trees; he and his co-pilot were killed in the crash.

Black Hills Aviation's run of bad luck continued, when on 16 April 1980, B-17G 44-85813/N6694C crashed at Bear Pen, North Carolina while fire-bombing. During 1985–90, Tom Reilly Vintage Aircraft at Kissimmee, Florida, used parts of the wreck to rebuild N5111N which had been badly damaged by a tornado at the Bradley Air Museum, Windsor Locks, Connecticut, in October 1979.

Another major operator of B-17s for fire-fighting work was Edgar A. Neeley's Fastway Air Service, of Long Beach, California. In 1959 the USAF decided to dispose of the majority of its stored B-17Gs, and 44-83546 was sold to the National Metals Co. in Phoenix; but rather than scrap the plane, the company sold it on to Fastway, who registered it as N3703G. It was painted in an attractive blue-and-white scheme, two 900-gallon (4,090l) tanks were installed, and starting in July 1960, N3703G began almost twenty-two years' continuous service as a fire-bomber.

Fastway operated N3703G, and B-17G-BO 43-38635/N3702G (which had served the Atomic Energy Commission), until 1982, when they were both purchased by TBM Inc of Tulare, California. TBM continued to use them in the fire-attack role. N3703G was eventually purchased by David Tallichet, and in 1986 was converted back to military configuration, while N3702G – or *Tanker Six-One*, as it was known – was acquired by Aero Union Corporation at Chico, California, on 1 November 1979. On 26 November, the Air Force Museum obtained the aircraft in a swap deal involving a C-54. The B-17 was repainted in the colours of the 94th Bomb Group, 8th Air Force, and named *Virgin's Delight*, and in October 1980 was placed on display at Castle AFB, California. The original *Virgin's Delight* was flown by Colonel (later Brigadier General) Frederick Castle (after whom the base is named), CO of the 94th Bomb Group, on several combat missions from Bury St Edmunds (Rougham) during World War II. General Castle was killed leading the 4th Wing on 24th December 1944. He was posthumously awarded the Medal of Honor for staying with the aircraft to allow his crew to bale out safely.

A sprayer of a different kind is B-17G-105-VE 44-85740, which was delivered to the military on 18 May 1945, too late to see combat duty. In July 1947, Universal Aviation Inc, of Tulsa, Oklahoma, bought the aircraft from Metal Products Inc, of Amarillo, Texas, for $1,800, thus saving it from the scrap smelter; it was registered N5017N. In August that year it was acquired by the Vero Beach Export and Import Co in Florida, and modified as a cargo-hauler for flying cattle between Florida and Puerto Rico. In mid-1949 it was bought by Aero Services for $28,000 and modified for high-altitude mapping operations in North Africa and the Far East; during the Vietnam War in 1958 it

B-17G-105-VE 44-85740 (N5017N) Aluminium Overcast **belonging to the Experimental Aircraft Association at Oshkosh, painted in the wartime colour scheme of 42-102516/H in the 601st Bomb Squadron, 398th Bomb Group, 8th Air Force, stationed at Nuthampstead, England.** EAA Warbirds of America

carried out all the early aerial photography of Vietnam. By 1966 the B-17 was owned by Dothan Aviation Corporation in Arizona, who modified it for fire and spraying duties by adding a hopper and chemical spraying system. In 1978 Dr. William E. Harrison, president of Condor Aviation of Tulsa, Oklahoma, bought the aircraft; but his organization known as B-17s Around the World', made up of a group of businessmen, was unable to restore and maintain the aircraft to airworthy condition because of insufficient funds. On 31 March 1981 the B-17 was donated to the Experimental Aircraft Association at Oshkosh, Wisconsin.

However, since it has been put back into flying condition it has used its original name once again *Aluminium Overcast*; it is one of only twelve Fortresses still flying in the world today.

Two further B-17s which fly in Europe and have yet to be mentioned are B-17G-85-VE 44-8846 F-AZDX *Pink Lady*, and B-17 Preservation's B-17G-105-VE 44-85784 *Sally B*. Both have been owned by the French Institut Géographique Nationale (IGN), a governmental cartographic photography company specializing in high-altitude work, based at Creil, near Paris. F-AZDX had served in the 351st and 305th Bomb Groups of the First Air Divi-

Schenectady, New York. Known now as an ETB-17G, with the Buzz-number 'BA-784', she served as a test vehicle for infrared tracking devices, fitted with man-carrying wing-tip pods and a nose-cone. On 7 February 1954 the ETB-17G was flown to the Ogden overhaul facility at Hill AFB, Utah, returned to a more conventional appearance, and then mothballed.

On 28 October 1954, 44-85784 was acquired by the Institut Géographique Nationale (which acquired eleven B-17s between 10 December 1947 and 6 April 1955). F-BGSR, as it was now known, landed at Paris-Le Bourget en route for Creil on 18 March 1958. In 1975 it was

B-17G/RB-17G-85-VE 44-8846 (F-AZDX) Pink Lady **pictured at the Great Warbirds Display, at Wroughton.**
Author

The Fortress retained its airworthy 'limited' classification (cargo only) while a restoration programme was put into action, and it was named *Aluminium Overcast*. In 1985 the name was changed to *Chief Oshkosh* to honour the crews of several aircraft which flew in World War II under the name of the great chief of the Menominee Indians. Also, *Chief Oshkosh* is symbolic of this aircraft's new home town of Oshkosh where the EAA Aviation Foundation maintains the aircraft.

sion in England in World War II before being acquired by IGN in December 1954.

44-85784 meanwhile rolled off the same Vega production line in the spring of 1945, and on 2 July was delivered to the modification centre at Nashville, Tennessee. Its combat equipment was removed, and in 1946 it was re-designated TB-17. For four years the aircraft served at the USAAF experimental station at Wright Field, Dayton, Ohio. In 1950 she was leased to the General Electric Flight Test Centre at

bought by Euroworld Ltd, and registered N17TE. The Fortress landed at Biggin Hill on 15 March, and then made Duxford airfield in Cambridgeshire its permanent home. In the summer of 1975, *Sally B* made her debut on the air-show circuit, and four years later Ted White and Elly Sallingboe created the company B-17 Ltd purely for her activities. Ted White was killed in an aircraft accident in June 1982, and Elly and her supporters have kept *Sally B* in airworthy condition ever since.

B-17 Preservation's B-17G-110-VE 44-85784 (G-BEDF) Sally B's alluring and distinctive nude nose-art, which is in sharp contrast to the more modest and fully clothed female forms who adorn the noses of US-operated B-17Gs like 'Texas Raiders', where even a cleavage is no longer permitted! Author

B-17 Preservation's B-17G-110-VE 44-85784 (G-BEDF) Sally B in formation with Mark and Ray Hanna's P-51D Mustang of the Old Flying Machine Company, painted to represent Big Beautiful Doll of the 78th Fighter Group, at an IWM Duxford air show. Sally B has tail markings taken from the 447th Bomb Group at Rattlesden, Essex. Author

B-17G-110-VE 44-85784 (G-BEDF) Sally B **in formation with Stephen Gray's P-51D 44-73149 Mustang 44-63221**
Candyman/Moose **of the 362nd Fighter Squadron, 357th Fighter Group, from The Fighter Collection, at an**
IWM Duxford air show in 1996. Author

Of course, funds generated by television, and movie work such as in *The War Lover*, and *Tora! Tora! Tora!*, has helped B-17s earn their keep and ensured that others in private hands remain flyable. In the summer of 1989, when a second *Memphis Belle* movie was filmed at the IWM airfield at Duxford, Cambridgeshire, *Sally B* appeared with two other IGN B-17Gs from France, and two B-17s from the USA: from France came 44-

85643 F-BEEA, and 44-8846 *Lucky lady* (now *Pink Lady*); from America came B-17G-85-DL 44-83546, flown by owner-operator Dave Tallichet (who flew twenty-one missions in the 350th Bomb Squadron, 100th Bomb Group at Thorpe Abbotts in World War II) and B-17F-70-BO 41-24335 N17W (piloted by Bob Richardson, whose company, Portage Bay Inc of Seattle, had bought the aircraft in 1985). The latter,

when a tanker, had already starred in the 1968 movie *The 1,000 Plane Raid*, and *Tora! Tora! Tora!* in 1969. For *Memphis Belle*, all four B-17G Fortresses had their chin turrets removed to resemble period B-17Fs, and olive drab paint was applied to all surfaces. But filming did not go smoothly. On 25 July, during follow-on shooting at RAF Binbrook, F-BEEA crashed on take-off and was destroyed. Incredibly, everyone managed to

B-17G-70-VE 44-8543 (N3710G) Chuckie, **owned by 'Doc' Hospers' BC Vintage Flying Machines, Fort Worth,**
Texas, and named after his wife, pictured at the Confederate Air Show, Harlingen, Texas, in October 1986.
The B-17 takes its colours from the 832nd Bomb Squadron, 486th Bomb Group, 8th Air Force. Author

B-17G/PB-1W-95-DL 44-83863 N5233V painted to represent B-17G-40-DL 44-6106 Gremlin's Hideout **in the**
563rd Bomb Squadron, 388th Bomb Group, 8th Air Force, on display at Eglin AFB Museum, Florida. The
original Gremlin's Hideout **survived the war and finished her days at Kingman, Arizona.** Author

B-17G-105-VE 44-85778 N3509G **which was finally restored to flying condition as** Miss Museum of Flying **at**
Santa Monica, California, in October 1991. Tony Plowright

B-17G-105-VE 44-85718 (N900RW) Thunder Bird **lifting off. This ex-IGN Fortress, owned by the Lone Star Flight Museum at Galveston, Texas, is painted to represent B-17G 42-38050/U of the 359th Bomb Squadron, 303rd Bomb Group, which flew from Molesworth, England, in World War II.** Author

B-17G-95-DL 44-83872 (N7227C) Texas Raiders **operated by the Gulf Coast Wing, CAF, and B-17G-85-DL 44-83514** Sentimental Journey, **operated by the Arizona Wing, pictured with** Diamond Lil **in the setting sun at Ellington Field, Houston, Texas, during the 'Wings Over Houston' Air-Show in October 1993.** Author

escape, though two people suffered a broken leg and one broken collarbone.

The loss of F-BEEA reduced the flyable B-17 population to thirteen. A year later, in April 1990, when Bob Richardson died suddenly, N17W passed to the Museum of Flight in Seattle, as per an agreement he had with the museum, who purchased the aircraft for $300,000, the same price Richardson had paid Globe Air for it in 1985. N17W has since been completely restored by a volunteer team of Boeing employees and former B-17 crew-members, and it rejoined the flying fraternity in 1998.

B-17s and parts of B-17s are still being found (two B-17s which landed in Green-land in bad weather on 15 July 1942 have been discovered under a 250ft (76m) deep ice-cap), and grandiose schemes evolve from time to time to turn these into flyable machines once more. One can only hope that Fortresses continue to be found and flown to delight future generations of aviation enthusiasts in the years to come.

APPENDIX I

Equipment Diagrams

Seat control and sight unit – Bendix chin turret, model 'D'

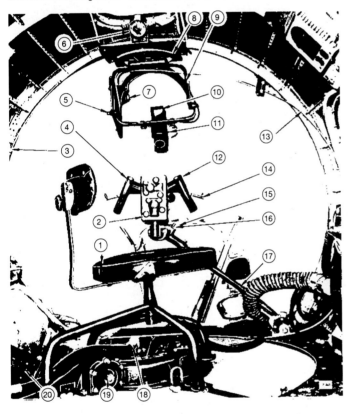

1. Seat
2. Controller (with gun-charger switch and main power switch*)
3. Azimuth drive cable
4. Control grip
5. Sight drive elevation
6. Rheostat
7. Elevation pinion
8. Azimuth sight drive
9. Supporting yoke
10. N-6 sight
11. Reserve filament switch
12. Trigger switch (forward side of grip)
13. Elevation drive cables
14. Safety (deadman) switch
15. Charger switch
16. Power switch
17. Controller arm
18. Hydraulic swivel gland*
19. Shifter shaft
20. Azimuth drive motor

* On early B-17G models

Drive mechanisms and limit stops let the turret move 360° (6,400 mils) in azimuth, and from 0°– 90° (–1600 mils) downward. Controlled power-drives gave tracing rates from 0°– 45° per second in azimuth and 0°– 30° per second in elevation. Bottom right is the bombardier's window defroster tube, known as the 'Elephant's pecker', which provided heat for the bombsight (deleted in this diagram) and optical glass. The compartments of the B-17G were heated by a glycol heating system in the No. 2 engine nacelle. Crew members could plug their electrically heated suits into rheostat controlled receptacles conveniently located at all crew stations in the aircraft. Bombardier's control panel is situated left. Boeing

Chin turret

A – power supply 24 volts
B – sight rheostat
C – to sight bulb
D – elevation drive cable
E – N-6 sight
F – azimuth drive cable
G – revolve control handle about this axis to move guns in elevation
H – hi-speed switch
I – trigger switch
J – gun charger switch
K – main power switch
L – controller and switch mounting bracket
M – safety switch
N – controller arm tube
O – rotate controller about this axis to move turret in azimuth
P – controller arm cable
Q – controller arm stop
R – release knob
S – hinge stop

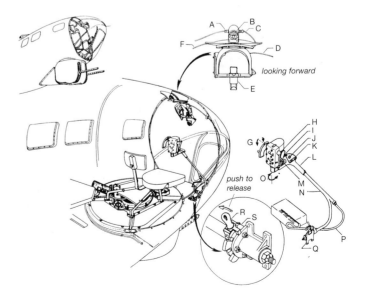

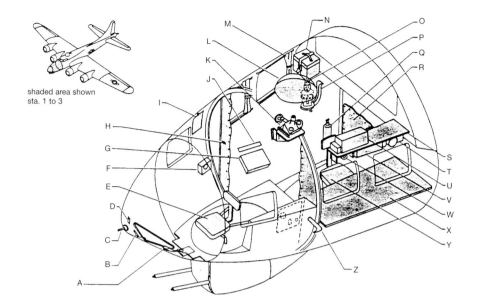

Equipment diagram, stations 1–3

A – bomb sight mount
B – dehydrator, windshield
C – thermometer, outside air type C13A
D – card, temperature correction type C–13
E – chair, bombardier's
F – intervalometer
G – box, bomb data card
H – curtain, bomber and navigator
    compartment blackout
I – clip board
J – holder, bomber's correction card
K – recorder, drift -type B–5
L – astrodome
M – curtain, bomber and navigator
    compartment blackout
N – lamp, signal – type C-3
O – astrocompass
P – astrocompass support
Q – extinguisher, fire (CO_2)
R – cover, door
S – shelf, navigators
T – compass, radio
U – remote compass
V – astrograph tye A–1
W – compass, navigator's
X – table, navigator's
Y – chair, navigator's
Z – mast, pitot, static

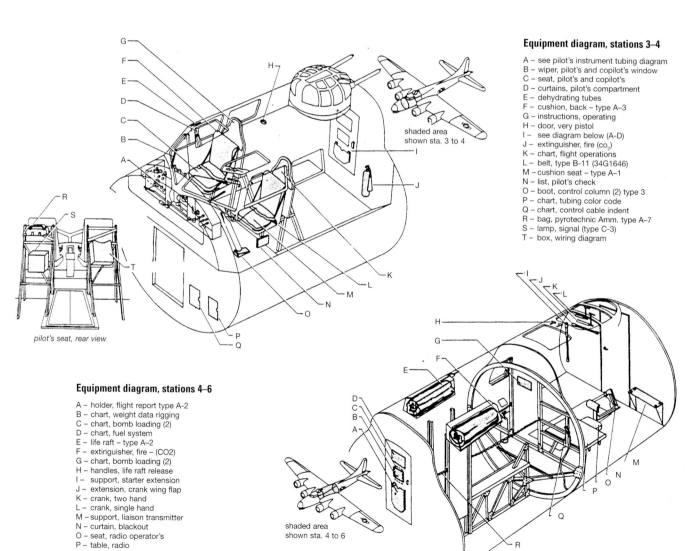

Equipment diagram, stations 3–4

A – see pilot's instrument tubing diagram
B – wiper, pilot's and copilot's window
C – seat, pilot's and copilot's
D – curtains, pilot's compartment
E – dehydrating tubes
F – cushion, back – type A–3
G – instructions, operating
H – door, very pistol
I – see diagram below (A-D)
J – extinguisher, fire (co_2)
K – chart, flight operations
L – belt, type B-11 (34G1646)
M – cushion seat – type A-1
N – list, pilot's check
O – boot, control column (2) type 3
P – chart, tubing color code
Q – chart, control cable indent
R – bag, pyrotechnic Amm. type A-7
S – lamp, signal (type C-3)
T – box, wiring diagram

shaded area shown sta. 1 to 3

shaded area shown sta. 3 to 4

pilot's seat, rear view

shaded area shown sta. 4 to 6

Equipment diagram, stations 4–6

A – holder, flight report type A-2
B – chart, weight data rigging
C – chart, bomb loading (2)
D – chart, fuel system
E – life raft – type A–2
F – extinguisher, fire – (CO2)
G – chart, bomb loading (2)
H – handles, life raft release
I – support, starter extension
J – extension, crank wing flap
K – crank, two hand
L – crank, single hand
M – support, liaison transmitter
N – curtain, blackout
O – seat, radio operator's
P – table, radio
Q – tube, emergency relief
R – guard rail rope

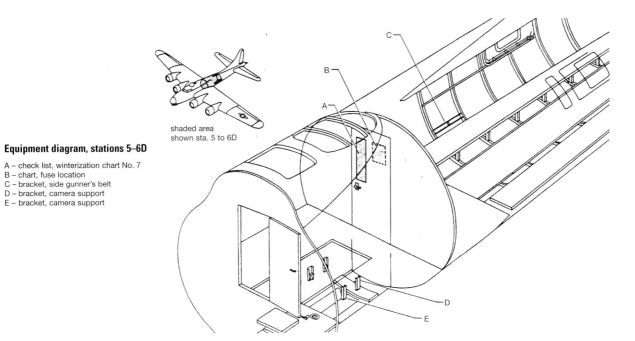

Equipment diagram, stations 5–6D

A – check list, winterization chart No. 7
B – chart, fuse location
C – bracket, side gunner's belt
D – bracket, camera support
E – bracket, camera support

shaded area
shown sta. 5 to 6D

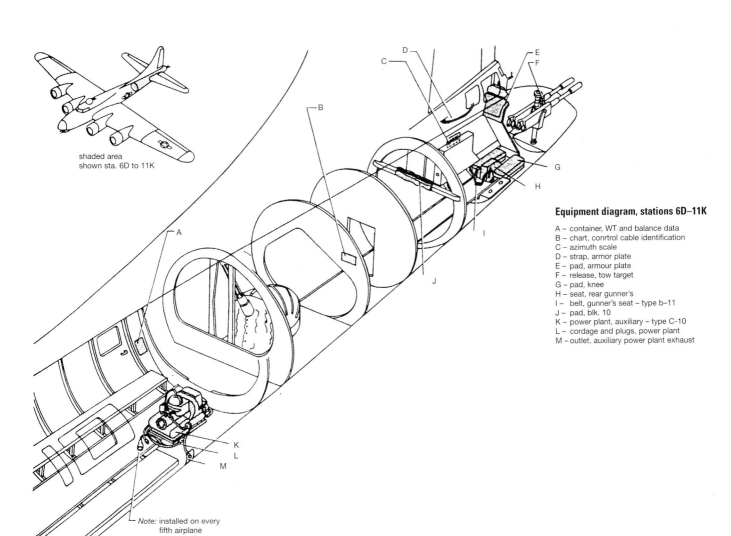

shaded area
shown sta. 6D to 11K

Equipment diagram, stations 6D–11K

A – container, WT and balance data
B – chart, conrtrol cable identification
C – azimuth scale
D – strap, armor plate
E – pad, armour plate
F – release, tow target
G – pad, knee
H – seat, rear gunner's
I – belt, gunner's seat – type b–11
J – pad, blk. 10
K – power plant, auxiliary – type C-10
L – cordage and plugs, power plant
M – outlet, auxiliary power plant exhaust

Note: installed on every
fifth airplane

(Below) **Miscellaneous electrical equipment**

A – flight gyro heater
B – spare lamp box
C – wiring diagram box and spare
   flourescent lamps
D – spare lamps box
E – top turret gun heaters
F – spare turbosupercharger amplifier
G – spare lamps box
H – radio compartment gun heater
I – rudder and elevation servo

J – tail gun heaters
K – spare resin (tail position) lenses
L – side gun heater
M – fuse chart
N – type G–3 signal lamp
O – C-1 autopilot operating
   instructions chart
P – external power plug
Q – aileron servo heater
R – flouuescent light headband
S – bombsight heating cover

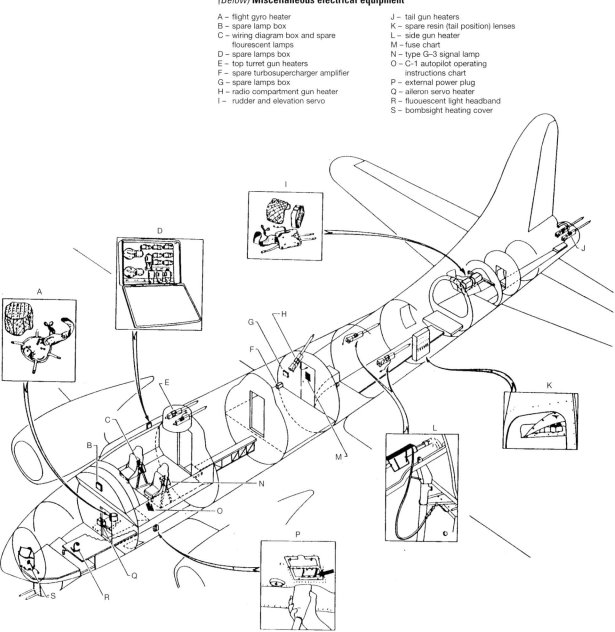

USAAF B-17 Medal of Honor Recipients 1942–44

DATE	RECIPIENT	USAAF UNIT
7 Aug 42	Captain Harl Pease Jr	19th BG/5th AF, Rabaul, New Britain+
18 Mar 43	1st Lt Jack Mathis	303rd BG/8th AF, Vegasack, Germany*
1 May 43	S/Sgt Maynard H. Smith	423rd BS 306th BG/8th AF, St Nazaire, France
16 Jun 43	2nd Lt Joseph R. Sarnoski	43rd BG/5th AF, Buka, Solomon Is*
16 Jun 43	Major Jay Zeamer Jr	43rd BG/5th AF, Buka, Solomon Is
26 Jul 43	Flt Off John C. Morgan	92nd BG/8th AF, Kiel, Germany
20 Dec 43	T/Sgt Forrest L. Vosler	303rd BG/8th AF, Bremen, Germany
20 Feb 44	1st Lt William R. Lawley	305th BG/8th AF, Leipzig, Germany
20 Feb 44	Sgt Archibald Mathies	351st BG/8th AF, Leipzig, Germany*
20 Feb 44	2nd Lt Walter E. Truemper	351st BG/8th AF, Leipzig, Germany*
11Apr 44	1st Lt Edward S. Michael	305th BG/8th AF, Brunswick, Germany
23 Jun 44	2nd Lt David R. Kingsley	97th BG/15th AF, Ploesti, Rumania*
2 Nov 44	2nd Lt Robert E. Femoyer	711th BS 447th BG/8th AF, Merseburg, Germany*
9 Nov 44	1st Lt Donald J. Gott	729th BS 452nd BG/8th AF, Saarbrücken, Germany*
9 Nov 44	2nd Lt William E. Metzger	729th BS 452nd BG/8th AF, Saarbrücken, Germany*
24 Dec 44	Brig Gen Fred W. Castle	4th BW/8th AF.*

+ Pease was executed by the Japanese on 8 Oct 42

* Posthumous Award

S/Sgt Maynard 'Snuffy' Smith, the first enlisted man in the 8th Air Force to receive the Medal of Honor. In an attack on St Nazaire on May Day 1943 the 306th Bomb Group lost six B-17Fs, and 42-29649, Lt Lewis P. Johnson Jr's aircraft in the 423rd Bomb Squadron, was hit several times and it caught fire in the radio compartment and in the tail area. Smith, ball turret gunner, who was on his first mission, hand-cranked his turret to get it back into the aircraft. He climbed out and discovered that the waist gunners and the radio operator had baled out. Smith remained in the aircraft and fought the fire with a hand extinguisher. The Fortresss did not show any signs of leaving formation so Smith assumed the pilots were still aboard and he went to treat the badly wounded tail gunner. Then he jettisoned the oxygen bottles and ammunition in the radio compartment, manned the waist guns during an attack by enemy fighters, stopping to dampen down the fires and treat the tail gunner. Johnson put the B-17 down at Predannack near Land's End after Smith had thrown out all expendable equipment. Richards' Collection

Surviving B-17 Flying Fortresses Around the World

MODEL			NAME	LOCATION
B-17D (RB-17D)	40-3097		*Swoose*	Paul E. Garber Rest Facility, Silver Hill, Maryland
B-17E	41-2446		*Swamp Ghost*	Agaiambo Swamp, Papua, New Guinea
B-17E (XC-108A)	41-2595			In storage at Galt Airport, Illinois
B-17E	41-9101			Abandoned in Greenland. Now under 260ft of ice
B-17E	41-9105			Abandoned in Greenland. Now under 260ft of ice
B-17E	41-9210	N8WJ		Scott D. Smith, Colorando Springs, CO
B-17F-10-BO	41-24485		*Memphis Belle*	Memphis Belle Memorial Association, Memphis, Tennessee
B-17F-50-BO	42-3374			In storage at Offut AFB, Nebraska
B-17F-70-BO	42-29782	N17W		Museum of Flight, Seattle, Washington
B-17G-35-BO	42-32076		*Shoo Shoo Baby*	Wright-Patterson AF Museum, Dayton, Ohio
B-17G-90-BO	43-38635	N3702G	*Virgin's Delight*	Castle Air Museum, Castle AFB, Merced, California
B-17G-50-DL	44-6393	CP-891	*2nd Patches*	March Field Museum, March AFB, California. (Painted 42-30092)
B-17G-70-VE	44-8543*	N3701G	*Chuckie*	BC Vintage Flying Machines, Fort Worth, Texas
B-17G-85-VE	44-8846*	F-AZDX	*Pink Lady*	Association Fortress 'Volante'. Jean Salis, Cerny, France
B-17G-85-VE	44-8889	F-BGSO		Musée De L'Air, Le Bourget, France
B-17G-75-DL	44-83316			Stored in pieces at Ocotillo Wells, California
B-17G-85-DL	44-83512		*Heavens Above*	Lackland AFB History and Tradition Museum, San Antonio, Texas
B-17G-85-DL	44-83514*	N9323Z	*Sentimental Journey*	Arizona Wing of the Condeferate Air Force, Mesa, Arizona
B-17G-85-DL	44-83525	N83525	*Suzy Q*	Stored in pieces Fantasy of Flight, Polk County, Florida
B-17G-85-DL	44-83542	N9324Z		Stored in pieces at Ocotillo Wells, California
B-17G-85-DL	44-83546*	N3703G	*Memphis Belle*	March AFB, California
B-17G-85-DL	44-83559		*King Bee*	Strategic Air Command Museum, Offutt AFB, Nebraska
B-17G-85-DL	44-83563*	N9563Z	*Fuddy Duddy*	National Warplanes Museum, New York
B-17G-85-DL	44-83575*	N93012	*909*	Collings Foundation, Riverhill Farm, Stow, Maine
B-17G-90-DL	44-83624			Dismantled for restoration, Dover AFB, Delaware
B-17G-90-DL	44-83663	N47780	*Short Bier*	Hill AFB Museum, Utah
B-17G-90-DL	44-83684	N3713G	*Picadilly Lilly*	Planes of Fame Museum, Corona del Mar, California
B-17G-95-DL	44-83690		*Miss Liberty Belle*	Grissom AFB Museum Foundation, Peru, Indiana
B-17H-95-DL	44-83718			Museu Aerospacial, Rio de Janiero, Brazil (also 44-83462)
B-17G-95-DL	44-83722			Stored in pieces at Ocotillo Wells, California
B-17G-95-DL	44-83728			Musée de L'Air, Le Bourget, France
B-17G-90-DL	44-83735	F-BDRS	*Mary Alice*	Imperial War Museum, Duxford, England
B-17G-95-DL	44-83785*	N207EV	*Shady Lady*	Evergreen Helicopters, Pinal Airpark, Marana, Arizona
B-17G-95-DL	44-83790			Abandoned in Newfoundland Canada 1947. Loc 1970 almost intact
B-17G-95-DL	44-83814	N66571	*Tanker 09*	In storage at Dulles Airport, nr Washington DC
B-17G-95-DL	44-83863	N5233V		USAF Armament Museum, Eglin AFB, Eglin, Florida
B-17G-95-DL	44-83868	N5237V		RAF Bomber Command Museum, Hendon, London
B-17G-95-DL	44-83872*	N7227C	*Texas Raiders*	Gulf Coast Wing, Confederate Air Force, Harlingen, Texas
B-17G-95-DL	44-83884	N5230V	*Yankee Doodle II*	8th Air Force Museum, Barksdale AFB, Bossier City, Louisiana
B-17G-95-DL	44-85583			On display at base area, de Recife, Brazil
B-17G-100-VE	44-85599		*Blackhawk*	Texas Museum of Military History, Dyess AFB, Abilene, Texas
B-17G-105-VE	44-85718*	N900RW	*Thunder Bird*	Lone Star Museum, Hobby Airport, Houston, Texas
B-17G-105-VE	44-85734	N5111N	*Five Engine*	New England Air Museum, Bradley Airport, Windsor Locks, CT
B-17G-105-VE	44-85738		*Amvet*	American Veterans Memorial, Tulare, California
B-17G-105-VE	44-85740*	N5017N	*Aluminium Overcast*	EAA Warbirds of America, Oshkosh, Wisconsin

MODEL			NAME	LOCATION
B-17G-105-VE	44-85778	N3509G		Semi-storage, Stockton, California
B-17G-105-VE	44-85784*	G-BEDF	*Sally B*	B-17 Preservation Ltd, (a/c based at Duxford)
B-17G-105-VE	44-85790			On top of Bomber Gas Station, Milwaukee, Oregon
B-17G-110-VE	44-85813	N6694C		Stored at Kissimmee, Florida
B-17G-110-VE	44-85825			Smithsonian Institute, Washington DC
B-17G-110-VE	44-85828	N9323R	*I'll Be Around*	390th BG Assn, Pima Air Museum, Tucson, Arizona
B-17G-110-VE	44-85829	N3193G	*Yankee Lady*	Yankee Air Force, Ypsilanti, Missouri

(BO) Boeing (DL) Douglas (VE) Lockheed Vega
* Flying Examples

B-17G-110-VE 44-85813 N6694C is one of two former five-engined test beds. This one was operated by Pratt and Whitney and is pictured at Tom Reilly's Bombertown restoration facility in May 1993.
NBS Aviation

B-17 Serials

USAAF SERIALS

TYPE	SERIAL	TYPE	SERIAL
Y1B-17	36-149/36-161	B-17F-30-VE	42-5855/42-5904
Y1B-17A	37-369	B-17F-35-VE	42-5905/42-5954
B-17B	38-211/38-220	B-17F-40-VE	42-5955/42-6029
B-17B	38-221/38-223	B-17F-45-VE	42-6030/42-6104
B-17B	38-258/38-270	B-17F-50-VE	42-6105/42-6204
B-17B	38-583/38-584	B-17F-55-BO	42-29467/42-29531
B-17B	38-610	B-17F-60-BO	42-29532/42-29631
B-17B	39-1/39-10	B-17F-65-BO	42-29632/42-29731
B-17C	40-2042/40-2079	B-17F-70-BO	42-29732/42-29831
B-17D	40-3059/40-3100	B-17F-75-BO	42-29832/42-29931
B-17E	41-2393/41-2669	B-17F-80-BO	42-29932/42-30031
B-17E	41-9011/41-9245	B-17F-85-BO	42-30032/42-30131
B-17F-1-BO	41-24340/41-24389	B-17F-90-BO	42-30132/42-30231
B-17F-5-BO	41-24390/41-24439	B-17F-95-BO	42-30232/42-30331
B-17F-10-BO	41-24440/41-24489	B-17F-100-BO	42-30332/42-30431
B-17F-15-BO	41-24490/41-24503	B-17F-105-BO	42-30432/42-30531
B-17F-20-BO	41-24504/41-24539	B-17F-110-BO	42-30532/42-30616
B-17F-25-BO	41-24540/41-24584	B-17F-115-BO	42-30617/42-30731
B-17F-27-BO	41-24585/41-24639	B-17F-120-BO	42-30732/42-30831
B-17F-1-DL	42-2964/42-2966	B-17F-125-BO	42-30832/42-30931
B-17F-5-DL	42-2967/42-2978	B-17F-130-BO	42-30932/42-31031
B-17F-10-DL	42-2979/42-3003	B-17G-1-BO	42-31032/42-31131
B-17F-15-DL	42-3004/42-3038	B-17G-5-BO	42-31132/42-31231
B-17F-20-DL	42-3039/42-3073	B-17G-10-BO	42-31232/42-31331
B-17F-25-DL	42-3074/42-3148	B-17G-15-BO	42-31332/42-31431
B-17F-30-DL	42-3149/42-3188	B-17G-20-BO	42-31432/42-31631
B-17F-35-DL	42-3189/42-3228	B-17G-25-BO	42-31632/42-31731
8-17F-40-DL	42-3229/42-3283	B-17G-30-BO	42-31732/42-31931
B-17F-45-DL	42-3284/42-3338	B-17G-35-BO	42-31932/42-32116
B-17F-50-DL	42-3339/42-3393	B-17G-80-DL	42-37714/42-37715
B-17F-55-DL	42-3394/42-3422	B-17G-10-DL	42-37716
B-17F-60-DL	42-3423/42-3448	B-17F-80-DL	42-37717/42-37720
B-17F-65-DL	42-3449/42-3482	B-17G-10-DL	42-37721/42-37803
B-17F-70-DL	42-3483/42-3503	B-17G-15-DL	42-37804/42-37893
B-17F-75-DL	42-3504/42-3562	B-17G-20-DL	42-37894/42-37988
B-17G-5-DL	42-3563	B-17G-25-DL	42-37989/42-38083
B-17F-30-BO	42-5050/42-5078	B-17G-30-DL	42-38084/42-38213
B-17F-35-BO	42-5079/42-5149	B-17G-1-VE	42-39758/42-39857
B-17F-40-BO	42-5150/42-5249	B-17G-5-VE	42-39858/42-39957
B-17F-45-BO	42-5250/42-5349	B-17G-10-VE	42-39958/42-40057
B-17F-50-BO	42-5350/42-5484	B-17G-40-BO	42-97058/42-97172
B-17F-1-VE	42-5705/42-5709	B-17G-45-BO	42-97173/42-97407
B-17F-5-VE	42-5710/42-5724	B-17G-15-VE	42-97436/42-97535
B-17F-10-VE	42-5725/42-5744	B-17G-20-VE	42-97536/42-97635
B-17F-15-VE	42-5745/42-5764	B-17G-25-VE	42-97636/42-97735
B-17F-20-VE	42-5765/42-5804	B-17G-3O-VE	42-97736/42-97835
B-17F-25-VE	42-5805/42-5854	B-17G-35-VE	42-97836/42-97935

TYPE	SERIAL	TYPE	SERIAL
B-17G-40-VE	42-97936/42-98035	B-17G-70-DL	44-6876/44-7000
B-17G-50-BO	42-102379/42-102543	B-17G-45-VE	44-8001/44-8100
B-17G-55-BO	42-102544/42-102743	B-17G-50-VE	44-8101/44-8200
B-17G-60-BO	42-102744/42-102978	B-17G-55-VE	44-8201/44-8300
B-17G-35-DL	42-106984/42-107233	B-17G-60-VE	44-8301/44-8400
B-17G-65-BO	43-37509/43-37673	8-17G-65-VE	44-8401/44-8500
B-17G-70-BO	43-37674/43-37873	B-17G-70-VE	44-8501/44-8600
B-17G-75-BO	43-37874/43-38073	B-17G-75-VE	44-8601/44-8700
B-17G-80-BO	43-38074/43-38273	B-17G-80-VE	44-8701/44-8800
B-17G-85-BO	43-38274/43-38473	B-17G-85-VE	44-8801/44-8900
B-17G-90-BO	43-38474/43-38673	B-17G-90-VE	44-8901/44-9000
B-17G-95-BO	43-38674/43-38873	B-17G-75-DL	44-83236/44-83360
B-17G-100-BO	43-38874/43-39073	B-17G-80-DL	44-83361/44-83485
B-17G-105-BO	43-39074/43-39273	B-17G-85-DL	44-83486/44-83585
B-17G-110-BO	43-39274/43-39508	B-17G-9O-DL	44-83586/44-83685
B-17G-40-DL	44-6001/44-6125	B-17G-95-DL	44-83686/44-83863
B-17G-45-DL	44-6126/44-6250	B-17G-95-DL	44-83864/44-83885
B-17G-50-DL	44-6251/44-6500	B-17G-95-VE	44-85492/44-85591
B-17G-55-DL	44-6501/44-6625	B-17G-100-VE	44-85592/44-85691
B-17G-60-DL	44-6626/44-6750	B-11G-105-VE	44-85692/44-85791
B-17G-65-DL	44-6751/44-6875	B-17G-110-VE	44-85792/44-85841

RAF SERIALS

TYPE	RAF SERIAL/MODEL		QTY
B-17C	AN518/537	Fortress I	20
B-17F-27-BO 41-24594/24599	FA695/700	Fortress II	6
B-17F	FA701/713	Fortress II	13
B-17E	FK184/213	Fortress IIA	30
B-17C	FL449/464	Fortress IIA	16
B-17G-40-BO 42-97098/97119	HB761/782	Fortress III	22
B-17G-50-BO 42-102434/102439	HB783/788	Fortress III	6
B-17G-60-BO 42-102940, 102941	HB789, 790	Fortress III	2
B-17G-40-VE 42-98021/98035	HB791/805	Fortress III	15
B-17G-45-VE	HB806/814	Fortress III	9
B-17G-45-VE 44-8082/8087	HB815/820	Fortress III	6
B-17G-55-VE 44-8240, 8241	KH998, 999	Fortress III	2
B-17G-55-VE 44-8242/8244	KJ100/102	Fortress III	3
B-17G-60-VE 44-8336/8343	KJ103/110	Fortress III	8
B-17G-70-VE 44-8534/8538	KJ111/115	Fortress III	5
B-17G-75-VE 44-8619/8628	KJ116/125	Fortress III	10
B-17G-85-VE 44-8861, 8862	KJ126,127	Fortress III	2
B-17G-85-VE 44-8863/8865	KL830/832	Fortress III	3
B-17G-90-VE 44-8966/8970	KL833/837	Fortress III	5

Glossary

AA	anti-aircraft fire, synonymous with *Flak*	*Crossbow*	allied bombing against German V1 and V2 sites	KIA	killed in action
AAC	Army Air Corps	CTO	Caribbean theatre of operations	Lt	Lieutenant
AAB	Army air base			Lt Col	Lieutenant Colonel
AAF	Army Air Forces, US Army	D-Day	day of Allied invasion of Normandy, France (6 June 1944)	Maj	Major
AD	air division			Maj Gen	Major General
AF	Air Force	DFC	Distinguished Flying Cross	*Manna*	USAAF supply missions to the Dutch, May 1945
AFB	Air Force base	DSC	Distinguished Service Cross	*Market-Garden*	Allied airborne and land-operations in Holland, September 1944
Air Corps	Army Air Branch 1926–41				
Air Service	Army Air Branch 1920–26	DUC	Distinguished Unit Citation		
AM	air medal (USAAF)			MIA	missing in action
AM	Air Marshal (RAF)	EM	enlisted men	'Mickey'	short for 'Mickey Mouse', an H_2X radar device
Argument	joint operation against German aircraft industry by 8th and 15th AFs, February 1944	ETO	European theatre of operations	MoH	Medal of Honor
				MPI	'mean point of impact': designated target point of maximum impact of bomb-load
ASW	anti-submarine warfare	FEAF	Far East Air Forces		
AVM	Air Vice Marshal (RAF)	Fg Off	Flying Officer (RAF); Flight Officer (USAAF)	M/Sgt	Master Sergeant
AWPD	Air War Plans Division			MTO	Mediterranean theatre of operations
		Flak	*Flieger-abwehr-kanonen*: German anti-aircraft forces		
BD	bomb division				
BG	bombardment/bomb group	Flt Lt	Flight Lieutenant (RAF)	NAAF	North African Air Forces
BG(P)	bomb group (provisional)	F/Sgt	Flight Sergeant (RAF)	napalm	incendiary bombs made from jellied gasoline
'Big B'	Berlin	*Frantic*	codename for shuttle-bombing attacks beginning 2 June 1944	'Noball'	V1/V2 target
Brig Gen	Brigadier General			nr	near
BS	bomb squadron				
BW	bomb wing	FTR	failed to return		
'buncher'	radio beacon used in assembling bomber formations	FTRLOC	failed to return, landed on Continent	ops	(RAF) short for operations (missions)
		Gee	navigational device (British)	*Overlord*	Allied invasion of German-held Europe, which began on D-day, 6 June 1944
Capt	Captain	GI	American soldier (literally 'government issue', an adjective applied to all things army)		
CBO	combined bomber offensive				
CBI	China-Burma-India theatre				
CBW	combat bombardment wing			Pte	Private
chaff	(US) metal foil strips used to 'snow' enemy radar	Gp Capt	Group Captain (RAF)	Pfc	Private First Class
		GP	general purpose (bombs)	PFF	pathfinder force, a radar-equipped unit or aircraft for bombing cloud-covered targets
Chowhound	USAAF supply missions to the Dutch, May 1945	HE	high explosive		
Clarion	comprehensive plan for co-ordinated air attacks on German transportation facilities ordered into effect by SHAEF on 22 February 1945	H_2X	a type of radar instrument used in bombing cloud-covered targets		
				Plt Off	Pilot Officer (RAF)
				Pointblank	American strategic bombing effort before the cross-Channel invasion, June 1943–May 1944
CO	Commanding Officer	IP	initial point, the geographic location marking the beginning of the bomb run		
Col	Colonel				
Cpl	Corporal			PoW	prisoner of war

radome	external housing of airborne radar instrument	SOP	standard operating procedure	U-boat	*Unterseeboot*: submarine
RAF	Royal Air Force	Sqn Ldr	Squadron Leader (RAF)	USASTAF	US Army Strategic Air Forces in the Pacific
RCAF	Royal Canadian Air Force	*Starkey*	deception plan to force the appearance of the *Lutfwaffe* over the English Channel in September 1943	USSTAF	US Strategic Air Forces in Europe
RCM	radio counter measures				
RP	rally point, the geographic location marking the re-assembly of a formation after the bomb run			*Varsity*	crossing of the Rhine operation near Wesel, 24 March 1945
		S/Sgt	Staff Sergeant		
		Swe	Sweden	VE-Day	Victory in Europe Day
R/T	radio telephone				
RZOI	returned to zone of the interior (the USA)	T/Sgt	Technical Sergeant	window	(British) metal foil strips used to 'snow' enemy radar
		10/10th	complete cloud cover: coverage of targets was expressed in tenths		
Schräge Musik	'Slanting Music' German night fighters' guns firing upwards			ZOI	zone of the interior (the USA)
		Torch	Allied invasion of Axis-controlled French North Africa which began on 8 November 1942		
Sgt	Sergeant				
SHAEF	Supreme Headquarters Allied Expeditionary Force				

In 1946 two B-17G-VEs were used as test beds for new Wright and Pratt & Whitney propeller-turbine engines. The first (44-85813/BA-813) was acquired by the Wright Aeronautical Co on a bailment contract as EB-17G (JB-17G in October 1956) to test the Typhoon propeller-turbine (pictured here). The second (44-85734) was used at Hartford, Conn. to test the Pratt & Whitney XT-34. via Jerry C Scutts

Index

Alconbury 76
Allen, Edmund 'Eddie' T. 8
Anderson, Brig Gen Fred L. 75, 86
Anderson, Brig Gen Orvill 86
Anderson, Gen Fred 131
Andrews, Gen Frank M. 7, 14
Anklam 83
Anvil, Operation 99–100
Argument, Operation 89–110
Armstrong, Col Frank A. 65–6
Arnold, Maj Gen Henry H. 22, 65, 70

Baldwin, Capt Irl E. 76–77
Barr, Maj Bernice 'Bernie' 42, 94, 93–4
Barton, Col Paul L. 89
Barwood, Gp Capt Antony J. OBE 25–6, 30–1
Bassingbourn 146
Berlin 113, 137, 139, 143
'Big Week' 89, 110, 113
Binbrook 176
Bismarck Sea, Battle of 50–1
Bisson, Lt William C. 86
Blechhammer 96, 103, 118
'Blitz Week' 79–80
Boast, Gp Capt Roy 15, 27, 29–30
Bowden, 2nd Lt William W. 128
Bowman, Col Harold W. 109
Bradley, Lt Jim 25–6
Brownlow, S/Sgt William C. M. 128
Brunswick 110–13, 116
Buono, 2nd Lt Thomas F. Cello 114–15
Bushey Hall 110

Cadillac, Operation 123–4
Campbell, Capt Claude 83
Carmichael, Maj Richard N. 44
Casablanca Conference 70, 146
Castle, Brig Gen Fred 133, 173, 182
Chelveston 65, 76, 119
Chowhound, Operation 144
Churchill, Winston 70, 72, 137
Clarion, Operation 137–8
Cohen, Lt Alfred B. 63–4
Coltishall, RAF 109
Combs, Maj Cecil 42
Connally, Capt James T. 25, 42
Crow, 2nd Lt George H. Jr 138

D-Day 122–3
Davies, Sqn Ldr Bob 150
Debach 128
Deese, S/Sgt Hayward F. Jr 130
Doolittle, Gen Jimmy 66, 88, 110, 125
Dragoon, Operation 100–1
Dresden 137, 139
Drone operations 165–6
du Frane, Lt J. L. 'Duke' 42–3
Duncan, Gen Asa N. 69

Eaker, Gen Ira C. 65–7, 69–70, 72, 75, 78–9, 85–6, 93, 110, 146
Eaton, Lt Fred 44–5
Edmundson, James 59
Eisenhower, Gen Dwight D. 92
Eubank, Col Eugene L. 38, 40
Everest, Col Frank F. 63

Faulkner, Capt Cecil 48
Feymoyer, Lt Robert 132, 182
Fields, Lt John W. 36–7, 44, 46–7
fire bombing 167–73
Fitzgerald, Lt Col Shepler 145–6
Framlingham 124
Frantic missions 93–5, 123–4
Fyler, Lt Carl 109

George, Col Harold L. 7, 14, 22
Gibbons, 1st Lt William F. 112–13
Gibbs, Maj David R. 40
Glatton 121
Goodspeed, 2nd Lt Russell A. 140
Gott, Lt Donald 132, 182
Grafton Underwood 65–66, 109
Great Ashfield 138
Great Massingham 25
Grow, Col Malcolm C. 71

Handrow, Horst 35, 48–9, 54–6, 58–9, 62–3
Haner, Gene 102–3
Hansell, Gen Haywood S. Possum 7, 22, 66, 71
Harding, Neil 14
Hardison, Capt Felix 48
Harriman, Averell 94
Harris, AM Sir Arthur 66

Haynes, Caleb 14
Hill, Major Ployer P. 'Pete' 11–12
Horham 119
Horowitz, Jules 89
Huls 79

Imrie, Sgt Tom 25, 30

Johns, T/Sgt Mike 92–3, 96
Johnsen, Fred 170–1
Johnson, Lewis 182
Johnson, 2nd Lt Richard R. 116, 120, 122–3
Johnson, Lt Lewis P. Jr 74

Kassel 79
Kelly, Capt Colin O. Jr. 38, 40
Kenny, Joe C. 94–7, 101
Kenney, Maj Gen George C. 49, 52
Kimbolton 65
King, 2nd Lt Miles 134
Kingsley, 2nd Lt David R. 95, 182
Kurtz, Col Frank A. 89
Kuter, Maj Larry S. 22, 70

Lauer, Col Ford J. 94
Lawley, Lt William Jr 110–12, 116, 182
Lawrence, Brig Gen Charles W. 94
Lay, Lt Col Beirne Ly Jr 80–1
LeMay, Curtis E. 14, 70–1, 79–82
Lewis, 1st Lt Richard B. 125–6

MacArthur, Gen Douglas 45, 49, 60
MacLaren, Sqn Ldr Andy 27, 30
Magdeburg 128–9, 135, 137
Magness, Ped G. 88
Mance, Lt George A. 141
Manning, Lt John P. 107–8
Marienburg 85
Martini, Capt Allen V. 72–4
Mathies, Sgt Archie 110–11, 182
Mathieson, Plt Off Alex 27–9
Mathis, Lt Jack 72, 182
McDougall, Wg Cdr J. 23, 26
Memmingen 95–6
Merseburg 131–3
Metzger, Lt William E. 132
Michael, 1st Lt Edward S. 114, 116, 182

Midway, Battle of 49
Mitchell, Gen Billy 7
Molesworth 65, 76–7, 116, 119–20
Morgan, 1st Lt John C. 'Red' 115, 182
Morgan, Capt Robert K. 78
Moss, Dr Sanford 18
Mulligan, Tony 29

Necrason, Maj Conrad F. 42–3

O'Donnell, Gen Emmett 'Rosie' 38, 42
Olds, Lt Col Robert C. 14, 17
Oslo 107
Oulton 154
Owen, Capt Roy 157, 159

Parsons, T/Sgt John R. 113
Pearl Harbor 34–6, 53–4, 65
Pease, Capt Harl Jr 49–50, 182
Peden, Flt Lt Murray 152–3
Ploesti 92, 95–7, 101–2
Plummer, John A. 100–1
Podington 65
Pointblank, Operation 77, 79, 89, 109
Polebrook 26, 29, 31, 65, 113

RAF Groups:
  2 Group 23
  15 Group (Coastal Command) 147–8, 152
  100 Group (RAF Special Duties) 149–54
RAF Squadrons:
  21 Squadron 23
  51 Squadron 25
  59 Squadron 147
  90 Squadron 23–32, 150
  101 Squadron 151
  199 Squadron 150
  206 Squadron 147–9, 151–2
  214 Squadron 150–1, 153–4
  220 Squadron 147–51
  223 Squadron 151, 154
  251 Squadron 147–9
  517 Squadron 147
  519 Squadron 147–8
  521 Squadron 147
Rasmussen, Maj 57
Rattlesden 136–7, 169
Regensburg 80–2, 89, 91, 113
Reunion, Operation 102
Rosenthal, Maj Robert 'Rosie' 137
Rougham 147, 173
Ruhrland 139–40

Sarnoski, 2nd Lt Joseph 50, 182
Saunders, Col Laverne G. 53–6, 59, 61–3

Sawicki, S/Sgt Joe 109
Schweinfurt 80–2, 85–6, 113
Sculthorpe 149
Seith, Capt Louis T. 99
Sewart, Maj Allan J. 55, 59, 61
Shuttle missions 93–5, 123–4
Slessor, AM 81
Smith, S/Sgt Maynard 'Snuffy' 74, 182
Snetterton Heath 149
Somers, Bill 104–6
Spaatz, Gen Carl 'Tooey' 66, 70, 110, 146
Spears, Richard 141
Spencer, 2nd Lt Charles 109
Story, Ray 35, 56
Stouse, Capt Harold 72
Sturmey, Plt Off Frank 27–31
Sudbury 133, 145
Sweeney, Lt Col Walter C. 47

Thorpe Abbotts 163, 176
Thurleigh 65
Tibbets, Maj Paul 65–6, 87
Tokarz, Capt Clement P. 48–9
Tower, Leslie 11–12
Truemper, 2nd Lt Walter 110–11, 182
Twining, Maj Gen Nathan F. 63, 93

Umstead, Capt Stanley 12–13
Units, Misc:
  69th Squadron (Israel) 159
Unruh Lt Col Marion L. 58, 63
US Air Forces:
  5th Air Force 50
  7th Air Force 38, 49, 63
  8th Air Force 65–87, 89, 91, 107–146
  12th Air Force 66, 87–8
  15th Air Force 99–106, 113, 118, 127
  20th Air Force 159
  USSTAF 110, 113
USSAF Air/Bomb Divisions:
  1st Air Division 135, 137
  3rd Air Division 135, 137
  1st Bomb Division 83, 86, 107, 109–10, 113, 123, 133, 134
  3rd Bomb Division 83, 86, 91, 107, 109–10, 113, 123, 125, 133–5
USAAF Bomb Groups:
  2nd Bomb Group 7, 13–14, 17–20, 87–9, 91, 93–4, 96, 101–3, 105, 118
  5th Bomb Group 36, 38, 56, 60, 62–3
  6th Bomb Group 38
  7th Bomb Group 7, 19–20, 36–7, 44
  11th Bomb Group 34–6, 38, 44, 47, 53–5, 58–63
  19th Bomb Group 7, 19–20, 36, 38, 40–4, 46, 48–50, 182
  25th Bomb Group 119

34th Bomb Group 65, 125
43rd Bomb Group 46, 50–2, 182
91st Bomb Group 112–13, 116, 132, 136, 146, 157–8
92nd Bomb Group 66–7, 74, 76, 143, 182
94th Bomb Group 68, 74–5, 79, 85, 111, 138, 148, 173
95th Bomb Group 74–5, 79–80, 111, 113, 119, 135, 138
96th Bomb Group 74–5, 79, 82, 86, 117, 124, 129, 131, 142, 145, 148–9
97th Bomb Group 65–7, 87–9, 91–3, 95, 105, 182
99th Bomb Group 87–9, 92–4, 96–7, 100–1, 104–6
100th Bomb Group 79–81, 83–4, 113, 125, 137, 163, 176
301st Bomb Group 65–7, 87–8, 92, 102
303rd Bomb Group 65, 72, 76, 80–1, 83, 107–9, 113–17, 119–20, 123, 143, 178, 182
305th Bomb Group 70, 72, 75–6, 86, 110–12, 114, 116, 119, 160, 182
306th Bomb Group 74, 86, 127, 182
351st Bomb Group 75, 110, 182
379th Bomb Group 78
381st Bomb Group 83, 160
384th Bomb Group 109
385th Bomb Group 79, 81, 115, 138, 142–3
388th Bomb Group 157, 177
389th Bomb Group 79, 83
390th Bomb Group 82, 84, 108, 110, 119, 124, 144, 164
398th Bomb Group 127
401st Bomb Group 107, 109, 119
447th Bomb Group 107, 109, 114, 122, 132, 134, 136–7, 139, 141, 169, 182
451st Bomb Group 105
452nd Bomb Group 115, 117, 121, 124, 129, 132, 134, 182
457th Bomb Group 121, 132, 171
463rd Bomb Group 88–9, 91, 93, 96, 100, 106
482nd Bomb Group 107, 115
483rd Bomb Group 88, 91, 93, 99, 103, 106
486th Bomb Group 125, 133, 145
487th Bomb Group 125
490th Bomb Group 125, 139
493rd Bomb Group 125–6, 128–31, 138, 140–2, 144, 164
504th Bomb Group 25
USAAF Bomb Wings:
  1st Bomb Wing 79–81, 83

3rd Bomb Wing 75, 80–1, 83
4th Bomb Wing 75, 79–80, 182
USAAF Combat Wings:
  1st Combat Wing 83
  4th Combat Wing 115, 123–4
  5th Wing 87–106
  58th Wing 63
  92nd Wing 125
  93rd Wing 125
USAAF Commands:
  V Bomber Command 40
  VII Bomber Command 110
  VIII Bomber Command 65–86
USAAF Fighter Groups:
  56th Fighter Group 79
  78th Fighter Group 79
  325th Fighter Group 93
  357th Fighter Group 86
USAAF Bomb Squadrons:
  14th Bomb Squadron 35, 38
  20th Bomb Squadron 13, 17–18, 118
  22nd Bomb Squadron 36, 44
  23rd Bomb Squadron 63
  26th Bomb Squadron 35, 53, 55, 59, 61
  28th Bomb Squadron 44
  36th Bomb Squadron 150, 153
  41st Recce Squadron 19, 38
  42nd Bomb Squadron 34–5, 53, 55, 60, 63
  49th Bomb Squadron 13–14, 89, 93–4, 96, 105
  63rd Bomb Squadron 51
  65th Bomb Squadron 50
  72nd Bomb Squadron 56, 60–2
  88th Recce Squadron 35–6, 44
  93rd Bomb Squadron 42, 48
  98th Bomb Squadron 53–4, 56–9, 61–2
  322nd Bomb Squadron 116
  323rd Bomb Squadron 136, 146
  324th Bomb Squadron 76, 78, 116, 132
  331st Bomb Squadron 68
  333rd Bomb Squadron 111, 148
  336th Bomb Squadron 111
  338th Bomb Squadron 82, 117, 131
  339th Bomb Squadron 117, 142
  341st Bomb Squadron 88–9, 95

346th Bomb Squadron 94, 96, 103
347th Bomb Squadron 92, 96, 97, 100, 105
348th Bomb Squadron 89, 104
349th Bomb Squadron 81
350th Bomb Squadron 176
351st Bomb Squadron 125
353rd Bomb Squadron 102
358th Bomb Squadron 76, 122
359th Bomb Squadron 72, 108, 122, 178
360th Bomb Squadron 114
364th Bomb Squadron 72, 110, 112, 114, 116
365th Bomb Squadron 75
366th Bomb Squadron 76, 160
367th Bomb Squadron 86
401st Bomb Squadron 112–13, 132, 158
410th Bomb Squadron 85
412th Bomb Squadron 119, 138
413th Bomb Squadron 124, 129
416th Bomb Squadron 93, 100
418th Bomb Squadron 81, 125
423rd Bomb Squadron 182
427th Bomb Squadron 113, 118, 122
429th Bomb Squadron 102
431st Bomb Squadron 53–4, 59, 62
435th Bomb Squadron 44
526th Bomb Squadron 78
533rd Bomb Squadron 83, 160
544th Bomb Squadron 109
550th Bomb Squadron 138, 143
562nd Bomb Squadron 157
563rd Bomb Squadron 177
568th Bomb Squadron 110
569th Bomb Squadron 108, 119, 144
570th Bomb Squadron 82, 84, 110
571st Bomb Squadron 110
603rd Bomb Squadron 127
615th Bomb Squadron 119
652nd Bomb Squadron 119
708th Bomb Squadron 136, 139, 169
710th Bomb Squadron 122, 134, 137
711th Bomb Squadron 182
728th Bomb Squadron 115, 121, 129

729th Bomb Squadron 134, 182
730th Bomb Squadron 124
75th Bomb Squadron 121
803rd Bomb Squadron 150
812th Bomb Squadron 115
815th Bomb Squadron 88
816th Bomb Squadron 99
817th Bomb Squadron 99, 101
835th Bomb Squadron 133
840th Bomb Squadron 99, 103
860th Bomb Squadron 129–30, 140
861st Bomb Squadron 126, 128, 140–2
862nd Bomb Squadron 138, 141, 164
863rd Bomb Squadron 130
USSAF Units, Misc:
  8th Weather Squadron (Prov) 119
  10th Emergency Rescue
  54th Troop Carrier Wing 52
  69th Troop Carrier Squadron 52
  433rd Troop Carrier Group 52
  6204th Photo Mapping Flight 163

Varnedoe, 2nd Lt William W. 138–9, 143
Vosler T/Sgt Forrest L. 182
Walker, Brig Gen Kenneth 7, 22, 50
Walsh, Maj Mike 23, 25
Waskowitz, Lt Frank 'Fritz' 53, 58
Watton 23–4
Wayman, Plt Off Mike 27–9
Weir, 1st Lt Gordon W. 126, 128–35
Werner, S/Sgt William T. L. 113
West Raynham 25
Westberg, Lt Franklin 114
Wheless, 1st Lt Hewitt T. 41
Wilhelmshaven 71
Willliams, Brig Gen Robert 80–1
Willing, Albert G. 92
Wilson, Brig Gen Russell 115
Wood, Sgt Tim 'Mick' 25–6, 29–30
Woodbridge 152
Woodward, 1st Lt Ellis M. 126, 128–9, 133
Wyler, Maj William 78

Zeamer, Capt Jay Jr 50, 182